COMPUTER SYSTEM SOFTWARE

The Programmer/Machine Interface

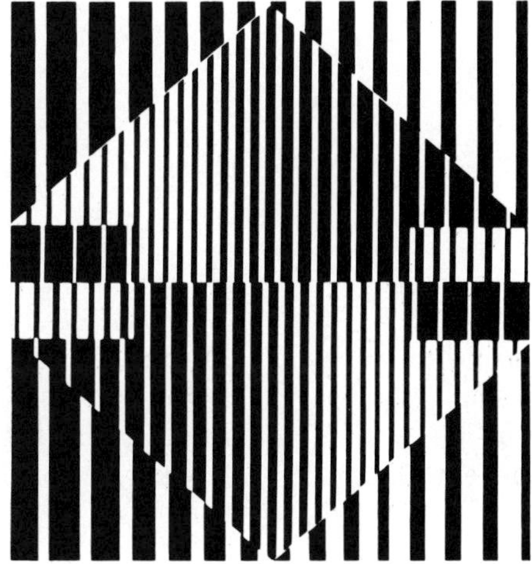

BY

ROY S. ELLZEY

Corpus Christi State University

SCIENCE RESEARCH ASSOCIATES, INC.
Chicago, Henley-on-Thames, Sydney, Toronto

An IBM Company

Acquisition Editor	Michael Carrigg
Project Editor	Byron Riggan
Compositor	Impressions, Inc.
Cover and Text Design	Kristin Nelson

Library of Congress Cataloging-in-Publication Data

Ellzey, Roy S.
Computer system software.

Bibliography: p.
Includes indexes.
1. Computer software. 2. Electronic digital computers—Programming. 3. Operating systems (Computers) I. Title.
QA76.754.E45 1987 005 86-1883
ISBN O-574-21965-X

Printed in the United States of America

10 9 8 7 6 5 4 3 2 1

*To all of my teachers,
beginning with my parents.*

TABLE OF CONTENTS

PREFACE

The primary purpose of this book is to give readers an understanding of: (1) the function of each of the major system software components that participate in the development and execution of application programs; (2) the point during the life cycle of a program from translation to execution that each function is performed; and (3) basically how each software component accomplishes its function(s). Another goal of this book is to provide a basis by which hardware functions and software functions can be distinguished as a computing system is viewed inward from the level of an application program.

The book is appropriate for the DPMA (Data Processing Managers Association) curriculum model course numbered CIS 8 entitled "Computer Software and Hardware Concepts" and also for the CSIS 8 course entitled "System Architectures," which was described as part of a proposed curriculum for small colleges in the June 1985 issue of the *Communications of the ACM* (Association for Computing Machinery). It is somewhat appropriate for the ACM curriculum 1978 course CS 6 entitled "Operating Systems and Architecture I." However, it is more appropriate for academic programs in which there is an overview course using this material followed by in-depth courses in computer architecture, programming languages and operating systems. The book could also be used as a basis for a first course in systems programming in an IBM mainframe environment; but in that case, supplementary material from the literature on systems programming as well as specific information from IBM reference manuals would be needed.

The focus of the book is more on the understanding of the functions of the software components rather than on specific techniques used to design and implement software components. Thus, in preparing the contents of this book, an effort was made to minimize the amount of mathematics needed to understand the material and to keep the discussions more descriptive than algorithmic. Some algorithmic development is necessary to better understand how software components function in general. Therefore, there is a stronger algorithmic development in the chapters on assemblers and loaders. This was done because these components offer a more simplified framework for studying the basic kinds of tasks that translators and other companion system programs perform in preparation for the execution of a program which was written in a source language.

Most ideas in the book are presented generically, but when a specific machine was needed to illustrate certain machine level techniques and procedures, a "generalized IBM mainframe" machine was chosen. This machine was simplified by using only a subset machine language consisting of 47 instructions that are common to all IBM mainframes starting with the System/360. An introduction to this machine is provided as well as enough of the corresponding assembly language needed to conveniently write programs for the machine, and enable students to understand any assembly language examples that are included. The book was written assuming that the readers will: (1) know at least one higher level programming language, (2) understand simple data structures such as lists, vectors, stacks and queues, and (3) have at least a minimal exposure to some assembly language. Students who have had little exposure to computer organization and assembly language will need to study Chapter 1 and the first two major sections of Chapter 2 carefully; others who have stronger backgrounds in this area can treat the material as a review or as a basis for simply learning a new machine.

The course for which we use this material at Corpus Christi State University is not primarily a programming course, however, some programming exercises are useful. Therefore, several programming exercises have been included to meet these needs as well as those for individuals who wish to use this book for a course more oriented to systems programming.

ACKNOWLEDGEMENTS

A number of people contributed to the development of this book and I am grateful to them all.

The college division staff at SRA were professional, responsive and a pleasure to work with. I am particularly indebted to Michael Carrigg, who recognized the value of the project and who supplied the leadership, energy and support to see it through. Next, there was Byron Riggan, who saw to it that a completed manuscript became a finished book and that all involved in the process (including the author) stayed on schedule.

I was fortunate to have had such an able and careful group of reviewers. They were invaluable to me in the development of the manuscript for this book, both from the standpoint of accuracy and coverage. They are:

Fran Gustavson, Pace University, New York
Fred G. Harold, Florida Atlantic University
Herbert R. Haynes, Corpus Christi State University
Douglas W. Jones, University of Iowa
James E. Miller, University of West Florida
David C. Perkins, Corpus Christi State University
Christopher W. Pidgeon, California State Polytechnic University
Les Waguespack, Bentley College
Robert F. Zant, North Texas State University

Finally, I would like to thank the faculty, staff members and students at Corpus Christi State University that participated in the development of this book. In order to provide classroom testing, Robert Diersing, Herb Haynes and David Perkins each used evolving versions of the manuscript in their sections of our course here. Georgia Lynn Porcher did a beautiful job on the working copies of the manuscript, both with respect to the word processing and the artwork, and Maureen Brown and Ruth Killins provided valuable proof-reading assistance for us all. The students who used the manuscript provided timely feedback concerning the clarity of the material and the logical sequencing of topics.

Roy S. Ellzey

CHAPTER

INTRODUCTION AND BACKGROUND

The modern computing system, as viewed by an applications programmer, is not simply a machine, but rather a combination of machine and system software. The function of the system software programs is to present the programmer and computer user with an enhanced or conceptually "extended" machine that is considerably more convenient to use than the underlying physical hardware system without the aid of system software.

OVERVIEW OF SYSTEM SOFTWARE

Computer system software refers to the collection of programs and routines that support the development and execution of other programs. This book deals primarily with the functional role of the major system software components, the point(s) during the development/execution cycle of a program at which they are active, and the interfacing and integration of these components in the process of program development and execution. In other words, in this book components are studied by examining each major software component that an applications program encounters from the time that it first enters a computing system in source form until it completes its execution. Our approach to the study of the major categories of system software will be approached more or less chronologically with respect to the development/execution cycle of a program. Within these major categories we will use a top-down approach in studying the components themselves. For our purposes, the major categories of software are defined as:

1. Language Processors
2. Loaders/Linkers
3. Operating Systems

Language processors include assemblers, compilers and interpreters. *Assemblers* and *compilers* (translators) receive programs or routines written in some programming language form (source programs) as input and produce a machine language program as output, which may or may not be in executable form. *Interpreters* receive source programs as input and dynamically translate and execute these programs on an instruction-by-instruction basis.

Loaders receive translated programs as input and place them in main memory for execution. If the translated program is not in executable form (which is usually the case), then the loader must also convert it to executable form in addition to loading it. If the program was translated in pieces (more than one module) and/or there are pretranslated library routines that must be included in the translated program, then a program called a *linker* collects these parts into one module for the loader. If the linking and loading functions are combined, the system program is called a *linking loader.*

An *operating system* is an integrated set of routines that function together to manage the resources of a computing system during its operation. This is by far the largest and most complex of this book's software categories and will be studied primarily from a conceptual level with references to several operating systems in common use today. The conceptual study divides the system management functions into memory management, pro-

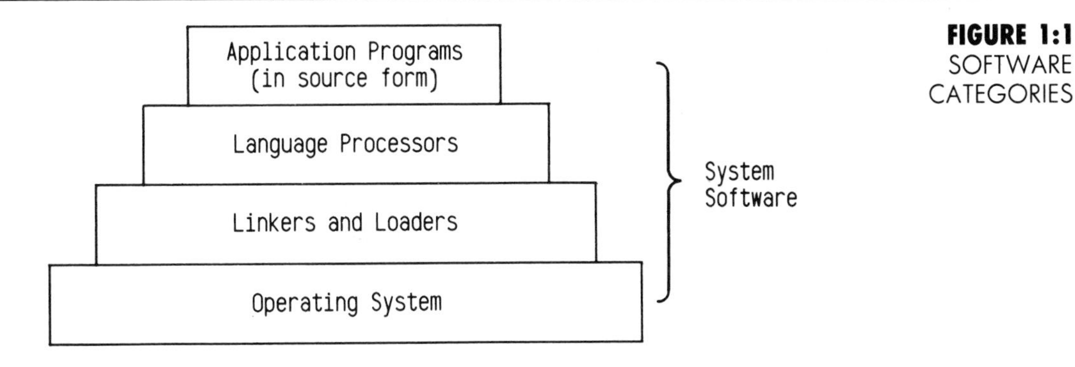

FIGURE 1:1
SOFTWARE CATEGORIES

cessor management, device management, and data/information management. A conceptual relationship of the software categories is shown in Figure 1.1.

A typical, more specific example of this relationship is illustrated in Figure 1.2 where the stages and flow of the development/execution cycle of a program using a translator are shown.

Before we continue our study of system software, it is useful to briefly discuss the historical development, since much of what we have today has evolved from that which came before instead of "springing full-grown from the head of Jove," so to speak. The fundamentals of hardware organization are then reviewed in some detail, since it is essential to understand how the basic hardware components of a computer system function, before we attempt to study the system software components that communicate with and control the hardware.

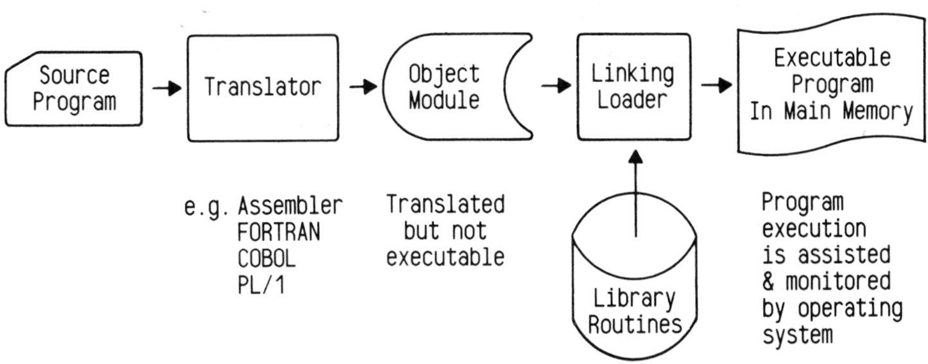

FIGURE 1:2
SEQUENCE OF SOFTWARE INTERACTION WITH AN APPLICATION PROGRAM

HISTORICAL DEVELOPMENT OF SYSTEM SOFTWARE

Since the main purpose of system software is to make computers more convenient for humans to use, it should not be surprising that, for the most part, historically system software development has been a response to the developments in hardware. Thus, as computer hardware became more powerful and sophisticated, software was developed to take advantage of these capabilities and also to insulate the user from the underlying complexities of the hardware. In more recent times this trend is not nearly so clear, and indeed the reverse situation is often seen in which hardware is designed to facilitate the use of a particular software product (for example, the Pyramid® computer was designed for the popular operating system UNIX).*

When the first stored-program computers were developed in the mid 1940s, there was no system software available. If a programmer wanted to write a program, it had to be written in machine language in complete executable form and entered in binary by hand for execution. By the late 1940s, machine language library routines begin to appear to assist in tasks such as I/O processing and floating point arithmetic, but programmers were still restricted to programming basically in machine language.

The first software efforts were focused mainly on the development of language processors so that programmers could express programs other than in machine language. These first language processors of the early 1950s were primarily low-level interpreters. But because of their relatively slow execution speeds, attention turned to the development of translator programs to produce machine language equivalents of the programs written in some form of "programming language."

There were two schools of thought concerning the form that the programming languages should take. One group held the view that programming languages should be as close as possible to the machine language of the computer that would execute the program; this group set out to develop assemblers. The other group felt that programming languages should be more functionally oriented than machine oriented; this group designed higher level languages (such as FORTRAN) and the compilers that would be needed to translate such languages. As one might expect, the development of assemblers slightly preceded the development of compilers, because both the design of an assembly language and implementation of the corresponding assembler were simpler. For example, assemblers were available during the mid-1950s, and although the first generally successful procedure oriented language (FORTRAN) was designed between 1954 and 1955, the first FOR-

*Registered trademark of Bell Laboratories

TRAN compiler was not available until 1957. By 1960, both COBOL and ALGOL had been developed, and compilers were available for them as well (LISP was also developed around this time, but was implemented as an interpretive language).

The development of translators necessitated the development of linkers and loaders with capabilities beyond the simple library routines that existed previously. Thus, the development of these software components progressed more or less concurrently with the development of translators. By the time the first translators (that is, assemblers) were available, at least basic forms of linkers and loaders were available also. The development of programming languages continued with enhancements and new definitions for the earlier languages already mentioned and with such notable new languages as: PL/1 (1964), BASIC (1965), Pascal and C (early 1970s), and Ada (early 1980s).

The development and availability of operating systems followed slightly behind the development of the other components already discussed. 1956 is often cited as a key year in operating system development, for it was this year that a simple operating system was developed by General Motors and North American Aviation for the IBM 704. However, basic operating systems were not generally available until the end of the 1950s. These early operating systems (often called *monitor systems*) were single-user, batch systems that provided automatic job to job transition, primitive I/O control systems, and automatic loading of object programs and library routines. When compared to the continued development of other software components since 1960, the development of operating systems has been much more dramatic than the others, largely because the role of operating systems has been greatly expanded since the early systems, particularly with respect to the development of multiuser systems.

The early 1960s saw the development of multiuser systems that were designed for a single mode of operations (that is, either batch, time sharing, or real time but not a combination of these modes). For example: CTSS was a time-sharing system developed under project MAC at the Massachusetts Institute of Technology in 1961, while the Burroughs Corporation produced a multiuser batch processing system known as MCP (Master Control Program) in 1963, and IBM followed with its multiuser batch system(s) known as OS/360 in 1964 (although Burroughs' MCP was a more sophisticated and advanced design involving such features as virtual memory and multiprocessing).

By the end of the 1960s, general purpose (that is, multimode) multiuser operating systems were available. Project MAC at MIT had expanded the concepts of CTSS and developed the Multics Operating System for the GE 645, and RCA had developed TSOS (Time Sharing Operating System, later named VMOS for Virtual Memory Operating System). The Multics system was larger and more powerful than TSOS, but both were truly multimode, both used virtual memory and both have continued in use into the 1980s (Multics is used by the high end Honeywell systems while VMOS is used on the Series 90 UNIVAC systems). IBM did not offer quite as complete a system of this type until MVS was introduced in 1974. However, IBM could create, more or less, the equivalent of such a system by a series of add-on packages used to enhance one or more of their earlier multiprogramming systems designed for batch processing. By the late sixties, IBM had offered a less-sophisticated virtual system called TSS that was developed for the IBM System/360/67. The development and refinement of general-purpose systems and special-purpose interactive systems has continued into the 1980s with emphasis on the adaptability of systems for networking and distributed processing.

So far the discussion on the development of operating systems has centered on those systems developed for mainframe computers, but with the current prominence of mini and microcomputer systems, the development of operating systems for them should also be addressed. Basically, the operating system features developed for mainframe computers between 1955 and 1980, typically appeared on mini computers five to ten years later, and on microcomputers five to ten years after that. For example, the first monitor type operating systems did not appear for minicomputers until the early 1970s, however these later implementations did take advantage of later knowledge and techniques that had been gained since the earlier mainframe versions. UNIX was conceived at Bell Labs as an interactive, single mode, multiuser system for the DEC PDP-7 in 1969, but by the early 1970s, it had been transported to the PDP-11 and from there its popularity grew rapidly. Besides being a very good product in its own right, UNIX's popularity continued to spread as it was transported to computers of several different types of architectures. This was an important event because in the past, operating systems were highly machine dependent and not typically transported between different architectures. This realization of a more or less standard operating system, such as UNIX, was a departure from the approach previously used for operating systems for mainframe computers. The trend toward more standard systems spread quickly to the microcomputer market with such products as CP/M (1975) and XENIX (the Microsoft version of UNIX) in the early 1980s. There has been little response toward standardized operating systems for mainframe computers, but in time, perhaps in this respect, the great will learn from the small.

For a more complete account of the history of software, the reader is directed to the *Encyclopedia of Computer Science and Engineering*, "A History of Operating Systems" (Weizer, 1981) and most of the other books on operating systems and programming languages listed in the references.

HARDWARE CONSIDERATIONS

It is essential that we understand the functional hardware characteristics of a typical computer if we wish to understand how and why system software components accomplish many of their tasks. A typical simple computer hardware configuration is shown in Figure 1.3.

The first concept to understand is that the actions of the computer are always controlled by a program or programs which are stored in the computer's main memory. If we ignore the asynchronous operation of the I/O processors for the moment and assume that our computer has only one CPU, then at any given instant only one program is in control of the computer and all others are dormant; this program may be either an application program or system program. A second and very closely related concept is that no program can have any effect on the computer until it is first loaded into the computer's main memory, and no data which initially resides outside of the main memory or CPU can be used by the computer until it is first placed (read) into main memory.

We will now take a closer look at the major hardware components. Referring to Figure 1.3, a simple computer consists of a central processing unit (CPU), a main memory, and some means (called the I/O subsystem here) for transferring information between main memory and the outside world. The CPU and main memory (called the primary subsystems here) form the most complex part of a computer and contain most of the indi-

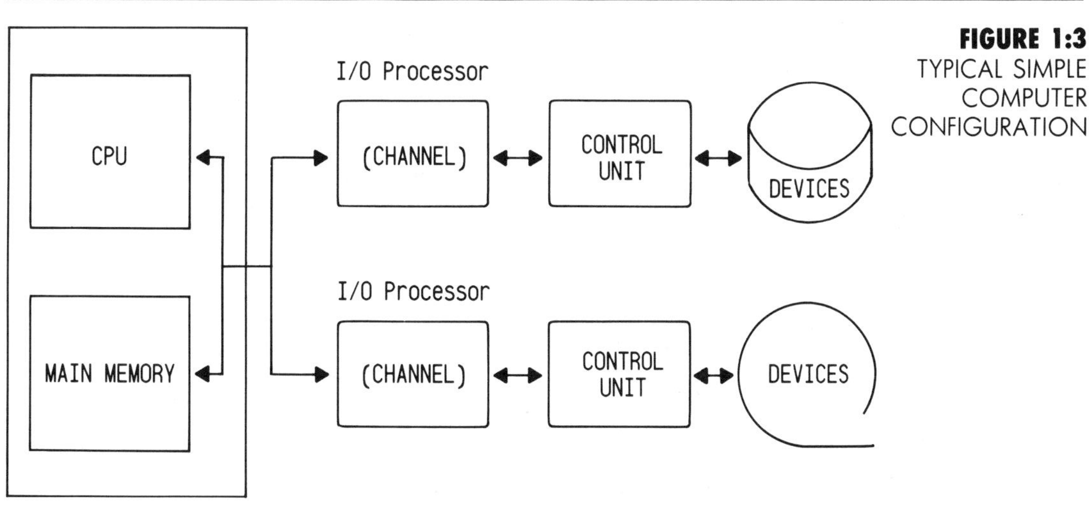

FIGURE 1:3 TYPICAL SIMPLE COMPUTER CONFIGURATION

vidualistic characteristics that distinguish one computer from another. The I/O subsystem consists of a set of peripheral devices (disk drives, printers, etc.) and an interface mechanism to the primary subsystems. This interface may be as simple as a single data path to the CPU or as sophisticated as a special-purpose processor (an I/O processor or channel) communicating with both the CPU and main memory (as is the case in most mainframe computers).

THE CPU

The Central Processing Unit is, as the name implies, the subsystem around which the activities of a computer are centered. In fact, all processing within a single-CPU system is either performed or initiated by the CPU. Overall, the two main functions of the CPU are the control of the other hardware subsystems attached to it and the execution of program instructions. Older views of major hardware components often separated the CPU into two subsystems; the control unit and the arithmetic and logic unit. This is rarely done today since several functions in this split view overlap and since physically, the CPU is built as one component; as a single chip in the case of most microcomputers.

CPU Contents and Functions The CPU is basically composed of registers, control logic, instruction logic, and some means of transferring data both internally and externally. A *register* is a high-speed memory device (typically about an order of magnitude faster than main memory) which is used for the temporary storage of small amounts of information during the operation of a computer. (Commonly a register holds a single word of information, but rarely is its size substantially more or less than a single word.) The CPU registers can be divided into two groups: those that are not explicitly addressable by an executing application program (these are commonly called *working registers*) and those that are generally addressable by any program.

Primary among the working registers is the *program counter* (PC). The PC always contains the address in main memory from which the next machine instruction will be fetched. Since program instructions are stored sequentially in main memory, each time the CPU fetches an instruction, the PC is routinely incremented by the length of the instruction. When a branch instruction is executed or an interrupt occurs, the PC is deliberately set to an address usually other than that of the next instruction. Other working registers include: the *instruction register* (IR), used to hold the current machine instruction that was fetched for execution; various status registers used to record conditions that affect the computing environment; and the *memory address register* (MAR) and the *memory buffer register* (MBR), which are used as follows. Whenever the CPU needs to fetch a word from main memory, the address of the word is placed in the MAR; this address and a "read" signal are then transmitted to the main memory subsystem. Then the desired word is returned to the MBR for use by the CPU. A store operation is quite similar, except that in addition to placing the desired address in the MAR, the CPU loads the MBR with the word and sends a "write" signal to the memory unit, along with the contents of both registers.

The generally addressable registers include the arithmetic registers and those used for address modification. The arithmetic registers may involve only an accumulator, an accumulator plus an extension register, or a set of registers; but in any case, these are the registers that hold the operands used in various arithmetic operations and may also be the principal locations in which the operations are performed. When a single accumulator register is used, one of the two operands for each arithmetic operation must be placed in the accumulator, while the other resides in main memory. After the operation, the result of the operation will remain in the accumulator. If an extension register is appended to the accumulator, then the accumulator will function basically as before. However, for some operations, the result of the operation will extend across both registers. For example, typically a multiplication operation uses the pair as a double-length register for the product, while the quotient from integer division is placed in the accumulator with the remainder in the extension register. A larger set of registers generally provides all of the capabilities provided by the accumulator and extension arrangement, plus added flexibility. Both operands for an arithmetic operation may be in registers, and/or there is a choice of registers in which to place operands instead of the required accumulator.

Address modification registers include index registers (for machines that use indexing) and base registers. Some systems such as the IBM mainframes, use general-purpose registers (GPR), which can be used as arithmetic, index, or base registers as the programmer desires. However, when used as arithmetic registers, the actual arithmetic operation is performed in nonaddressable working registers, and the result is placed back in the corresponding GPR.

The basic control logic within the CPU includes the logic that is used to perform the overall instruction execution cycle, the logic needed to receive and post status information, the logic to control the operation of the other subsystems (I/O and main memory) and the logic required to incorporate an interrupt mechanism.

During the operation of a computer, the CPU is normally limited to the execution of a single machine language instruction set referred to as the machine language of the computer. This machine language cannot be changed during normal operation and is rarely changed at all by any of the users of a particular computer; to do so would render the computer incompatible with all software written under the original machine language, including the operating system.

The machine language instruction set logic is stored in the CPU, typically in the form of microcode routines which usually reside in a high-speed memory referred to as the *control store* which is not altered during normal computer operation. There is a low-level microcode routine within the control store for each machine language instruction, creating in effect a computer within a computer, but the microcode instructions are at a much more primitive level than those of the host computer's machine language. Earlier computers contained the machine language set in the form of hard-wired logic, but this technique is no longer common.

While a computer is in operation, the CPU performs a continuous cycle of (1) *fetching* an instruction from main memory located at the address in the PC; (2) *decoding* the instruction, and (3) invoking the microcode routine which performs the instruction's *execution.* The execution of an instruction frequently requires additional fetches from main memory to provide the operands required by the instruction. For example: the instruction,

```
ADD 1000,1004
```

might be decoded to mean "add the word found at location 1004 to the word found at location 1000." In addition to fetching the instruction, the CPU would have to perform two additional fetches to obtain the desired words at locations 1000 and 1004 and then perform a store to record the results of the add.

Machine Languages As indicated earlier, for all practical purposes, the machine language for a particular computer is fixed. Contrary to the efforts at standardization made in higher level programming languages, machine languages tend to be highly individualized, since they are usually designed to take advantage of the underlying architecture of their target machines. Given this individualistic nature of machine languages, we can still find some properties which are common to all and others that are likely to be found in one group of machines but absent from others.

For binary digital computers, all machine languages are written in some form of binary code. Every machine language instruction must contain a field which identifies the operation that the instruction will perform (the operation code) and zero or more fields that specify the location or value of the operand(s) needed by the operation. There must be instructions that:

1. provide for storing and retrieving information to and from main memory and the CPU.

2. perform basic arithmetic operations on at least one numeric data type. (Practically all computers will contain instructions to perform binary integer arithmetic, and most larger computers contain instructions for floating point or decimal arithmetic as well.)
3. allow some form of branching so that the fetching of instructions does not have to be a purely sequential process.
4. provide means of comparing operands.
5. perform or, at least, initiate I/O operations.
6. provide for some form of logical operations such as AND, OR, shifts, etc.

Given the few basics stated in this list, machine languages tend to increase in sophistication and computing power along the scale from personal computers to mainframes. As mentioned before, a mainframe computer will typically provide instructions for performing arithmetic operations on more than one numeric data type; and, within a particular data type, provide operations for more than one operand length. Mainframe computers frequently have instructions for more complex data manipulation, such as data conversion from one numeric type to another. Personal computers typically provide only binary arithmetic instructions and other numeric types must be handled by software routines that simulate the necessary operations. In addition, small computers do not generally possess the complex data manipulation instructions found on the mainframes.

Instruction sets are sometimes classified by the number of operands that can be specified in an arithmetic operation. As could be expected, the logic necessary to incorporate an instruction with two operand addresses is more complex and thus more costly than a similar instruction with only one operand address. Therefore, the instruction sets with multiple operands tend to be found on larger machines. The advantage in having multiple operands is that a particular computation task can be accomplished with fewer machine instructions. For example, suppose we want to add two numbers located in main memory and store their sum at a third location. The process in machine language for three representative machine types could appear as:

1. Compute C = A + B using a one-address machine

CODE COMMENTS

```
LOAD   A     Place value at A in the accumulator
ADD    B     Add value at B to contents of accumulator
STORE  C     Store contents of accumulator at C
```

2. Compute C = A + B using a two-address machine

CODE		COMMENTS
MOVE	C,A	Copy value at location A to location C
ADD	C,B	Add value at location B to value at C

3. Compute C = A + B using a three-address machine

CODE		COMMENTS
ADD	A,B,C	Add the values at A and B, copy sum to C

In this example, observe that as we increase the number of operands from one to three, we reduce the number of machine instructions required to perform the ADD from three to one instruction. All other things being equal (word size, cycle time, and so on), the single ADD A,B,C, instruction cannot be expected to execute as fast as the single ADD B instruction (if for no other reason than the first requires three memory accesses while the other requires only one); but, the single three-address ADD will execute more quickly than the three-instruction sequence required on the one-address machine to perform the same task.

Unfortunately, no one can devise a four-address machine that can perform an ADD with no machine instructions! However, it is possible to create a zero-address machine for arithmetic instructions that performs an ADD in four instructions. Zero-address machines (also called *stack machines*) use a stack structure in which both operands for an arithmetic operation are placed in the top two positions of the stack. Then the operation is performed by first "popping" the stack twice to obtain the operands and then pushing the result of the operation onto the top of the stack. An example of the machine language for this type machine would appear as:

CODE		COMMENTS
LOAD	A	Push A onto stack.
LOAD	B	Push B onto stack.
ADD		Pop A, B; push A + B onto stack.
STORE	C	Store sum at location C.

Since three-address machines tend to be overly expensive to implement for the comparative gains, and since zero-address machines are somewhat inconvenient (and slower) to use, most computers are either one-address or two-address machines, with small and special-purpose scientific computers (little nonnumeric work required) tending toward the one-address type and the larger and general data processing machines tending toward the two-address type.

Machine Language Addressing Schemes A very important property of any machine language is the format for expressing main memory addresses within the machine language instructions themselves. As mentioned before, when the CPU needs to fetch an operand from main memory, it must place the *absolute* address of this operand into the MAR so that the memory unit can then place the operand (or part of it) into the MBR. The address of the operand is obtained by the CPU from the machine language instruction that is being executed, but the form of the address in the machine language instruction may not be in the absolute form required by the MAR; in fact, it usually is not. We will now examine several addressing schemes used in the machine languages of various computers.

1. **Absolute**—Main memory is divided into addressable cells (typically bytes or words) that are numbered by consecutive integers starting with zero. This cell number represents the absolute or physical address marking the location of the operand and is carried unchanged in the instruction. This form is not common in the machine languages of modern computers; however, this is the form of the address for IBM mainframe channel instructions called channel command words (CCWs).

2. **Relative**—This refers to any type of addressing in which the address carried in the instruction is based on some variable starting location (in terms of a cell number). It may appear very much like an absolute address (same size) except that this address is added to a beginning program or segment address that is maintained in a register. It may also be an address expressed in terms of a specified base register that contains an address within main memory and a displacement from the location in the base register to the desired operand. Several forms of relative addressing are:

    a. *Zero Relative.* In zero relative addressing, all instruction addresses are generated as if the program (or program segment), of which the instruction is a part, starts at absolute location zero. A fixed machine register will always carry the actual starting address of the given program. Thus the CPU calculates the absolute main memory addresses by adding the contents of this program origin register or segment origin register to the zero relative addresses carried in the instructions. (See Figure 1.4).

    b. *Base and Displacement.* In base and displacement addressing, the instruction has two parts. The first part specifies a base register which is chosen under direct program control from a set of registers available as base registers. The base register must be loaded as part of the housekeeping chores of the program that uses it and must contain the absolute address of some location within the program (machines that use base and displacement addressing will have at least one machine instruction that will accomplish this, such as the Branch And Link Register (BALR) instruction on IBM mainframes.) The second part of the address is the displacement from the location in the corresponding base register to the desired operand.

c. *Indexing.* Indexing is actually a means of modifying an address expressed in one of the primary modes such as absolute, zero relative, or base displacement; but, we will still treat it as a form of relative addressing. If the machine language does allow indexing, then the contents of a program specified *index register* is added by the CPU to the primary address carried in the instruction in a manner similar to that used with base registers. The principal function of index registers is to allow a convenient means of accessing elements in structures such as tables or arrays.

d. *Indirect addressing.* In all of the addressing forms described previously for absolute and relative schemes, the instruction address given represented *the address of the desired operand.* In indirect addressing, the instruction address represents *the location of where the operand address will be found.* Some machines allow multiple levels of indirect addressing and in these cases, the target address in the machine instruction can refer to a location that in turn contains another indirect address. Indirect addressing can be useful in situations in which actual operand locations must be determined dynamically during program execution. Indirect addressing is not available on the IBM mainframes but is found on the DEC PDP-11 and VAX-11 series machines and also on several microcomputer systems such as those that utilize the MOS Technology 6502 microprocessor.

Having defined indirect addressing, we are now faced with an interesting if not confusing problem with addressing terminology. If indirect addressing refers to an addressing scheme in which the operand address must be found by following one or more indirect addresses (much as one follows clues in a treasure hunt), it seems reasonable to refer to schemes in which the instructions carry the actual operand addresses as direct addresses. Unfortunately, other treatments on addressing modes use the terms "absolute" and "direct" interchangeably. Nonetheless, for Figure 1.4 showing examples of the various addressing schemes, there is a break with tradition and direct is used to mean the opposite of indirect; after this example, the problem is avoided by not using the term direct address again.

Figure 1.4 represents the various forms of addressing discussed previously by using a simple hypothetical computer with a machine language in which the machine instructions contain only one main memory address. We illustrate each addressing mode using the same basic add operation in which we add the value at main memory location 10,800 (decimal) to the contents of the accumulator; however, we represent the same operand address differently in each example (fortunately, our hypothetical machine can change addressing modes at will without going into all of the details!).

In order to conveniently compare the addressing mode examples, assume a program is loaded at starting location 10,000. The common form of the add instruction in assembly language is ADD X, where X is a symbolic main memory operand to be added to the accumulator. Alternate forms of representing the address of X are shown in Figure 1.4.

Machine States When describing the operation of the CPU, it is helpful to define certain CPU *states of operation*.

The *execution state* refers to whether the CPU is running, waiting or stopped. In the *running state*, the CPU is executing instructions and can receive interruptions (interrupts are explained in the next section). In the *waiting state*, the CPU is not executing instructions but can receive interruptions. In *the stopped state*, the CPU is not executing instructions and cannot receive interruptions.

In most CPUs there is an *execution mode state*. This state may vary from a basic arrangement of just two states of either problem or privileged (IBM mainframes), or to a set of states allowing degrees of privilege or selectivity (the VAX-11 has four). In the basic arrangement, the *problem state* is intended for application programs and during this state, certain machine instructions such as those that perform I/O operations, cannot be executed. While the CPU is in the *privileged state*, any instructions in the CPU's machine language can be executed. This state is intended for use by the operating system so that users in the problem state can be protected and controlled.

Lastly, an *interruption state* is defined as either masked or interruptable. In the *masked state*, some, if not most, interrupts will not be accepted. This state is intended largely for the operating system routines that need to be

FIGURE 1:4
ADDRESSING MODE SCHEMES

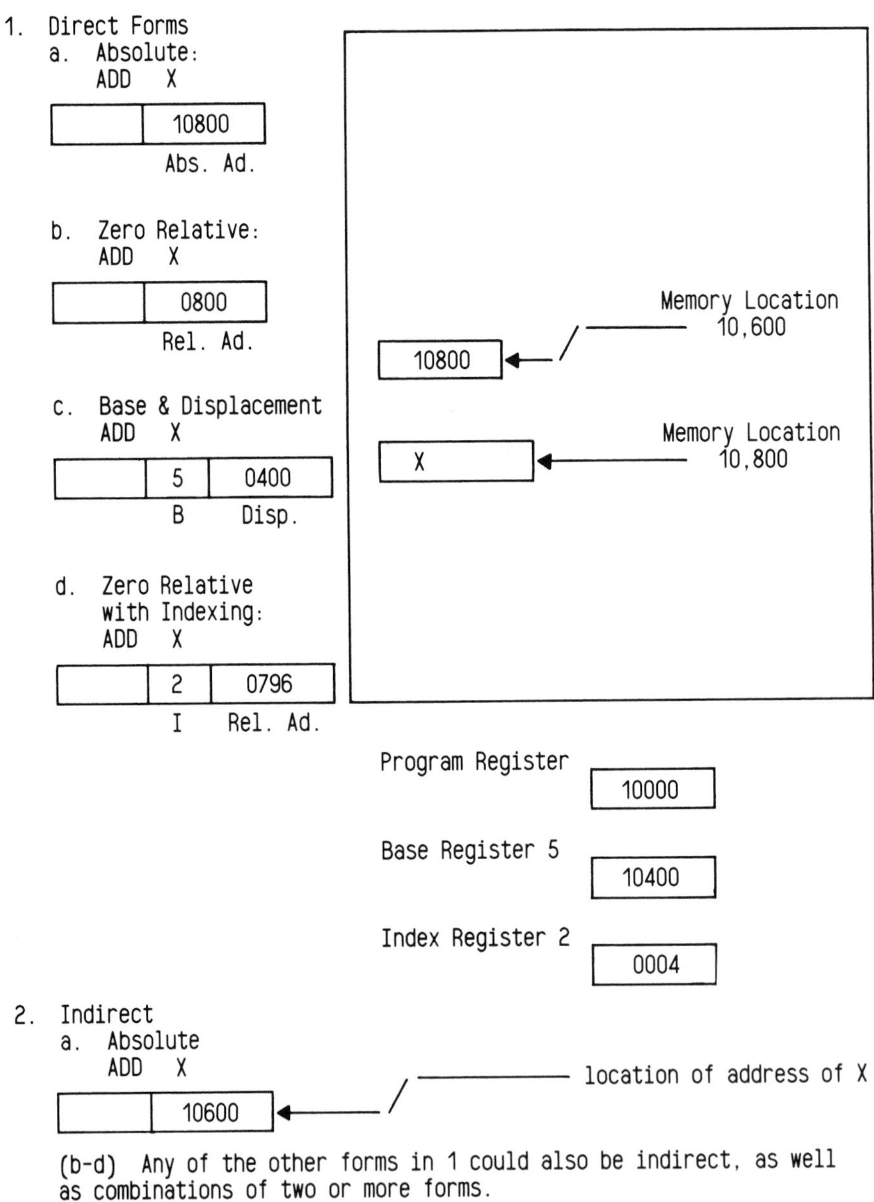

that need to be completed before attending to routine requests generated by interrupts. In the *interruptable state*, all interrupts not under immediate program control will be accepted (it is possible in some machines for an application program to mask out certain interrupts which are not critical to the overall computing environment).

Because each of these various operational states represents a different view of the same operating environment, we can more completely describe the operating environment by specifying a set containing one state type from each of the three operational states. (For example, the CPU could be operating in the running, privileged and masked states and it could later be in the waiting, problem and interruptable states.)

Interrupts An *interrupt* is a hardware feature that automatically changes control of the CPU due to an event that has occurred. Interrupts are used as a means of passing control to the operating system when service is needed. An operating system is said to be *interrupt driven* if all operating system processing is initiated by interrupts. In other words, the operating system can only gain control of the CPU when it is needed.

The alternative to an interrput driven system is to routinely pass control of the CPU to the operating system at regular time intervals or at the completion of certain events or both. Thus, at some predetermined time, the operating system goes through a "shoulder tapping" or polling process in which various devices and programs are checked to see if they need service. This technique is not generally as effective as interrupts since first, the operating system may often get control when it is not needed. And second, a process or device needing service is forced to wait until "asked," thus, effective scheduling of concurrent processes such as computation and I/O can be severely limited.

The interrupt technique is so generally successful at improving the performance of a computing system that most computers (large or small) designed and built since the introduction of the so-called "third generation" computers of the early to mid 1960s have been interrupt driven systems.

The automatic transfer of control is usually accomplished by basically one of two ways, both requiring the use of fixed locations in main memory. A *fixed location* is a location in main memory that is restricted to a single use by machine design. The fixed location is usually imbedded in the area of memory occupied by the operating system.

In the first basic technique, the interrupt causes an automatic branch to a location in main memory that contains either the first instruction of the operating system routine that will analyze the interrupt or a branch instruction (called an *interrupt vector*), which causes a transfer to the analyzer routine.

In the second technique, the fixed location contains an image of the PC or its equivalent (IBM mainframes), and this image is swapped with the current contents of the PC, causing an automatic transfer to the desired interrupt analyzer routine. (This technique will be explained more fully when we study the IBM mainframe organization.)

The CPU may be able to distinguish classes of interrupts, such as I/O completion or program error, and thus perform the first level interrupt analysis by routing CPU control to a different operating system analyzer routine for each interrupt class, or it may send all interrupts to the same routine to do the first-level analysis. But since the interrupt mechanism is so closely related to operating system functions, further discussion is deferred until Chapter 5, at which time we will study the total environment of which interrupts are an important part.

Multiprocessor Systems So far in the discussion of CPUs, it was assumed that each computer has only one CPU; and indeed, this will be the assumption for the rest of this book, as this is by far the most common case. But when we look at the very large mainframe computers, we frequently find more than one CPU. The additional CPUs will provide greater computation power without having to duplicate the other subsystems or peripheral devices. There will be a relatively small cost in performance due to the system overhead to coordinate the operation of multiple CPUs. It is common to refer to two CPU systems as *duplex systems* and systems with *n* CPUs as *n-plex systems*. Readers wishing to pursue the subject of multiple CPU systems are directed to more extensive treatment of computer organization in books such as Stone's *Introduction to Computer Architecture.*

BUSES

In order for the CPU to communicate with another subsystem unit such as main memory, there is a set of parallel communication lines each capable of transmitting a single bit of information at one time. This set of communication lines is called a *bus*. The bus lines are usually divided into three groups: those that carry data, those that carry addresses and those that carry control signals. Buses are not only used for CPU communication with other subsystems but for all intersubsystem communication. Figure 1.5 shows two common bus structures found in computers.

Figure 1.5a, shows a two-bus structure in which all subsystem communication must pass through the CPU; however, both buses can be active simultaneously. Figure 1.5b, shows a single-bus structure in which all subsystems share a common bus. In the latter, the CPU can be removed from direct participation in communication between the I/O subsystem and main memory, but in all cases, only two subsystems can be active on the bus at one time.

Other more sophisticated computer organizations provide for multiple bus structures that are conceptually combinations or extensions of the two basic arrangements shown in Figure 1.5. The multiple bus structures allow for more simultaneous intersubsystem and intrasubsystem communication

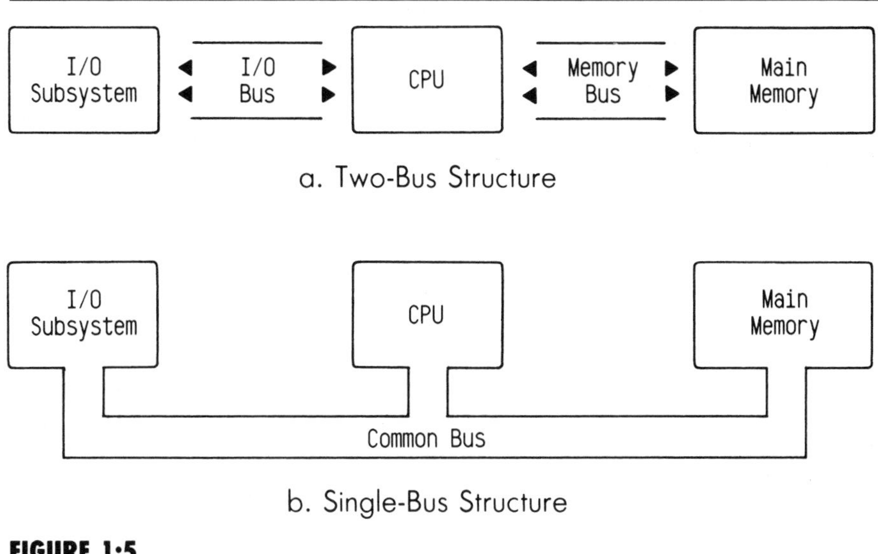

FIGURE 1:5
SINGLE AND TWO-BUS COMMUNICATION STRUCTURES

(for example, multiple instruction fetches) but for the purposes of this book, these multiple bus structures are basically a means of increasing the effective speed of a computer and will not be discussed further.

MAIN MEMORY

The purpose of main memory is to store programs and data for use by the CPU. Indeed, the basic concept of any stored program computer is that the CPU can only fetch instructions for execution from its main memory and also that no data originating from outside the two primary subsystems can be accessed by the CPU for processing until it is first stored into main memory. This means the CPU cannot access operands directly from a record stored on disk; the record must first be transferred into main memory and then the CPU will access it there for processing, even if the initial transfer to main memory was performed by the CPU.

Basic Properties Main memory is organized as a system of many small storage cells that are directly addressable by the CPU. This direct addressability of the individual storage cells is why main memory is often described as *random access memory* (RAM). A second property of a RAM is that, in general, the time to access any cell is the same (excepting, for the time, advanced features such as interleaving and classes of memory which are described later. The addressable storage cells consist of a set of logically consecutive bits that are either one byte (eight bits) or one word in length. One common definition of a computer *word* is the width (in bits) of the data path between the CPU and main memory; which means the word is defined as the number of bits that the CPU can store or fetch with one access to main memory.

Another definition of a word is the bit size of the basic fixed-point numbers in the system. For example, the VAX-11™ is a byte addressable machine with a 32-bit data path between the CPU and main memory and a word size of 16 bits which is the size of a fixed point number. However, the VAX-11 also provides for long-word integers of 32 bits. IBM appears to follow the fixed point number size definition for its byte addressable "families" of mainframe computers starting with the System/360, yet this constant word size of 32 bits was also the size of the data path of a computer that was roughly in the center of the product line. We will use the "data-path-width" meaning of word size in this book unless referring to a specific machine. Word-addressable machines are more likely to be found in an environment intended for scientific computing while byte-addressable machines are more common in environments requiring general computing and particularly for those environments intended for commercial applications.

There are two measures for the speed of a particular main memory: access time and cycle time. *Access time* is defined as the time required to perform a single memory operation, such as a read or write. *Cycle time* is the minimum time between two successive memory operations, but since the time between two successive memory operations requires, in addition, a control signal indicating the completion of the operation, the cycle time is usually slightly more than the access time.

Memory Protection It is usually desirable to restrict an application program from accessing (or at least altering) areas of main memory that were not originally assigned to it for its execution. Even in a single user operating environment, memory is usually divided into a user area and an area for the operating system. In a multiuser system, the user area is usually further subdivided into separate areas for each user. (These concepts will be developed much more fully in Chapter 5.) Without some form of main memory protection, an application program, either through error or mischief, can raise havoc with the intended execution of other programs which happen to share main memory, particularly when the other program happens to be the operating system. Regardless of the protection scheme used, the result is the same—any attempt by a program to violate a protected area ends in a protection interrupt, and control passes to the operating system, which normally terminates the errant program. All but the more basic types of computer systems (such as the IBM PC and most other personal computers) provide some means of memory protection. Descriptions of several techniques follow.

Memory Bounds Registers: In a computer system intended as a single user system, a single memory bounds register within the CPU will suffice. This register contains the address below which (or above which, depending on whether the operating system resides in high or low memory) attempted access by an application program (or any other problem state program) results in a protection interrupt. When the system is intended to protect multiple users from each other as well as the operating system, a pair of memory bounds registers is used. Each time a new application program gains control of the CPU, the beginning and ending addresses of the memory space assigned to that program are placed in the two bounds registers. Every main memory access attempted by the program is checked by the CPU to see if the corresponding memory location lies between the addresses specified by the bounds registers; if not, an interrupt occurs.

A slight variation of the pair of memory bounds registers is to use one register to carry the beginning address of the current user's memory space and the other register to carry the length of the user's memory area. The CPU can then calculate the upper bound address by adding the contents of the two registers. Both techniques require that the user's memory area (space) reside in one contiguous section of main memory.

Memory Keys: A slightly more flexible technique (not requiring a single contiguous memory segment) is the use of memory keys. In this technique, main memory is physically divided into blocks of some fixed size (IBM uses 2048 byte blocks for its mainframe machines), and each memory block has a hardware key (several bits) that can be set by the operating system. As a new application program is loaded into main memory, all memory blocks assigned to that program have their keys set to the same value which is unique to that user. Each time an application program gains control of the CPU, its memory key value is carried in a status register in the CPU. All attempted accesses to main memory by a program are checked by comparing the key value in the status register with the key value attached to the corresponding memory block. If the keys match, the access is allowed, if not, an interrupt occurs. In this scheme, the operating system is given a "master key" value which allows access to any area of memory. (For IBM, the operating system has a key value of all binary zeros.)

Address Translation: Virtual memory machines use a technique whereby all instructions carry virtual addresses. The virtual addresses are mapped onto real memory addresses by a translation process which is usually a combination of hardware and software processes. This mapping can be controlled such that all mappings result in "legal" accesses to main memory or in invalid addresses which in turn cause an interrupt. Virtual memory systems are heavily related to the operating systems that use them; therefore, a much fuller discussion of this topic is presented in Chapter 5 after the development of a foundation by which the operating system participation in the process can be understood.

Additional Features The following features are typically found in the larger mainframe computers and are intended to improve the speed in which main memory can be accessed since, in general, the CPU is capable of processing instructions and data faster than either can be obtained from a basic main memory. Particular machines may contain some or all of these features.

Cache Memory: A cache memory is a very high speed (and relatively expensive) memory that is inserted between the CPU and the larger main memory. Main memory is arranged into blocks that can be conveniently copied into the cache memory. By placing copies of the blocks containing the most recently or heavily referenced instructions and operands in the cache and relying on the property that programs tend to use the same instructions and operands repeatedly, there is a high probability that a good percentage of main memory fetches will be successful in the cache without proceeding on to main memory. Thus the average main memory cycle time is reduced.

Interleaved Memory: Another way to increase the speeds by which memory can be accessed is to arrange memory in several modules with CPU access buses to each module. By placing *n* logically consecutive words, one word to a module, in each of the n memory modules in a "round robin" fashion, the CPU can initiate fetches to each of the modules in the time normally required for a single memory cycle. For example, in a two-way, interleaved memory the even numbered addresses are in one module while the odd numbered addresses are in a second. As the CPU requests an access from an even numbered address, it can immediately initiate a request to the next odd-numbered address (or word). Once again, this relies on the sequential nature of programs which leads to the assumption that usually the next sequential word will be needed by the CPU. Thus, the average speed in accessing main memory is improved.

Associative Memory: An *associative memory* is one in which each word in the memory can be accessed simultaneously by the CPU by comparing the content of each word to a given value. This technique is used primarily to improve address translation in virtual memory systems, which will be discussed in Chapter 5.

I/O SUBSYSTEMS

The I/O subsystem has been mentioned several times in the previous pages. The *I/O subsystem* is the means by which information passes between the outside world and main memory. There are basically three ways of implementing an I/O scheme: direct program control, direct memory access, and I/O processors.

Direct Program Control This is the most basic of the three schemes and is most likely to be found on basic personal computers. In this technique, an I/O program must be executed by the CPU to transfer data one word at a time over the I/O bus to or from the involved I/O device or its controller. The CPU must, therefore, store every word of input to main memory and fetch every word of output from main memory. Thus, in this scheme, the CPU is performing the I/O operations and cannot be available for other processing, which is highly undesirable in a multiuser environment. In this case, the I/O subsystem beyond the CPU is hardly more than an I/O bus coupled with a storage area (called a *buffer*) to hold or receive data.

Direct Memory Access In this technique, a direct memory access (DMA) control unit is capable of directly transferring data to or from main memory once the control unit has been properly initiated by the CPU. The DMA control unit contains a data address register and a data length register plus some means of recognizing control signals from the CPU. The CPU under program control must load the data address register with the starting main memory address of the data block to be transferred in or out, and also place the length of the block in the data length register. The CPU then signals the DMA controller to "read" or "write" and the operation is completed by the control unit without further involvement of the CPU, thus freeing the CPU to continue fetching and executing other instructions on a cycle stealing basis (explained later) as the I/O operation progresses. This is the common technique found on mini computers and virtually all microcomputers with capability for using a hard disk.

I/O Processors Most mainframe computers require a degree of flexibility and speed beyond that of the DMA and thus separate I/O processors are used. *An I/O processor* is a separate processor (usually simpler, but similar in operation to a CPU) with its own machine language. Once initiated by the CPU, the I/O processor can execute its own I/O programs stored in the computer's main memory (and thus freely access data areas in main memory). In other words, the I/O processor is another processor that shares main memory with the CPU but can only be activated by the CPU. IBM refers to its mainframe I/O processors as *channels.* (Channels will be discussed more fully later in this chapter under IBM mainframe organization).

Cycle Stealing: A DMA controller or an I/O processor usually operates at speeds much slower than the CPU such that both types of I/O subsystems are capable of using only about one in ten available memory cycles. By giving these slower I/O subsystems priority over the CPU in accessing main memory once their operations have been initialized, the DMA and I/O processor are said to be "stealing cycles" from the CPU. However, the CPU is free to use the memory cycles between those used by the I/O subsystem and therefore runs in only a slightly degraded state.

BASIC IBM MAINFRAME ORGANIZATION

In a treatment of computer system software, it is often useful to refer to the machine language and organization of a particular computer in order to provide program segments of common machine level techniques. In choosing a specific machine for our purposes, we have basically two choices: use an existing machine that is commonly described in the literature, or invent a hypothetical machine that possesses the properties we desire, yet is simple enough to learn quickly. Recognizing the merits of both approaches, a modified version of the first choice was made.

Starting with the IBM System/360 and following the evolution of that line of mainframe computers through the System/370 computers and onto the later 4300, 303X, 308X and 309X series systems, we find a set of consistent properties (including a majority subset of the machine language instructions) that more than meet our needs. Descriptions of the basic organization of these computers together with their largely compatible machine languages, are widely available (if not the most available) in the literature; thus, for these reasons, a "basic IBM mainframe machine" composed of a subset of these common, real properties was chosen. This basic IBM mainframe machine is more than adequate for the teaching purposes of this book and would serve as a good introduction to the study of any of the specific machines within the IBM mainframe group. However, every machine within the group is more complete (and complex) than the basic machine described here; therefore, anyone wishing to write system software for any specific IBM mainframe must go well beyond this presentation before embarking on such an undertaking.

SUBSYSTEM STRUCTURE

The subsystem structure of the basic IBM mainframe is essentially that shown in Figure 1.3. The minimum configuration consists of a CPU, main memory and at least two I/O processors (called channels). There is a multiple bus structure such that the CPU and the channels can each access main memory independently on a cycle stealing basis. One of the channels is called a *multiplexor channel,* since it is capable of communicating with several slow-speed devices (such as printers, card readers or terminal controllers) simultaneously by multiplexing their information onto a common data path. The other channel (or channels) must be of the *selector channel* type. Selector channels can only communicate with one device at a time. Selector channels are intended for high-speed I/O devices such as disk drives.

THE CPU

The CPU contains a number of working registers and two sets of programmer addressable registers called the *general purpose registers (GPRs)* and the *floating point registers (FPRs).* The discussion of the working registers is limited to the *program status word (PSW),* which is the functional equivalent of several of the generic working registers described for the CPU early in this chapter. Also the discussion of the programmer-addressable registers is limited to the GPRs, since the FPRs are intended for binary floating-point arithmetic, which will not be discussed.

The PSW is a 64-bit register that contains a 24-bit program counter and the equivalent of several other status registers. The exact content (and format) of the PSW depends on whether the CPU is operating in the basic control mode (BC) or under the extended control mode (EC). System/360 mainframes use only the BC mode but System/370 and later mainframes could run in either mode. Fortunately, there are four fields (each serving a unique function) within the PSW that are common to either mode of operation and these are the fields that most affect the description of the basic machine. These fields are: the program counter (PC), the condition code (CC), the protection key, and the program mask. Figure 1.6 shows the structure of the PSW in the extended control mode with only the four common fields specified.

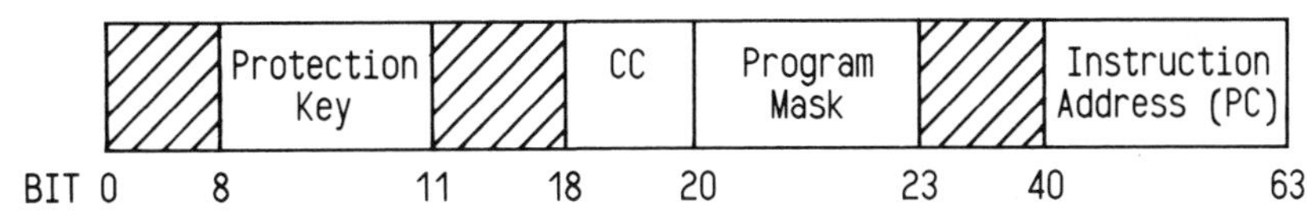

FIGURE 1:6
FORMAT OF THE PSW REGISTER (EC MODE)

The function of each of the PSW fields shown in Figure 1.6 is:

1. The instruction address is the program counter discussed in the CPU contents and is the absolute address of the location from which the CPU will fetch the next instruction. Even though this field is not directly available to the programmer in the problem state, the programmer can affect its contents through the execution of branching instructions and can cause the value of the PC to be copied into a program specified GPR on the execution of a branch and link instruction.

2. The condition code (CC) is a two-bit field (with no pun intended) that is primarily used to specify the result of a compare instruction ($<$, $>$, $=$) or arithmetic instruction ($+$, 0, $-$, overflow). It is the object of the test in the conditional branch instructions.

3. The protection key contains the value that was assigned to the memory keys of all blocks of main memory storage that were assigned to the current user. (This process was described in Memory Protection early in this chapter.)

4. The program mask consists of four bits, each of which represents a program interrupt condition that can be enabled/disabled by the programmer through the execution of a set program mask (SPM) instruction.

The general purpose registers (GPRs) form a set of sixteen 32-bit registers which are available to the programmer for a variety of uses. They are the primary receptacles by which a program transfers data between main memory and the CPU. In addition to this function, they can be used as: base registers, index registers, or registers for data manipulation or binary arithmetic as the programmer sees fit. However, in the case of arithmetic, the actual computation is performed in nonaddressable working registers and the result is placed back in the corresponding GPRs.

MAIN MEMORY

Memory is organized by words, but is byte addressable. IBM defines a "word" as 32 bits for all mainframe machines, however, the actual data path from the CPU to main memory varies in size within models for a particular mainframe line (such as S/360, S/370, or 4300 series). In modern IBM mainframes this data path is at least 32 bits. The maximum addressable memory space is 16MB at any given instant since this is the maximum value that can be specified with a 24-bit absolute address (the memory space can be extended by using multiple virtual memories, discussed in Chapter 5).

There are 512 contiguous bytes of *fixed memory locations* starting at address absolute zero. These fixed locations are limited by machine design to specific functions which cannot be changed by programs running in the problem state and must not be changed from their intended use by programs in the privileged state, if the computing system is to operate properly. These fixed locations, for example, are used by the CPU interrupt mechanism and by the I/O channels.

THE INTERRUPT SYSTEM

The IBM mainframes use the swapping technique described earlier in this chapter to implement interrupts. More specifically, these machines have six pairs of PSW images located in the fixed portion of main memory (see Figure 1.7). Each pair of these images is used for a particular class of interrupt; thus, there are six classes of interrupts, which are:

	Interrupt	Example of a cause for interrupt
1.	restart	Pressing start button on console
2.	external	Computer operator interrupt
3.	supervisor call	Program request to read a record
4.	program	Program error(such as protection)
5.	machine check	Power failure
6.	I/O	Completion of a channel I/O program

By dividing interrupts into six classes, the hardware performs the first level of the analysis in determining exactly what caused a particular interrupt; the rest of the process is performed by the operating system. Each pair of PSW images is divided into a new and old image. The new PSW image contains the instruction address of the beginning of the operating system routine that analyzes interrupts in a particular class. The corresponding old PSW image is used to save the current PSW contents when the interrupt occurrs.

Each time an interrupt occurs, the CPU first stores the current contents of the PSW in the old PSW image for the specific class of interrupt and then places the corresonding new PSW image for the interrupt class in the PSW (this is called *PSW swapping*). The PSW swapping, therefore, causes an automatic branch to a location that must (by machine design) contain the first instruction of a routine that will perform the interrupt analysis for the corresponding interrupt class (see Figure 1.7). As soon as the CPU

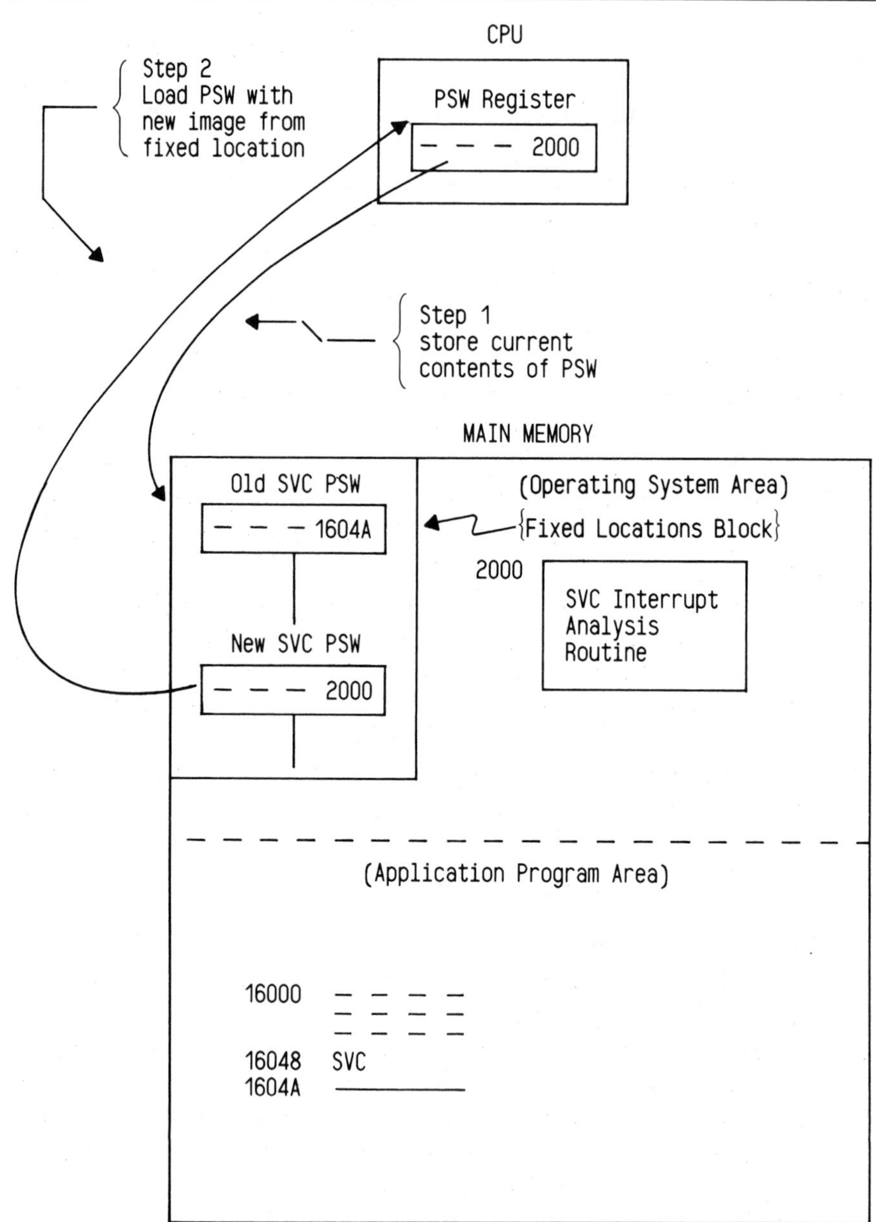

FIGURE 1:7
STEPS AND RESULT OF AN SVC INTERRUPT

performs the PSW swapping the interrupt has occurred; what immediately follows is called *interrupt handling* and is performed by the operating system. Interrupt handling is covered in much greater detail in Chapter 5 when we study operating systems, but for now only the interrupt mechanism is described.

Figure 1.7 presents a partial picture of memory and the PSW immediately after an interrupt has occurred. The machine instruction SVC, located at 16048, is a supervisor call which causes an interrupt for a program request. During the execution cycle of the SVC instruction, the PSW was updated to show the next instruction address but when the interrupt occurred, the current contents of the PSW were automatically stored at the location for the OLD SVC PSW and replaced (swapped) with the contents from the location of the NEW SVC PSW. This effects a transfer to the SVC interrupt analysis routine located at 2000.

DATA TYPES

The IBM mainframes have a rich assortment of data types on which their machine instructions can operate directly. For instance, in addition to strings of characters or other data, there are typically five distinct numeric types and a set of machine instructions that perform the usual arithmetic operations for each arithmetic type. These five numeric types include two forms of binary integers (16 bit and 32 bit), single and double precision floating point numbers, and packed decimal integers. However, data types used for this book are limited to a working subset using only four of the available data types. These are sufficient for our examples throughout the book and are commonly found on most other computers. Also, this choice simplifies our discussion of the IBM mainframe and allows us to greatly reduce the size of the machine language subset that we will need later. The four data types are: hexadecimal digit strings, binary integers, memory addresses and character strings.

Hexadecimal strings (basically the same as bit strings) are composed of any combination of an even number of hexidecimal digits ranging from one to 256 bytes in length. In a byte addressable machine all operands must be in multiples of a byte, thus bit strings could be expressed in terms of eight bits per byte or two hexadecimal digits per bytes. However, the value is the same, therefore the shorter notation was chosen.

Binary integers (the longer form) are expressed as a 31-bit binary integer preceded by a one-bit sign for a total of 32 bits. A sign value of 0 is positive while a value of 1 is negative. For example, the binary equivalent of decimal 37 is

$$0000\ 0000\ 0000\ 0000\ 0000\ 0000\ 0010\ 0101_2 = 00\ \ 00\ 00\ 25_{16}$$

Negative binary integers are stored in the *two's complement form.* Converting from a positive integer to its negative complement can be easily computed by simply subtracting 1 and then inverting all 32 bits (or by inverting the bits and adding 1). For example, converting 37_{10} to -37_{10} is accomplished by:

```
Step 1   0000 0000 0000 0000 0000 0000 0010 0101
                                              -1
         ---------------------------------------
         0000 0000 0000 0000 0000 0000 0010 0100
Step 2   1111 1111 1111 1111 1111 1111 1101 1011₂ = -37₁₀
```

Likewise, converting a negative integer to its positive complement is also accomplished by subtracting 1 and inverting the bits. Keeping with the example above, we can convert -37_{10} back to 37_{10}.

```
Step 1   1111 1111 1111 1111 1111 1111 1101 1011
                                              -1
         ---------------------------------------
         1111 1111 1111 1111 1111 1111 1101 1010
Step 2   0000 0000 0000 0000 0000 0000 0010 0101₂ = 37₁₀
```

The real advantage in using the two's complement form for negative numbers is that when two integers of opposite sign are added, they can be treated as simply two 32-bit unsigned integers and added, with any carry into an imaginary 33-bit position being ignored (commonly said to fall into the "bit bucket"). Continuing with our previous example, we can add 37_{10} and -37_{10} and get 0 (See figure 1.8).

Memory addresses are simply 24-bit nonnegative binary integers which represent corresponding byte locations in main memory. These are treated separately from numeric data types because the machine will treat them differently from a binary integer data type, even though the address is often transferred as part of a right justified 32-bit operand.

Character strings are similar to hexadecimal strings except that each byte in a character string is assumed to contain a bit configuration (two hexadecimal digits) which corresponds to a character in the Extended Binary Coded Decimal Interchange Code (EBCDIC). EBCDIC is an eight-bit binary code used (primarily by IBM) to identify a character set that contains less than 256 characters. Since there are 256 possible bit combinations in an

FIGURE 1:8
ADDITION OF COMPLEMENTS

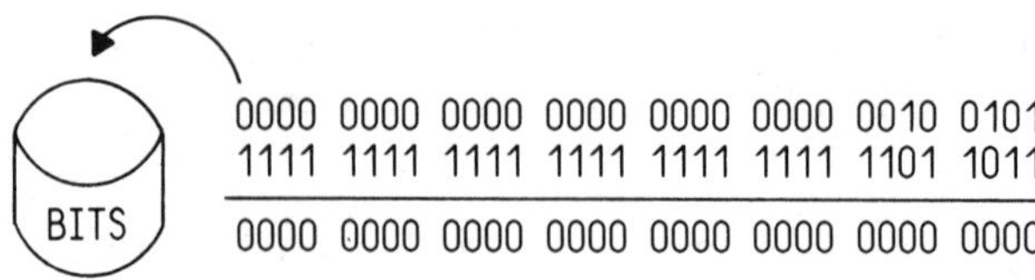

eight bit field, a character string byte is restricted to a value that represents a character from EBCDIC while a byte in a hexadecimal string may contain any of the 256 possible values. Actually, most machine instructions that operate on strings of either type do not distinguish between the two, however, it is more convenient in later discussions when we use assembly language, to be able to distinguish the two types of strings.

Figure 1.9 lists some of the more common characters from the EBCDIC system. (A complete table is given in Appendix B.)

CHARACTER	EBCDIC CODE		
	Binary	Hex	
Null	0000 0000	00	
Space	0100 0000	40	
.	0100 1011	4B	
,	0110 1011	6B	
A	1100 0001	C1	
|	|	|	*
I	1100 1011	C9	
J	1101 0001	D1	
|	|	|	*
R	1101 1001	D9	
S	1110 0010	E2	
|	|	|	*
Z	1110 1001	E9	
0	1111 0000	F0	
|	|	|	*
9	1111 1001	F9	

*Omitted characters that follow the indicated sequences will have corresponding sequential code values.

FIGURE 1:9
ABBREVIATED TABLE OF
CHARACTERS WITH EBCDIC CODES

IBM MAINFRAME MACHINE LANGUAGE

The machine language for the IBM mainframe computers is a powerful and flexible language designed to support a generalized computing environment and meet the needs of most classes of computing tasks. Using the terminology developed earlier in the CPU section, the IBM mainframe machine language is a two-address language using base and displacement addressing for main memory operands (see Machine Language Addressing Schemes earlier in this chapter). The language utilizes six instruction types of which indexing is allowed only for instructions belonging to one type, RX.

Instruction Formats The six instruction types range from two to six bytes in length with a unique instruction format for each type. The name of each instruction type is based on the location of its operands (with respect to main storage, GPRs, and so forth) for the majority of the instructions of the type. In many cases there are equivalent instructions that perform the same operation for each of several different instruction types. This allows an operation to be performed without first having to load the operands into a pair of registers (GPRs) and thus execution performance is improved. In most cases, the first operand in a two-operand instruction will receive the result of the operation.

Each instruction type contains an operation code in the first byte but other than that, the format for each instruction type is different. Descriptions of the six instruction types follow, using the notation that is consistent with that found in IBM reference manuals:

Register and Register (RR): This is the simplest of the instruction types. Each operand resides in one of the 16 GPRs, whose register number can be expressed with a single hexadecimal digit (0-F) in machine language (see Figure 1.10a). (There are instructions of this type that are exceptions to the operand location rule, but these are relatively rare and must be learned individually when needed.)

Using absolute assembly language notation to improve readability, an example of an RR instruction that adds the contents of GPR 6 to GPR 5 is: AR 5,6. In machine language this is 1A56. (See figure 1.10b)

FIGURE 1:10a
RR INSTRUCTION FORMAT

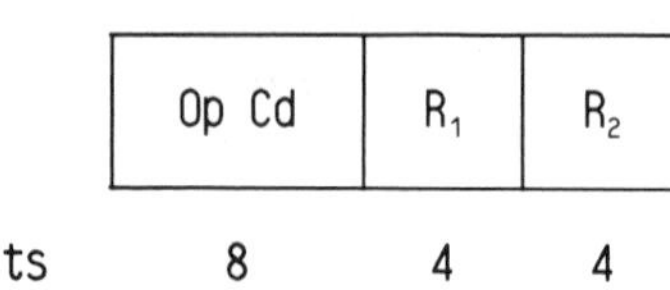

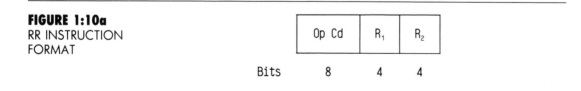

Op	R_1	R_2
1A	5	6

FIGURE 1:10b
RR EXAMPLE

Register and Indexed Main Storage (RX): In this instruction type, the first operand resides in one of the GPRs and the second operand is in main memory. The main memory operand may be indexed (see Machine Language Addressing Schemes), which is an option that is not provided by any other instruction type. The lack of indexing for other instruction types is not a serious problem, since most of the instructions that would benefit from indexing of main memory operands (such as basic load and store instructions, binary and floating point instructions, etc) are of the RX type. In fact, the RR and RX instructions together form the core of the machine language set and offer a complete computing set which is similar to many smaller and simpler machines.

When indexing is not desired for an RX instruction, an index register of 0 is specified in the machine language instruction. Actually, the GPR 0 is ignored by the CPU for any form of address computation whether the case is an index, base register or target of a branch. The omission of GPR 0 from use in addressing saves the programmer from having to zero out an index register to avoid unwanted indexing.

The format of an RX instruction is shown in Figure 1.11 where X_2, B_2, D_2 are the index, base register and displacement used in computing the address of the second operand which resides in main storage.

For an example of an RX instruction, the RR example is modified so that we now add the contents of a four byte (full word) operand in memory to the contents of GPR 5. The address of the memory operand is specified by base register 3 and a displacement of 04C; no indexing is used. (Note: Decimal numbers are used in absolute assembly language.)

A 5,76(0,3) in machine language is 5A50304C, as shown in Figure 1.11b.

	Op Cd	R_1	X_2	B_2	D_2
Bits	8	4	4	4	12

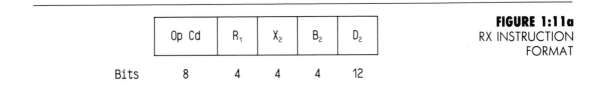

FIGURE 1:11a
RX INSTRUCTION FORMAT

FIGURE 1:11b
RX EXAMPLE

Op	R_1	X_2	B_2	D_2
5A	5	0	3	04C

Register and Main Storage (RS): RS instructions are somewhat similar to RX instructions, but the index register of the second operand of the RX instruction has been replaced by a third register type operand in the RS format. Actually, the RS instruction is the maverick of the instruction types, with almost as many exceptions as there are examples of the basic instruction design. Since exceptions must be handled individually, they are not presented here. The basic instruction format is shown in Figure 1.12a.

An example of an RS instruction is the Load Multiple instruction, in which consecutive GPRs are loaded with consecutive words from memory starting with the B_2 D_2 address. The registers are treated as if they were arranged in a circle in clockwise ascending order, and loading progresses from R_1 around the circle to R_3. For instance, if we wish to load four registers (9,10,11,12) with words starting at a 0 displacement from base register 1, we would have:

LM 9,12,0(1) which in machine language is: 989C1000 as shown in Figure 1.12b.

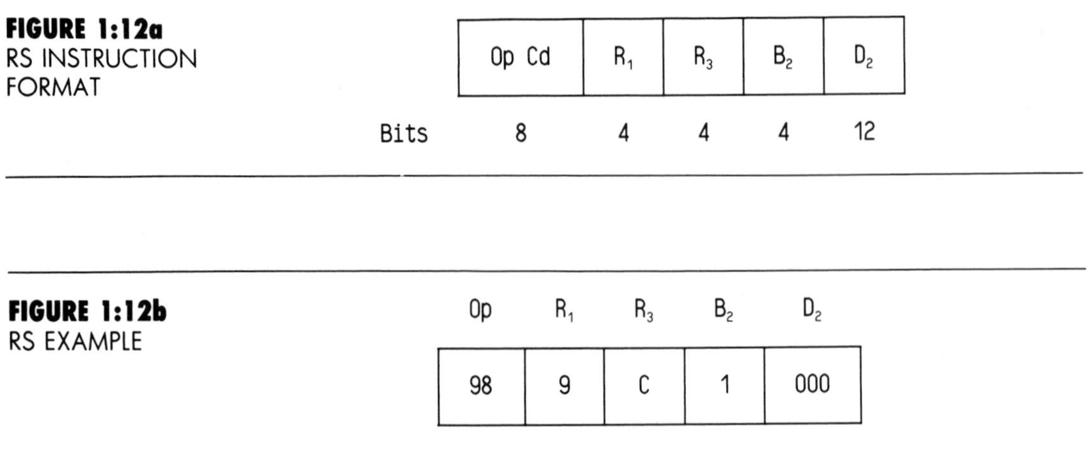

FIGURE 1:12a
RS INSTRUCTION
FORMAT

	Op Cd	R_1	R_3	B_2	D_2
Bits	8	4	4	4	12

FIGURE 1:12b
RS EXAMPLE

Op	R_1	R_3	B_2	D_2
98	9	C	1	000

Storage and Immediate Operand (SI): This instruction type is intended for use with two one-byte operands, of which one is in main storage and the other is carried directly in the instruction. Since the memory operand is the receiving field for instruction operations, it is referred to as the first operand even though it follows the immediate operand in the instruction format shown in Figure 1.13a.

For an example, this instruction type would be used to compare a byte in memory to a blank. Thus, we could have:

CLI 48(3),C' ' which in machine language is 95403030 (note that C' ' $= 40_{16}$ in machine language), as shown in Figure 1.13b.

Storage and Storage (SS): SS instructions allow operations to be performed on two main storage operands. Because each base and displacement address requires two bytes, four bytes are needed for the pair of main memory operand addresses. There is another byte that provides a length modifier used in separate ways for the two subclasses of instructions belonging to this type. The first subclass is intended primarily for character manipulation, and the entire length modifier byte is used to specify the length of the first (receiving) operand. Thus, in this case, an operand can be from 1 to 256 bytes in length. The second subclass of SS instructions is intended primarily for packed decimal arithmetic (which is not covered in this book). The length modifier byte for this group of instructions is split into two four-bit length modifiers; one for each operand. In this case, the maximum length of an operand is 16 bytes. (In both cases, *the machine language length in the instruction is one less than the actual operand length*, which allows maximum

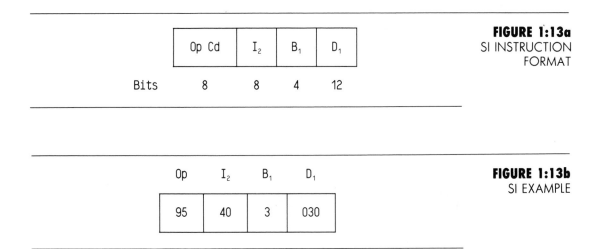

	Op Cd	I_2	B_1	D_1
Bits	8	8	4	12

FIGURE 1:13a
SI INSTRUCTION FORMAT

Op	I_2	B_1	D_1
95	40	3	030

FIGURE 1:13b
SI EXAMPLE

lengths of 256 and 16, instead of 255 and 15.) The SS instruction format is shown in Figure 1.14a.

For an example of an SS instruction with a single length modifier, suppose we wish to "move" (copy) a 132 character header to a print buffer. An instruction which does this is:

MVC 90(132,3),0(4) which in machine language is D283305A4000 as shown in Figure 1.14b.

For an example of an SS instruction with two length modifiers, an add packed instruction is used to add two packed decimal numbers from main memory. Thus we could have:

AP 0(9,5),0(7,6) which appears in machine language as FA8650006000, as Figure 1.14c shows.

FIGURE 1:14a
SS INSTRUCTION FORMAT

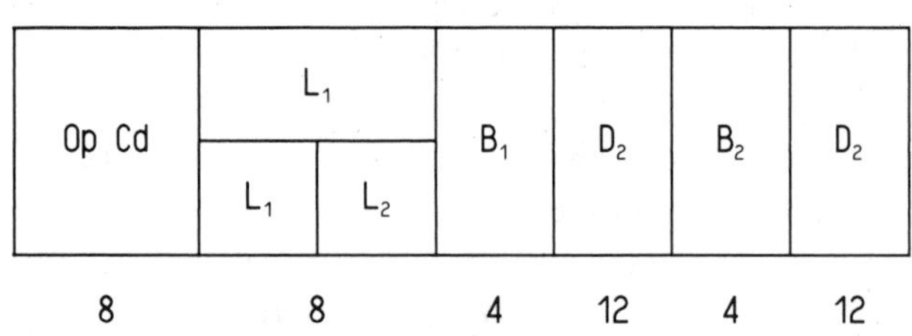

Op	L	B_1	D_1	B_2	D_2
D2	83	3	05A	4	000

FIGURE 1:14b
SS EXAMPLE FOR SUBCLASS WITH ONE LENGTH MODIFIER

Op	L_1	L_2	B_1	D_1	B_2	D_2
FA	8	6	5	000	6	000

FIGURE 1:14c
SS EXAMPLE FOR SUBCLASS WITH TWO LENGTH MODIFIERS

	Op Cd	B_1	D_1
Bits	16	4	12

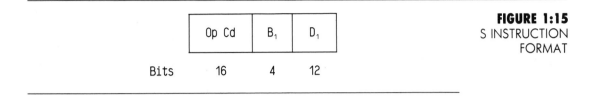

FIGURE 1:15
S INSTRUCTION FORMAT

Storage (S): Finally, there is the S type instruction which has as its only operand a single main memory operand. This instruction type is only used for instructions that execute in the privileged state. The op code is expanded to 16 bits (although the second byte of the op Code is basically a modifier to the first) and the single operand is specified with a base and displacement address. The S format is given in Figure 1.15.

Since the treatment of this instruction is highly nonuniform, and since privileged instructions are not used in the coding examples, a specific example does not appear here.

Machine Language Subset The complete machine language set for the IBM mainframes contains nearly 200 machine instructions. This far exceeds the needs of this book in choosing a machine language to demonstrate certain common computing concepts and techniques that are associated with system software. Furthermore, a machine language of this size would distract from the overall purpose of this book and place too great a burden on the reader. Therefore, this text uses a subset of 47 machine instructions which provide the following:

1. a machine language that is logically complete. In other words we can still program practically any application that we could with the full set (even though it might take considerably more instructions and execution time to do so).
2. a machine language that is functionally similar in many ways to subsets of those found on other machines.
3. a subset that still provides a sound introduction to and preserves the characteristics of the full IBM mainframe machine language.
4. a subset that can be mastered quickly by anyone familiar with another machine language.
5. a machine language that is complete enough to provide a solid foundation for anyone studying a machine language in depth for the first time.

In order to facilitate the study of the machine language subset, the instructions are organized into functional groupings that correspond to the instruction groupings in our general discussion of machine languages earlier. Each instruction is then described with the following information:

1. **Instruction mnemonic.** This is the mnemonic operation code which is used in the assembly language described in Chapter 2.
2. **Instruction operation code (hexadecimal).**
3. **Instruction type.** This includes RR, RX, RS, SI, SS, or S.
4. **Instruction name.** For example; LR is "Load Register"
5. **Instruction function.** This is described in an abbreviated notation based on the convention used in IBM reference manuals for defining the machine instruction formats. More specifically:
    a. *Operands* are identified as they were in the instruction formats by R (for registers), I (for immediate operands), and S (for storage operands, instead of B and D).
    b. The *contents at the location* specified by an operand is denoted as c(operand). For example: $c(R_1)$ or $c(S_2)$.
    c. The *address of a storage operand* is indicated by $a(S_1)$ or $a(S_2)$.
    d. *Transfer of information* is shown by an arrow pointing to the receiving field. For example: $c(R_2) \rightarrow c(R_1)$.
    e. Instructions that cause the setting of the condition code in the PSW are indicated with a *cc* at the end of the function description.
    f. The *testing of a value* is shown by *t*(value). For example, if the condition code is tested, t(cc) is included in the function description.
    g. A branch is indicated by b(location). For example: $b(S_2)$ or $b(c(R_2))$.

A complete list of the machine instructions for the IBM 4300 processor family is given in Appendix A with the subset instructions indicated. The instruction subset can now be presented using the conventions that have been defined. To illustrate the execution of representative instructions including the effects on memory, registers, and so on, examples are presented using the absolute assembly language format which is explained fully at the beginning of the next Chapter. The only purpose of this section is to describe the machine language on an instruction-by-instruction basis. Because programming at machine level is normally done in assembly language, most programming considerations will be discussed in chapter 2.

1. Instructions that transfer data between main memory (storage) and the CPU or between registers.

Mnemonic	Op Cd	Type	Name	Function
LR	18	RR	Load Register	$c(R_2) \longrightarrow c(R_1)$
L	58	RX	Load (4 bytes)	$c(S_2) \longrightarrow c(R_1)$
LTR	12	RR	Load & Test Register	$c(R_2) \longrightarrow c(R_1)$; cc
LA	41	RX	Load Address	$a(S_2) \longrightarrow c(R_1)$; *
LM	98	RS	Load Multiple	$c(S_2, S_2 + 4, \ldots) \longrightarrow c(R_1, \ldots, R_3)$
IC	43	RX	Insert Character	$c(S_2) \longrightarrow$ c(right byte R_1)
ST	50	RX	Store (4 bytes)	$c(R_1) \longrightarrow c(S_2)$
STC	42	RX	Store Character	c(right byte R_1) $\longrightarrow c(S_2)$
STM	90	RS	Store Multiple	$c(R_1, \ldots, R_3) \longrightarrow c(S_2, S_2 + 4, \ldots)$

*Since the address of S_2 is only 24 bits, the LA instruction loads the 24-bit address in R1 right justified and zero fills the high order 8 bits of the register.

EXAMPLES:

			Contents of:	Before	After
a.	LR	5,6	GPR 5	00000000	0000001C
			GPR 6	0000001C	same
b.	LTR	5,6	GPR 5	00000000	0000001C
			GPR 6	0000001C	same
			CC	?	"+"
c.	L	7,0(0,3)	GPR 0	Anything	same
			GPR 3	00064000	same
			GPR 7	F1F2F3F4	00000100
			Word@ 064000	00000100	same

d.	L	7,0(4,3)	GPR 3	00064000	same
			GPR 4	00000004	same
			GPR 7	F1F2F3F4	00002244
			Word@ 064004	00002244	same
e.	LA	7,0(4,3)	GPR 3	00064000	same
			GPR 4	00000008	same
			GPR 7	F1F2F3F4	00064008
f.	LA	5,1(0,0)	GPR 0	Anything	same
			GPR 5	FFFFFFFA	00000001
g.	LM	5,7,0(3)	GPR 3	00004000	same
			GPR 5	Anything	0017A800
			GPR 6	Anything	0017B000
			GPR 7	Anything	FFFFFFFF
			word@ 004000	0017A800	same
			word@ 004004	0017B000	same
			word@ 004008	FFFFFFFF	same
h.	IC	8,0(0,4)	GPR 0	Anything	same
			GPR 4	0017AC42	same
			GPR 8	C1C2C3C4	C1C2C3E9
			Byte@ 17AC42	E9	same

i. ST, STC, and STM are similar to L, IC, and LM, respectively, except the transfer of data is in the opposite direction (that is, from register to memory instead of vice versa).

2. Instructions for performing full-word (32 bit) binary integer arithmetic. The multiply and divide instructions use an even-odd pair of registers as the object of the operation, such that the registers function as a double sized (64 bit) register. R_1 is always the even register with $R_1 + 1$ as the implied odd register. A multiply will right justify its result and sign fill (that is, zeros for nonnegative numbers or ones for negative numbers) the rest of the 64 bits; a divide assumes the dividend is in this same format.

Mnemonic	Op Cd	Type	Name	Function
AR	1A	RR	Add Register	$c(R_1) + c(R_2) \rightarrow c(R_1)$;cc
A	5A	RX	Add (word)	$c(R_1) + c(S_2) \rightarrow c(R_1)$;cc

SR	1B	RR	Subtract Register	$c(R_1) - c(R_2) \longrightarrow c(R_1)$;cc
S	5B	RX	Subtract (word)	$c(R_1) - c(S_2) \longrightarrow c(R_1)$;cc
MR	1C	RR	Multiply Register	$c(R_1 + 1) * c(R_2) \longrightarrow c(R_1 \,\&\, R_1 + 1)$
M	5C	RX	Multiply (word)	$c(R_1 + 1) * c(S_2) \longrightarrow c(R_1 \,\&\, R_1 + 1)$
DR	1D	RR	Divide Register	$c(R_1 \,\&\, R_1 + 1)/c(R_2)$, Quotient$\longrightarrow c(R_1 + 1)$, Remainder$\longrightarrow c(R_1)$
D	5D	RX	Divide (word)	$c(R_1 \,\&\, R_1 + 1)/c(S_2)$, Quotient$\longrightarrow c(R_1 + 1)$ Remainder$\longrightarrow c(R_1)$

Note: Since the dividend is often loaded directly into $R_1 + 1$ (not the result of a multiply), care must be taken that R_1 contains zeros in the case of a positive integer, or all binary ones in the case of a negative dividend.

Examples:

			Contents of:	Before	After
a.	AR	4,5	GPR 4	0000E231	000106A4
			GPR 5	00002473	same
			CC	?	"+"

b. The A instruction is similar to AR, except that the second operand is a word in main memory instead of a register. Likewise the SR and S instructions are similar in every way to AR and A, except that the second operand is subtracted from the first.

			Contents of:	Before	After
c.	MR	4,7	GPR 4	Anything	00000000
			GPR 5	00000005	00000014
			GPR 7	00000004	same

d. The M instruction is similar to the MR, except that the second operand resides in a word in main memory.

			Contents of:	Before	After
e.	DR	6,10	GPR 6	00000000	00000001
			GPR 7	00000009	00000004
			GPR 10	00000002	same

f. The D instruction is similar to the DR, except that the second operand (the divisor) resides in a word in main memory.

3. Instructions that perform branching. In these instructions, GPR 0 is ignored as the object of a branch. As stated before, GPR 0 is always ignored as a base register in the computation of any base and displacement address.

Mnemonic	Op Cd	Type	Name	Function
BALR	05	RR	Branch and Link	$c(PC) \longrightarrow c(R_1), b(c(R_2))$
BAL	45	RX	Branch and Link	$c(PC) \longrightarrow c(R_1), b(a(S_2))$
BCR	07	RR	Branch on Condition Register	t(cc), if true $b(c(R_2))$
BC	47	RX	Branch on Condition Register	t(cc), if true $b(a(S_2))$
BCTR	06	RR	Branch on CounT Register	$c(R_1) - 1 \longrightarrow c(R_1)$ and $t(c(R_1))$, if $\neq 0$ then $b(c(R_2))$
BCT	46	RX	Branch on CounT	$c(R_1) - 1 \longrightarrow c(R_1)$ and $t(c(R_1))$, if $\neq 0$ then $b(a(S_2))$

The BALR instruction serves two important functions. First, it is the principle mechanism for subroutine linkage, because in addition to branching to a given subroutine, the instruction provides for the passing of the return address in a programmer-specified register. Secondly, when register zero is specified as the object of a branch, the branch is ignored and the instruction provides a convenient way of loading a base register.

In the two branch on condition instructions (BC and BCR) the R_1 operand is used as a mask value by which the condition code is tested. Thus, the actual value of R and not its content ($c(R_1)$) is used for the test. Each bit in the four-bit (one hexadecimal digit) mask represents one of the four possible settings of the condition code. Each of the 16 possible values of the mask (ranging from 0 to F_{16}) corresponds to one of the 16 combinations that can result from the four possible settings of the condition code (that is, 00, 01, 10, 11). Therefore, a single test can be made for a compound condition such as "less than or equal" (01 or 00). In this scheme, each bit in the value of R_1 corresponds to one of the four conditions. Thus:

cc value	mask value	meaning: compare	meaning: arithmetic
00	8 (1000)	=	0
01	4 (0100)	<	—
10	2 (0010)	>	+
11	1 (0001)	(none)	overflow

Therefore, to branch to the address in GPR 3 on a condition code of 01 or 00 (less than or equal), we would use a mask value of 8 + 4 or 12 and write: BCR 12,3.

Examples:

The six instructions in this group basically reduce to three operations, which may be specified in either the RR or RX format. Therefore, only the more common format for each pair is shown.

	Instruction Address			Contents of:	Before	After
a.	0620A4	BALR	14,15	GPR 14	Anything	**0620A6
	0620A6	---		GPR 15	00064000	same; branches to this location
				PC(of PSW)	000620A4	00064000
b.	050004	BALR	3,0	GPR 0	Anything	same
	050006	---		GPR 3	Anything	**050006
				PC(of PSW)	00050004	00050006

Note: The high order byte resulting from the BALR instructions in example (a) and (b) also comes from the PSW and cannot be determined from these examples alone.

c.	003000	BC	8,0(0,4)	GPR 0	Anything	same
				GPR 4	00004000	same
				CC	''=''(00)	same, branch is taken
d.	005040	BCT	5,0(0,4)	GPR 0	Anything	same
				GPR 4	00005000	same
				GPR 5	0000000A	00000009, branch taken

e. 005000	BCT	5,0(0,4)	GPR 0	Anything	same
			GPR 4	00005000	same
			GPR 5	00000001	00000000 No Branch

4. The compare instructions compare the first operand to the second and then set the condition code accordingly. The first two instructions (CR and C) perform arithmetic compares and treat the operands as signed binary integers. The rest of the compare instructions (CL, CLC, CLI) perform logical compares in which the operands are treated as an unsigned string of bits.

Mnemonic	Op Cd	Type	Name	Function
CR	19	RR	Compare Register	$c(R_1):c(R_2);cc$
C	59	RX	Compare (word)	$c(R_1):c(S_2);cc$
CL	55	RX	Compare Logical (word)	$c(R_1):c(S_2);cc$
CLC	D5	SS	Compare Logical Character	$c(S_1):c(S_2);cc$
CLI	95	SI	Compare Logical Immediate	$c(S_1):I_2\ ;cc$

Since the compare instructions in each format cause only the setting of the condition code (explained previously) and nothing else, only one example is shown:

		Contents of:	Before	After
CR	8,9	GPR 8	00000005	same
		GPR 9	0000000A	same
		CC	?	"<" (01)

5. There are generally two instructions needed to perform an I/O. The first instruction (SVC) is executed in preparation for an I/O operation. It causes an interrupt and identifies the I/O operation needed; the second instruction (SIO) starts the channel that will perform the I/O. The full process is explained in I/O Processing, later in this chapter.

Mnemonic	Op Cd	Type	Name	Function
SVC	0A	RR	Supervisor Call	value of R_1 R_2 byte identifies request
SIO	9C	S	Start I/O	starts channel using device whose address is S_2;cc

The execution of the SIO instruction is much more involved than its simple S format would indicate and is almost a subset of instructions in itself. The explanation is well beyond what is needed for this book; therefore, for a complete explanation, refer to the *Principles of Operations* reference manual for any of the IBM mainframe computers. For this text's purposes, it will suffice to view SIO as the instruction that activates a channel.

6. Instructions that perform the logical operations AND, OR and XOR (exclusive OR). In these instructions, the desired logical operation is performed on a bit-by-bit basis, and the resulting value is placed in the corresponding bit position of the first operand. The results of the possible logical operations are:

Operand 1	Operand 2	AND	OR	XOR
0	0	0	0	0
0	1	0	1	1
1	0	0	1	1
1	1	1	1	0

The following are full-word (32-bit) logical instructions:

Mnemonic	Op Cd	Type	Name	Function
OR	16	RR	OR Register	$c(R_1)$OR $c(R_2) \longrightarrow c(R_1)$;cc
O	56	RX	OR (word)	$c(R_1)$OR $c(S_2) \longrightarrow c(R_1)$;cc
XR	17	RR	XOR Register	$c(R_1)$XOR $c(R_2) \longrightarrow c(R_1)$;cc
X	57	RX	XOR (word)	$c(R_1)$XOR $c(S_2) \longrightarrow c(R_1)$;cc
NR	14	RR	AND Register	$c(R_1)$AND $c(R_2) \longrightarrow c(R_1)$;cc
N	54	RX	AND (word)	$c(R_1)$AND $c(S_2) \longrightarrow c(R_1)$;cc

Examples:

			Contents of:	Before	After
a.	OR	5,6	GPR 5	00000005	00000007
			GPR 6	00000003	same
			CC	?	01(''some ones'')
b.	XR	5,6	GPR 5	00000005	00000006
			GPR 6	00000003	same
			CC	?	01(''some ones'')
c.	XR	5,5	GPR 5	00000005	00000000
			CC	?	00(all zeroes)
d.	NR	5,6	GPR 5	00000005	00000001
			GPR 6	00000003	same
			CC	?	01(some ones'')

7. Miscellaneous instructions. The following group of instructions are provided for convenience in coding examples and to enable the examples to be more representative of those commonly used in IBM mainframe machine language. Their operations generally require more explanation than can be expressed with the earlier notation; therefore, the group is listed alphabetically and then their operations are explained.

Mnemonic	Op Cd	Type	Name
CVB	4F	RX	ConVert to Binary
CVD	4E	RX	ConVert to Decimal
MVC	D2	SS	MoVe Characters
MVI	92	SI	MoVe Immediate
OI	96	SI	Or Immediate
PACK	F2	SS	PACK
SLL	89	RS	Shift Left single Logical
SRL	88	RS	Shift Right single Logical
SLDL	8D	RS	Shift Left Double Logical
SRDL	8C	RS	Shift Right Double Logical
UNPK	F3	SS	UNPacK

CVB and CVD are inverse instructions, such that the object of one is the result of the other. CVB takes a packed decimal integer right-justified in a double-word (eight-byte) field and converts the decimal number to an equivalent binary integer residing in the R_1 operand of the instruction. CVD does just the opposite; namely, the binary integer contained in R_1 is converted to a packed decimal integer right-justified in a double-word field in main memory (packed decimal integers are explained under the PACK and UNPK instructions). These instructions greatly simplify the process of converting character string representations of integers to binary and vice versa.

Examples:

		Contents of:	Before	After
CVB	5,0(0,6)	GPR 0	Anything	same
		GPR 5	Anything	00000009
		GPR 6	00050000	same
		Word@ {050000	00000000	same
		Word@ {050004	0000009F	same
CVD	5,0(0,6)	GPR 0	Anything	same
		GPR 5	00000009	same
		GPR 6	00050000	same
		Word@ {050000	Anything	00000000
		Word@ {050004	Anything	0000009C

Note: The CVD instruction (and any other instruction that computes a positive packed decimal result) forms a sign of C (instead of F), which is also recognized by the CPU as a positive sign.

The *MVC* instruction copies data from the S_2 location in main memory to the S_1 location one byte at a time until the length of the data "moved" is equal to $L + 1$, which will range from 1 to 256 bytes. This movement of one byte at a time allows a single character (such as a blank) to be propagated through a field by storing the character at location S_2 and then setting $S_1 = S_2 + 1$. The *MVI* instruction simply copies the byte I_2 to the location S_1. Following is an illustration of the propagation of a space through a 132-byte field using the two move instructions.

```
MVI  20(3),C' '
MVC  21(132,3),20(3)
```

The *OI* instruction is simply the immediate form of the OR instruction explained under the logical instructions earlier in this section. It is very useful in adjusting signs when converting from numeric to character formats.

The *PACK and UNPK* instructions constitute another pair of inverse instructions. The intent of the PACK instruction is to convert a character string representation of an integer (which we will call a character integer) located at S_2 to a packed decimal integer at S_1, while the intent of the UNPK is to convert a packed decimal integer at S_2 to a character integer at S_1. However, the instructions do not check the data type of the fields that are being converted; therefore, their operation must be explained more generally. While packed decimal numbers are not treated as a basic data type in this abbreviated IBM mainframe machine, they are introduced here as an intermediate data type used in the conversion of character data to computational form and vice versa. In order to understand the conversion process to and from packed numbers, it is helpful to now examine the formats of character and packed decimal integers.

A *character integer* is a string of eight-bit character digits (EBCDIC) in which the leftmost four bits (called the zone) are $1111 = F_{16}$ and the rightmost four bits range from 0000 to 1001 or from 0_{16} to 9_{16}. Thus, the character equivalent of the integer 1234 is F1F2F3F4. The packed decimal equivalent of this number is 01234F, which is accomplished by reversing the hexadecimal digits of the rightmost byte of the field and then stripping off the zones of the remaining digits so that, except for the rightmost digit, the other digits are "packed" two for one in the bytes of the receiving field; this is exactly what the PACK instruction does.

The UNPK instruction reverses the process. Once again, the rightmost byte has its hexadecimal digits reversed, and all remaining bytes are expanded two for one by inserting an F before each of the original hexadecimal digits. For example, 0635780F becomes F0F6F3F5F7F8F0. Both the PACK and UNPK instructions operate on one byte at a time from right to left, and if the receiving field is too short, truncation will occur. Zero padding to the left is performed when the receiving field is longer than is needed.

Examples:

			Contents of:	Before	After
a.	PACK	0(3,3),0(5,4)	0(3)	?	12345F
			0(4)	F1F2F3F4F5	Same
b.	PACK	0(3,3),0(3,4)	0(3)	?	00123F
			0(4)	F1F2F3	Same
c.	UNPK	0(4,3),0(2,4)	0(3)	?	F0F1F2F3
			0(4)	123F	Same
d.	UNPK	0(3,3),6(3,3)	0(3)	?	F3F4F5
			0(6)	12345F	Same

Since packed decimal arithmetic will not be used in this book other than in passing from character integers to binary, there is no need to carry the discussion further.

SLL, SRL, SLDL and SRDL are logical shift instructions (that is, shifting is done without regard to a sign). In the case of SLL and SRL, the contents of the register operand R_1 is shifted left (SLL) or right (SRL) by the number of bits specified by the low-order six bits of a(S_2). Bits moving out of the register in the direction of the shift are discarded, while bits entering at the end of the register opposite to the shift direction are set to zero. Usually the S_2 address is coded as a displacement equal to the size of the shift and with a base register equal to zero (which will be ignored). The SLDL and SRDL operate quite similarly to SLL and SRL except that the R_1 operand is an even-odd register pair that functions like a single 64-bit register. In all shift instructions, the R_3 operand is ignored.

Examples:

		Contents of:	Before	After
SLL	10,4	GPR 10	20000005	00000050
SLDL	10,8	GPR 10	00000000	000000F1
		GPR 11	F1F2F3F4	F2F3F400

I/O PROCESSING

As we mentioned earlier in the section on I/O Subsystems, the IBM mainframes use two or more I/O processors (called *channels*) to perform all input/output operations. The channels have their own machine language and service I/O requests by executing programs that reside in main memory in much the same manner as the CPU executes programs residing in main memory. However, channel programs tend to be quite short (one to several instructions) and the machine language of the channels is much simpler than that of the CPU. More specifically, the machine language for the channels consists of a single instruction type called a Channel Command Word (CCW). A CCW is a 64-bit (double-word), fixed-format instruction that contains four information fields, which are: (1) the command code, (2) the data address, (3) the flags field, and (4) the byte count (see Figure 1.16).

The *command code* is simply an operation code and identifies which operation the channel is to perform (such as READ, WRITE, and SEEK).

The *data address* is the main memory address of an I/O area (buffer) that is used to receive or send a record for a READ or WRITE operation. The I/O buffer must be contained within the memory area allocated for the application program requesting the operation, otherwise, memory protec-

FIGURE 1:16
CCW FORMAT

	Command Code	Data Address	Flags	00		Byte Count
Bits	0-7	8-31	32-37		40-47	48-63

tion features would prevent the program instructions from accessing the information in the buffer (see Figure 1.17).

The *flags* field consists of six bits, each of which can (when set) cause the execution of the instruction to be modified in some way. Two of these modifications are *command chaining* and *data chaining*. Command chaining indicates to the channel that there are more instructions to be executed before it completes its I/O program. The last CCW in the I/O program will have this flag set to zero, and the channel will then terminate its execution with an I/O completion interrupt. *Data chaining* indicates to the channel that the current operation is to be repeated using the I/O area specified in the next CCW. This allows "scatter" loading into noncontiguous areas or "gather" writing from noncontiguous areas.

The *byte count* is just the length of the data to be read or written in a particular I/O operation.

In order to execute a channel program (that is, an I/O program), two actions must be taken. First, the address of the channel program must be loaded into a fixed memory location called *the Channel Address Word (CAW)* found at fixed memory address 72. Then a Start I/O (SIO) instruction must be executed by the CPU, which signals the proper channel to begin operation. (These two functions are performed by the operating system which will be discussed in Chapter 5.) At this point, the channel will fetch the address of its program from the CAW and then, starting with this address, begin to fetch and execute instructions from main memory just as any other processor would.

Once the channel starts its operation, the channel will execute independently of the CPU until one of three events occurs: (1) the channel completes its I/O program (the usual case), (2) an error occurs or (3) the CPU executes a Halt I/O (HIO) instruction stopping the channel. While the channel is executing, the CPU is free to perform other tasks. When there is contention between a channel and the CPU for access to main memory, the channel is given priority on a cycle stealing basis as was explained earlier in the section on I/O Subsystem. Contention between channels is handled by hardware queueing techniques.

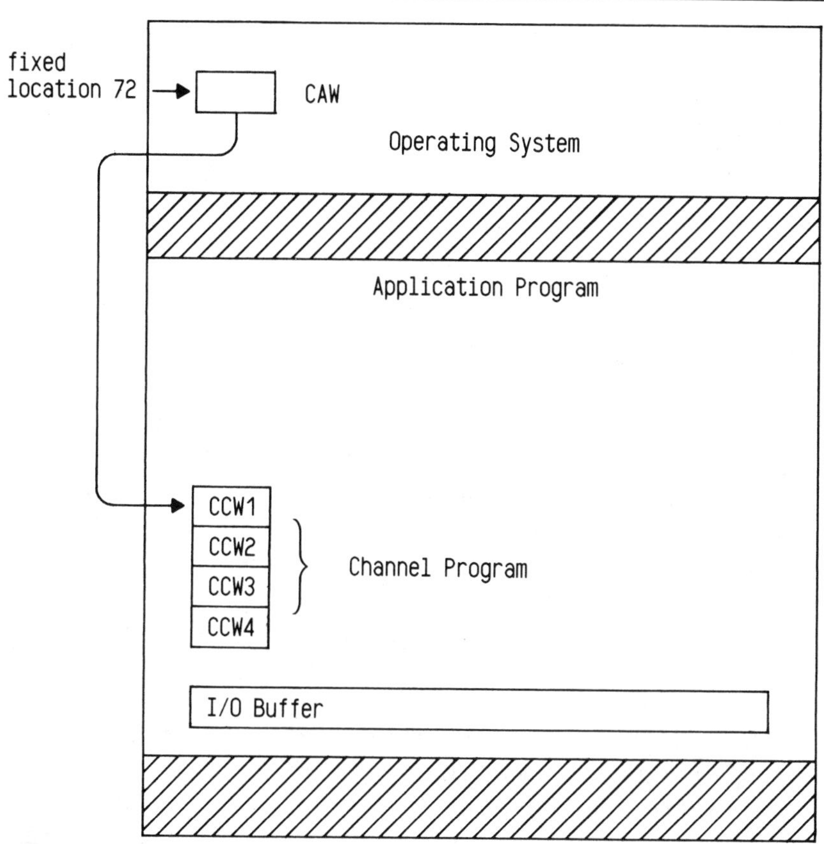

FIGURE 1:17
PRINCIPAL AREAS OF MAIN MEMORY INVOLVED IN AN I/O OPERATION

A full discussion of I/O processing in an IBM mainframe environment requires considerable involvement of the operating system, therefore we will defer the rest of the discussion until Chapter 5.

REVIEW QUESTIONS AND EXERCISES

1. Define or explain briefly:
   a. Interrupt
   b. Interrupt driven
   c. Problem/privileged states
   d. Word
   e. Access/cycle time
   f. Bus
   g. I/O Processor
   h. Cycle stealing
2. A main memory operand is located at absolute address 24000 (decimal). Show how this address would be expressed (using decimal numbers for simplicity) in the alternate forms that follow according to the formats indicated if:
   a. The address were zero relative based on a program load address of absolute 20000. __________
   b. The address were in base and displacement form using base register 5, which has been loaded with absolute 23600. __________ (BDDD)
   c. The address were in zero relative based on program load address plus index form such that the program load address is 20000 and the index register 6 contains 200. __________ (XRRR)
   d. The address were in base and displacement form, plus indexing where base register 3 contains 23400 and index register 4 contains 400. __________ (XBDDD)
3. Compare the memory protection schemes using memory bounds registers or memory protection keys.
4. Given the following segment of IBM mainframe machine language code together with the mnemonic operation code of each instruction, identify the parts of each machine code instruction (such as operation code, register operand, or index register) and state briefly what the instruction does.

Operation	Machine Instruction
STM	90ECD00C
LR	183F
LA	41D030C0
ST	50D030C4
LM	98451000
MVI	92014000
MVC	D2135000309E

5. Main memory operand addresses are represented in base and displacement format in IBM mainframe machine language with the possibility for indexing in the RX instruction type. Calculate the equivalent absolute address from the machine language address given the GPR3 contains 000140C8, GPR4 contains 00000008, and GPR 0 contains 000000A4.

Machine Language Address			Absolute Address
X	B	D	
	3	0 1 8	
	3	F 2 4	
4	3	2 0 0	
0	3	4 0 8	
	0	0 4 8	
	3	F 3 8	

6. Answer the following brief questions concerning the operation of an IBM channel.
   a. What initiates the operation of the channel?
   b. How does the channel locate its I/O program?
   c. Where is the channel program stored?
   d. Where are the I/O areas used by the channel located?

ASSEMBLERS

An *assembler* is a program whose function is to translate a source program written in some specific assembly language into an equivalent machine language program for a particular computer. This translated program may or may not be in executable form, depending on the design and implementation of the assembler used.

TYPES OF ASSEMBLERS

Because the input to an assembler is in the form of some specific assembly language, we need to examine the various types of assembly languages in order to better understand the rationale behind the design of a particular assembler. First, any assembly language is basically a symbolic machine language. Therefore, every assembly language will be limited to one specific type of computer or at least to a family of machine language compatible computers such as IBM's S/370 computers or DEC's PDP-11 and VAX-11 families. Thus, the first step in classifying an assembly language is to identify the hardware for which it is intended. Second, we also classify assembly languages by the amount of abstraction that they provide from the target machine, particularly in the way operands are specified. Thus, the assembly languages are referred to as absolute, symbolic, or macro assembly languages. To illustrate this second area of classification, we will use program segments that would be typical of assembly languages intended for the IBM mainframe computers.

Suppose that we wish to write instructions to add one binary number to another where both numbers initially reside in main memory.

A machine language segment for the IBM mainframe model that accomplishes this is:

```
                              Comments

5840301C               Load register 4 with 1st number
5A403020               Add second number
5040301C               Store sum at 1st location
```

The least amount of abstraction from machine language is an *absolute assembly language.* This type of assembly language provides for mnemonic operation codes and allows decimal numbers to be used instead of hexadecimal numbers in defining operands, but allows for no symbolic operands. This means that when an equivalent machine language instruction carries a main memory address, the address must be determined manually by the programmer. An absolute assembly language improves readability through spacing and groupings of specific instruction parts (such as separating operation codes from operands by spaces and separating multiple operands by commas). Instructions are easier to recognize and to remember because of the mnemonic operation codes, but for all practical purposes, the programmer must think at machine language level. In absolute assembly language, the above machine language example would appear as:

```
                                   Comments
L    4,28(0,3)            Load register 4 with 1st number
A    4,32(0,3)            Add second number
ST   4,28(0,3)            Store sum at 1st location
```

Since an absolute assembly language requires explicit addresses, main memory addresses are tedious to work with. This is particularly true for forward references, which the programmer is usually forced to fill in later. A notable improvement is provided by a *symbolic assembly language*, in which operands and other instruction parts can be referenced symbolically. The programmer chooses a name or symbol to represent an operand address or other machine instruction component. Then this symbol is used in place of the corresponding explicit address when writing assembly language instructions. The symbol value is fixed by the programmer by placing the symbol in the definition field of the assembly language instruction at the desired location in the program. Symbol values can also be assigned through the use of a specific assembler directive or pseudo instruction. The actual value used to replace the symbol is usually calculated by the assembler; and thus, the programmer is spared this task. In addition, if symbolic names are chosen mnemonically, they can greatly enhance the readability of a program.

In a symbolic assembly language the previous example might now appear as:

```
L    4,STUCNT
A    4,CLASSCNT
ST   4,STUCNT
```

The use of symbolic assembly language can give added meaning to the addition of two binary numbers. Here we are adding the number of students in one class to a total of all students in some higher classification. The programmer still must think at machine level with respect to machine operations, but now symbolic operands can be used.

A step above symbolic assembler language is *macro assembly language.* A macro assembly language is usually a symbolic assembly language that provides for the definition and use of macro instructions. A *macro instruction* is actually a request to the assembler to generate a set of assembly language source statements (assembly language text) that will then be translated as if they were coded directly by the programmer. Macros happen to belong to a particular class of subroutines that will be discussed later in the chapter, but obviously, a macro is a means to extend the power and productivity of the programmer. For example, if we were using a macro assembly language and had previously defined a macro called TOTAL, that adds two binary numbers, we could write

```
TOTAL    STUCNT,CLASSCNT
```

This would cause the exact same machine code to be generated as in the previous examples.

Generally, the capabilities for an assembler that can process an absolute assembly language are contained in an assembler that processes symbolic assembly language for the same system. Likewise, a macro assembler for the same system will be an extension of the capabilities of the symbolic assembler. Thus, we can view an absolute assembler as a subset of a symbolic assembler which is, in turn, a subset of a macro assembler.

To restrict this discussion of assemblers to just absolute assemblers would omit one of the most valuable concepts involved in programming languages: the concept of symbolic operands and how they are processed at a very basic level. However, to pursue the design of a macro assembler in detail is beyond the intent of this book. Therefore, most later discussions on the design and implementation of assemblers will concentrate on symbolic assemblers.

With this in mind, the following more complete example illustrating the difference between absolute and symbolic assembly language is given.

ABSOLUTE ASSEMBLER EXAMPLE

```
Location          Source Code

  000          START
  000          BALR          2,0
  002          L             4,14(0,2)
  006          A             4,18(0,2)
  00A          ST            4,22(0,2)
  00E          BR            14
  010          DS            F
  014          DS            F
  018          DS            F
  01C          END
```

SYMBOLIC ASSEMBLY LANGUAGE EQUIVALENT

```
Location                      Source Code

  000          ADD2     START
  000                   BALR     2,0
  002                   USING    *,2
  002                   L        4,FIRST
```

```
006                   A      4,SECOND
00A                   ST     4,SUM
00E                   BR     14
010          FIRST    DS     F
014         SECOND    DS     F
018            SUM    DS     F
01C                   END
```

*Note: * is a symbol substitute representing the current location, that is the current value of the location counter.

IBM MAINFRAME ASSEMBLY LANGUAGE

Because a generalized (and abbreviated) IBM mainframe machine was adopted as a teaching machine for this book, it now becomes essential to describe an assembly language for that machine. This will allow us to conveniently write examples at machine level and to present assembler concepts specifically.

The assembly language for the IBM mainframes is basically the same across the product line and can be classified as a macro assembly language. In fact, this assembly language has a very powerful facility for defining and generating macros well beyond what this book will attempt to describe. This discussion of the language will concentrate on those basic symbolic assembler features that will allow us to write routine assembly language examples using the machine instruction subset presented in Chapter 1 so that representative features likely to be found in many assembly languages can be presented.

LANGUAGE STRUCTURE AND SYNTAX

A program written in IBM mainframe assembly language consists of a set of physically sequential statements of which the first statement must be a START (or CSECT) and the last statement must be an END. The format of each statement (except a comment) is basically the same and consists of four positional fields (the *name, operation, operands* and *comment* fields) of which the first three are ended by one or more spaces. We may view a statement as one or more lines of text of up to 71 characters in length. The vast majority of statements do not exceed one line in length, but when necessary, a nonblank character is placed in byte position 72, and the statement is continued in the next line of text. When the name field is used, it must begin in the first byte of a statement, but other fields are free form with respect to byte position as long as they maintain their relative positions to each other (that is, the name field followed by operation, operands, and comment fields, in that order). However, convention has established a statement coding format that improves readability and is strongly recommended for those who use the language. (See Figure 2.1)

The name field is used to equate a symbol (name) to a specific location in a program. Naming a location in a program allows the use of symbolic address instead of the explicit form. Symbols are composed of from one to eight alphabetic and/or numeric characters, of which the first character must be alphabetic. A symbol is defined by placing it in the name field of exactly one statement. Using the same symbol in the name field of more than one statement is not allowed, since this would result in an attempt to assign multiple locations to the same symbol, thus making translation ambiguous. By contrast, it is permissible to assign the same location or value to more than one symbol.

The operation field is used to specifically identify the statement type. It may contain an operation from any one of three statement types, which are:

1. machine instructions (specified by any of the mnemonic operation codes given in Chapter 1).
2. pseudo instructions (sometimes called *assembler directives*) which are explained in the next section.
3. macros.

Anything else that appears in the operation field is considered a mistake (which should perhaps be considered the fourth statement type, since the assembler must be able to process these too!).

The operand field may contain from zero to several operands, depending on the operation. When there are two or more operands, they are separated by commas. Since the coding formats for operands are dependent on the statement type and operation, they will be covered in the next section.

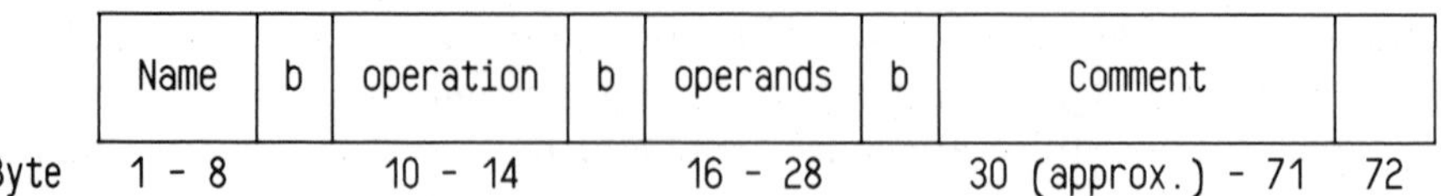

	Name	b	operation	b	operands	b	Comment	
Byte	1 - 8		10 - 14		16 - 28		30 (approx.) - 71	72

FIGURE 2.1
CONVENTIONAL ASSEMBLY LANGUAGE CODING FORMAT

The comment field follows the operand field and is the last field in any statement type. Comments are for program documentation only and are ignored by the assembler, except that it copies them to the source listing verbatim. Since no attempt is made to analyze a comment, it may contain any sequence of characters (including blanks), but hopefully its contents will make the source code more clear. If a comment is to be placed on a statement with no operands, a comma must be placed in the operand field to indicate their absence.

STATEMENT TYPES

Now that the statement structure has been defined, the assembly language statement types can be examined in greater detail. This discussion is not meant to be exhaustive, but should provide enough information to write simple assembly language programs and to understand the symbolic assembly language examples that occur in the book.

Machine Instructions Ordinarily, most of the statements in an assembly language program will be a symbolic form of a single machine instruction. Therefore, it is not surprising that the coding format of this statement type is quite similar to the actual machine instruction it represents. However, in some cases, the operands in an assembly language machine instruction have a different order from their machine language counterparts. For that reason the following rules are given to help clarify the coding formats for the various types of operands.

1. All numeric values are represented by decimal integers, not hexadecimal, unless they are part of a *self-defining term*, such as X'F0'.

2. The position of an operand in a list of operands follows the position order of operands in the machine language formats explained in Chapter 1, except for SI machine instructions, in which case the operand order is reversed (for example, MVI FLAG,C' ').

3. When base and displacement addresses are written explicitly, the register or registers (in case of indexing) are placed in parentheses preceded by the displacement, such as $D_2(B_2)$ or $D_2(X_2,B_2)$.

4. Any simple base and displacement address, such as D(B), can be represented by a symbol. If indexing is desired, the index register is placed in parentheses following the symbol, such as TABLE(4).

The coding formats for each of the six machine language instruction types is as follows:

Type	Explicit Form		Symbolic Example	
RR	OP	R_1, R_2	AR	5,6
RX	OP	$R_1, D_2(X_2, B_2)$	L	9,TABLE(8)
RS	OP	$R_1, R_3, D_2(B_2)$	LM	3,7,PARMS
SI	OP	$D_1(B_1), I_2$	MVI	PLINE,C' '
SS	OP	$D_1(L_1, B_1), D_2(B_2)$	MVC	HERE(10),THERE
S	OP	D(B)	SIO	X'242'

To help programmers use the conditional branching instructions (BC and BCR), the IBM assembler includes a set of extended mnemonics. Each extended mnemonic represents one of the two conditional branch instructions, plus the conditions that cause the branch to be taken. Thus, the programmer can code the extended mnemonic instruction, and the assembler will generate a BC or BCR instruction together with the proper mask value (M_1). A partial list of extended mnemonics and their equivalents follows:

Name	Extended Mnemonic Form		Instead Of	
(unconditional Branch)	B	DONE	BC	15,DONE
(unconditional Branch on Register)	BR	14	BCR	15,14
(Branch on Equal)	BE	FOUND	BC	8,FOUND
(Branch on Not Equal)	BNE	AGAIN	BC	7,AGAIN
(Branch on Low)	BL	LOOP	BC	4,LOOP
(Branch on High)	BH	TOOBIG	BC	2,TOOBIG
(Branch on Not High)	BNH	LTOREQ	BC	13,LTOREQ
(Branch on Not Low)	BNL	GTOREQ	BC	11,GTOREQ
(No Operation)	NOP	0	BC	0,0
(No Operation Register)	NOPR	0	BCR	0,0

By using the extended mnemonic version of the conditional branching instruction, the programmer is spared the task of determining the correct mask value. The extended mnemonics are placed in the operation code table (explained later) so that translation of these instructions can be performed like the machine instructions they represent.

Pseudo Instructions *Pseudo instructions* (also called *directives* or simply *pseudos*) provide information or directions to the assembler that affect the translation process. Pseudos are used for such things as: marking the start and end of a program segment, declaring a base register, and defining a constant. In most cases, the pseudos are simply interpreted by the assembler without producing any object code. The obvious exceptions to this are the DS (Define Storage) and DC (Define Constant) explained later.

The IBM assemblers contain an extensive repertory of pseudos. However, this discussion is confined to only those that are most common and those that are needed in the coding examples that follow. In addition, the discussion of those pseudos covered is restricted to the most common uses; for a complete discussion of all pseudos, refer to the *IBM Assembly Language Reference Manual* No. GC33-4010. In specifying the coding format for each pseudo, the operation field (also the pseudo name) is always required and is written in uppercase letters. Programmer-supplied fields are in lowercase letters and *are underlined when required or strongly recommended.*

1. START and CSECT. Every program segment must begin with a START or CSECT, which identifies the beginning and the name of a program segment. The only difference between the two is that any segment may begin with a CSECT whereas only the first segment in a program can begin with a START. Frequently, an assembly language program consists of a single segment in which case either pseudo may be used. The format is:

   ```
   Symbol    START   value
   ```

   or

   ```
   Symbol    CSECT
   ```

   (The value in the operand field of a START is to provide for a relative starting address that is other than relative zero.)

2. END. An END is used to identify the physical end of the last segment defined in a source module. If a source module contains more than one segment, other segments are ended by declaring a new segment (control section) with a CSECT. The format for an END is:

   ```
   blank    END
   ```

3. USING. The USING pseudo declares one or more base registers that the assembler is to use in generating base and displacement addresses for symbols. USING simply tells the assembler which register(s) *will be loaded* for addressing; it is the program's responsibility to actually load these registers as declared during ex-

ecution. If more than one base register is declared with a single USING, the assembler assumes that they will be loaded with addresses that are exactly 4096 bytes apart.
The format is:

```
blank     USING   relocatable expression,R1,R2,...
```

(the relocatable expression is commonly a single symbol)

4. DS and DC. The DS (define storage) and DC (define constant) pseudos are both used to reserve a specified amount of storage within a program or program segment. They are identical in every way except one; the DC instructs the assembler to initialize the storage area with a value (that is, a constant) while the DS does not. The operand field for a DS or DC is composed of four positional components, of which only the type component is always required. More specifically, the formats are:

```
Symbol     DS   dtl'v'
           or
Symbol     DC   dtl'v'
where: d represents an integer duplication factor
       t represents the type (see Figure 2.2)
       l represents the length modifier which is
           written as L followed by an integer
           (e.g. L3 or L256).  If this component
           is omitted, for a DS the implied length
           for the type is used and for a DC the length
           of the string is used.
       'v' represents the initial value to be
           placed in an area for a DC.  This
           component is ignored for a DS.
```

There are a number of different storage and constant types, but for our future examples and discussion, we can limit ourselves to the five types shown in Figure 2.2.

Examples of the use of DS and DC are:

Code			Generates
ONE	DC	F'1'	'00 00 00 01'
WORD	DS	F	4 byte field (word)
NAME	DS	CL20	20 byte field
TABLE	DS	10F	Table of 10 fullwords

t (field type)	Name	Implied Length
F	fullword binary	4 bytes
C	character	1 byte
X	hexadecimal	1 byte
A	internal address*	4 bytes
V	external address*	4 bytes

24 bit address, right justified and zero filled. Logically, these constants may usually be thought of as absolute addresses, although they will usually require relocation at load time.

FIGURE 2.2
SELECTED DATA TYPES WITH IMPLIED LENGTHS

```
         DS   0F                   causes fullword alignment
                                   (address divisible by 4)
                                   may generate slack bytes
         DC   2C'JOHN'             'JOHNJOHN' in EBCDIC
PARMS    DC   A(PLIST)             relative address of PLIST
                                   (Loader will replace with
                                    absolute address)
```

5. Literals. Literals are not pseudos per se, but they cause the assembler to generate the equivalent of a DC. Therefore, we describe them here. A literal may be used in place of a storage operand of constant value by simply coding the literal instead of a symbolic reference to a programmer defined constant. The assembler will generate the appropriate constant together with all other literal references in an area known as the *literal pool.* Literals are denoted by writing an equal sign followed by a minimum of the constant type and value (for example, =F'1' or =C' '). If desired, the literal may contain a duplication factor and/or length modifier.
   The IBM assembler places the literal pool at the end of the first program segment (CSECT) unless instructed otherwise.

6. LTORG. This is the pseudo that instructs the assembler to generate a literal pool. Each time a LTORG is encountered, the assembler will place all literals since the last LTORG at this spot in the program. In a multisegment program, an LTORG should be written in each segment using literals, otherwise, addressability

errors will occur since each segment has its own addressing environment. The format is:

```
symbol     LTORG
```

7. EQU. EQU equates a symbol to a location or value. The format is:

```
symbol     EQU    value or location
```

Examples:

```
REG1      EQU   1
HANDLE    EQU   NAME
```

Comment Statements A comment statement is denoted by placing an "*" (asterisk) in byte position one of an assembly language statement. Once this is done, the entire statement is treated as a single line of text to be used for program documentation only. Any sequence of characters may be used and no object code will be produced from a comment statement. Example:

```
* BEGINNING OF SHELL SORT ROUTINE.
```

Macros A macro instruction is actually a call to the macro generator portion of the assembler to generate a set of assembly language source statements at this point in the program according to a specific definition for the macro. Because a macro is a form of subroutine (open subroutine), it will be discussed more fully in the sections under assembly language subroutines.

IMPLEMENTATIONS OF ASSEMBLERS

Now that we have described what assembly languages are in general and also what IBM assembly language (at least a working subset of it) is in particular, assemblers can be examined more closely. As stated before, an assembler is a translator program whose function is to convert a source program written in assembly language to an equivalent machine language program. Thus, the role of an assembler is similar to that of other language processors, yet by studying assemblers, we are afforded an opportunity to study on a more simple scale many of the tasks that are common to most translators and other language processors.

Furthermore, many of the tasks that we encounter in studying assemblers are common to a wide spectrum of computing applications besides language processors. For example, hashing and the creation of symbol tables are common activities in file processing. Hence, the design of an assembler provides a framework for developing algorithms that are fundamental to many computing activities.

When we turn our attention to the specific tasks involved in the implementation of an assembler, there are several major questions that must be answered before we start to design algorithms. After the choice of an absolute, symbolic, or macro assembler is made, we need to decide if the design is to be a load-and-go assembler or a module assembler.

A *load-and-go assembler* is one that translates a source program into an executable program residing in main memory and then allows the program to execute if the translation is successful. This design is easier for the implementor and offers a considerable advantage in speed for a combination translation and execution; but there are several disadvantages for the user. First, a program must be retranslated every time before it can be executed, since the only copy of the translated program resides in a work area that is part of the assembler itself and is not saved after the execution (see Figure 2.3). Second, the size of the translated program is more restricted because the translated program shares memory with the assembler. In addition, the use of preassembled subroutines is restricted to those which can reside in predetermined areas outside of the main work area (many load-and-go assemblers simply do not allow for the inclusion of preassembled routines at

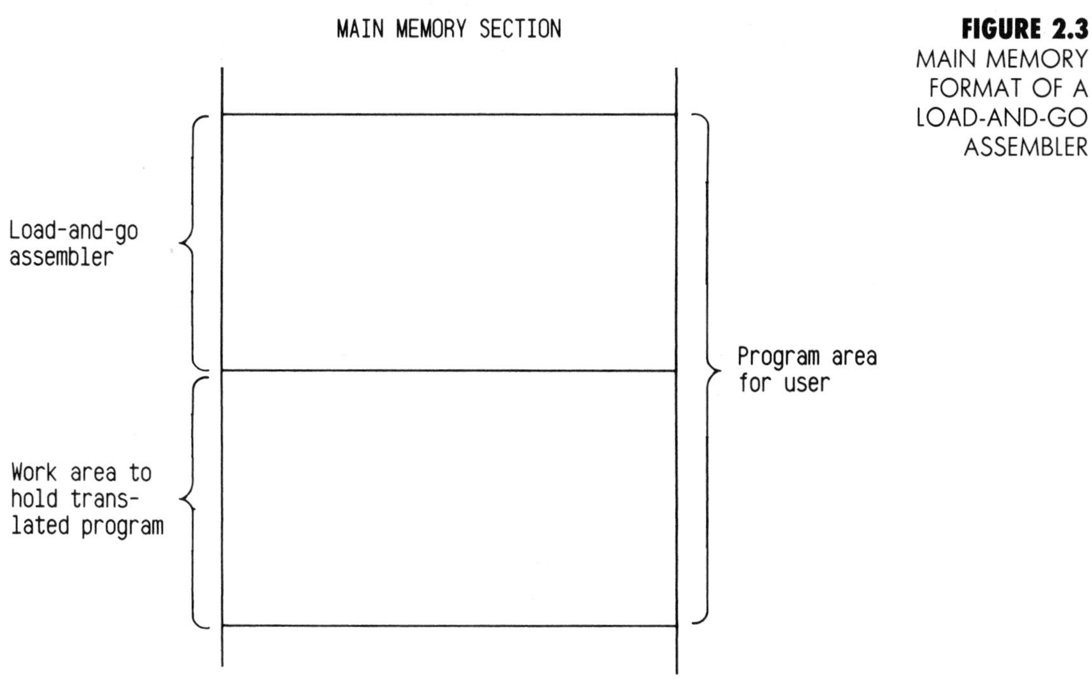

FIGURE 2.3 MAIN MEMORY FORMAT OF A LOAD-AND-GO ASSEMBLER

all). Therefore, the modular development of a large program is severely limited.

The alternative to a load-and-go assembler is a *module assembler*, which allows a program to be written in segments that can be assembled separately and combined later for execution. Of course, the segments can also be assembled together, but the choice is up to the programmer(s). The output of a module assembler is stored on an external medium, such as a disk or tape, and is not in executable form; this output is commonly called an *object module.* Object modules contain translated code in machine language. However, absolute addresses that will depend on where the module will be loaded in main memory are incomplete. In addition, the object module also contains tables (or some other information structure) to assist in the relocation of these absolute addresses and to combine this module with other object modules if needed.

A module assembler will be more difficult to implement than an equivalent load-and-go assembler, and for a combination translation and execution, it will be slower. However, it offers a number of advantages. After a program has been completed, it can be assembled once and stored in object form. Thus, future executions can bypass the translation step, which will save time for commonly used programs. (A load-and-go assembler saves time only when a new translation is needed, such as in a test or program development environment which is the usual case in a student environment, but not in a production or service environment.) Because the output from a module assembler is written to an external medium, it is not necessary for the executable program and assembler to share memory. Therefore, more memory will be available for the translated program when it is loaded for execution. Because of the relocatable properties of object modules, a module assembler provides much greater flexibility in the use and modification of subroutines. In fact, it is common to combine subroutines produced by a module assembler with those translated from another source language, and vice versa. Given these advantages, it is not surprising that most commercially available assemblers are indeed module assemblers.

After we have decided on the type of assembler that we want to implement, we can turn our attention to the design of the assembler. At the beginning of this chapter an assembler was defined as a translator, which is a program that receives statements written in one language (the source module) as input and produces a logically equivalent module in some other language as output. Thus, we wish to design a program that will accept statements written in assembly language and produce their equivalent in the machine language for a particular computer. In other words, given a statement such as:

```
LA      1,PARMLST
```

our assembler must be able to translate this into

```
41103248
```

if we accept the address of PARMLST to be 3248 without going into detail.

Therefore, when we view the assembly process from the highest level, we see two fundamental tasks:

1. Analyze the source statements (*Analysis*)
2. Generate the corresponding object code (*Synthesis*)

These two fundamental tasks of analysis and synthesis are the same for all translators. However, the tasks are usually considerably simpler for assemblers than compilers, primarily because analysis and generation are basically performed on a statement-by-statement basis in assembly language. In a higher level language, the scope of analysis and generation may extend well beyond the current source statement under examination. (The discussion of how compilers approach the tasks of analysis and synthesis is deferred until Chapter 4, when we study higher level programming languages and their language processors.)

Other than the processing of symbols, the translation of the statements in an assembly program can generally be performed on an individual statement basis. Because of this, once a statement has been analyzed, machine code generation is straightforward and presents less of a problem to the implementor of an assembler than does analysis.

Analysis is traditionally described in terms of three subtasks: lexical analysis, syntactic analysis and semantic analysis.

Lexical analysis is the task of dividing each source statement into a string of language "tokens" and identifying each token according to type. *Tokens* are defined as the basic units of a language which convey meaning (symbols, machine operations, integers, delimiters, and so on).

In assembly language, the lexical analysis is simplified because of the uniform structure of each statement type (that is, for our subset of assembly language used in this book each statement contains the identical four major fields separated by one or more spaces excepting, of course, a comment statement which is treated as a single token).

Syntactic analysis is the task of recognizing and identifying structures in the language. More specifically, syntactic analysis is the task of examining the string of tokens obtained from the lexical analysis to see if the sequence of tokens form a valid structure (such as a statement) in the language and to identify what the structure is. In the case of the assembly language we have described, syntactic analysis is primarily concerned with the analysis of the operands field, since the name, operation and comment fields contain, at most, a single token.

Semantic analysis is the task of determining the meaning of a valid structure (statement) in the language. In assembly language, semantic analysis is concerned with the definition and evaluation of symbols, the evaluation of expressions and the interpretation of pseudos.

For example, in the analysis of the statement

```
LA     5,INREC+6
```

the lexical analysis would tell us that we have:

1. a null name field
2. a machine instruction in the operation field
3. a string of tokens in the operands fields consisting of: an integer, a comma, a symbol, a plus sign and an integer
4. a null comment field

The syntactic analysis would tell us that we have a valid LA (load address) instruction with an expression for the second operand. The semantic analysis would evaluate the expression in the instruction, including determining the value of the involved symbol (such as, INREC).

For any given structure in the language, we must always perform the analysis subtasks in the same order (lexical, syntactic and semantic). However, for a given implementation of an assembler when analyzing a statement, it may be more convenient and/or efficient to alternate between the functions of lexical, syntactic and semantic analysis rather than doing each subtask completely before moving to the next. For example, during the first pass of a two-pass assembler (described later), it may be more appropriate for a function of the syntactic analysis to ask for a lexical analysis of the operands field for some statements but not for others that have no effect during the first pass. It may also be appropriate to define a symbol (a function of semantic analysis) before completing the lexical or syntactic phases. This avoids undefined references in other statements that may have referenced an invalid statement that was rejected in the earlier stages of analysis. Therefore, as we examine specific implementations of assemblers, there is no attempt to develop each design into distinct sections representing the subtasks of analysis and generation, but, it is suggested that these implementations be reviewed keeping in mind the conceptual subtasks to which the functions belong.

The next consideration in the design and implementation of an assembler is how many passes of the source code will be used to perform the translation. By a *pass*, we mean a complete scan of all the source statements. In general, convenience and flexibility in writing an assembly language program will increase as the number of passes increases. Conversely, as the number of passes increases, so does the time for translation. Therefore, most module symbolic assemblers are implemented with two passes since this choice is generally accepted to provide the best compromise between speed and convenience. One-pass assemblers are more likely to be used for load-and-go symbolic assemblers, because the assembly language for these is more restrictive to begin with, and for absolute assemblers, because there are no forward references to be determined by the assembler. A *forward reference* occurs when a symbolic operand is encountered prior to the point at which the symbol is defined. Since the physical order of a source language module is generally identical to the physical order of the corresponding translated module, translation is basically a sequential process. Therefore, the technique for resolving forward references is a central concern in the design of a symbolic assembler.

A two-pass symbolic assembler solves the problem of forward references by creating a table of symbols and their corresponding locations or values on the first pass and then uses this table (appropriately called the *symbol table*) on the second pass to replace symbolic operands with their explicit values (locations or absolute values, as the case may be). In a simplified view of a two-pass assembler, the main function of the first pass is to create the symbol table, while the main task of the second pass is to generate the object code.

We have already examined the general tasks required of an assembler with respect to analysis and synthesis, but before pursuing the intricacies of either a one-pass or two-pass implementation, we need to identify the major, specific tasks of any symbolic assembler. The overall task is, of course, to translate a program written in assembly language to its equivalent in machine language; but, this overall task may be broken down into a series of smaller tasks. We have already addressed the task of replacing symbols with their respective values; this will require the construction and use of some type of symbol table. Closely related to the construction of the symbol table is the initialization and maintenance of the *location counter*. The location counter is an internal software counter that contains the current relative location within the object program being created.

The assembler must replace mnemonic operation names with the proper machine operation codes. A predefined table within the assembler matching mnemonics with machine codes is needed for this. There are times when the programmer wishes to provide information or instructions to the assembler about the program that is being assembled. This is the purpose of pseudo instructions, described earlier, and they too must be processed by the assembler. Typical examples of pseudo instructions are: START, END,

DS, and DC. Most assembly languages provide for the use of literals, also described earlier. Literals must be recognized and defined by the assembler. Examples of literals are: =C'NAME' and =F'1'. Values for literals are maintained in an area called the *literal pool*, which will be attached to the object program. Finally, the assembler must provide a listing if one is desired, which is usually the case. Other implementation-dependent tasks are addressed later.

IMPLEMENTATION OF A TWO-PASS ASSEMBLER

If we now return to the implementation of a two-pass symbolic assembler, we can summarize the major tasks for each pass as:

PASS 1

1. Perform lexical and syntactic analysis needed for PASS 1.
2. Create the symbol table.
3. Maintain the location counter.
4. Interpret pseudo instructions (according to needs of first pass).
5. Create literal table (At the end of first pass assign addresses).
6. Generate intermediate code. (This is an optional step, but is one technique for reducing duplication of effort during the second pass.)

PASS 2

1. Perform all lexical and syntactic analysis needed and not saved from PASS 1.
2. Interpret pseudo instructions (according to needs of second pass).
3. Maintain location counter if not saved as part of intermediate code or if no intermediate code was produced.
4. Generate machine code
    a. replace mnemonic operations with machine codes
    b. replace symbols and expressions with values
    c. replace explicit values with hexadecimal equivalents
    d. generate data for defined constants (This function is also related to No. 2.)

5. Generate listing.

In PASS 1, step 1 is self explanatory, while steps 2 through 6 are part of the semantic analysis. In PASS 2, steps 2 and 3 belong to the semantic analysis while steps 4 and 5 form the program synthesis. It is necessary to interpret the pseudo instructions on each pass since some (such as DC) are needed in both passes while some are used only during the first pass (such as LTORG) and others are only used during the second pass (such as USING).

To accomplish these major tasks, the design of a two-pass assembler requires four files and four tables. (Additional tables may be needed depending on special characteristics of the specific assembly language being translated and design preference.)

The four files are the:

Source Program: the input to Pass 1

Intermediate File: the input to Pass 2 (optional)

Object Module: the primary output of Pass 2

Listing: an optional output of Pass 2

Any of these files could be memory resident during some part of the translation process, however, we will view them as residing principally on secondary storage with no more than a few records from each file being memory resident at any time. Of these files, the source program and listing need no explanation. The object module was already discussed briefly, and will be covered in depth when loaders are discussed in the next chapter. Therefore, only the intermediate file needs further explanation here.

The purpose of the intermediate file is to reduce the amount of work required during the second pass, primarily by saving the assembler from repeating processes performed in the first pass—particularly repeating all of the searches of the machine operations table and the pseudo instruction table that are required as part of the lexical analysis. The intermediate file contains a modified copy of the input program, in which either: (1) some parts of the input statement have been translated (such as operation codes substituted for mnemonic operations); or (2) the source statements have been appended with descriptive information and pointers to elements in assembler tables that were located during the first pass and will be needed again in the second pass. The IBM assemblers take this second approach and append to each source statement information which, among other things, identifies the statement type (machine instruction, pseudo, macro, or comment) and provides a pointer to the specific entry in any table that was used in the first pass and needed again in the second pass to complete translation.

For example, in order to identify a source statement as a machine instruction or a pseudo, the assembler must search tables containing all valid entries for each type. This same entry is needed in the second pass to replace the mnemonic operation with its equivalent operation code. Thus, in the second pass, the assembler can go directly to the proper translation routine (that is, the one for machine instructions or pseudos) and then immediately access the correct entry in the appropriate table by using the pointer instead of repeating a table search.

By creating an intermediate file that simply enhances the source file from the first pass, the original source file is not needed for the second pass, and the object module and listing can be produced entirely from the intermediate file during the second pass.

Even though the creation of an intermediate file reduces the amount of work that an assembler must perform during the second pass, there is reason to question its value when the total efficiency of an assembler is analyzed. The intermediate file is normally written to secondary storage, such as magnetic disk, and the actual time to create this new file can far exceed the time saved by reducing the internal workload of the assembler. The descrepancy between CPU and I/O speeds has widened in recent years to the point that in the time required to write a single record to disk, tens of thousands of machine instructions could be executed. To be more specific, a very modest average execution time for many CPUs is on the order of one microsecond per instruction, while the best average access times available on the fastest disk devices are measured in terms of tens of milliseconds (and this does not include the operating system overhead required to initiate the I/O operation). Of course, the final analysis will depend on such factors as whether an I/O processor or DMA controller is actually performing the I/O operation; and if the assembler is running in a multiuser environment, whether there is a net savings in CPU time to benefit other users, even though the total assembly time (clock time) may be slower. All things being considered, the design of the two-pass assembler described below still includes the creation and use of an intermediate file. This is basically the approach used by IBM for some time; however, it would be a simple matter to modify the design to eliminate the intermediate file.

Of the four basic tables needed by the assembler, two are predefined and static (the contents do not change) and two are created dynamically by the assembler as part of the translation process. The two static tables are the *machine operation table* and the *pseudo table*, while the dynamic tables are the symbol table and the literal table.

The machine operation table matches assembly language mnemonic machine operations with their equivalent machine language operation codes. Besides the two basic components (mnemonics and operation codes) found in each table element, the table may also contain additional information about each individual instruction. The IBM assemblers also include the machine instruction type, length, and mask value where appropriate (see Figure 2.4).

Since a search of the machine operation table is made using the mnemonic operation as the search argument, the table is typically ordered on this field so that a rapid searching technique (such as a binary search) can be used.

The pseudo table is used to identify valid pseudo operations. But, since a pseudo must be interpreted instead of translated like a machine operation, the pseudo table simply contains the pseudo name and the address of the corresponding assembler routine that will interpret it (see Figure 2.5). The table is typically ordered by the pseudo operation name to provide rapid searching as with the other tables.

The symbol table equates locations or values to symbolic operands. Each time the assembler encounters a symbol definition during the first pass, the symbol—together with its corresponding value—is placed in the symbol table. During the second pass, each time a symbol is encountered in the operand field, the symbol table is searched in order to replace the symbol with its equivalent value or location. Besides the basic matching of symbols to values, the symbol table will usually contain other information concerning additional attributes associated with each symbol (e.g. the length and type with respect to defined constants).

Mnemonic Operation	Operation Code	Instruction Type	Instruction Length	Mask
A	5A	RX	4	
AR	1A	RR	2	
B	47	RX	4	15
BAL	45	RX	4	
BALR	05	RR	2	
BC	47	RX	4	
.	.	.	.	.
.	.	.	.	.
.	.	.	.	.

FIGURE 2.4
LOGICAL DESIGN FOR AN IBM MACHINE OPERATION TABLE USING MACHINE LANGUAGE SUBSET (INSTRUCTION LENGTHS AND TYPES WOULD ACTUALLY BE IN CODED FORM.)

FIGURE 2.5
LOCAL DESIGN FOR AN IBM PSEUDO OPERATION TABLE USING THE LANGUAGE SUBSET

Pseudo Operation	Address of Processing Routine
CSECT	A(CSECTRTN)
DC	A(DCRTN)
DS	A(DSRTN)
END	A(ENDRTN)
EQU	A(EQURTN)
.	.
.	.
.	.

Since the creation and use of the symbol table is so central in the design of a symbolic assembler, these tasks are examined in some detail at this point.

It is highly desirable that the symbol table be created as a data structure that can be searched quickly during the second pass, and created in such a manner that multidefined symbols (i.e. assigning more than one value to the same symbol) can be easily detected during the first pass.

One way of achieving this goal is to create the symbol table by inserting new definitions in an ordered list which can then be searched using a binary search both during creation and after the table is complete. However, maintaining a physically ordered list during creation can be time consuming for a list of more than a few dozen symbols. Therefore a variation of this technique, in which the symbol table is created as a balanced binary tree, is likely to be generally more satisfactory. Both techniques are explained in detail in *Data Structures for Computer Information Systems* (Ellzey, 1982), as well as other standard texts on data structures.

Another technique for creation of the symbol table involves hashing. This method, as presented here, was described in *Assemblers and BAL* (Flores, 1971), but the basic concepts can be found in most any data structures textbook that covers hashing. This method is presented in detail because, in general, it should provide a faster means of creating a symbol table than either of the other two methods. It is simpler to implement than the balanced binary tree insertion, and it can provide the desired rapid search times, as long as a good hashing algorithm is chosen. The major disadvantage of this technique is that if a poor hashing algorithm is chosen, search times may be degraded to the point that they approach those of searching a linear list.

In this technique, symbols (together with their values) are placed in the symbol table (SYMTAB) in the same physical order that they are defined in the source program, however, each symbol table entry is linked logically to the set of all other entries whose symbol produced the same hashing value (HV). Thus, the symbol table is composed of a set of linked sublists, in which the membership in any particular sublist is based on a common value obtained from hashing the symbol and not on the physical position in the table. Each time a new symbol definition is encountered, the symbol is placed in the next physical location in the symbol table, the symbol is hashed to produce a hash value, and the table entry is linked to the other entries whose symbols produced the same value. If a symbol produces a hash value that has not been produced before, a new sublist is started.

The search procedure that is used for symbol evaluation on the second pass is also used to link the new symbol to the proper sublist during the first pass. The procedure uses a hash table (HASHTAB) in which the starting address for each sublist is kept in the hash table entry that corresponds to the hash value for a particular set of symbols (for example, the location for the sublist whose symbols hash to a value of 2 would be found at HASHTAB(2)). Thus, the search for any symbol begins by obtaining the hash value for the symbol (HV) and starting the search at the address found at HASHTAB(HV). If HASHTAB(HV) produces a null address on the first pass, a new sublist is started; if this occurs on the second pass, the symbol is undefined. Figure 2.6 shows an example of the use of this technique, and Figure 2.7 presents an algorithm for its implementation.

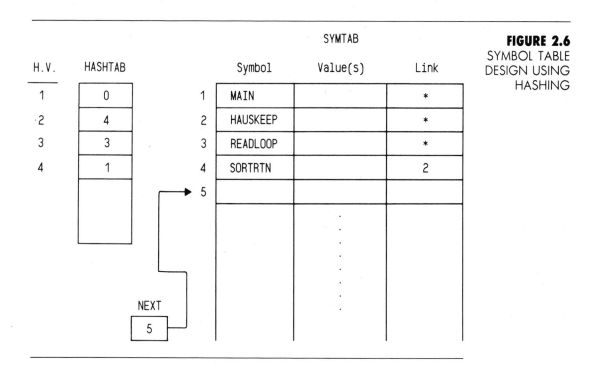

H.V.	HASHTAB
1	0
2	4
3	3
4	1

NEXT: 5

SYMTAB

	Symbol	Value(s)	Link
1	MAIN		*
2	HAUSKEEP		*
3	READLOOP		*
4	SORTRTN		2
5			
		⋮	

FIGURE 2.6
SYMBOL TABLE DESIGN USING HASHING

FIGURE 2.7
LOGIC TO CREATE SYMBOL TABLE

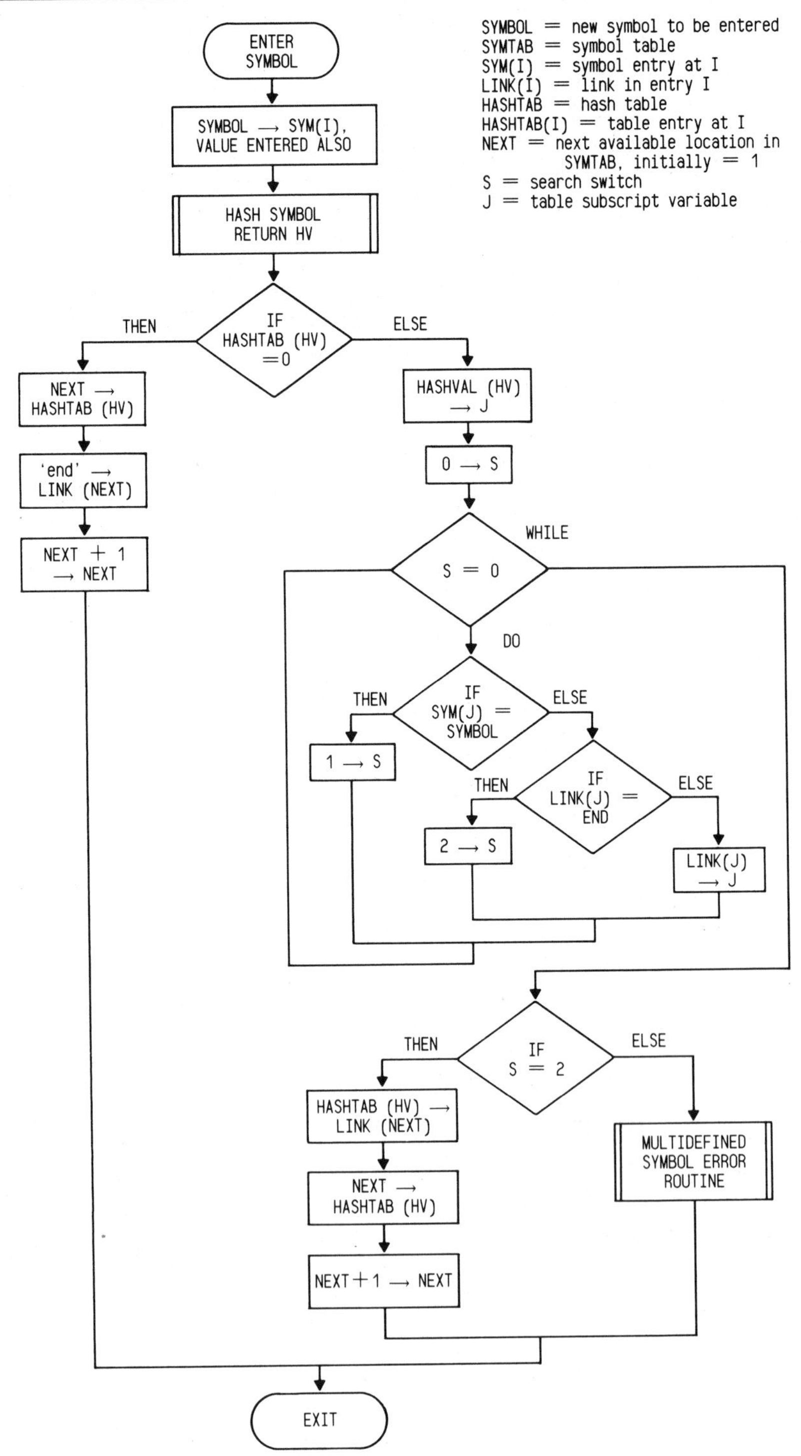

Following is a generally satisfactory hashing algorithm based on the division method. The symbol is PACKED into a five-byte field, which is the size needed to accommodate a maximum length symbol of eight bytes. This compresses the symbol by eliminating the zone portion of each byte—which is the portion of each byte that offers the least variety, since a field composed of alphabetics and/or numerics has only C, D, E, or F (in hexadecimal) in the zones.

Since the SYMBOL often ends in one or more blanks (assuming the symbol has been isolated left-justified in a field, which is eight bytes long) the left portion of the packed field is likely to provide more variety. Therefore, the leftmost four bytes of this packed field are then loaded into a register (treated as a binary positive integer) and divided by the number of sublists desired. The remainder of this division is treated as the hash value. The number of sublists should be prime (or as least odd); otherwise, the distribution may be poor. For a fuller discussion of hashing techniques, see *Key-To-Address Transform Techniques* (Lum, 1971).

```
*HASHING ALGORITHM
        PACK    PKSYM(5),SYMBOL(8) COMPRESS SYMBOL
        L       7,PKSYM            LOAD LEFT 4 BYTES OF PKD.SYM.
        SR      6,6                CLEAR EVEN REG FOR DIV,SETS SIGN
                                   TO +
        D       6,LSTCOUNT         DIVIDE BY NO. OF SUBLISTS
                                    (PRIME NO.)
        ST      6,HASHVAL          SAVE THE HASH VALUE
*TO ACCESS STARTING ADDRESS OF LIST FROM HASHTAB
        SLL     6,2               MUL. HV BY 4 FOR ADDRESS LENGTH
        L       5,HASHTAB(6)       GET LIST ADDRESS
```

Figure 2.7 shows the logic (in structured flowchart form) to create a symbol table using the hashing technique. The search portion of this algorithm can easily be modified to perform the search procedure needed in Pass 2 of an assembler.

The *literal table* is formed by placing each new literal encountered in the operand field of an instruction in a table containing the literal and its machine language value. If a literal (such as =F'0') appears in more than one assembly language statement, only one copy will be placed in the literal table. Literal table order is often based on a scheme that makes the most efficient use of memory. Since the literal table is generally composed of a relatively small number of entries, a sequential searching technique can be used without serious problems in assembler execution time overhead. However, no matter what ordering scheme is used, the assembler will assign locations to the literals at the end of the first pass, thus making the creation of the literal table a simpler task than that of creating the symbol table.

FIGURE 2.8
OVERVIEW OF PASS I OF A TWO-PASS ASSEMBLER

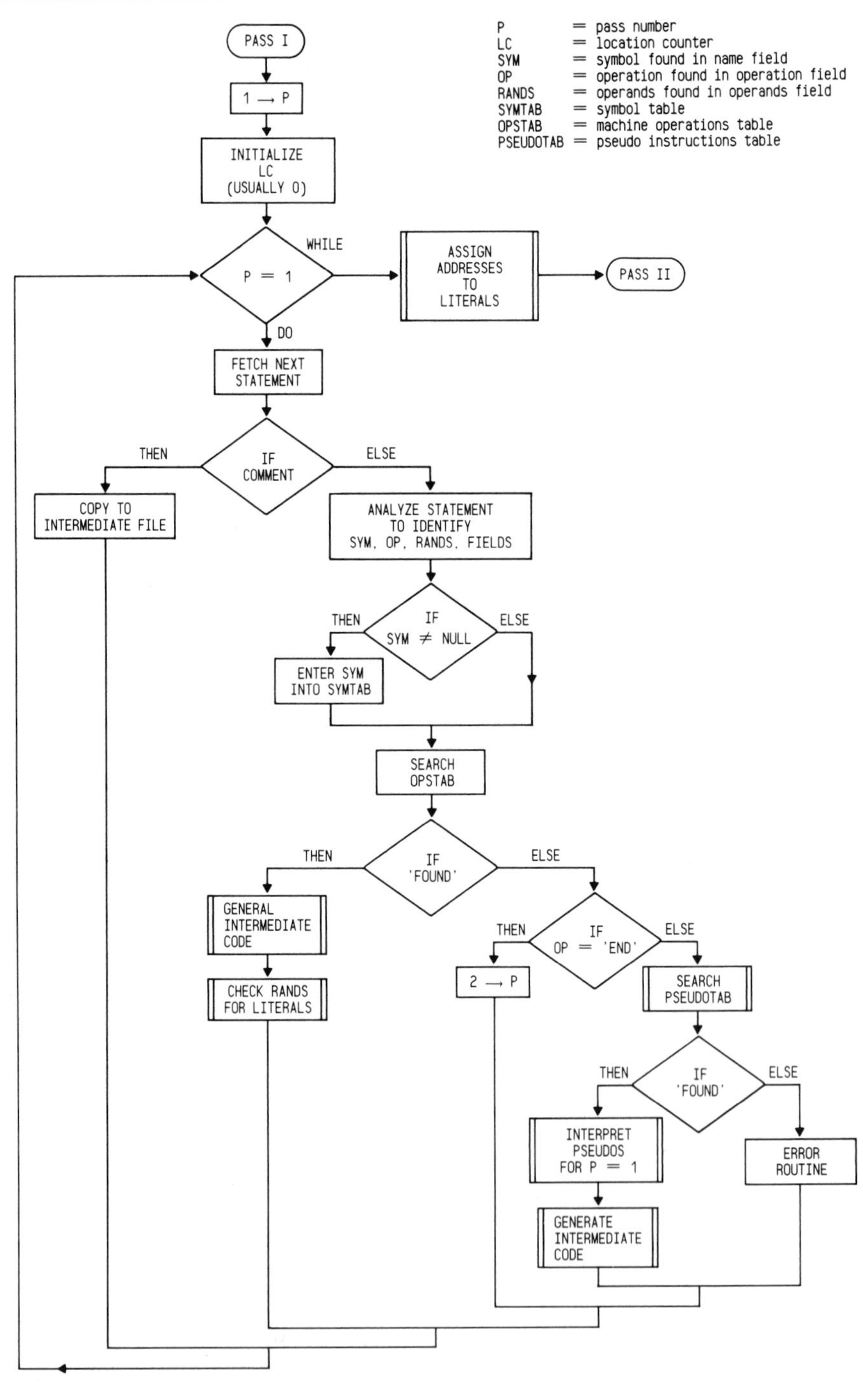

t	Loc.	Seg.No.	TBL PTR	Source Statement

```
            t = statement type:
                  machine instruction
                  pseudo instruction
                  comment
                  error (at this point, the result of an
                         invalid operation field)
                  (A macro assembler would also classify a
                   macro type)
         Loc. = location counter value
      Seg. No. = segment number (value is 1 for all statements
                          in a single segment program)
Table pointer = pointer to specific entry in the table of
                operations for the statement type (e.g. if
                the statement operation has a value of
                ''LA'', pointer is the address of the LA
                entry in the machine operations table
                (OPTAB).).
```

FIGURE 2.9 FORMAT OF INTERMEDIATE FILE RECORD

An overview of the logic for a complete two-pass assembler is shown in Figures 2.8, 2.9, and 2.10.

IMPLEMENTATION OF A ONE-PASS ASSEMBLER

A one-pass assembler must obviously perform all major tasks in the one pass; however, to do this, certain additional tasks and/or restrictions must be imposed. These additional tasks and/or restrictions are mainly associated with the treatment of forward references; otherwise, any of the previously listed major tasks for both passes of a two-pass assembler could be performed in one pass. Obviously, any pseudo instruction must be placed in the source code at a point that will precede any other source statements that are affected by it, but this is basically true of two-pass assemblers as well. One restriction that can be imposed to reduce (but not eliminate) the occurrence of forward references is to require the programmer to define all data areas in front of the executable portion of the code; thus, the only undefined forward references would be in the form of forward branches. This restriction is somewhat inconvenient—but not unreasonable—and can result in a slightly easier

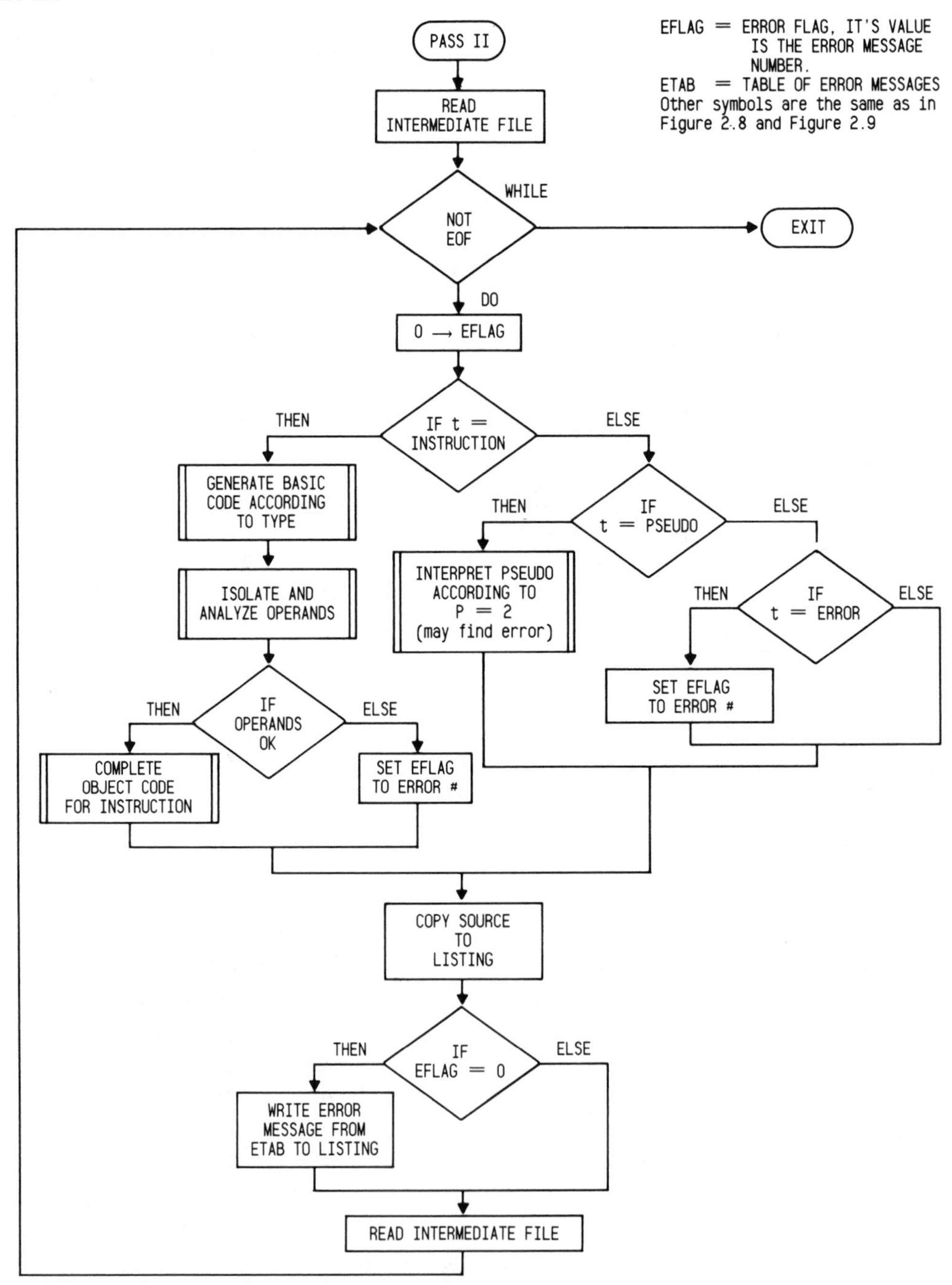

FIGURE 2.10
OVERVIEW OF PASS II OF A TWO-PASS ASSEMBLER

job for the implementor with a slight improvement in assembler efficiency. Still, forward references must be dealt with in either case.

One technique for handling forward references is to place a symbol in the symbol table the first time it is encountered, either by definition or reference and associate with it an indicator marking the symbol as defined or undefined. If the symbol is placed in the symbol table as the result of a definition, then it is marked as defined, and its corresponding value or location is entered as well. Future references to the symbol can be resolved directly by accessing the symbol table. Otherwise, if the symbol is placed in the symbol table as the result of a reference, the symbol is marked as undefined and the value field for the symbol will carry a pointer to the "chain" or list of unresolved references to this symbol. Each undefined symbol has its own separate chain which is implemented as a linked list with the most recent reference at the head (a LIFO or stack structure). All reference chains can be carried in a single table. (See Figure 2.13.)

Consider the following assembly language segment (Figure 2.11), which is a subroutine that calculates the value of N! for a given integer N where $0 \leq N \leq 12$ (as a matter of interest, N! for $N > 12$ would exceed the word size for a 32-bit word). When the one-pass assembler has reached location 040 (just before the point where CONT has been defined), the symbol table and table of reference chains would appear as shown in Figure 2.12. A second view of these tables is shown in Figure 2.13 which depicts a later stage in the assembly process, when the assembler has reached location 056.

We assume that the symbol table was created according to the method described for a two-pass assembler in which symbols are positioned in the symbol table in the order that they are encountered in the text. In that method (see Figures 2.6 and 2.7), we achieved rapid table searching through hashing, however, the resulting linked lists of synonyms are not shown in Figures 2.12 and 2.13 because the focus of this discussion is on resolution of forward references. Also, the search method used is not restricted to a particular technique such as hashing.

Literals, such as =F'0' that appears at location 016 in Figure 2.11, will be handled very much like undefined symbols. Actually, a literal is a symbol that the assembler is asked to define for the programmer. Each new literal is entered in a literal table, and a reference chain is started for all references to it. When the assembler reaches the end of the source module or when it processes the pseudo LTORG that instructs specific placement of the literal pool, it will create the literal pool and resolve all resulting reference chains.

An algorithm showing the major structure of a one-pass assembler utilizing the technique for resolving references described above is given in Figure 2.14. Since the creation and use of the symbol table is perhaps the most significant difference between a one-pass assembler and a two-pass

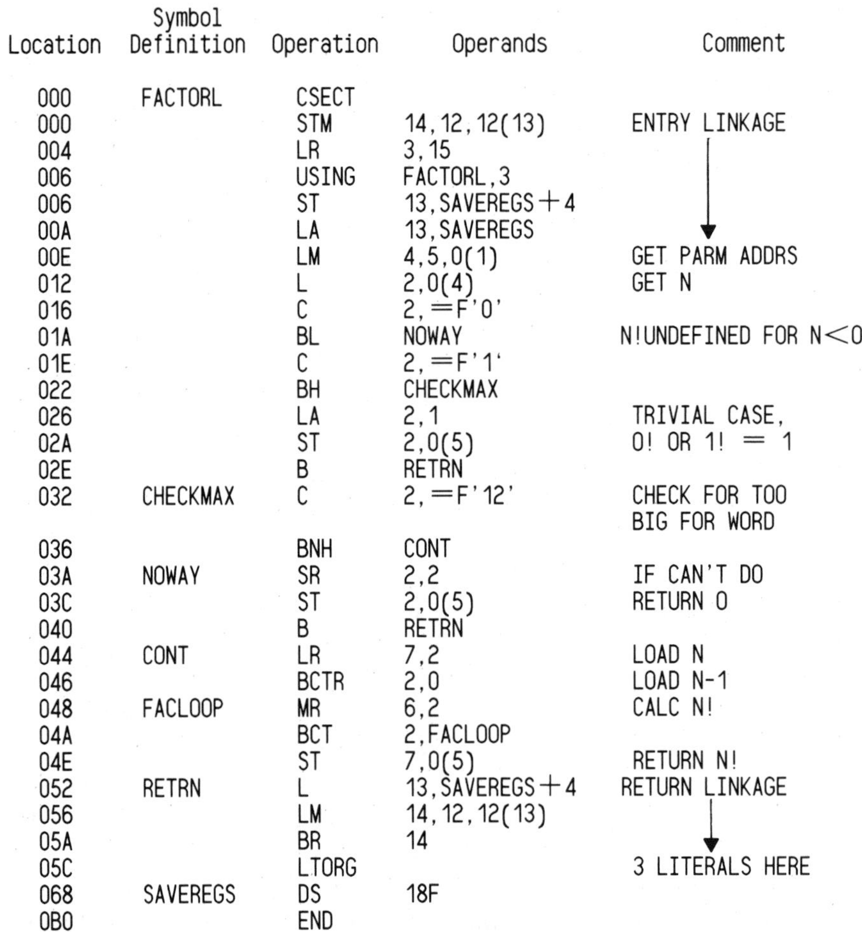

Location	Symbol Definition	Operation	Operands	Comment
000	FACTORL	CSECT		
000		STM	14,12,12(13)	ENTRY LINKAGE
004		LR	3,15	
006		USING	FACTORL,3	
006		ST	13,SAVEREGS+4	
00A		LA	13,SAVEREGS	
00E		LM	4,5,0(1)	GET PARM ADDRS
012		L	2,0(4)	GET N
016		C	2,=F'0'	
01A		BL	NOWAY	N!UNDEFINED FOR N<0
01E		C	2,=F'1'	
022		BH	CHECKMAX	
026		LA	2,1	TRIVIAL CASE,
02A		ST	2,0(5)	0! OR 1! = 1
02E		B	RETRN	
032	CHECKMAX	C	2,=F'12'	CHECK FOR TOO BIG FOR WORD
036		BNH	CONT	
03A	NOWAY	SR	2,2	IF CAN'T DO
03C		ST	2,0(5)	RETURN 0
040		B	RETRN	
044	CONT	LR	7,2	LOAD N
046		BCTR	2,0	LOAD N-1
048	FACLOOP	MR	6,2	CALC N!
04A		BCT	2,FACLOOP	
04E		ST	7,0(5)	RETURN N!
052	RETRN	L	13,SAVEREGS+4	RETURN LINKAGE
056		LM	14,12,12(13)	
05A		BR	14	
05C		LTORG		3 LITERALS HERE
068	SAVEREGS	DS	18F	
0B0		END		

FIGURE 2.11
ASSEMBLY LANGUAGE SEGMENT TO DEMONSTRATE HANDLING OF FORWARD REFERENCES BY A ONE-PASS ASSEMBLER

assembler, Figures 2.15a and 2.15b are given to expand that part of the algorithm that involves the use of the symbol table so that the extra steps required of a one-pass assembler can be seen.

The algorithm for entering symbol definitions (see Figure 2.15a) needs some further explanation for processing an unresolved reference chain. The basic method behind the creation and processing of these chains was already discussed, but the actual value stored at each unresolved reference point may require additional information beyond the value (such as a relative address) for a particular symbol. For example, in the case of an assembler

SYMBOL TABLE

Symbol	Defined Flag	Location
FACTORL	D	000
SAVEREGS	U	2
NOWAY	D	03A
CHECKMAX	D	032
RETRN	U	3
CONT	U	4

REFERENCE CHAINS TABLE

	Reference Location	Link
1	006	end
2	00A	1
3	02E	end
4	036	end

FIGURE 2.12
FIRST VIEW OF A SYMBOL TABLE CREATION FOR A ONE-PASS ASSEMBLER (AT LOCATION 040 IN FIGURE 2.11)

SYMBOL TABLE

Symbol	Defined Flag	Location
FACTORL	D	000
SAVEREGS	U	3
NOWAY	D	03A
CHECKMAX	D	032
RETRN	D	052
CONT	D	044
FACLOOP	D	048

REFERENCE CHAIN TABLE

	Reference Location	Link
1	006	end
2	00A	1
3	052	2

FIGURE 2.13
SECOND VIEW OF SYMBOL TABLE CREATION FOR A ONE-PASS ASSEMBLER (AT LOCATION 056 IN FIGURE 2.11)

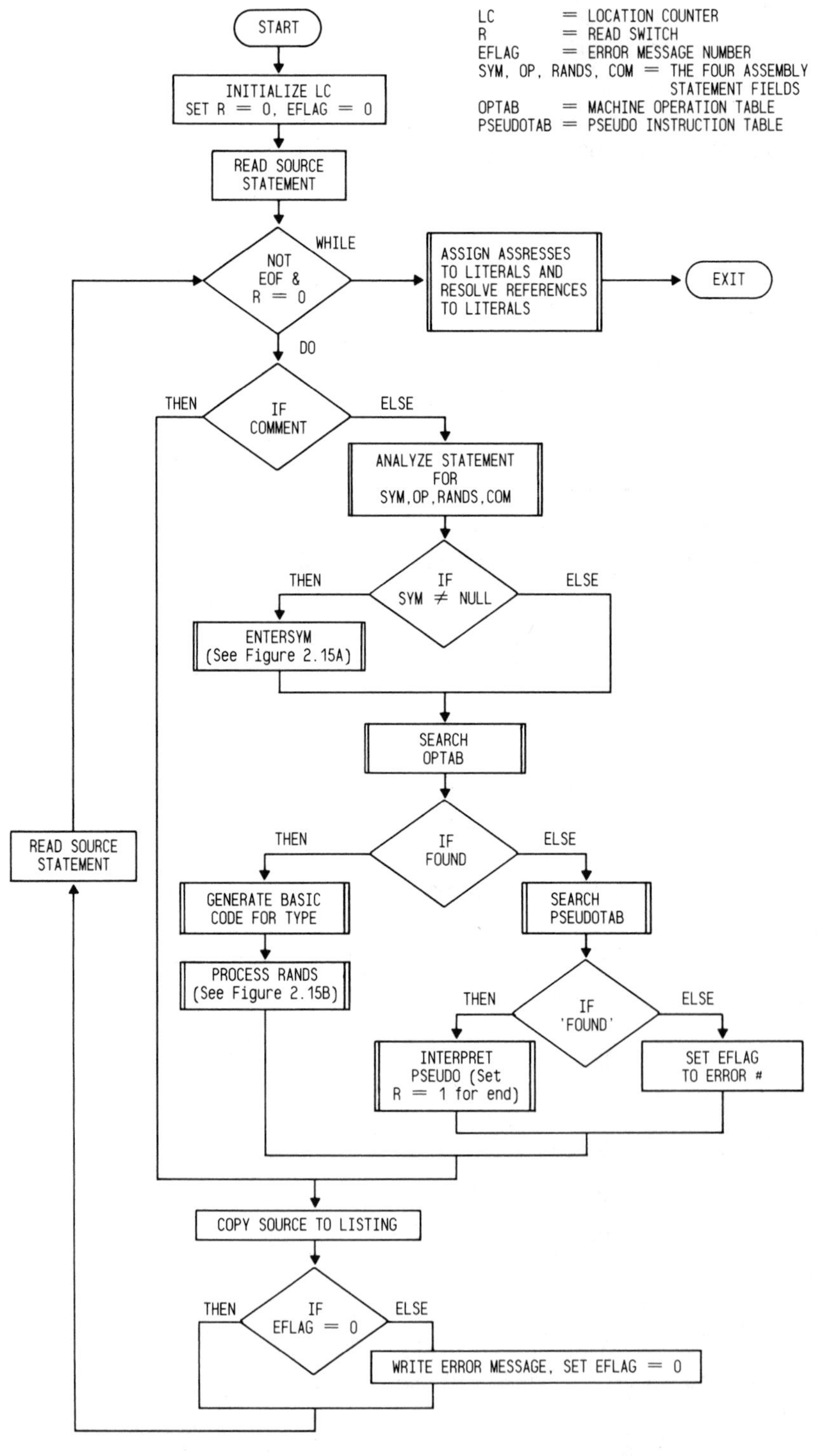

FIGURE 2.14
GENERAL ALGORITHM FOR A ONE-PASS ASSEMBLER

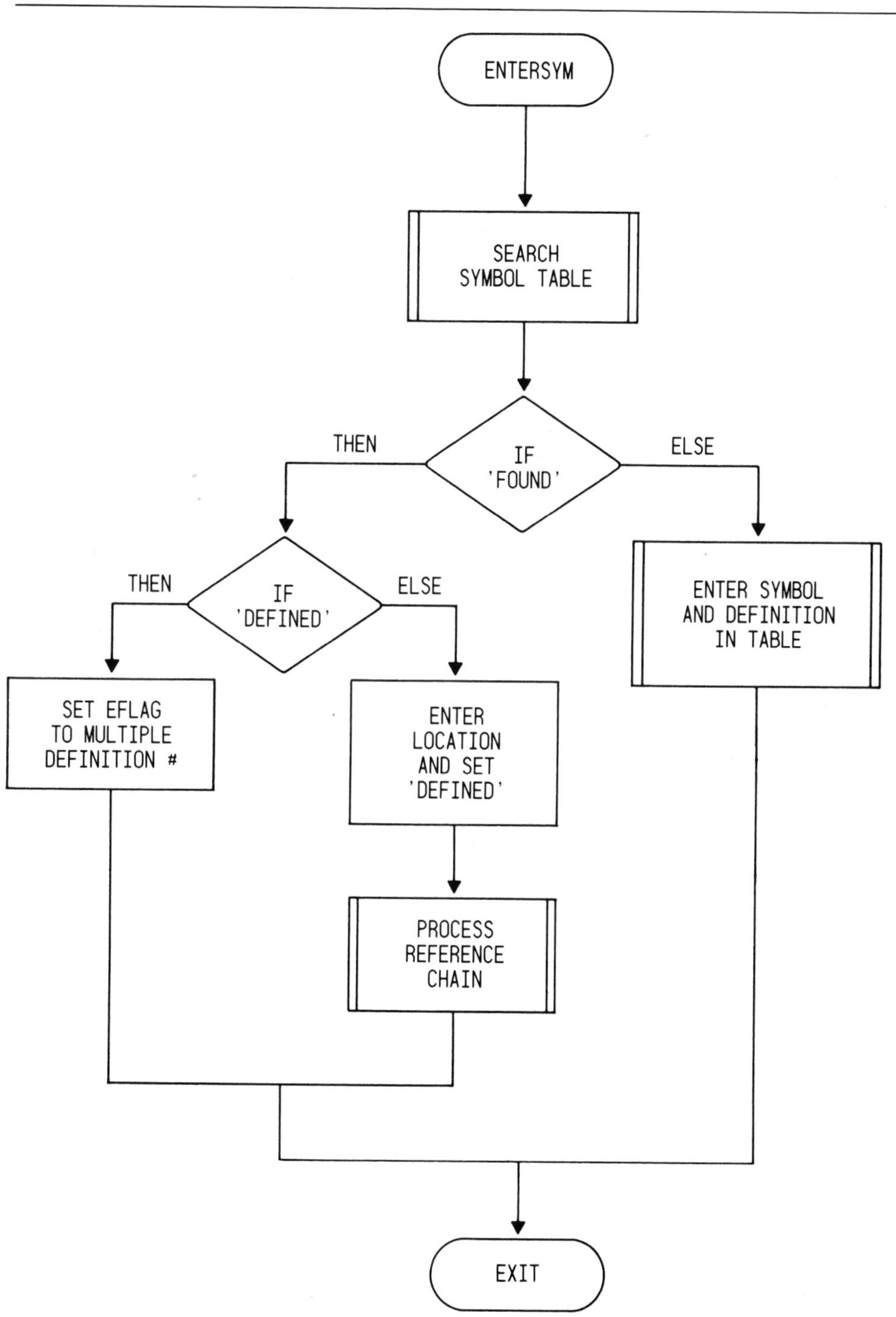

FIGURE 2.15a
PROCESSING OF SYMBOL DEFINITION

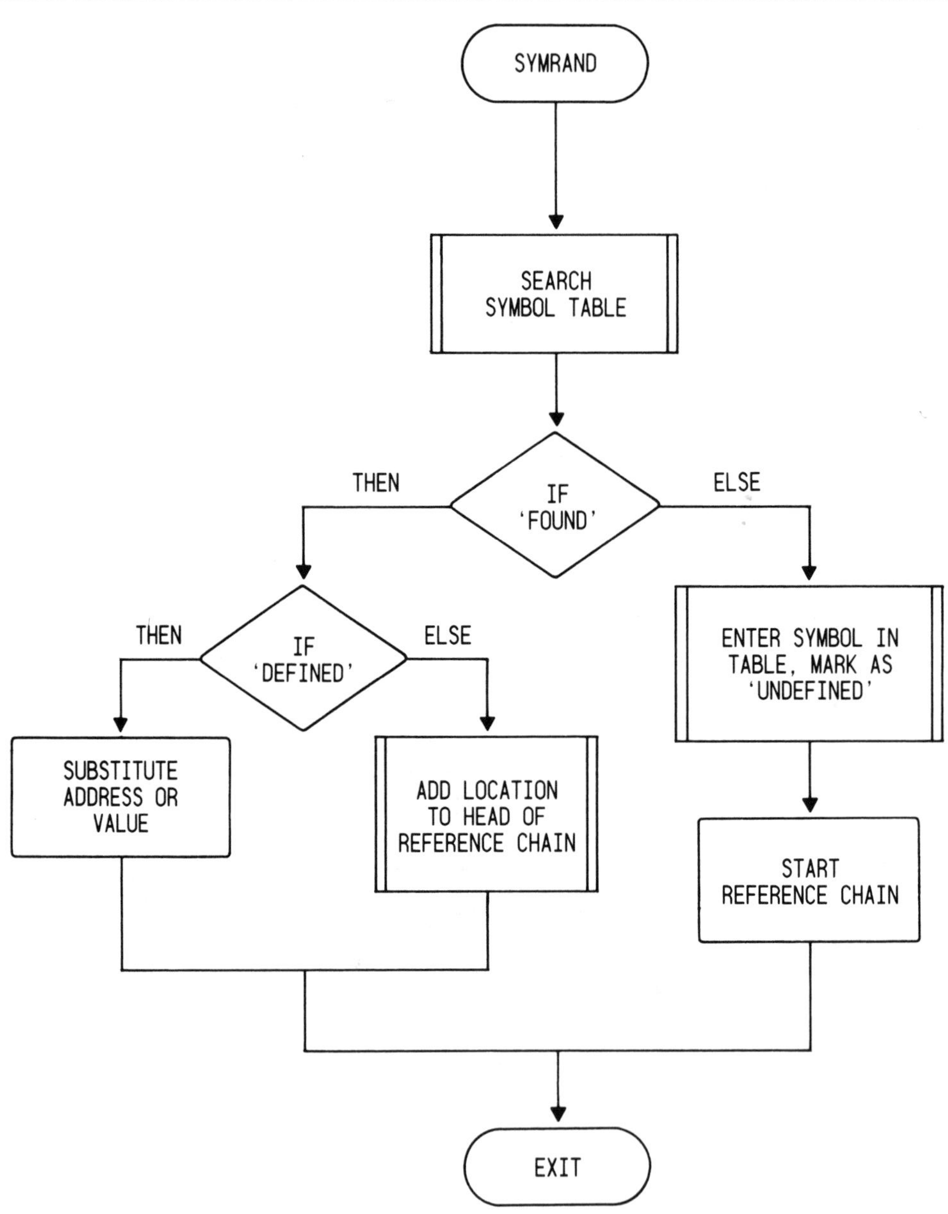

FIGURE 2.15b
PROCESSING OF SYMBOLIC OPERAND

for IBM assembly language, instruction addresses are written in base and displacement form. Therefore, a table of base registers and their relative reference points must be maintained so that base and displacement addresses can be calculated. This table of base registers could be maintained as part of the routine that interprets the USING pseudo, but the information must be available.

In case the unresolved symbol was part of an expression (such as NAME+6), it is also necessary to retain the rest of the expression so that the desired value can be calculated when the symbol is defined. By restricting expressions to a single symbol involving an offset (that is a symbol ± some integer constant), the offset can be stored in the chain entry or simply placed at the reference point that will carry the final value (such as in the address portion of an instruction).

While the algorithms given in Figures 2.14 and 2.15 are not completely explicit at the lower logic levels, they should provide a basis for understanding the major processes involved and the relationships between these processes.

SUBROUTINES

Subroutines play an important part in assembly languages, as they do in most higher level programming languages as well. There are two basic types of subroutines: closed and open. A *closed subroutine* sits apart from its calling routines. Therefore, a calling routine must branch to the subroutine in order to execute it, and upon completion of its execution, the subroutine must branch back (return control) to the calling routine. In order to provide an orderly entry to and return from the closed subroutine, assembly language programmers are asked to adopt a *linkage convention* which was developed by the operating system designers. This linkage convention consists of a standard sequence of assembly language instructions to be used in calling and returning from subroutines including the passing of parameters between routines. A linkage convention not only ensures that the subroutine will not adversely affect the execution of the calling routine, and vice versa, but it also provides for a policy that allows for the incorporation of the subroutine in any other programs that follow the convention. It must be emphasized that a standard linkage convention is not inherent to the particular assembly language or its target machine (particularly if parameter passing is involved) and a programmer may choose not to use it. However, this is an unwise practice since it tends to increase the likelihood of errors and greatly reduces the portability of the subroutine. The assembly language segment shown previously in Figure 2.11 is an example of a closed subroutine that was written following the standard IBM linkage convention.

An *open subroutine* is a subroutine that is inserted directly into the calling program at the point it is called. This direct insertion into the calling program affects the value of the location counter. Therefore, the open subroutine is usually stored in source form and participates in the entire assembly process, as with macros which are examples of open subroutines. The open subroutine needs no linkage instructions; thus, it will always execute faster than an equivalent closed subroutine; and, when compared to an equivalent closed subroutine on a one-to-one basis, the open subroutine will reduce the size of the program by the amount of storage required for the linkage instructions. This apparent savings in program size can be misleading, for if a particular open subroutine is called multiple times in a program, a new copy is inserted for each call. Conversely, if a closed subroutine is called multiple times, only one copy of the subroutine is needed, and only the call linkage is repeated. Since the call linkage usually requires only a few machine instructions, the size of the body of the routine will usually substantially outweigh this. Therefore, in the case of multiple calls to a specific subroutine, the closed version normally reduces program size. Another advantage of closed subroutines is that the subroutine can be assembled separately and stored in object form for incorporation in future programs without reassembling. Thus, program translation time is reduced. An added benefit of storing subroutines in object form is that they can be more easily incorporated in programs written in other source languages. Figure 2.16 illustrates the basic physical properties of open and closed subroutines.

CLOSED SUBROUTINES IN IBM ASSEMBLY LANGUAGE

The closed subroutines written in IBM mainframe assembly language are expected to follow well-defined conventions for calling the subroutine, returning to the routine that initiated the call, and for passing parameters between the two routines. This same convention is also used in the machine language code generated by IBM-supported compilers for languages that pass parameters by reference (or location, see Chapter 4). In other words, assembly language routines that are written using these conventions and translated into object module form will be in the proper form for use by programs that are written in COBOL, FORTRAN, or PL/1.

The linkage conventions achieve three needed functions:

1. The assignment of specific functions to specific GPRs (general Purpose Registers).
2. A policy for the saving and restoring of the register contents of the GPRs for the calling routine.
3. A policy for the passing of parameters.

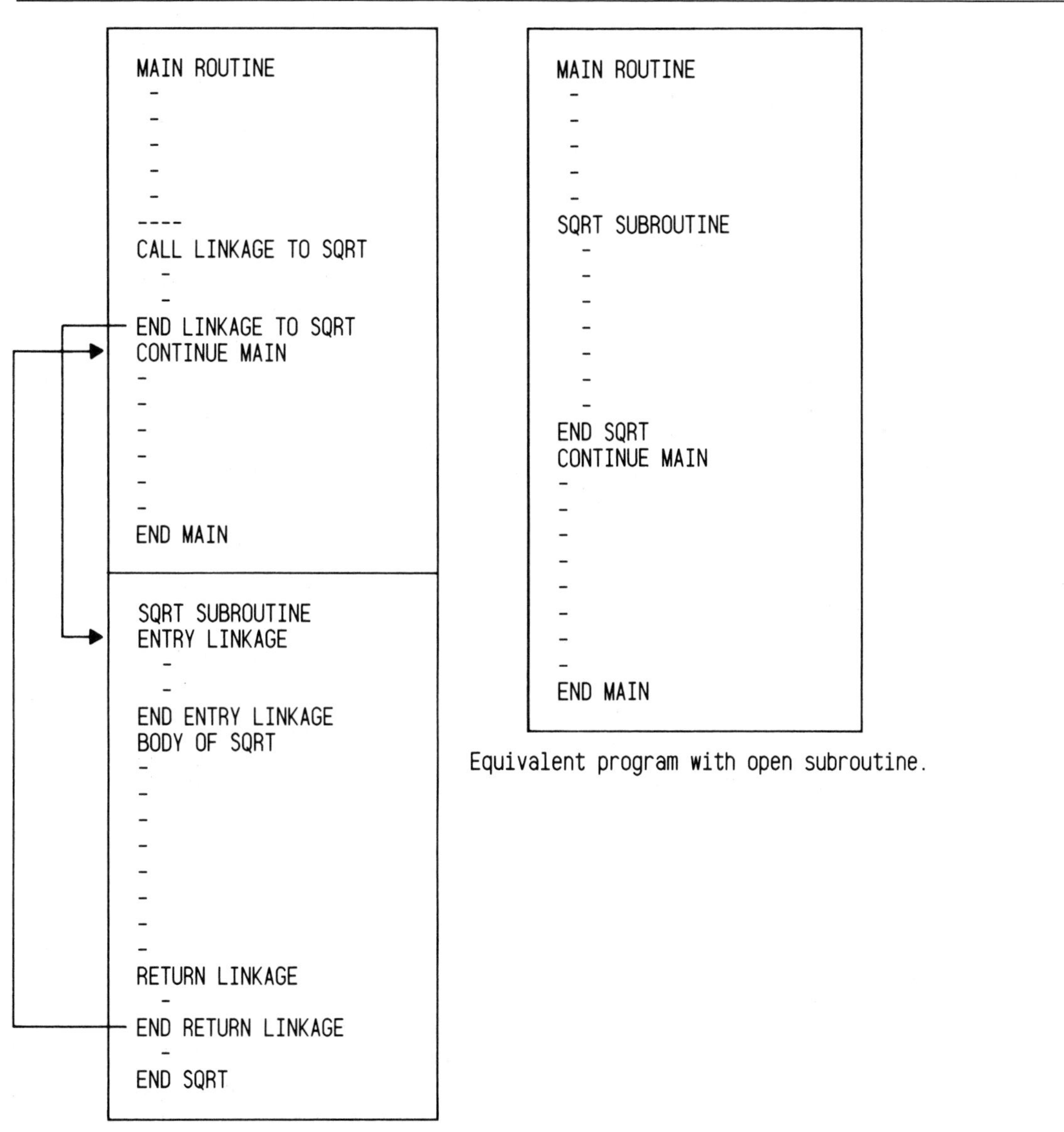

Program with closed subroutine

Equivalent program with open subroutine.

FIGURE 2.16
COMPARISON OF THE RELATIONSHIP OF OPEN AND CLOSED SUBROUTINES TO A PROGRAM

The use of specific registers for specific functions, involves five GPRs. Upon entry to the called routine:

GPR 15 will contain the address of the called routine.
GPR 14 will contain the return address to the calling routine.
GPR 13 will contain the address of the save area in the *calling* routine.
GPR 1 will contain the address of the parameter list in the calling routine.
GPR 0 is used to return the result of an integer type function subroutine such as IABS in FORTRAN.

Since all routines must share the same set of GPRs, a policy is needed to provide for the orderly saving and restoring of register contents upon passing from one routine to another. The policy used is that upon entry, and before any register contents are altered, the called routine will store the contents of all GPRs, except GPR 13, in a save area (See Figure 2.17) provided by the *calling routine.* Since GPR 13 contains the pointer (address) to the calling routine's save area, the contents of GPR 13 must be stored

FIGURE 2.17
SAVE AREA FORMAT

Word	Displacement (bytes)	
1	+ 0	(Used by PL/1 only)
2	+ 4	Pointer to save area in calling routine (GPR 13)
3	+ 8	Pointer to save area in routine called by this routine
4	+12	For use to save contents of GPR 14 of this routine
5	+16	For use to save contents of GPR 15 of this routine
6	+20	For use to save contents of GPR 0 of this routine
7	+24	For use to save contents of GPR 1 of this routine
.	.	
.	.	
.	.	
18	+68	For use to save contents of GPR 12 of this routine

(saved) within the *called routine.* In this way, the called routine can access the save area in the calling routine and restore the original GPR contents as part of the return linkage to the calling routine.

The save area has a fixed format, consisting of 18 fullwords (72 bytes). Each routine must have its own save area using the identical format (actually, if a routine never issues a call to another routine, it only needs to provide for the saving of the contents of GPR 13, but for simplicity, we will assume that every routine has a uniform save area). The last 15 words of a save area are used to save the contents of registers 14,15,0,1,—,12 for the routine that contains the area if it calls another routine (even though the saving is done by the called routine). Words two and three are used for pointers between save areas of calling and called routines. More specifically, word two always points to the save area of the calling routine. Word three (when used) provides a reverse link from the calling routine save area to the save area of the called routine save area. (This link is not needed for the return, but is sometimes useful for debugging purposes.) Thus, the save areas for a set of routines that are called serially form a linked list that is operated as a stack structure.

Parameter passing is achieved by passing a pointer to the called routine in GPR 1. This pointer points to a list *of the addresses* of the parameters that are defined in the calling routine (or a higher level routine). Therefore, by passing the address of a parameter, the called routine can access the parameter directly (that is, the called routine can access memory locations defined in the calling routine). This technique is called *passing parameters by reference* (discussed with other means of parameter passing more fully in Chapter 4).

Since GPR 1 contains only the address of a list of addresses, the parameter addresses must be loaded into registers so that the parameters can be accessed by normal base and displacement addressing. This is achieved in Figure 2.19 by the LM 4,5,0(1) instruction which places the address of the parameter N in GPR 4 and the address of the parameter N! in GPR 5.

A complete example of the use of a closed subroutine is shown in Figures 2.18 and 2.19. Figure 2.18 illustrates a call from a routine named MAIN to the subroutine named FACTORL (Figure 2.19) which was used previously in Figure 2.11 to illustrate a one-pass assembler. However, in the case of Figure 2.19, the optional backward link to the calling routine's save area is included. This backward link places the address of the subroutine's save area in the third word of the calling routine's save area. This option is not needed for normal linkage and return from a subroutine, but can be useful for debugging purposes in certain unrecoverable error situations. More specifically, in case of a program "crash," if the backward link option is used, the main program's save area can be examined to determine the last subroutine called prior to the crash.

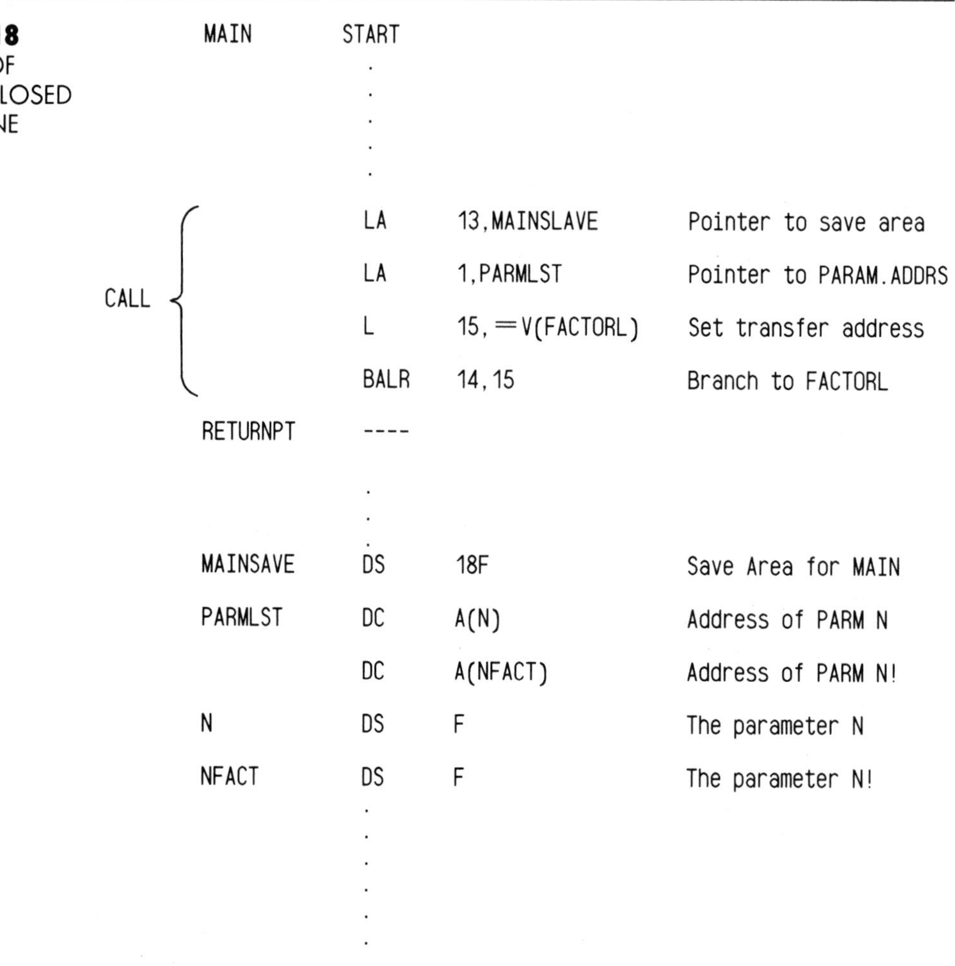

```
          MAIN        START
                        .
                        .
                        .
                        .
                        .
       (                LA      13,MAINSLAVE       Pointer to save area
       |                LA      1,PARMLST          Pointer to PARAM.ADDRS
CALL  <
       |                L       15,=V(FACTORL)     Set transfer address
       (                BALR    14,15              Branch to FACTORL
          RETURNPT      ----
                        .
                        .
                        .
          MAINSAVE      DS      18F                Save Area for MAIN
          PARMLST       DC      A(N)               Address of PARM N
                        DC      A(NFACT)           Address of PARM N!
          N             DS      F                  The parameter N
          NFACT         DS      F                  The parameter N!
                        .
                        .
                        .
                        .
                        .
                        .
```

FIGURE 2.18 EXAMPLE OF CALL TO CLOSED SUBROUTINE

CREATION AND USE OF MACROS

In assembly language, formal open subroutines are represented by macros. As was stated in the introductory discussion of subroutines, an open subroutine is inserted directly in a program at the point of call. This affects the value of the location counter and is why open subroutines, and therefore macros, are stored in source statement form. In fact, a call to an open subroutine is a request to the language processor (the assembler, in the case of a macro) to include a set of source statements at a particular point in the source program for translation along with the rest of the program. Thus a macro call is executed by the assembler (or by an extension of the assembler called a *macro processor*) *at translation time*, while a call to a closed subroutine is executed by the program *during program execution*.

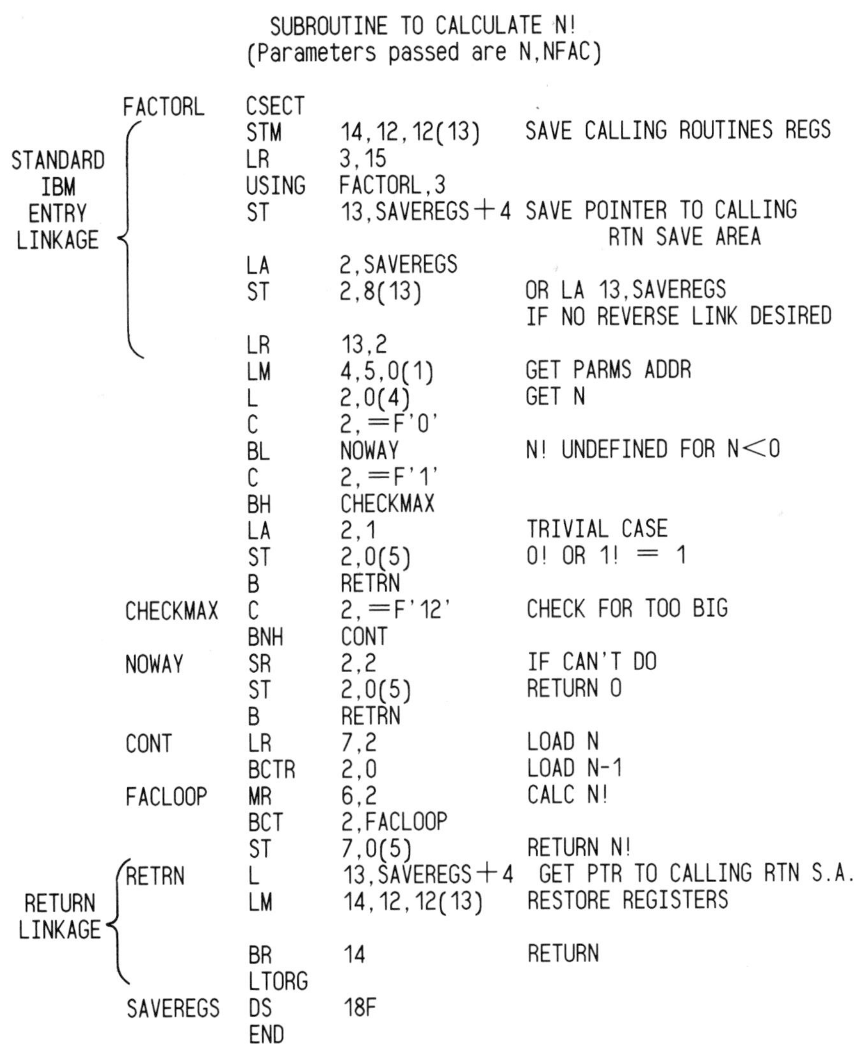

```
                    SUBROUTINE TO CALCULATE N!
                  (Parameters passed are N,NFAC)

          FACTORL  CSECT
                   STM    14,12,12(13)     SAVE CALLING ROUTINES REGS
STANDARD           LR     3,15
  IBM              USING  FACTORL,3
 ENTRY             ST     13,SAVEREGS+4    SAVE POINTER TO CALLING
LINKAGE                                              RTN SAVE AREA
                   LA     2,SAVEREGS
                   ST     2,8(13)          OR LA 13,SAVEREGS
                                           IF NO REVERSE LINK DESIRED
                   LR     13,2
                   LM     4,5,0(1)         GET PARMS ADDR
                   L      2,0(4)           GET N
                   C      2,=F'0'
                   BL     NOWAY            N! UNDEFINED FOR N<0
                   C      2,=F'1'
                   BH     CHECKMAX
                   LA     2,1              TRIVIAL CASE
                   ST     2,0(5)           0! OR 1! = 1
                   B      RETRN
          CHECKMAX C      2,=F'12'         CHECK FOR TOO BIG
                   BNH    CONT
          NOWAY    SR     2,2              IF CAN'T DO
                   ST     2,0(5)           RETURN 0
                   B      RETRN
          CONT     LR     7,2              LOAD N
                   BCTR   2,0              LOAD N-1
          FACLOOP  MR     6,2              CALC N!
                   BCT    2,FACLOOP
                   ST     7,0(5)           RETURN N!
          RETRN    L      13,SAVEREGS+4     GET PTR TO CALLING RTN S.A.
 RETURN            LM     14,12,12(13)     RESTORE REGISTERS
LINKAGE
                   BR     14               RETURN
                   LTORG
          SAVEREGS DS     18F
                   END
```

FIGURE 2.19 CLOSED SUBROUTINE EXAMPLE

If we wanted simply to insert a set of unaltered source statements at some point within our program, we could achieve this with some sort of pseudo instruction COPY statement. But this would require a complete knowledge of any symbols used in the set of source statements to be included and the integration of these symbols throughout our program. This is generally too restrictive and inconvenient for most of the reasons that a programmer would choose to use a subroutine in the first place. Fortunately, macros provide the facility of modifying the source statements generated according to the needs and convenience of the programmer.

Basic Macros Throughout this section, all of our examples are written in IBM macro assembly language and thus many of the comments about macros are intended specifically for this language. However, at the level of this discussion, most of the concepts (if not the particulars) will have their equivalents in other macro assembly languages as well.

The use of a macro in an assembly language program involves three components:

1. A macro definition
2. A macro call (also called a *macro reference*)
3. A macro generation.

The macro definition is written in a macro definition language, which is composed of:

1. Macro definition language statements
2. Pure assembly language statements
3. Assembly language statements that include variable components from the macro definition language
4. Conditional assembly statements.

Each macro definition consists of four parts:

1. *A header* to indicate the beginning of a macro definition
2. A *prototype statement* that defines the format of the macro call
3. A *body* that defines the specific assembly language statements that will or can be generated
4. A *trailer* to indicate the end of the definition.

A very basic macro definition written in IBM macro assembly language is shown in Figure 2.20. This definition defines a macro that will clear a 132-byte field intended for printing, by propagating a blank through the field, given the symbolic location of the field. In this example, &NAM and &PLINE, which appear in the prototype statement, are *symbolic parameters*. These symbolic parameters will be replaced throughout the definition body of the macro by the character strings (symbols) that are used in corresponding positions in the macro call statement in generating source statements. Symbolic parameters are written as *variable symbols*, which are 1–7 character symbols prefixed by an &.

```
header                        MACRO
prototype  &NAM               CLEARPL     &PLINE
body       { &NAM             MVI         &PLINE,C' '
           {                  MVC         &PLINE+1(131),&PLINE
trailer                       MEND
```

FIGURE 2.20
BASIC MACRO DEFINITION EXAMPLE

For example, a call to the macro CLEARPL which could appear in an assembly language source program is shown by:

```
WIPEOUT    CLEARPL    PRINTLN
```

in which case, WIPEOUT and PRINTLN correspond to the symbolic parameters &NAM and &PLINE, respectively. Thus, the call will cause the generation of the following source statements:

```
WIPEOUT     MVI     PRINTLN,C' '
            MVC     PRINTLN+1(131),PRINTLN
```

The generation is performed by the macro processor, either before or during the first pass of the assembly process described earlier for one- and two-pass assemblers. The macro processor will apply the components of each macro call to the corresponding macro definition and generate the appropriate assembly language statements. In order to do this, the macro processor must have access to every macro definition prior to processing a call to the macro in the source program. Thus to achieve this, the IBM assembler requires any macro definition(s) that the assembler uses to reside in a macro library, or that the macro definition(s) precede the START statement in the source program.

Since macro generation often requires the use of forward references beyond the scope of the statements generated by a single macro call, the macro processor usually makes one or more passes over the source program *in addition* to those required by the translation process. The number of extra passes (sometimes called *prepasses*) required by the macro processor will depend partly on the features offered by the macro definition language (such as symbol attributes) and partly on the design of the assembler itself. Both the IBM mainframe assembler and the VAX-11 macro assembler integrate the macro processor functions as part of the assembler, while other designers treat the macro processor and assembler separately.

Another simple macro definition is shown in Figure 2.21. In this case, two fixed point numbers are to be added together and their sum is to be stored at a specified location (which could be the same as either of the first two operands).

```
header                               MACRO
prototype  &NAM                      ADDSTOR    &A,&B,&SUM
         ( &NAM                      L          14,&A
body    {                            A          14,&B
         (                           ST         14,&SUM
trailer                              MEND
```

FIGURE 2.21
MACRO DEFINITION WHICH ACHIEVES SUM = A + B

The use of &NAM on two statements in Figurre 2.21 is an IBM language convention that is required in order to place a symbol at the location corresponding to the point of call. It must be placed on the prototype statement and on any statement(s), which, if generated, will result in the definition of the symbol at translation time. &NAM may legally appear on more than one source statement if no more than one of these will be generated for any particular call (this involves conditional assembly which is explained shortly).

A call of:

```
          ADDSTOR    CNT1,CNT2,TOTAL
```

would cause the generation of:

```
          L          14,CNT1
          A          14,CNT2
          ST         14,TOTAL
```

while the call

```
NEWTOTAL  ADDSTORE   TOTAL,COUNT,TOTAL
```

would generate

```
NEWTOTAL  L          14,TOTAL
          A          14,COUNT
          ST         14,TOTAL
```

In this second call, the macro ADDSTOR is used simply to increment a running total. It is worth noting that in the first call statement, no value was used in the position that corresponds to &NAM in the prototype statement, and nothing was generated for the variable symbol &NAM. But the second call uses the parameter NEWTOTAL in that position; thus, NEWTOTAL appears in the same field of the first generated statement. This illustrates the fact that macro generation is the generation of text which is intended to be in the form of assembly language statements. Therefore, the omission of a symbolic parameter will cause a null character string to be generated in the text at every corresponding point from the definition. Thus a call of:

```
         ADDSTOR   TOTAL
```

would generate:

```
         L         14,TOTAL
         A         14,
         ST        14,
```

which gives two invalid statements.

So far our examples have been relatively bland, but through the use of conditional assembly, macro definitions can become much more creative and useful.

Macros and Conditional Assembly It has been shown that by using symbolic parameters in a macro definition, the programmer is free to choose the actual symbols that will be generated in the source statements resulting from a particular call of the macro. However, the definitions that were given in the last section will always generate the same set of assembly language statements with respect to type and function (the only things that change are the symbols used in forming the statements, but not the number or basic form of the statements themselves).

With *conditional assembly*, the programmer can direct the assembler to generate or not generate a particular statement or group of statements, based on some condition that is true or not true. Thus, conditional assembly provides greater flexibility in the generation of text within a single statement beyond that of simple symbol substitution. Conditional assembly can be used practically anywhere in a source program, but its greatest and most common use is in creating macro definitions.

The conditional assembly feature is implemented through the use of the *conditional assembly language*, which is a simple, special-purpose language that is processed (interpreted) by the assembler prior to the translation process of the basic assembly language statements. Through the use of this conditional assembly language, we are able to "program" the assembler to modify a source language module before it is translated.

The conditional assembly language consists of variables, expressions, conditional assembly statements, sequence symbols, and data attributes. (Although conditional assembly language can be used in the open code of an assembly language program, we will, in general, confine our discussion to its use in defining macros.)

There are two classes of *conditional assembly variables*: local and global. A *local variable* is defined only within the span of the macro definition in which it is declared (it exists in only one macro definition). A *global variable* is defined for all macro definitions that are available to the assembler and which have declared the same global variable. This brings up an important requirement for the use of variables. *All* variables must be declared in *every* macro definition in which they are used, prior to their use in the body of the macro definition. Local variables are far more common in macro definitions than global variables but when global variables are used, they must be declared before the declaration of the local variables.

A variable can represent one of three data types: arithmetic (integer), character, and Boolean. Figure 2.22 shows the form for the declaration of local and global variables of each of these three types.

For example, to declare two local arithmetic variables &A and &B, we would write: LCLA &A,&B

Values are assigned to variables using set symbol statements that correspond to the three data types. Boolean variables are assigned a bit value of 1 or 0 representing true or false, respectively. Figure 2.23 shows the formats of the set symbol operation.

If we assume that &COUNT, &TYPE, and &TEST have been declared as local arithmetic, local character, and local Boolean variables, respectively. Examples of the use of the set symbol statement are:

```
&COUNT    SETA    1
&TYPE     SETC   'F'
&TEST     SETB   (&COUNT LT 10)
```

FIGURE 2.22
DECLARATION STATEMENTS FOR VARIABLES

Arithmetic
Boolean
Character

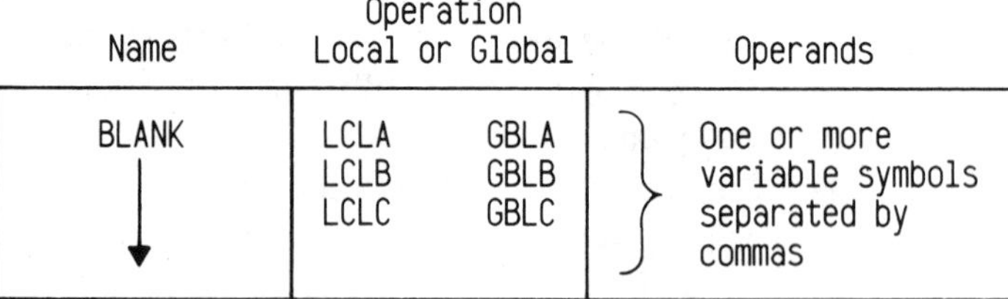

Name
Operation
Local or Global
Operands
BLANK
LCLA GBLA
LCLB GBLB
LCLC GBLC
One or more variable symbols separated by commas

FIGURE 2.23
SET SYMBOL FORMATS

	Name	Operation	Operands
Arithmetic	Variable Symbol	SETA	Arithmetic expression
Boolean	↓	SETB	Logical expression
Character		SETC	Character string

Name	Operation	Operands
Optional Sequence Symbol	AGO	Sequence Symbol

FIGURE 2.24
FORMAT OF AGO STATEMENT

Besides being able to declare variables and assign values to them, there are three conditional assembly statement types that provide the basic capability of sequence control within the processing of a macro definition. They are:

```
AGO
AIF
ANOP
```

Since all three statement types use sequence symbols in their descriptions, they are defined here. A *sequence symbol* is a symbol used in conditional assembly to name a location within a macro definition for the purpose of branching. Once the conditional assembly process is complete, they *will not* be present in the resulting source module. A sequence symbol is written in the form of a 1–7 character symbol preceded by a period. A sequence symbol is defined by placing it in the name field of a conditional assembly or regular assembly language statement.

The AGO statement is a simple GO TO, or unconditional branch, statement. Its format is shown in Figure 2.24.

```
EXAMPLE:            AGO      .DONE
```

The MEXIT statement can be considered as a special case of a conditional assembly branch and is equivalent to an AGO to the end of the macro definition. It simply provides a shorthand means of skipping the rest of the macro definition instead of requiring the placement of a sequence symbol on the MEND statement and then specifying an AGO to that symbol. The MEXIT statement has the same format as the AGO statement, except MEXIT appears in the operation field, and the operand field is not used.

The ANOP statement simply provides a place to GO TO as the object of a conditional assembly branch. It is a passive statement that performs no operation, but it is useful when we want to branch to a statement that already contains a symbol or variable symbol in its name field (the object of a conditional assembly branch *must* be a sequence symbol). Its format is shown in Figure 2.25.

FIGURE 2.25
FORMAT OF ANOP STATEMENT

Name	Operation	Operands
Sequence Symbol or blank	ANOP	Not Used

The AIF statement is basically a restricted form of the IF-THEN statement type without the ELSE option. The statement evaluates a logical expression and if the expression is true, there is a branch to a specified sequence symbol; otherwise, sequence control passes to the next physical statement. Its format is shown in Figure 2.26.

Example: Assuming &COUNT is a local arithmetic variable that counts iterations of a loop, we might find:

```
AIF    (&COUNT LT 10).LOOP
```

The rules for forming conditional assembly expressions are lengthy and will not be covered in any detail here. For a complete discussion, see the *IBM OS/VS-DOS/VSE-VM370 Assembler Language Reference Manual (GC33-4010-X)*, but in general:

1. Arithmetic expressions are formed similar to those found in FORTRAN, COBOL, and Pascal with the same basic operators of +, −, *, / and with the same precedence in evaluating the expression.

2. Logical expressions may contain:

   a. logical constants 1 (true) and 0 (false)

   b. relational operators:
      EQ (Equal)
      NE (Not equal)
      LT (Less than)
      GT (Greater than)
      LE (Less than or equal)
      GE (Greater than or equal)

FIGURE 2.26
FORMAT OF AIF STATEMENT

Name	Operation	Operands
Sequence Symbol or blank	AIF	(logical expression) sequence symbol

c. logical operators: AND, OR, and NOT.

d. arithmetic or character expressions

3. Character expressions are either:

a. strings

b. substrings

c. or the concatenation of strings and/or substrings

It is important to understand that a conditional assembly branch is a branch that is taken by the assembler *at assembly time.* Thus, any statements (conditional or otherwise) that are skipped as the result of this type of branch will not be processed by the assembler and will not be part of the assembler output (i.e., the object module). Hence, the programmer is able to "program" what the assembler (more particularly the macro processor) will generate for a specific macro call by incorporating logical combinations of AIF, AGO, and MEXIT statements within a macro definition.

In stating that conditional assembly branches are branches that are taken by the assembler at assembly time, it is also important to emphasize that *all conditional assembly statements and features are processed during assembly time.* Therefore, conditional assembly statements will not be part of the translated program and must not be used in an attempt to affect sequence control of a program at run time (that is, conditional assembly statements do not exist in a program after translation time).

Data attributes are used to describe the named instructions, constants (DC), and storage areas (DS) of a source module. They may be used in pure assembly language code, but are frequently used in conditional assembly language statements for creating expressions of all types. Each symbol defined in a source module has associated with it a set of data attributes which describe certain properties of the data object that the symbol defines. These attributes are specified explicitly in the case of DS and DC statements and are implied by other statements, such as machine instructions. In order to make these attributes available during conditional assembly, conceptually the macro processor must make a pass (prepass) through the source module prior to macro generation to create a symbol table containing the symbols and their corresponding attributes. Afterwards, the macro processor uses this table in evaluating expressions that contain data attributes as terms. There are six data attributes available for each symbol; they are shown in Figure 2.27, together with a brief definition of each. The first three attributes shown are the most commonly used and only they appear in the coding examples that follow.

FIGURE 2.27
DATA ATTRIBUTES

Attribute	Name	Description
T'	Type	The data type-a single character (e.g., 'F', 'C', 'A')
L'	Length	The integer length of the data as in: A DS CL50, thus L'A = 50
K'	Count	The count of the number of characters in a symbol
N'	Number	The count of parameters in a parameter sublist
S'	Scaling	Used to specify the decimal position in an arithmetic constant
I'	Integer	The number of significant digits in a number (used with S')

For a coding example of the use of data attributes we have:

```
         MVC     PLINE(L'A),A
                 .
                 .
                 .
                 .
A        DS      CL50
```

In this case, the MVC instruction will be translated by the assembler exactly as if it had been written as

```
         MVC     PLINE(50),A
```

since the length attribute of A (L′A) is equal to 50.

This concludes the overview of the conditional assembly language, but there are a few additional elements of the macro definition language that are extremely useful in the creation of macro definitions that must be mentioned.

There are several *system variable symbols* which are maintained by the assembler that are available to the programmer. Each of these symbols begins with the prefix &SYS (for example, &SYSNDX and &SYSLIST) and is reserved for a specific purpose. The most generally useful of these system variable symbols is &SYSNDX. *&SYSNDX* is used to count macro calls encountered in the source program; all calls are counted together instead of using separate counts for each different definition. The purpose of &SYSNDX is to avoid multiple definitions of a symbol that result from multiple calls of the same macro by appending the current value of &SYSNDX to a fixed symbol prefix. This is possible if the prefix does not exceed four characters, since the value of &SYSNDX is always given as a four-digit integer in *character form.* For example, if the definition W&SYSNDX DS 2F appears in the definition of a macro that is being expanded as the result of the fourth macro call in a program, the generated statement will be:

```
W0004    DS    2F
```

Finally, we have the MNOTE statement. This provides us with the mechanism for displaying a message to the programmer in the listing of his or her program.

The operands field of the MNOTE statement contains an integer severity code (chosen by the programmer in the range from 0-255) and the desired message in single quotes. The format of the MNOTE statement is shown in Figure 2.28. (Note: If the severity code is replaced with an * (asterisk), the message will be generated as a comment.)

Now for a complete example of a macro definition using conditional assembly we will return to our first macro example in which we cleared a fixed length field of 132 bytes. However, the redefined macro in Figure 2.29 has been redesigned to clear a field of any length between 1 and 256 bytes in length. This improved definition also checks for an error in the call statement (a symbol that has a count attribute of 0 contains 0 characters; thus, it is missing!). In addition, by checking the length attribute, no attempt will be made to clear a field of more than 256 bytes in length.

Name	Operation	Operands
Variable Symbol or blank	MNOTE	Code,'messeage'

FIGURE 2.28 FORMAT OF MNOTE STATEMENT

FIGURE 2.29 MACRO DEVINITION USING CONDITIONAL ASSEMBLY

```
header                          MACRO
prototype      &NAM             CLEAR     &LOC
                                LCLA      &LEN
                                AIF       (K'&LOC GT 0).CONT
                                MNOTE     1,'OPERAND MISSING,
                                          CALL IGNORED'
                                MEXIT
body           .CONT            AIF       (L'&LOC GT 256).TOOBIG
               &LEN             SETA      L'&LOC-1
               &NAM             MVI       &LOC,X'40'
                                AIF       (&LEN GT 0).MORE
                                MEXIT
               .MORE            MVC       &LOC+1(&LEN),&LOC
                                MEXIT
               .TOOBIG          MNOTE     1,'LENGTH OF FIELD
                                          EXCEEDS 256, CALL
                                          IGNORED.'
trailer                         MEND
```

Examples of calls to CLEAR are:

```
(a)                      CLEAR     MESSAGE
                           .
                           .
                           .
                           .
          MESSAGE        DS        CL20
```

which generates

```
                         MVI       MESSAGE,X'40'
                         MVC       MESSAGE+1(19),MESSAGE
```

```
(b)       WIPEOUT        CLEAR
```

which generates no source statements, but displays in the program listing:

```
1,OPERAND MISSING,CALL IGNORED
```

Another example which builds on a previous one is to write a macro definition that will generate a subroutine call to a closed subroutine. For this example, the parameter sublist option is used to account for the variable number of parameters that would be required of a generalized subroutine call. In this option, whenever a symbolic parameter (in this case &PLST) represents a list of parameters, the corresponding list in the macro call statement is enclosed in parentheses.

For example, the call to the subroutine FACTORL would appear as:

```
        CALL       FACTORL,(N,NFACT),SAVREGS
```

in which N represents &PLST(1) and NFACT represents &PLST(2). Using the definition given in Figure 2.30 and assuming &SYSNDX has a value of 0005, the above call would generate:

```
           LA      13,SAVREGS
           LA      1,PRM0005
           L       15,=V(FACTORL)
           BALR    14,15
           B       C0005
PRM0005    DC      A(N)
           DC      A(NFACT)
C0005      NOPR    0
```

The creation of macro definitions can provide insight to the kinds of processes that higher level languages perform in moving the programmer above the level of machine language. For our last example of macro definitions, we will examine a definition that performs only a subset of the functions performed by a very common statement type in a very common language—the ADD-GIVING statement from COBOL. The statement provides for the addition of a list of numeric variables of possibly different data types and the assigning of the sum to another variable, which may or may not be the same data type as one or more elements from the list. This statement not only (1) requires the checking of data types but (2) causes the generation of conversion routines to temporarily convert all variables to a common type for the addition, and, (3) possibly causes another conversion for the assignment operation. The statement has the form:

```
ADD     A,B,C     GIVING     TOTAL.
```

Since our machine language subset accommodates only integer and character types for numbers (and also because a complete simulation of the statement is more of a lesson than is needed to make a point), a restricted version of this process is presented in the macro ADDABGIV. In this macro

```
               MACRO
&NAM           CALL      &SUB,&PLST,&SAVE
               LCLA      &PCNT
               AIF       (K'&SUB EQ 0 OR N'&PLST EQ 0 OR
                            K'&SAVE EQ 0).ERR
               LA        13,&SAVE
               LA        1,PRM&SYSNDX
               L         15,=V(&SUB)
               BALR      14,15
               B         C&SYSNDX
&PCNT          SETA      1
PRM&SYSNDX     DC        A(&PLST(1))
.LOOP          AIF       (&PCNT GE N'PLST).DONE
&PCNT          SETA      &PCNT+1
               DC        A(&PLST(&PCNT))
               AGO       .LOOP
.DONE          ANOP
C&SYSNDX       NOPR      0
               MEXIT
.ERR           MNOTE     2,'OPERAND MISSING,
                         CALL IGNORED.'
               MEND
```

FIGURE 2.30
MACRO DEFINITION TO GENERATE CLOSED SUBROUTINE CALLS

the sum of exactly two nonnegative integer variables (in either binary or character form) is assigned to a third variable (which should be a repetition of the data type of one of the first two).

Type checking is performed on the first two operands; however, if the type of the &SUM operand is not integer (fixed point), the result is simply stored in character form. A structured flowchart of the logic of this macro

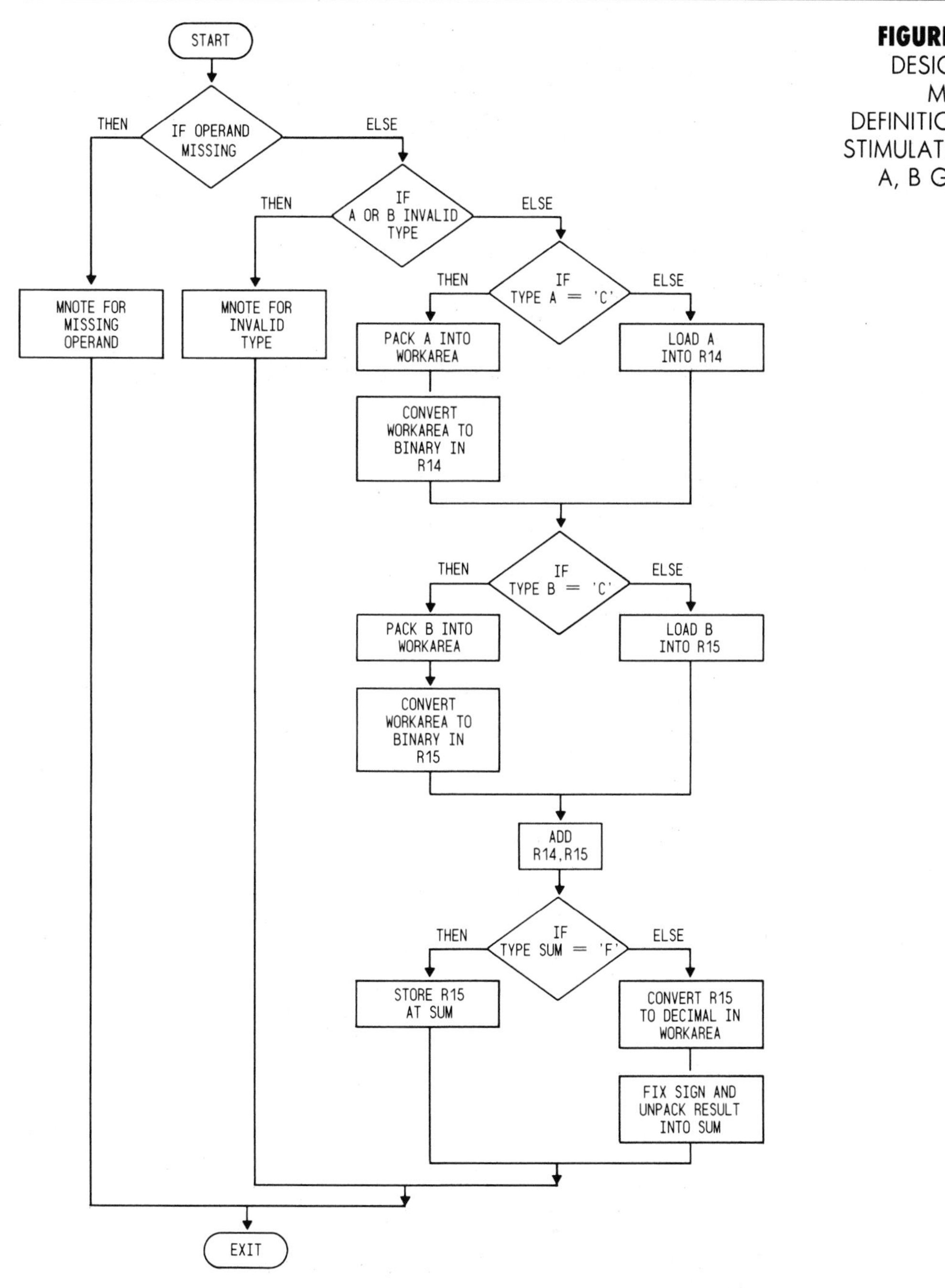

FIGURE 2.31 DESIGN OF MACRO DEFINITION TO STIMULATE ADD A, B GIVING SUM

definition is shown in Figure 2.31 with the actual definition given in Figure 2.32. For example, if we have

```
COUNT     DS     F
NEW       DS     CL5
TOTAL     DS     CL7     and  &SYSNDX=0006
```

then a call of:

```
NEWTOT    ADDABGIV    COUNT,NEW,TOTAL
```

```
                    MACRO
&NAM                ADDABGIV      &A,&B,&SUM
                    AIF           (K'&A NE 0 AND K'&B NE 0 AND
                                    K'&SUM NE 0).CKTYPE
                    MNOTE         2,'OPERAND MISSING, CALL IGNORED'
                    MEXIT
.CKTYPE             AIF           ((T'&A EQ 'F' OR T'&A EQ 'C')
                                   AND (T'&B EQ 'F' OR T'&B EQ
                                   'C')).TYPEOK
                    MNOTE         2,'INVALID OPERAND TYPE'
                    MEXIT
.TYPEOK             AIF           (T'&A EQ 'C').PACKA
.&NAM               L             14,&A
                    AGO           .GETB
.PACKA              ANOP
&NAM                PACK          W&SYSNDX,&A     CONVERT CHAR OPERAND
                    CVB           14,W&SYSNDX
.GETB               AIF           (T'&B EQ 'C').PACKB
                    L             15,&B
                    AGO           .ADD
.PACKB              PACK          W&SYSNDX,&B     CONVERT CHAR OPERAND
                    CVB           15,W&SYSNDX
.ADD                AR            14,15
                    AIF           (T'&SUM NE 'F').CHAR
                    ST            14,&SUM
                    AGO           .DONE
.CHAR               CVD           14,W&SYSNDX
                    OI            W&SYSNDX+7,=X'0F'      FIX SIGN
                    UNPK          &SUM,W&SYSNDX(8)CONVERT CHAR OPERAND
.DONE               B             SKIP&SYSNDX
W&SYSNDX            DS            2F
SKIP&SYSNDX         NOPR          0
                    MEND
```

FIGURE 2.32
MACRO DEFINITION TO PERFORM SIMPLIFIED ADD-GIVING FOR TWO NON-NEGATIVE VARIABLES

would generate

```
NEWTOT    L     14,COUNT
          PACK  W0006,NEW     CONVERT CHAR OPERAND
          CVB   15,W0006
          AR    14,15
          CVD   14,W0006
          OI    W0006+7,X'0F'     FIX SIGN
          UNPK  TOTAL,W0006(8)
          B     SKIP0006
W0006     DS    2F
SKIP0006  NOPR  0
```

Thus, when called correctly, the ADDABGIV macro will cause the generation of 46 or 48 bytes of machine language code (depending on the alignment at the two fullword work area). A simulation of the full ADD . . . GIVING statement from COBOL could generate more machine code and would require a considerably more complex version of the macro definition for ADDABGIV. We would have an incomplete picture of the role of a translator for a higher level language if we viewed a program written in a higher level language as just a series of macro calls. However, the previous example does address part of the process involved; the full scope of the process will be discussed further in Chapter 4.

REVIEW QUESTIONS AND EXERCISES

1. Define or explain briefly:
   a. Absolute assembly language
   b. Symbolic assembly language
   c. Macro assembly language
   d. Pseudo instruction
   e. Literals
   f. Load and go assembler
   g. Module assembler
   h. Object module
   i. Forward reference
   j. Symbol table
   k. Location counter
   l. Open subroutine
   m. Closed subroutine
   n. Conditional assembly

2. Perform the role of a load-and-go assembler and translate the program segment into executable machine language. Assume X and Y are at relocatable 600 and 64C. Also show relative location values.

```
Location
 0000    BEGIN  STM    14,12,12,(13)
                LR     2,15
                USING  BEGIN,2
                ST     13,X+4
                LA     13,X
                MVI    Y,X'40'
                MVC    Y+1(10),Y
                LA     5,4
                L      6,Y(5)
```

3. Show the results after the execution of each of the following instructions with respect to contents of involved registers and memory locations (refer to the memory locations by their symbolic names (for example, the word at M)). Recall that * used as a symbol means the current value (position) of the location counter.

```
SR     4,4
LA     5,20
L      6,=F'4'
DR     4,6
STM    4,6,M
C      4,=F'2'
BL     *+8
LA     5,1(5)
CVD    5,DOUB
```

4. Write assembly code to:
   a. Perform a loop to sum 10 words containing binary numbers starting at TABLE. Use Register 5 for the total and Register 4 as an index.
   b. Rewrite exercise *a* so that the integers in the table are stored in character form (EBCDIC) and must be converted to binary before the addition. Leave the sum in binary.
   c. Compute Y = (X + 5)/8, where X and Y are words in memory containing binary numbers.
   d. Compute C = (F − 32) * 5/9, where C and F are words in memory containing binary numbers. (Hint: be sure to multiply (F − 32) by 5 and then divide the product by 9).

5. The following is an assembly language program segment in which PRINTLN is a macro and SQRT is a closed subroutine.

```
         .
         .
         LA        13,SAVE
         LA        1,PARMLST
         L         15,=V(SQRT)
         BALR      14,15
         PRINTLN   N,ROOT
         L         6,=F'3'
LOOP     L         5, ROOT
         ST        5,N
         LA        1,PARMLST
         L         15,=V(SQRT)
         BALR      14,15
         BCT       6,LOOP
         PRINTLN   N,ROOT
         .
         .
         .
```

Based on the segment shown (assuming SQRT and PRINTLN are not used elsewhere), complete the following table. (Note: GPRs 1, 14, 15 must be restored in the loop since they may have been used by the macro PRINTLN).

	PRINTLN	SQRT
Times called		
Times executed		
Copies in program		

6. Given the following definition for a macro that adds a list of fixed point numbers, show the source code that will be generated for the accompanying macro calls.

```
         MACRO
&NAM     ADDBLST   &SUM,&BLST
         LCLA      &LCNT
         AIF       (K'&SUM EQ 0 OR N'&BLST LT 1).ERR
&NAM     L         14,&BLST(1)
&LCNT    SETA      2
```

```
.LOOP       AIF         (&LCNT GT N'&BLST).DONE
            A           14,&BLST(&LCNT)
&LCNT       SETA        &LCNT+1
            AGO         .LOOP
.DONE       ST          14,&SUM
            MEXIT
.ERR        MNOTE       2'OPERAND MISSING, CALL IGNORED.'
            MEND
```

```
a.               ADDBLST     MTOTAL,(WK1,WK2,WK3,WK4)
b.   PERMTR      ADDBLST     TRI,(A,B,C)
c.               ADDLST      X,Y
d.               ADDLST      TOTAL
```

PROGRAMMING EXERCISES

The following programming exercises are described for an IBM mainframe environment. If such an environment is not available (or desired), these exercises can be modified for other environments while still preserving the main concepts.

1. Write a program using the CALL macro (Figure 2.30) to call the FACTORL subroutine (Figure 2.19) to calculate values for N! given input values for N. The program should read a series of records, each containing a value for N and then print N and the corresponding value for N!.

2. Write a program that will assemble RX instructions written in absolute assembly form into executable machine language form. The program should store the translated instructions in a self-contained area ready for execution. (In other words, you are to write a limited load-and-go assembler that only translates RX instructions in absolute assembly language form). Store the translated instructions in an area named "CODE" which is defined as CODE DS 100F.
   Test the program by translating the following segment which is intended to sum the elements in a table and return.

```
A      5,0(6,7)
LA     6,4(0,6)
BCT    8,0(0,4)
BC     15,0(0,14)
```

Set up the execution of the segment by including the following instructions (or their equivalent) in the assembler program.

```
L      8,=F'10'    SET COUNTER FOR NO. OF ELEMENTS
LA     7,TABLE     GET TABLE ADDRESS
SR     5,5         CLEAR ACCUMULATOR
SR     6,6         SET INDEX TO 1st ELEMENT
BAL    14,CODE     LINK TO CODE AREA
---                RETURN POINT
```

SEMESTER PROJECT

Write a one pass, load and go, symbolic assembler for the instruction subset and pseudos given in this book.

In order to simplify the problem of I/O, include additional pseudos READ, WRITE and/or PRINT which will cause the inclusion of instructions to load the address of the desired I/O area in GPR1 and branch and link (BALR 14,15) to a segment in your assembler that contains the appropriate I/O MACRO (GET or PUT) to perform the operation plus a move of the data to the desired area and then return. Limit I/O operations to the most basic form of reading and writing of single records available (such as card input and printer output, or terminal input and output for an interactive system).

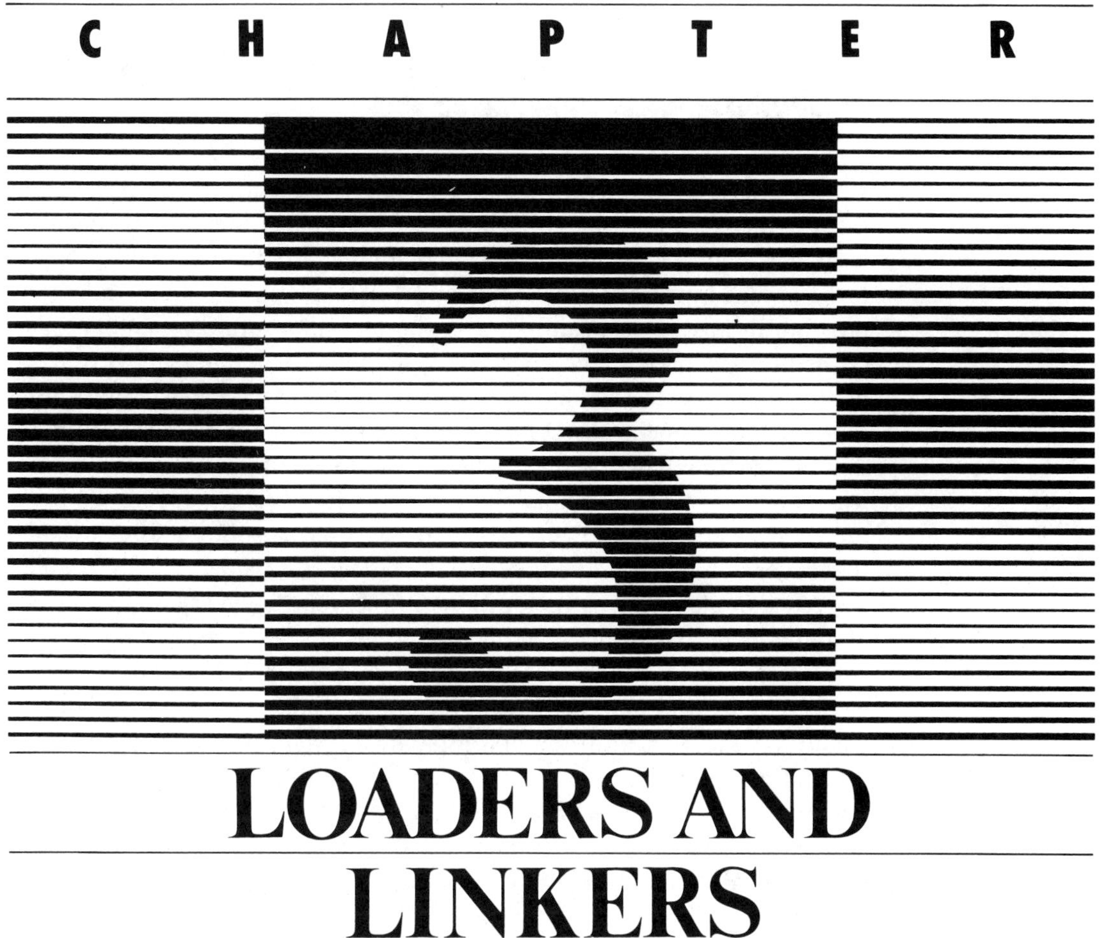

CHAPTER 3

LOADERS AND LINKERS

Loaders and linkers were among the first system software programs developed. Indeed, without loaders, programs would have to be entered into main memory by hand one word at a time. Without linkers, all subroutines referenced by a program would have to be present at translation time.

Loaders and linkers may be implemented as separate system programs or combined as a single program (that is, a linking loader). The merits for both approaches are discussed later in this chapter. However, the combination of functions performed in linking and loading is essentially the same in either arrangement. Therefore, the details of linking will generally be treated as part of the evolution from the development of the simplest loaders through linking loaders. This approach allows us to concentrate on the more basic process of loading first. Thus, a better basis for understanding the linking process is provided, because the output of the linking phase is dependent on the design of the loader.

FUNCTIONS AND CONCEPTS

A *loader* is a program that places a machine language program in main memory in executable form. Every loader must perform at least two simple tasks. These are: (1) to obtain space in main memory to receive the program to be loaded (memory allocation) and (2) to physically place the object program in this space (loading). The memory allocation is usually accomplished by a request to the operating system and is not actually performed by the loader itself. The loading task is relatively simple and requires little more than reading the object program records into main memory and moving the machine language instructions into consecutive memory locations which were allocated to hold the program. If the input to the loader is intended to be an object program that has fixed absolute addresses, then the loader is called an *absolute loader*. This type of loader will always load a given module at the same locations in memory for every execution. An absolute loader is simple to implement, but would cause considerable inconvenience and probably wasted machine time in a multiprogramming environment, since another program requiring addresses already allocated would have to wait until the first program completed its execution before it could be loaded. The bootstrap loader for the Initial Program Load of an operating system (IPL is described in chapter 5) is an appropriate use for an absolute loader, since, by machine design, a portion of the operating system usually must reside in or around fixed memory locations.

An algorithm for a simple absolute loader is shown in Figure 3.1. The object module input to this sample absolute loader consists of three types of records (also shown in Figure 3.1):

1. A single header record identifying the object program, its length and its required load point (starting address).
2. A set of one or more machine code records. Each record contains a string of executable machine language together with the length of the string.
3. A single trailer record marking the end of the object module.

As mentioned before, the loader obtains storage for the object program by calling an operating system routine and passing the required starting address and the length of storage needed. If the storage is available, the loader is notified by way of the status flag S and continues with the loading process.

At the completion of a successful loading process, the loader would normally either initiate the execution of the program just loaded by branching to its beginning, or return control to the operating system to schedule the new program for execution according to some selection criteria.

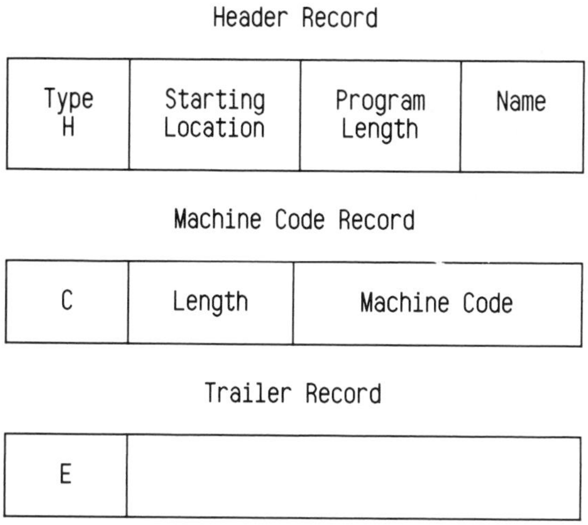

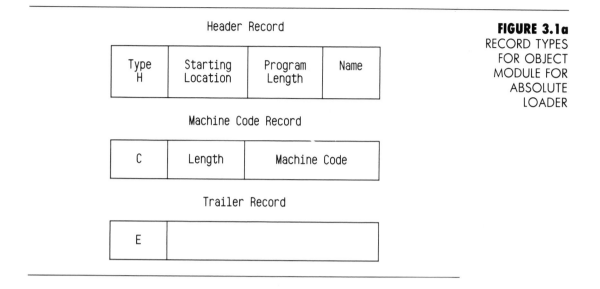

Header Record

Type H	Starting Location	Program Length	Name

Machine Code Record

C	Length	Machine Code

Trailer Record

E	

FIGURE 3.1a RECORD TYPES FOR OBJECT MODULE FOR ABSOLUTE LOADER

If a loader is designed so that it receives an input object program in a form that can be placed in different locations for different executions, then it is called a *relocating loader*. A relocating loader offers the obvious benefit of allowing a program to run in any region of memory that is large enough to accommodate the program instead of waiting until some fixed region is available for use (as was the case with an absolute loader). Relocation is then the third task which may be (and usually is) performed by a loader.

RELOCATION SCHEMES

To facilitate the loader's task of relocating addresses that are load-location dependent, an assembler or other language translator produces addresses which are relative to an assumed load point at those locations in the machine code for which absolute addresses are required at execution time. Normally, the assumed load point is zero. The loader can then calculate a relocation factor by subtracting the relative load point from the actual load point (see Figure 3.2). Thus, program relocation is achieved by simply adding this relocation factor to each location in the object program that contains an address which must be converted to absolute (that is, relocated).

RELOCATION BITS

A relocating loader must be supplied with information specifying exactly which locations within a machine language program (object program) need to be relocated for a variable starting load address. Therefore, the language

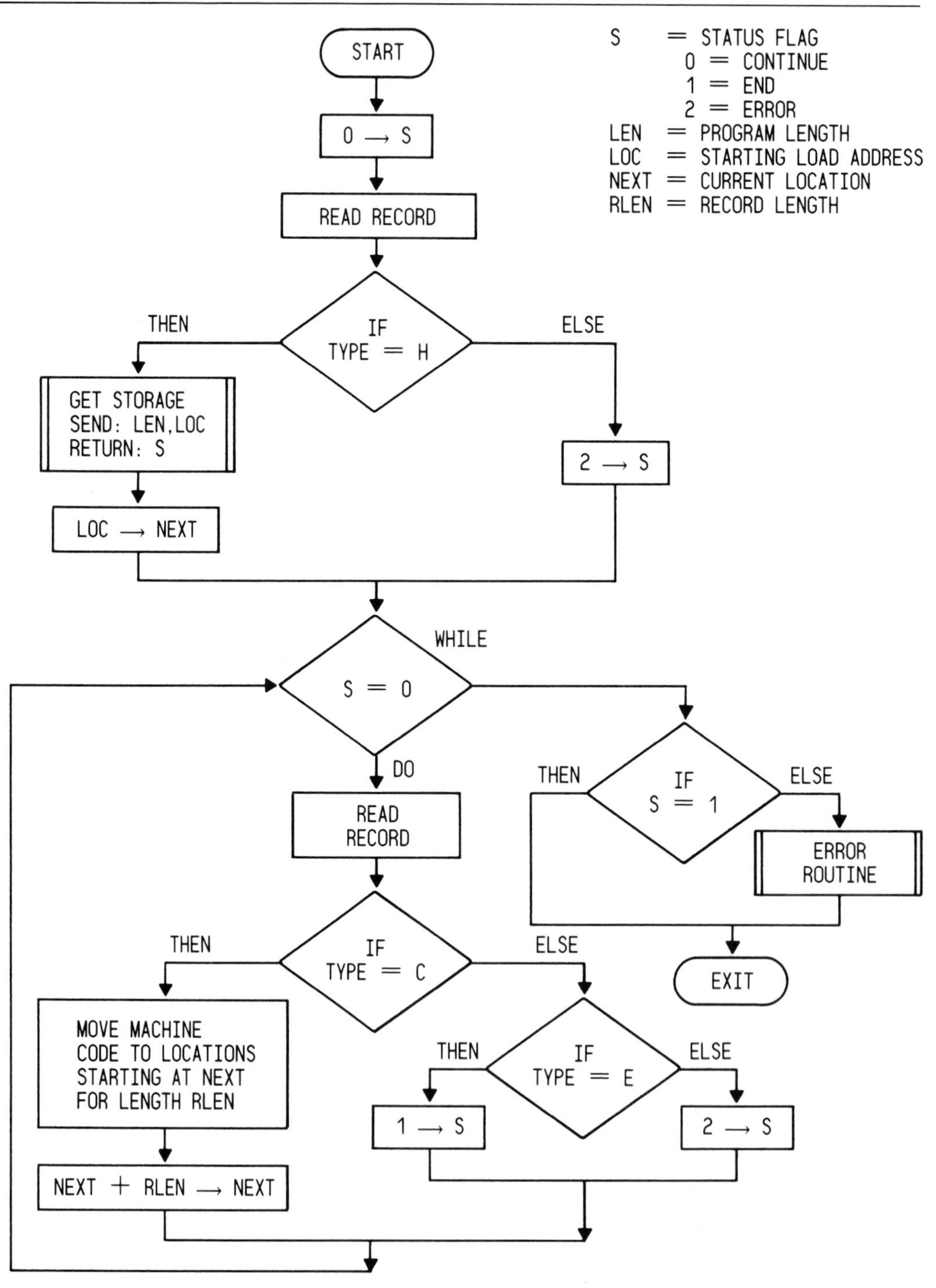

FIGURE 3.1b
ALGORITHM FOR ABSOLUTE LOADER

	1	2	3
Actual Load Point	12000	12000	12000
Relative Load Point	0	10000	20000
Relocation Factor	12000	2000	- 8000

FIGURE 3.2
EXAMPLES OF PROGRAM RELOCATION

translator must determine this information for the loader during the translation process (for example, assembly time) by identifying the locations that need relocation. There are two common techniques for accomplishing this. In the first technique a relocation bit is associated with each machine instruction or word of the object program (constants must be included in the scheme). To perform relocation, the loader makes a complete scan of the object program and examines the relocation bit for each instruction or word. If the bit is set, the loader will add the relocation factor to the associated address; otherwise, it makes no adjustment and moves to the next instruction. This technique is intended for a machine with fixed length instructions which, in addition, carry absolute addresses or segment relative addresses in the instructions. A machine of this type will normally need relocation for a high percentage of its instructions; therefore, a scheme that requires examination of every instruction is reasonable.

It is awkward to demonstrate the relocation bit technique using IBM mainframe assembly/machine language, since these machines use neither fixed length instructions nor absolute addresses in the machine instructions. However, it is less desirable to introduce another totally new machine (real or imaginary) for this discussion; therefore, let us consider a computer that has only the RR and RX instructions of the familiar machine. All instructions perform exactly the same operations as before and have the same format except that the 16-bit memory operand address in RX instructions is now an absolute address instead of the normal format using a 4-bit base and 12-bit displacement (see Figure 3.3). In addition, the RR format is expanded to four bytes so that all instructions are the same length.

This is the same modification to the RX instruction format that was proposed by Donovan (1972) in his explanation of the same loading process. The modified version of the RR instructions is included to give us more realistic programming examples. The modification expands the two-byte RR instructions to four bytes with the rightmost two bytes unused. This provides us with a computer with fixed length instructions of exactly one word in length, which allows a relocation bit to be assigned to each word

FIGURE 3.3
MODIFIED RX INSTRUCTION FORMAT

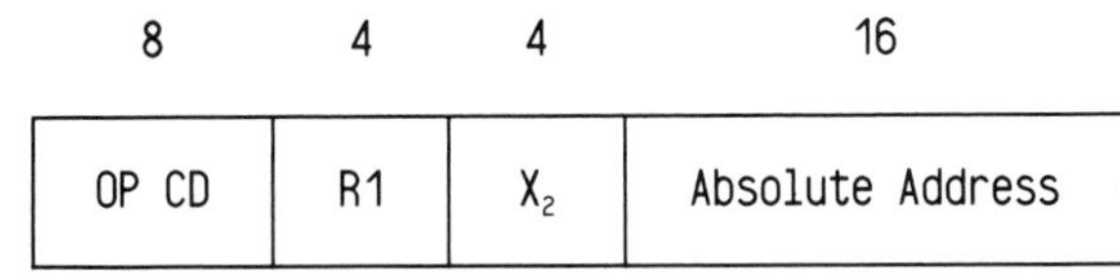

of the object program produced by the translator (for example, the assembler) including constants and data areas. But since the RR instructions do not reference main memory operands, their relocation bits would always be zero. In addition, all address constants are required to be right-justified in a four-byte field (which is the usual form of an A or V constant in IBM mainframe assembly language); therefore, anytime the loader finds a relocation bit set, it can simply add the relocation factor to the rightmost 16 bits of the corresponding four-byte field. Thus, all relocation is performed by the same simple procedure, regardless of whether a word contains an instruction or an address constant. Of course, with an absolute address space defined by 16 bits, our modified machine would be limited to 64K of main memory.

Using our modified machine, the entire process from source code through assembly to loading can now be demonstrated. The following program segment (Figure 3.4) sums the elements in a ten-element table.

An algorithm for a relocating loader using the relocation bits technique is shown in Figure 3.5. The object module intended for this type of loader has the same three record types that were used with the absolute loader. However, the formats of the header and machine code records are slightly different (shown in Figure 3.5 also). There is no longer a starting address

FIGURE 3.4a
SOURCE CODE

```
Relative
Location

 100              SR    3,3         CLEAR ACCUM
 104              SR    4,4         SET INDEX TO 0
 108              L     5,=F'10'    SET LOOP COUNTER
 10C     LOOP     A     3,TABLE(4)  SUM ELEMENTS
 110              A     4,=F'4'     INCREMENT INDEX
 114              BCT   5,LOOP
  .                .
  .                .
 140     TABLE    DS    10F
  .                .
  .                .
 170     =F'4'    DC    F'4'        LITERAL POOL
 174     =F'10'   DC    F'10'
```

Relative Location	Relocation Bit	Generated Code
		address
100	0	1B330000
104	0	1B440000
108	1	58500174
10C	1	5A340140
110	1	5A400170
114	1	4650010C
.	.	
.	.	
140-167	0	-------
.	.	
.	.	
170	0	00000004
174	0	0000000A

FIGURE 3.4b
TRANSLATED CODE FROM SPECIAL ASSEMBLER FOR MODIFIED IBM MACHINE LANGUAGE

Physical Location	Executable Code	
8100	1B330000	
8104	1B440000	
8108	58508174	Instructions with relocated addresses (8108–8114)
810C	5A348140	
8110	5A408170	
8114	4650810C	
.	.	
.	.	
8170	00000004	
8174	0000000A	

FIGURE 3.4c
RELOCATED EXECUTABLE CODE FOR MODIFIED IBM MACHINE LANGUAGE USING RELOCATION FACTOR OF 8000

in the header record, since this will be obtained by the loader at load time. The machine code record contains a code length (in words) and a field contains a relocation bit for each machine code word in the record. For example, using two bytes for this field, relocation bits would be assigned to a maximum of 16 words in the machine code portion of the record, where (moving from left to right) the nth relocation bit corresponds to the nth machine code word.

FIGURE 3.5a RECORD TYPES FOR OBJECT MODULE FOR RELOCATING LOADER USING RELOCATION BITS

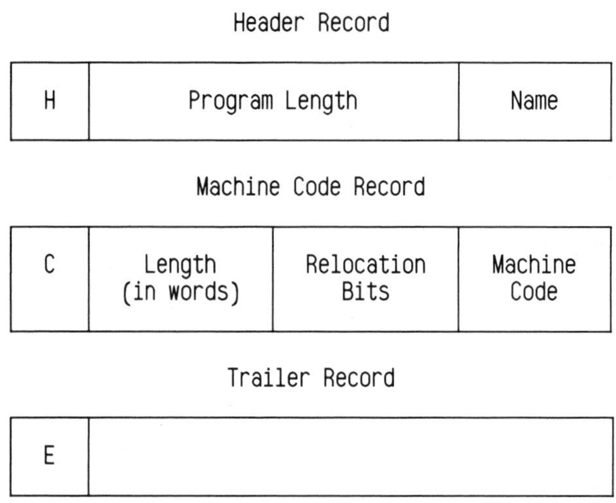

In this algorithm it is assumed that the intended machine is word addressable, therefore, in the case of a byte addressable machine, we would have to increment the NEXT address by four instead of one to move to the next available word in memory.

RELOCATION TABLES

Machines which use some form of relative addressing such as base and displacement, will normally require much less relocation activity by the loader. The second technique for providing relocation information to the loader is intended for these machines and involves supplying the loader with a table of all locations that must be relocated. The loader can then make one scan of the table and adjust only the locations listed, without examining other instructions or locations.

Since IBM mainframe machine languages use the base and displacement form of specifying main memory addresses within the actual machine instructions, relocation for these addresses is achieved automatically at execution time when the appropriate base register is loaded. (See previous discussion on IBM Assembly/Machine Language in Chapter 1). As a result of this type of addressing scheme, loaders for the IBM mainframes only need to relocate address constants. Since address constants usually amount to a very small portion of the object code for a program, the usual design for an IBM mainframe loader employs the relocatible locations table technique for identifying which locations must be relocated. For example, consider the following segment of a program which is long enough to require

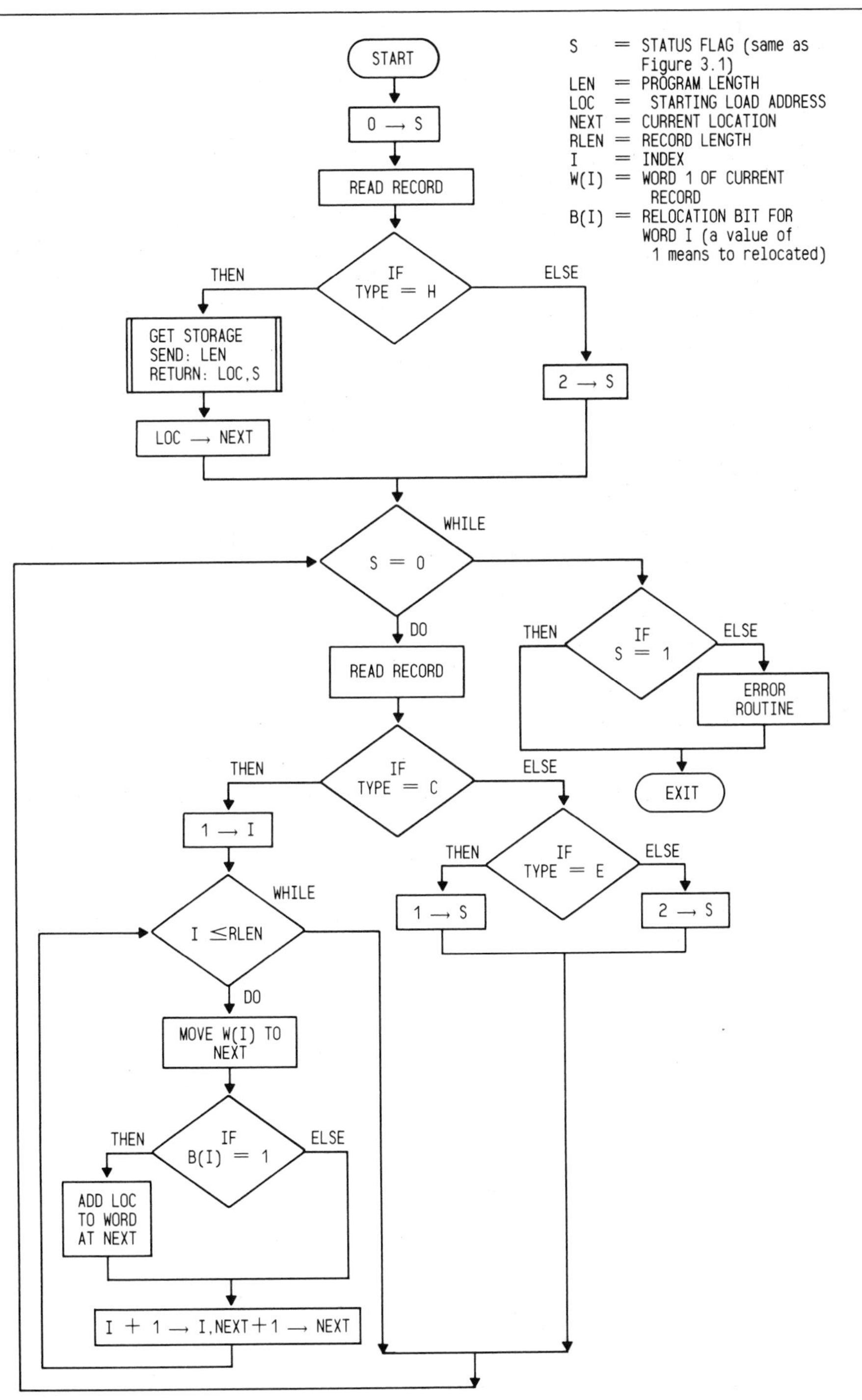

S = STATUS FLAG (same as Figure 3.1)
LEN = PROGRAM LENGTH
LOC = STARTING LOAD ADDRESS
NEXT = CURRENT LOCATION
RLEN = RECORD LENGTH
I = INDEX
W(I) = WORD 1 OF CURRENT RECORD
B(I) = RELOCATION BIT FOR WORD I (a value of 1 means to relocated)

FIGURE 3.5b
ALGORITHM FOR RELOCATING LOADER USING RELOCATION BITS

that several implied base registers be given to the assembler to use in translating the program. (A simplified object module design is used to illustrate the basic procedure.)

The example shown in Figure 3.6 is 9,216 bytes (2400_{16}) long, yet the relocatable locations table contains only two entries. This, of course, assumes that there are no additional address constants needed in the program, which is not unreasonable, provided that the program consists of a single module and does not call any subroutines.

In order to present a basic algorithm that achieves relocation through the use of a relocatable locations table (RLT), we will need to define an object module that contains four types of records. The records are composed of the same three types that were used for the other loader models, plus a record type for the entries in the relocatable locations table (the formats for these records are shown in Figure 3.7 a).

The algorithm for the loader is given in Figure 3.7b. Notice, that in this algorithm the machine code is first moved into the acquired memory area without any adjustments, just as with the absolute loader. Then the locations are adjusted as needed as each RLT record is processed. Since each RLT record contains a series of zero relative addresses to be relocated, relocation can be achieved by adding the load address to a RLT relative address (to yield the program address to be relocated) and then adding the load address to the value found at this program address. Or, we can load the relative address entry, R(I), into an index register X and add the load address to the beginning program address (LOC) indexed by X.

Since most popular programming languages support calls to subroutines and since the concept of modular programming encourages the use of routines (modules) that call each other, long single segment programs are less common. We now come to the fourth and final task that may be required of a loader; the task of linking.

FIGURE 3.6a
SOURCE

```
Relative
Location                      Source Code

  0000       LDREXM            START
  0000       BEGIN             BALR      2,0
  0002                         USING     *,2,3,4
  0002                         LM        3,4,ADCONS
  0006                         B         SKIPCONS
  000C       ADCONS            DC        A(BEGIN+4098)
  0010                         DC        A(BEGIN+8194)
  0014       SKIPCONS          SR        5,5
   .                            .
   .                            .
  2400                         END
```

FIGURE 3.6b
ASSEMBLED MODULE (OBJECT MODULE)

```
Relative
Location          Object Code

  0000            0520
  0002            9834200A
  0006            47F02012
  000A            ---          (slack bytes from address
  000C            00001002      constant alignment)
  0010            00002002
  0014            1B55
   .                .
   .                .
  2400            ----

      Relocatable Locations Table

              000C
              0010
```

```
Absolute
Location          Executable Code (Loaded Code)

  8000            0520
  8002            9834200A
  8006            47F02012
  800A            ----
  800C            00009002 }  These locations
  8010            0000A002 }  have been
  8014            1B55        relocated
   .                .
   .                .
   .                .
  A400            ——
```

FIGURE 3.6c
PROGRAM LOADED AT LOCATIONS STARTING AT ABSOLUTE 8000

LINKING SCHEMES

Linking (sometimes referred to as binding or collecting) is the process of combining a set of independently translated subroutines or modules into a complete program, most commonly represented as one composite block of object code ready for loading. It is often desirable to include in a program, modules that have been previously translated and stored in object form; the linking process performs this function for us. I/O requests in source

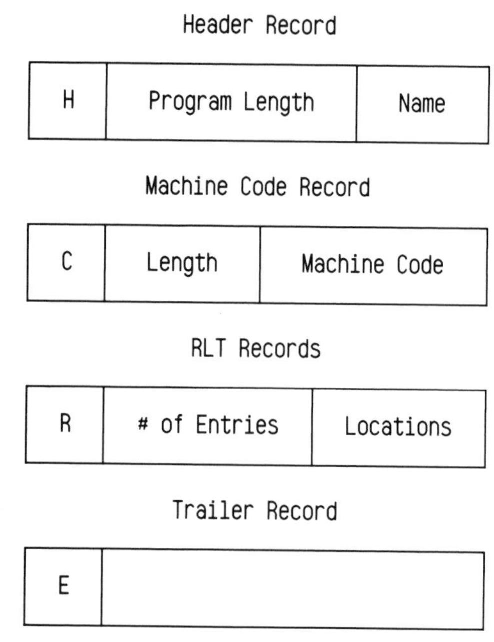

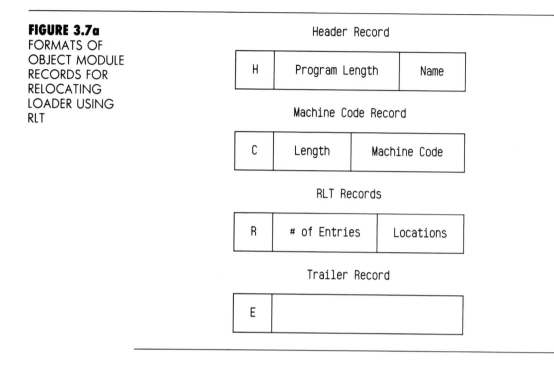

FIGURE 3.7a FORMATS OF OBJECT MODULE RECORDS FOR RELOCATING LOADER USING RLT

programs are commonly translated into calls to subroutines that are included at link time; FORTRAN math functions are also usually handled in this manner. The linking process provides us with a convenient means of reusing modules again and again, both at the system software level and at the applications program level. Once a procedure or function has been developed, it can be translated and stored in object form for incorporation in other programs, thus saving not only translation time during program testing, but program development time as well. Linking may occur at several stages, ranging from translation time to execution time (dynamic linking). However, most commonly, linking occurs after translation and prior to loading. This may be performed in two ways, either by a separate linker program (for example, a linkage editor) prior to the execution of the loader or by the first phase of the loader itself, in which case the loader is called a *linking loader.* Both of these two common approaches to linking and loading have advantages, given different sets of conditions.

In a production environment where programs are typically run many times without need for retranslation, the two-step approach to linking and loading between translation and execution is more efficient, since a program can be linked once and stored as a single load module. Thus, the loader's job is reduced to the tasks of allocation, loading, and relocation, and the task of linking is not needlessly duplicated for each execution. On the other

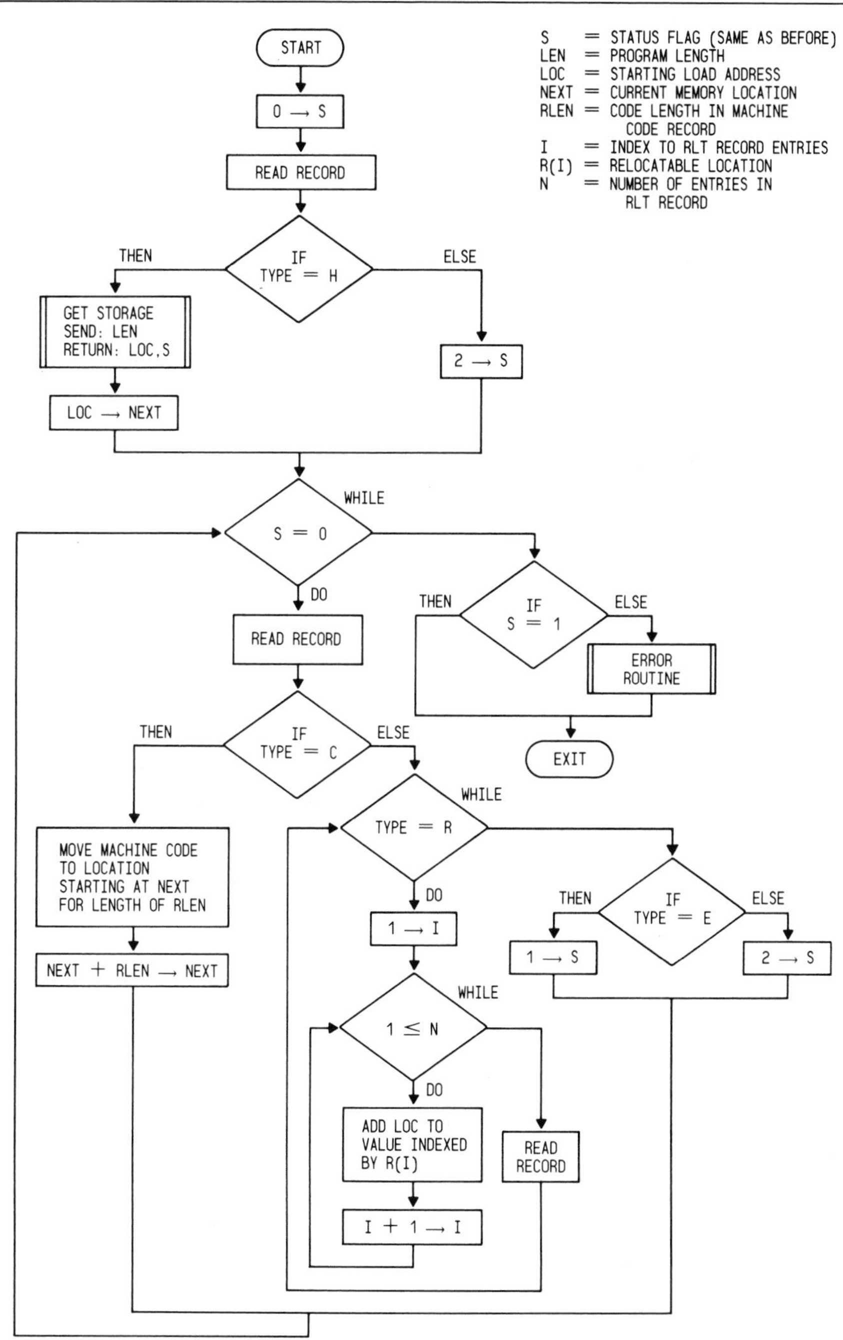

FIGURE 3.7b
ALGORITHM FOR RELOCATING LOADER USING RELOCATABLE LOCATIONS TABLE

hand, in a program test environment (such as student jobs in a programming class) programs (or at least some modules of the programs) must be retranslated before each execution, and therefore, relinked each time the program is tested. In this case, the use of a linking loader reduces the overhead of loading and executing two separate systems programs (the linker and then the loader); and reduces the total job time for a given program test.

As a rule, the later the linking or binding process, the greater the flexibility to the user of the program. For example, if linking is postponed until execution time, there is no need to load subroutines unless they are required for a particular execution of the program. If programs have a large set of subroutines, and only some are needed for any given execution, using dynamic linking could save memory space and loading time. However, the price we pay for late linking is a cost in operating system overhead.

Most of the benefits to be gained by dynamic linking are also provided by the virtual memory systems explained in Chapter 5, therefore, any further discussion of dynamic linking is deferred until then. The present discussion of linking concentrates on that which occurs after translation and prior to program execution.

Two schemes for the design of a linking loader are now considered. (Separate designs for independent linker programs will not be presented, since they could be readily extracted from the combination programs.)

In order to better understand the linking process, it is helpful to reexamine certain physical properties of a modular program and how the modules (subroutines) communicate with each other. At execution time, the modular program will appear as a set of closed subroutines; therefore, communication between modules basically amounts to a branch from the first module to the second and a return to the first upon completion of the execution of the second. Obviously, the first module must have the load address of the second module in order to branch to it and, since the loader determines the load address for a module, it follows that the loader must provide modules with the address of the corresponding modules that they need to communicate with (call). It also follows that the loader must somehow be informed of the addresses needed by particular modules. And since the input to the linking loader is supplied by a translator, the translator must inform the loader of the addresses that are needed. But since a translator simply translates a source program into object form, the programmer must follow a language convention for specifying which subroutines will eventually be needed (ignoring implicit calls to system subroutines such as I/O subroutines, which are supplied by the translator or operating system). In assembly language, a programmer will explicitly identify the name of a subroutine as an external name; in a higher level language, the subroutine's name will typically be given in some type of CALL statement whose format dictates the use of an external module. The translator can now supply a list of external subroutines needed for each module and the loader will supply these addresses at load time.

TRANSFER VECTORS

The first scheme described for linking routines is primarily intended for machines with fixed length machine instructions that carry absolute main memory addresses. This scheme employs a technique known as a *transfer vector* which is created in the following manner. First, the translator creates a vector at the beginning of the object code in which each element of the vector is the name of an external subroutine referenced within the corresponding source module. At each point in the source program where a branch to an external subroutine is needed, the translator replaces this branch with a machine instruction that branches to the element in the vector with the corresponding subroutine name. Then, when the linking loader loads the module, it replaces each element (name) in the vector with a machine language branch instruction that will branch to the subroutine that corresponds to the name that was replaced; thus the name transfer vector. To illustrate this type of loader, we will return to the modified IBM machine used in the example for Figure 3.4, in which relocation was achieved using relocation bits. To simplify the linking process, subroutine names are restricted to a length of four bytes and must be declared at the beginning of the source module. Each subroutine name is declared by using the EXTRN pseudo (See Figure 3.8a). In addition to the object module containing a

```
Relative
Location                Source Code

  000      PASS         START
  000                   EXTRN RTNA
  004                   EXTRN RTNB
  008      BEGIN        ST          14,RETN      SAVE RETURN ADDR
  00C                   LA          1,BUFF       MESSAGE BUFFER ADDR
  010                   L           15,=F'1'     CODE TO SEND
  014                   BAL         14,RTNA      CALL SENDING RTN
  018                   LA          1,BUFF       RESTORE BUFFER ADDR
  01C                   L           15,=F'2'     CODE TO RECEIVE
  020                   BAL         14,RTNB      CALL RECEIVING RTN
  024                   L           14,RETN      GET RETURN ADDR
  028                   BR          14           RETURN
  02C      RETN         DS          F
  030      BUFF         DS          20F          MESSAGE BUFFER
                        END
  080      =F'1'                        (Literal Pool)
  084      =F'2'
```

FIGURE 3.8a
SOURCE CODE FOR MESSAGE PASSING ROUTINE

FIGURE 3.8b
OBJECT CODE FOR MODIFIED MACHINE

Relative Location	Relocation Bit	Generated Code	Comments
000	0	'RTNA'	(will actually
004	0	'RTNB'	be in character code)
008	1	50E0002C	
00C	1	41100030	
010	1	58F00080	
014	1	45E00000	(BAL to vector)
018	1	41100030	
01C	1	58F00084	
020	1	45E00004	(BAL to vector)
024	1	58E0002C	
028	0	07FE0000	
02C	0	----	
030	0	----	
.		.	
.		.	
080	0	00000001	
084	0	00000002	

DESCRIPTION RECORD: MODULE LENGTH=088 VECTOR LENGTH=08

Location	Executable Code	Comments
5000	47F06000	(vector elements now
5004	47F07000	contain branch instr-uctions)
5008	50E0502C	
500C	41105030	
5010	58F05080	
5014	45E05000	(BAL to 1st.Elm. in vector)
5018	41105030	
501C	58F05084	
5020	45E05004	(BAL. to 2nd.Elm. in
5024	58E0502C	vector)
5028	07FE0000	
.	.	(uninitialized
.	.	storage area)
5080	00000001	
5084	00000002	

FIGURE 3.8c
RELOCATED EXECUTABLE CODE FOR MODIFIED IBM MACHINE WITH ROUTINE PASS LOADED AT ABSOLUTE 5000 AND ROUTINES RTNA AND RTNB LOADED AT ABSOLUTE 6000 AND 7000 RESPECTIVELY

vector whose elements are the external subroutine names, the translator must also provide the loader with some form of a descriptor record giving the length of the program including the transfer vector. The entire process is shown in Figure 3.8.

REFERENCE TABLES

The other common scheme used in the design of a linking loader to provide the information needed to identify all the program modules that must be linked is to provide a table of all external references for each module. During the linking phase, the loader collects the set of modules or segments named in the external reference table for the first module and then repeats this collecting process for any new modules referenced in the external reference tables of all other modules collected. When the set of all modules referenced by any of the member modules has been collected, the modules are linked as one program module in main memory ready for relocation.

IBM mainframe linking loaders and linkage editors make use of this second scheme for linking; therefore, as an example of this scheme, a module is traced from source module form to executable code in main memory using the common design followed by the IBM translators and loaders.

The output of each IBM mainframe translator that produces an object module that will be processed by a linking loader, or by a linkage editor followed by a relocating loader, has the following format. Each object module is divided into three principal parts followed by a trailer record identifying the end of the module. These three parts are: (1) the external symbol dictionary (*ESD*), (2) the program text (*TXT*) and (3) the relocatable locations directory (*RLD*). This format is shown in Figure 3.9.

No attempt is made to provide an exact description of each field in the ESD, TXT and RLD records; however, descriptions are provided from a

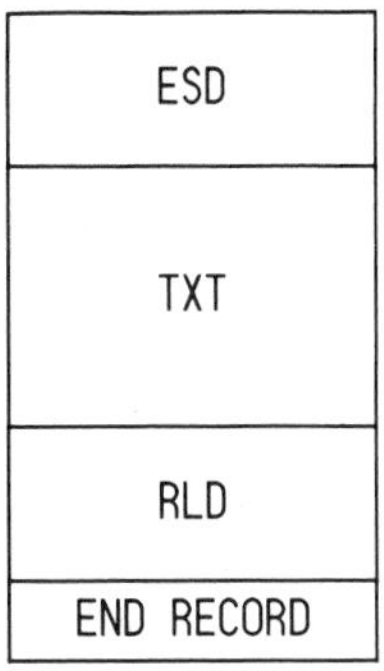

ESD
TXT
RLD
END RECORD

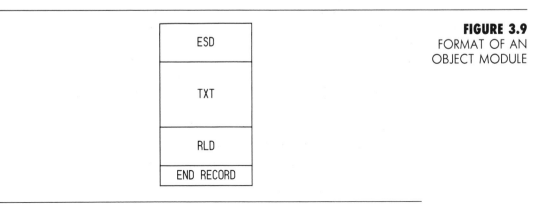

FIGURE 3.9
FORMAT OF AN OBJECT MODULE

conceptual viewpoint that include the most important contents for each of the record types that comprise an object module.

The ESD for a given module contains symbols that are referenced in the module but are defined in other modules. The ESD also contains symbols that are defined in the given module that have been designated so that they can be referenced by other modules. The ESD is organized as a list of records such that there is one record for each symbol. Each record contains a symbol and a set of descriptive information about the symbol. Besides the symbol the three descriptive fields in each record which have bearing on this discussion are: (1) the symbol type, (2) the value or relative location assigned to the symbol and (3) the length of the segment represented by the symbol (see Figure 3.10). There are three common symbol types. These are external reference (ER), segment definition (or section for IBM definition) (SD), and local definition (LD).

A segment (section) definition usually occurs in assembly language by way of a START or CSECT psuedo. This definition specifies the name of a section in the same fashion that a program name or subroutine name is specified in a higher level language program. For a segment definition, the value field is the relative location of the segment within the module (it is possible to have more than one segment in a module). The length field contains the length of the pure machine code within the module (the length is the exact length of the executable machine language that the loader will produce from the object module).

In assembly language, an external reference occurs as the result of a V type address constant or by declaration using an EXTRN psuedo. In a higher language, external references are commonly the result of a subroutine named in a CALL statement. ESD records for an external symbol carry null values for the value and length fields, since these are unknown at translation time.

Local definitions are declared by use of an ENTRY pseudo. Any location within a module can be accessed directly by another module if the location has been declared as an entry point. However, in strict modular programming methodology with one entry and one exit point, local definitions are not used; thus, this symbol type is becoming less common. For local definitions, the value field contains the relative location of the symbol within the module while the length field is null.

Symbol	Type	Value	Length

FIGURE 3.10
SUMMARY FORMAT OF AN ESD RECORD

Symbol	Flag	Length	Relative Location

FIGURE 3.11
SUMMARY FORMAT OF RLD RECORD

The text section of any object module is essentially the translated machine code from the source language program. Addresses that must be relocated carry only module relative addresses. And there is additional control information attached to each TXT record (such as the original source statement number); but for our purposes, we can consider the TXT section as simply relocatable machine language code.

The relocatable locations directory section of an object module contains a list of records, one for each location in the machine language program that must be relocated. Each record contains: (1) the relative location within the module of the field that must be relocated, (2) the length of the field to be relocated, (3) the segment name (symbol) that the relative address is based on, and (4) a flag denoting whether the relocation factor must be added or subtracted to the value that must be relocated (see Figure 3.11).

AN EXAMPLE FROM TRANSLATION THROUGH LOADING

Figure 3.12a on page 136 gives a complete example in which a source module represents the mainline of a program that calls a subroutine (READLN) to read a value N. Next, the mainline calls the subroutine (FACTORL) used before to calculate N!, then calls a subroutine (WRITEM) to write out the values of N and N! (I/O is messy, therefore we let subroutines do it). Finally, the mainline calls a subroutine (EOJRTN) to perform some exit housekeeping and exits the program. Figure 3.12b shows the object module produced by the assembler. Continuing with example figures 3.12a and b, if MAIN is loaded at 17A078, with READN, FACTORL, WRITEM, and EOJRTN loaded at 17A110, 17A420, 17A4C0, and 17A800, respectively, then the program loaded into memory for execution would be identical to the generated TXT for relative locations 000–077; however, the following locations would be changed by the loader as follows:

Rel. Loc.	New Contents	Which Represents
078	0017A0E4	A(MAIN) + 00006C
07C	0017A0E8	A(MAIN) + 000070

(continued on page 138)

FIGURE 3.12a THE SOURCE MODULE TO BE TRANSLATED

Rel. Loc		Source		Comments
	MAIN	START		
000		BALR	2,0	
002		USING	*,2	
002		LA	13,SAVE	PREPARE TO CALL SUBROUTINES
006		LA	1,PRMLST	
00A		L	15,=V(READN)	CALL 1st SUBROUTINE
00E		BALR	14,15	
010		L	15,=V(FACTORL)	CALL 2nd SUBROUTINE
014		BALR	14,15	
016		L	15,=V(WRITEM)	CALL 3rd SUBROUTINE
01A		BALR	14,15	
01C		L	15,=V(EOJRTN)	PREPARE TO EXIT PROGRAM
020		BR	15	EXIT PROGRAM
024	SAVE	DS	18F	
06C	N	DS	F	
070	NFAC	DS	F	
074	COUNT	DS	F	
078	PRMLST	DC	A(N)	THE PARAMETER LIST CONTAINS
07C		DC	A(NFAC)	THREE INTERNAL ADDRESS CONSTANTS
080		DC	A(COUNT)	THAT MUST BE RELOCATED
		END		
084			=V(READN)	THE LITERAL POOL CONTAINS
088			=V(FACTORL)	FOUR EXTERNAL ADDRESS CONSTANTS
08C			=V(WRITEM)	THAT MUST BE RELOCATED
090			=V(EOJRTN)	

OBJECT MODULE

ESD

Symbol	Type	Rel.Loc.	Length
MAIN	SD	0	094
READN	ER	-	-
FACTORL	ER	-	-
WRITEM	ER	-	-
EOJRTN	ER	-	-

TXT

Rel. Loc.	Object Code
00	0520
02	41D02022
06	41102076
0A	58F02082
0E	05EF
10	58F02086
14	05EF
16	58F0208A
1A	05EF
1C	58F0208E
20	07FF
22-77	-
78	00 00 00 6C
7C	00 00 00 70
80	00 00 00 74
84	00 00 00 00
88	00 00 00 00
8C	00 00 00 00
90	00 00 00 00

RLD

Symbol	Flag	Length	Rel. Loc.
MAIN	+	4	078
MAIN	+	4	07C
MAIN	+	4	080
READN	+	4	084
FACTORL	+	4	088
WRITEM	+	4	08C
EOJRTN	+	4	090

FIGURE 3.12b
THE OBJECT MODULE PRODUCED FROM THE SOURCE MODULE IN FIGURE 3.12a

Rel. Loc.	New Contents	Which Represents
080	0017A0EC	A(MAIN) + 000074
084	0017A110	A(READN)
088	0017A420	A(FACTORL)
08C	0017A4C0	A(WRITEM)
090	0017A800	A(EOJRTN)

It must be emphasized that in this loading scheme, the only changes to the object program made by the loader are found at the locations referenced in the RLD. In each case, the value changed by the loader was obtained by adding the load address of the appropriate segment (named by the symbol) to the value found at the corresponding location listed in the relocatable locations directory (RLD).

A second example of the complete process from translation to loading, involves a subroutine written in assembly language which could be called by a FORTRAN mainline to handle the conversion of character integers into binary or vice versa. The subroutine shown in Figure 3.13 (CONV4FOR) acts as an interface to two lower level subroutines that actually perform the conversions (this is better for our linking example and also easier to write!). CONV4FOR receives a parameter list referencing three parameters; only the third parameter, which is a course-of-action code, is used by this routine in order to call the proper conversion routine (either CONV2BI or CONV2CH). If an invalid code is received by CONV4FOR, it will return all binary 1s in the code field.

Figure 3.14 presents a diagram of how a program called FMAIN that uses CONV4FOR would appear in main memory assuming that FMAIN (and any other unmentioned routines) immediately precede CONV4FOR, CONV2BI, and CONV2CH.

If we assume that CONV4FOR is loaded at location 12000 in main memory with CONV2BI and CONV2CH immediately following at 120A8 and 120E0 respectively (See Figure 3.14), then only two four-byte fields (words) in CONV4FOR would require relocation. These two words are part of the literal pool of CONV4FOR and must contain the addresses of CONV2BI and CONV2CH at execution time. Therefore, the changes made by the loader are:

Rel.Loc	Loaded at	Changed to
9C	1209C	000120A8
A0	120A0	000120E0

The diagram in Figure 3.14 provides us with an example in which we can summarize the processes of linking and loading utilizing reference tables.

```
         CONV4FOR    CSECT    (Routine converts character to
         *                     binary numbers and vice versa
         *                     using two lower level routines)
00                   STM      14,12,12(13)
04                   LR       2,15          LOAD BASE REG
                     USING    CONV4FOR,2
06                   ST       13,SAVER+4
0A                   LA       13,SAVER
0E                   L        3,8(1)        GET ADDR OF CODE
12                   L        4,0(3)        GET CONVT CODE
16       CH2BI       C        4,=F'0'        CHECK FOR CHAR
                                            TO BINARY
1A                   BNE      BI2CH
1E                   L        15,=V(CONV2BI)
22                   BALR     14,15
24                   B        RETURN
28       BI2CH       C        4,=F'1'        CHECK FOR BINARY
                                            TO CHAR
2C                   BNE      ERROR
30                   L        15,=V(CONV2CH)
34                   BALR     14,15
36                   B        RETURN
3A       ERROR       MVC      0(4,3),=X'FFFFFFFF' BAD CODE
40       RETURN      L        13,SAVER+4
44                   LM       14,12,12(13)
48                   BR       14            RETURN TO CALLING
                                            RTN
4C       SAVER       DS       18F
                     END
94                            =F(0)
98                            =F(1)
9C                            =V(CONV2BI)
A0                            =V(CONV2CH)
A4                            =X'FFFFFFFF'
```

FIGURE 3.13a SOURCE MODULE TO BE TRANSLATED

The linker examines the external symbol dictionary of FMAIN and encounters an external reference to CONV4FOR; this causes the linker to locate the subroutine and attach it (along with others not mentioned in the example) to FMAIN as part of the load module. In linking CONV4FOR to FMAIN, the linker also encounters external references to CONV2BI and CONV2CH within the external symbol dictionary of CONV4FOR. Thus, these two subroutines are also located and included as part of the load module which now typically contains a composite ESD and a composite RLD instead of separate tables for each routine.

The loader places the machine language component of the load module (that is the complete program in executable format) in main memory at continuous locations starting at 10000. Then, using the relocatable locations table, the loader adjusts those values (addresses) that need relocation. For example, the subroutine CONV4FOR contains two values that represent

FIGURE 3.13b OBJECT MODULE CREATED FROM SOURCE IN FIGURE 3.13a

ESD

SYMBOL	TYPE	Rel.Loc	Len
CONV4FOR	SD	00	A8
CONV2BI	ER	-	-
CONV2CH	ER	-	-

TXT

Rel.Loc	CODE
00	90ECD00C
04	182F
06	50D02050
0A	41D0204C
0E	58301008
12	58403000
16	59402094
1A	47702028
1E	58F0209C
22	05EF
24	47F02040
28	59402098
2C	4770203A
30	58F020A0
34	05EF
36	47F02040
3A	D203300020A4
40	58D02050
44	98ECD00C
48	07FE
4C-93	
94	00000000
98	00000001
9C	00000000
A0	00000000
A4	FFFFFFFF

RLD

SYMBOL	FLAG	LENGTH	Rel.Loc
CONV2BI	+	4	9C
CONV2CH	+	4	A0

NOTE: A separate parameter list is not defined in CONV4FOR. The parameter list sent to this routine is simply passed along to each of the two lower level routines.

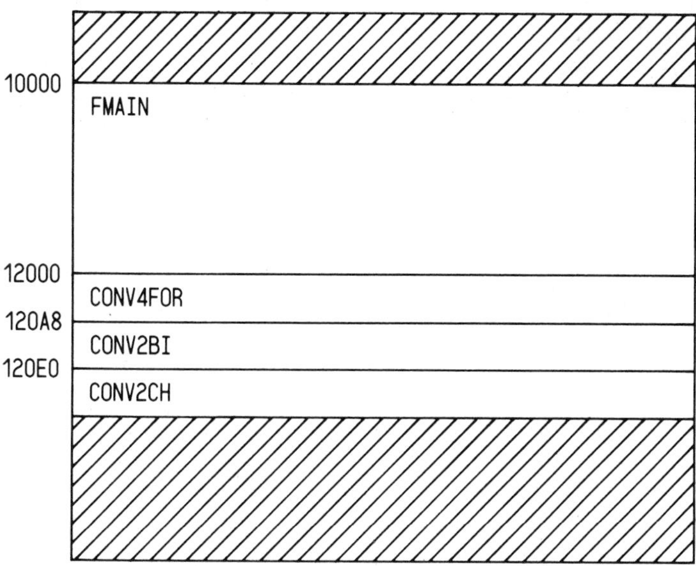

FIGURE 3.14
DIAGRAM OF PROGRAM LOADED IN MAIN MEMORY USING ROUTINES PREVIOUSLY DESCRIBED

the addresses of CONV2BI and CONV2CH which will be changed (relocated) by the loader. After all locations referenced in the relocatable locations table have been processed by the loader, the program FMAIN is ready for execution.

REVIEW QUESTIONS AND EXERCISES

1. Define or explain briefly:
   a. Absolute loader
   b. Relocating loader
   c. Linker
   d. Linking loader
   e. Relocation factor
   f. Relocation bits
   g. Relocatable locations table
   h. Transfer vector
   i. External symbol table
2. Given the following source code for the subroutine RELAYMES written in IBM assembly language. This subroutine passes a message, its

length, and a code (RELAYCD) to one of two other subroutines depending on the value of a pass code. Notice that the parameter list for this subroutine contains only one assembly time address constant, although at execution time the list will contain three absolute addresses (two are simply copied from the calling routine).

a. Show the object module (IBM format) that will be created from this source module.
b. If RELAYMES is loaded at location 42000, with RTNA and RTNB at 420E0 and 42200 respectively, show which locations will be changed by the loader and what their values will be.

```
Relative
Location

000      RELAYMES  CSECT
000                STM     14,12,12(13)
004                LR      2,15
006                USING   RELAYMES,2
006                ST      13,SAVER+4
00A                LA      13,SAVER
00E                LM      3,5,0(1)       GET PARAMETER
                                          ADDRESSES
012                STM     4,5,PASSPRMS   PASS PARAMETERS
016                L       6,0(3)         GET PASS CODE
01A                C       6,=F'1'
01E                BE      CALLA
022                C       6,=F'2'
026                BE      CALLB
02A                L       6,=F'15'        RETURN ERROR CODE
02E                B       RETURN
032      CALLA     MVI     RELAYCD,C'A'
036                LA      1,PARMLST
03A                L       15,=V(RTNA)
03E                BALR    14,15
040                B       GOODPASS
044      CALLB     MVI     RELAYCD,C'B'
048                LA      1,PARMLST
04C                L       15,=V(RTNB)
050                BALR    14,15
052      GOODPASS  SR      6,6            RETURN SUCCESS ONE
054      RETURN    ST      6,0(3)
058                L       13,SAVER+4
05C                LM      14,12,12(13)
060                BR      14
```

```
064     SAVER      DS    18F
0AC     PARMLST    DC    A(RELAYCD)
0B0     PASSPRMS   DS    F            WILL HAVE MESSAGE
                                        ADDRESS
0B4                DS    F            WILL HAVE MESSAGE
                                        LENGTH ADDRESS
0B8     RELAYCD    DS    CL1
                   END
0BC                      =V(RTNA)       LITERAL POOL
0C0                      =V(RTNB)
0C4                      =F'1'
0C8                      =F'2'
0CC                      =F'15'
0E0
```

PROGRAMMING EXERCISES

1. Rerun program 1 from Chapter 2 such that the main routine and the subroutine FACTORL are assembled separately and then linked together for execution.
2. Replace the main routine in programming exercise 1 by one that is functionally equivalent but written in a higher level language such as FORTRAN or COBOL. Compile the new main routine, assemble FACTORL as before, link them together and execute the program.
3. Write a relocating loader using the relocatable locations table format shown in Figure 3.7. To test the loader, you will need to create a short load module by hand (this may be almost as much trouble as the program). Since the load module may be more conveniently entered in character form instead of hexadecimal (182F in character form would enter memory as F1F8F2C6). The following subroutine (CHAR2HEX) is provided which will convert a character string to the equivalent string of hexadecimal digits that it represents. The subroutine expects three parameters
    1. a word containing the binary length of the character string
    2. the character string to be converted
    3. the area to receive the hex string

    in that order. The output string needs an area only half as long as the input string since two characters will convert to one hexadecimal byte. (Note: A full 18-word save area is included for consistency, although a single word to save GPR13 will suffice, since no lower level subroutines are called).

```
CHAR2HEX  CSECT                      CONVERT CHARACTERS TO HEX
          STM     14,12,12(13)
          LR      2,15
          USING   CHAR2HEX,2
          ST      13,CSAVE+4
          LA      13,CSAVE
          LM      3,5,0(1)           GET PARAMETER ADDRESSES
          L       6,0(3)             GET DATA LENGTH
          SR      7,7                CLEAR BYTE COUNT
          SR      9,9                CLEAR WORK REGISTER
LOOP      IC      9,0(4)             GET NEXT EBCDIC CHARACTER
          C       9,=F'240'            CHECK FOR CHARACTER DIGIT
          BL      ALPHA
          S       9,=F'240'            CONVERT TO 0-9 HEX
          B       CONT
ALPHA     S       9,=F'183'            CONVERT TO A-F HEX
CONT      SLL     9,28               LEFT JUSTIFY HEX DIGIT
          SLDL    8,4                CAPTURE HEX DIGIT
          A       7,=F'1'              COUNT BYTE POSITION
          C       7,=F'2'
          BL      NEXTIN
          STC     8,0(5)             STORE HEX BYTE IN OUTPUT
          SR      7,7                CLEAR BYTE POSITION COUNT
          LA      5,1(5)             NEXT OUTPUT LOCATION
NEXTIN    LA      4,1(4)             NEXT INPUT CHARACTER
          BCT     6,LOOP
          L       13,CSAVE+4
          LM      14,12,12(13)
          BR      14
CSAVE     DS      18F
          END
```

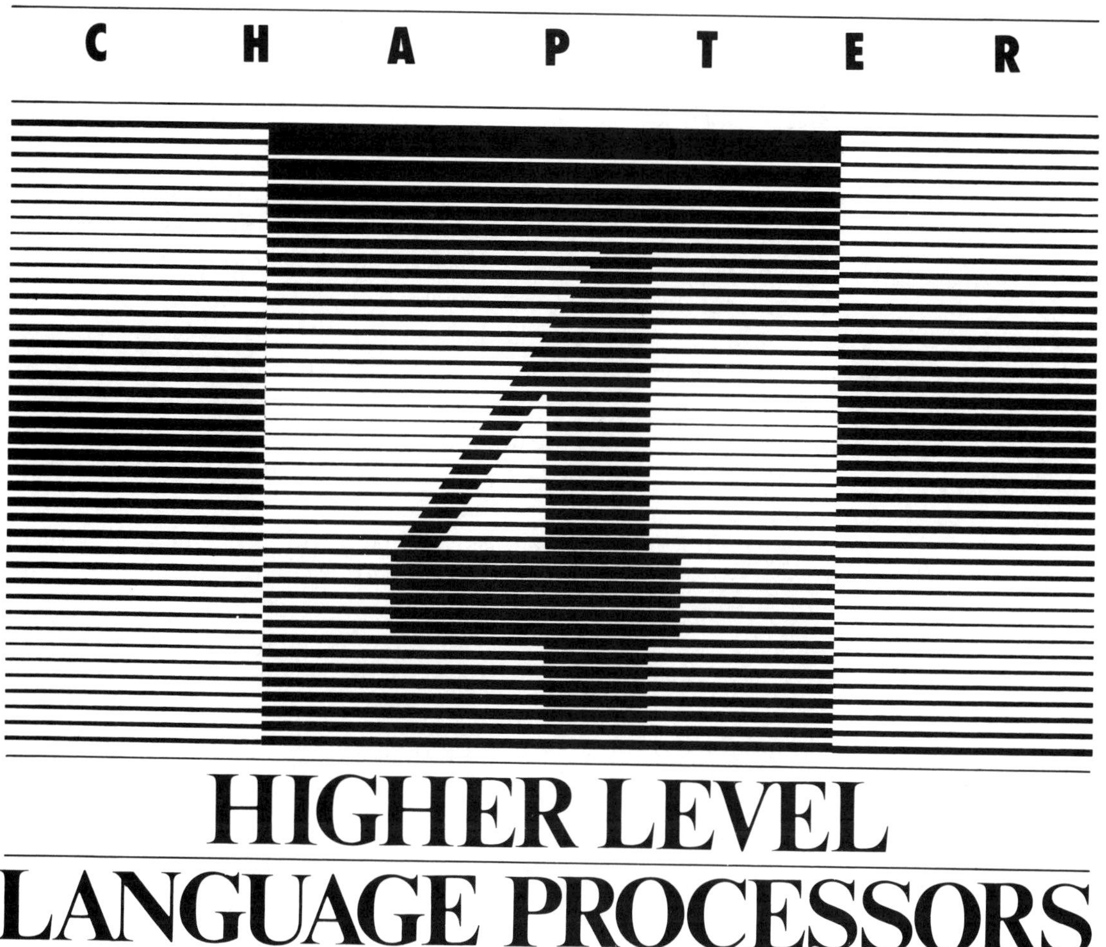

HIGHER LEVEL LANGUAGE PROCESSORS

Given the prominence of high-level programming languages, we are naturally interested in the processes by which a program written in a high-level language is executed on a computer that can only execute programs composed of instructions from its machine language. It may be convenient for the programmer to think of the target computer as a machine that simply executes the programming language used (such as, a Pascal machine or a COBOL machine), but in the end, the target computer must have either (1) an equivalent machine language program to execute or (2) a set of machine language routines that simulate the execution of the high-level language version of the program. System programs that perform either of these two functions for programs written in a high-level language are called *high-level programming language processors.*

INTRODUCTION

A *high-level programming language* is a programming language that is designed to be independent of any particular machine language (as opposed to an assembler language, which is heavily dependent on a particular machine language). In addition, high-level programming languages provide a level of abstraction above a machine or assembly language so that programmers can more conveniently: (1) define a process by which a problem may be solved or (2) define a problem for which a process will be invoked. In general, not only is the programmer provided with an abstraction from typical machine-like functions such as LOAD and STORE, but he or she gains considerable power over a machine/assembly language in expressing and solving problems. This gain is such that a typical statement in a high-level language will require several or perhaps many machine language instructions to implement. For example:

Suppose we want to add two binary integers and store the result at SUM. A minimum assembly language routine would be:

```
L     5,A
A     5,B
ST    5,SUM
```

But in FORTRAN, we would simply write: `SUM = A + B`
which is similar to Pascal's: `SUM := A + B`
or the COBOL equivalent: `ADD A, B GIVING SUM`

If the high-level language is chosen wisely for a particular programming task, the programmer is provided with a language that allows a more natural expression (for humans) of the problem at hand. This provides a means of expression that can greatly reduce programming time and reduce the risk of errors. As might be expected, we do pay a price for the convenience, power, and security gained in using a high-level language instead of an assembler language and this price is program overhead, both with respect to program size and execution time. However, when we consider the benefits already stated and the added attraction that programs written in a suitable high-level language are easier to maintain and more portable, the benefits usually outweigh the cost in most program implementations. In fact, the great majority of programs written today are written in high-level languages instead of assembler languages and in all likelihood, this trend away from programming at machine level will only increase.

In the literature it is common to drop the term "high-level" and simply refer to assembly languages and assemblers as separate from programming languages and programming language processors. Hereafter, this abbrieviated convention is adopted for this book.

There are two broad classes of programming language processors: compilers and interpreters. A *compiler* is a language processor that accepts as input a source language program written in some programming language and translates this source program into an equivalent machine language program. This machine language program may or may not be in executable format. Some compilers produce an equivalent assembly language or metalanguage program that must in turn be processed by a lower level processor, but for our purposes, the output of a compiler is considered to be in a given machine language.

An *interpreter* is a language processor that accepts a source language program as input and dynamically translates and executes the program statement by statement. This type of processor requires a set of routines that can simulate the execution of each statement type. Some interpreters make a partial translation of the source program producing an intermediate form of the program and then interpret the intermediate code in order to improve execution time, but for this discussion of language processors, interpreters are considered as processors that function purely from source statement to execution.

In comparing compilers to interpreters we find that each has some advantages and disadvantages. The compiler's advantages are mainly in relation to the efficiency of the program translation and execution. Since the compiler only translates a statement *once* per program translation, this is a considerable savings over the interpreter, which translates a statement every time it is encountered during the logical execution of the program. For example, in the case of a loop, the interpreter will retranslate every statement in the body of the loop on each iteration. Also, since the compiler creates a complete machine language version of the source program, it can perform certain optimizing techniques on the initial translated code so that the substructures of the program interface with each other more efficiently. This is not feasible in an interpretive scheme, where each statement is translated independently of other past or future translations. In addition, once a program is completed, it can usually be compiled once and stored in *object form* so that future executions require no translation. The interpretive program, by contrast, is stored in *source form* and retranslated statement by statement for every execution. Finally, the compiler offers a greater degree of security for developers of software packages sold to multiple customers. It is far more difficult to pirate someone's ideas and procedures from a program that is supplied in machine language form than one that is sold in source language form.

The interpreter's advantages are ease of implementation and minimal resources required to use the language processor. As a rule, for a given programming language, a compiler is much more difficult to write than an interpreter (this will be addressed in more detail in the discussion of the translation process later in the chapter). Because the compiler is a more complex program, it is usually considerably larger than a corresponding interpreter. Therefore, the interpreter requires less memory to execute, which is the reason that BASIC was so popular on the early microcomputer systems with their very limited main memories. Compilers also typically need additional work space on external units, such as disks, in order to create a complete machine language copy of a program while interpreters do not generally need this. Thus, even greater demand is made by compilers on the resources of a minimal computer system such as a basic personal computer.

One other software category that is very closely related to language processors is the preprocessor. A *preprocessor* is a program that accepts as input a program written in an extended form of some programming language and produces an equivalent source program in the standard form of the language. Assembly language macro processors are frequently implemented as preprocessors. Another typical example is a FORTRAN source program that includes data manipulation statements for a particular data base management system (DBMS). The preprocessor simply replaces the DBMS statements with equivalent routines written in FORTRAN source code so that the resulting program can then be translated by a standard FORTRAN compiler. Macro processors have already been briefly introduced, but other preprocessors are not discussed further because they fall outside the basic set of system software for this book and, except for macro processors, they tend to be more the exception than the rule in a routine computing environment.

So far we have seen what language processors are and very generally what they do. In order to be more specific about what a given language processor does, a brief overview of the various features that distinguish one programming language from another is needed. These features may affect the way in which a source program is processed. The intent here is to establish an appreciation of both common tasks and language-specific tasks required to process programs written in different languages, for example, the major tasks performed by a COBOL processor versus tasks required of a Pascal processor.

PROGRAMMING LANGUAGES

The discussion of programming languages is directed toward three goals:

1. Define and explain a set of terms and features which are commonly used to describe programming languages.

2. Adopt a framework organized around the features in (1.) by which we can analyze a programming language, given the particular set of features that the language possesses.
3. Use the framework to examine several programming languages.

These three goals are generally basic to the study of programming languages. There are several excellent books that treat this material in much greater depth than presented here. Two such publications are *Programming Languages: Design and Implementation* (2nd ed.) by Pratt (1984) and *The Programming Language Landscape* by Ledgard and Marcotty (1981).

After addressing the three goals, consideration will then be given to the implementation of language processors.

COMMON CLASSIFICATIONS OF PROGRAMMING LANGUAGES

In discussing programming languages, several terms are used to broadly classify and characterize a particular language.

In a *procedural language* the programmer specifies the sequence in which statements are performed in a given program or routine. Examples of procedural languages are: FORTRAN, COBOL, BASIC, Pascal, Pl/1 and Ada. In computer science most of the study of programming methodology assumes the use of a procedural language. Going one step further, it can be reasonably argued that the very term programming implied that the programmer will define the required procedure even though the use of very high-level languages require less and less procedure specification and more automatic generation.

A *nonprocedural* language is one that does not in general permit the "programmer" to specify the sequence of steps to be performed to accomplish a given task. Instead, the language provides a means of defining a problem together with its input and output requirements, and the language processor generates or, more commonly, tailors a general program to meet the needs of the specific problem. Each nonprocedural language is intended for a well-defined class of applications and is not suitable for applications outside of its intended class. RPG is an example of a nonprocedural language.

A *scientific programming language* is one that is intended for the processing of numeric data and the evaluation of mathematical expressions. Since many scientific applications require high levels of computation for a relatively small amount of I/O, scientific programming languages tend to have very limited file handling capabilities. FORTRAN is the best known scientific programming language; APL is another example.

A *commercial programming language* is one that is intended primarily for the manipulation of nonnumeric data, particularly in relation to file handling and report generation. COBOL and RPG are examples of commercial programming languages.

Additional terms and detailed language features will be presented as the framework for evaluating a programming language is explained. The framework itself is based largely on a logical grouping of language features which helps provide a structured approach toward the study of these features.

HISTORICAL DEVELOPMENT

In Chapter 1 a brief history of the development of software was presented in which programming languages played a prominent part. At this point, it is helpful to return to the historical development of programming languages in order to appreciate the evolution of programming language design and also to point out certain factors that contributed to this evolution. Factors that have led to the popularity of one language over another are also discussed. Figure 4.1 provides a list of popular programming languages and the year that each language was implemented (that is, a language processor was available so that the language could be used on a computer).

The 10 languages listed in Figure 4.1 have all changed and evolved from their original design. And, as might be expected, the older languages have generally undergone greater change than the more recent ones. However, in each case the design philosophy, structure, and intended use for the language have remained basically the same. From the standpoint of use, the most successful of the earlier languages were COBOL and FORTRAN. The designs of these languages were influenced by a strong concern that their compilers produce equivalent machine language programs that were efficient both in execution speed and program size. The importance placed on the production of highly efficient programs was, in part, related to the relatively slow internal speeds, limited memory sizes, and high costs of the computers that were available at the time.

ALGOL, for example, was developed as an alternative to FORTRAN for scientific applications, but was only moderately successful in competition with FORTRAN for the intended market. ALGOL's design caused some sacrifice in program efficiency in exchange for power, flexibility, and clarity in expressing algorithms. Even though ALGOL is rarely used today, it has had much greater influence than FORTRAN on the designs of the major programming languages developed since the late 1960s (such as Pascal, C and Ada). This has been due, in part, to the fact that computers have increased in capability and decreased in cost while people costs have increased.

LANGUAGE	INTENDED USE	IMPLEMENTATION
FORTRAN	Scientific applications	1957
ALGOL	Scientific applications	1960
COBOL	General commercial/ administrative applications	1960
LISP	List processing	1962
RPG	Limited commercial applications	1964
PL/1	General purpose language	1964
BASIC	Teaching programming	1965
Pascal	Teaching programming	1970
C	Systems programming	1972
Ada	Embedded systems applications	1983

FIGURE 4.1
PROGRAMMING LANGUAGES WITH RESPECTIVE IMPLEMENTATION DATES

Thus, it is now generally considered more important to save people time than machine time.

FORTRAN is still an important language in the area of scientific and engineering applications. Given the large number of existing production programs written in this language, its importance is likely to continue for years to come. However, FORTRAN's dominance of the scientific/engineering programming market is on the decline, and it has been virtually replaced by Pascal as the standard language used to introduce programming at the university level. The decline in the use of FORTRAN may be attributed to its limited ability to define and manipulate data structures (other than homogeneous arrays) and to its lack of power in expressing certain types of algorithms (such as, recursive algorithms) that occur frequently in scientific applications. However, its strongest quality, computational efficiency, must not be overlooked. In fact, no other commonly available language (including those listed in Figure 4.1) can, in general, match FORTRAN for the production of efficient programs to perform heavy numerical computation.

Other languages have dominated certain areas of programming activity. LISP, for example, has been the primary language used for a wide class of applications associated with artificial intelligence. However, any discussion of dominant languages must include COBOL, since no other programming language has experienced its magnitude of dominance. COBOL is not only the dominant programming language used in commercial and administrative data processing, but it is by far the most commonly used language in all areas of programming activity taken as a whole. Several studies conducted between the late 1970s and 1985 estimated that approximately half of all production programs in the United States are written in COBOL! This was several times the frequency for the next most common languages, RPG and FORTRAN. There are several reasons for this massive use of COBOL:

1. COBOL was designed for commercial and administrative data processing, which comprise the majority share of all programming activity taken as a whole. Therefore, dominance in these areas would practically guarantee dominance of programming activity in general.

2. The needs of these application areas typically involve the requirement to create, access, and maintain large external files containing highly variable forms and types of data. Meanwhile, the amount of computation performed on individual data items is relatively simple and straightforward. This is almost the opposite of the requirement for scientific applications. Thus, an appropriate programming language for the commercial/administrative areas must have powerful file handling abilities, requiring (in general) only a modest degree of sophistication in expressing algorithms and need support only basic arithmetic operations directly.

3. Of the languages listed in Figure 4.1, only COBOL and RPG were intended specifically for the commercial/administration applications areas. However, RPG is appropriate for only a restricted subset of these applications. Thus, RPG is typically found in smaller commercial organizations where the primary data processing needs are relatively standard (e.g., billing, payroll, and so on) and there is little or no need to create and manipulate data structures internally.

4. Compared to the other languages listed in Figure 4.1, only PL/1 possesses file handling capabilities that generally match those found in COBOL. Without question, PL/1 is the more powerful and flexible language in the expression of algorithms. However, PL/1's additional capabilities are not commonly needed in the com-

mercial/administrative data processing areas. The cost for these additional capabilities is the learning of a more complex language that requires longer compilation time to generate larger programs that execute more slowly than their COBOL counterparts. Thus PL/1 has not been successful in replacing COBOL in the market place.

5. COBOL is highly portable. There is a strong tendency among the various computer systems vendors to follow the ANSI COBOL standards in the version of the language that they offer (at least as a majority working subset). Adherence to ANSI standards, together with the fact that the file operations are part of the standards (contrary to languages that omit or severely limit file operations, such as MODULA-2), have made COBOL programs highly portable from operating system to operating system and vendor to vendor.

In explaining why COBOL has been so successful in its intended applications areas there has been no intent to portray COBOL as the best of all possible languages; it is not! It is simply very likely the best standard language currently available to meet the programming needs of the largest segment of the present day programming market. Heaven forbid if the programmers at NASA were required to write their tracking programs for the space shuttle in COBOL or systems programmers were forced to write operating systems in COBOL!

In the future, should file processing activity usually be separated from the programming language (such as could be done through the use of a standardized DBMS with host programming languages) or should a generally better programming language with a powerful file system be developed, then COBOL's popularity will certainly decline. Although a decline would most likely be quite gradual given the huge investment in COBOL programs worldwide. Currently there are no challengers to replace COBOL as the most widely used language in all "programmingdom" in the near future.

Two other languages that are considerably different from each other were developed for a common reason: the teaching of programming. These languages are BASIC and Pascal.

BASIC was developed in the mid-1960s as a minimal language to teach beginning programming. The design of the language borrows heavily from FORTRAN to the point that if we ignore the extensions found in the many dialects of BASIC, we could view the common set of statements in BASIC as simplified forms of a subset of the statements in FORTRAN. By contrast, BASIC was conceived as an interpreted language to be used interactively, while FORTRAN was intended as a compiled language primarily for batch processing.

Any discussion of BASIC leads almost immediately to the question of which BASIC? BASIC had no ANSI standard until 1978, and even that had only a modest effect on the implementors of the language. We now have almost as many dialects of BASIC as implementations. Fortunately, the differences between dialects occur primarily in the extensions to the original version of the language (basic BASIC!) so that most of the major characteristics of the language are preserved between dialects even if programs are not readily portable.

BASIC gained much of its popularity not on the particular merits of the language, but because it became, almost by default, the standard programming language supplied or made available for the early minicomputers and early personal computers. Even though these two classes of computers were introduced several years apart, there were common reasons for choosing BASIC. The primary reason was, that at their introduction, both minicomputers and personal computers typically had very small main memories (of about 16K–32K) and BASIC was a small, interpretive language that could be comfortably implemented in such limited space. Second, BASIC was conceived to be used interactively, which coincided with the intended use for personal computers and many of the minicomputers as well. Thus, as the popularity of minicomputers and (then later) microcomputers increased, so did the use of BASIC.

Even though BASIC was not originally intended as a serious candidate for technical or commercial applications, the very fact that it was often the only programming language commonly available for large classes of computers led to the inevitable: all sorts of application packages, written in BASIC, were developed and marketed. These packages covered the gambit of applications from engineering to business and from education (such as computer-assisted instruction, CAI) to computer games. In many (if not most) cases these packages written in BASIC could have been improved, had other programming languages been generally available. As there were no generally available alternatives, questioning the use of BASIC was rather like criticizing the early settlers for using horse-drawn ploughs instead of tractors.

BASIC was designed without many of the features and capabilities found in larger, more powerful languages so that it could be learned quickly by a beginning programmer. This has turned out to be a mixed blessing, as learning a programming language quickly does not imply the person will program well, and quickly-ever! It is certainly possible to use good programming methodology and techniques (that is, program well) using BASIC. However, it is, perhaps, easier to avoid using good programming methodology when programming in BASIC than other languages, if for no other reason than the fact that many of the methodology concepts involved (especially structured programming) are not supported directly by the language.

Pascal was designed to teach programming and to encourage good programming methodology. For example, a programmer has to go out of his or her way to write an unstructured program in Pascal, while almost the reverse is true with BASIC. Pascal was designed at a time when more had been learned about the advantages of modular and structured programming, and at a time of growing concern about the correctness and maintainability of large programs and systems of programs. As we study the next section on the design and implementation features of programming languages, it will be helpful in understanding the evolution of languages to note those features from earlier languages that were and were not included in Pascal.

Not all exclusions from Pascal are necessarily desirable for all programming applications. Since Pascal was designed for the teaching of good programming practices, not as an applications language per se, more attention was directed toward designing a language to express a large variety of algorithms and data structures directly and clearly. Less attention was paid to such things as:

1. file processing (which is desirable for commercial applications)
2. an extensive mathematical function library (which is desirable for scientific applications)
3. the ability to combine separately compiled modules (which is desirable in production programming environments in general).

Nonetheless, Pascal is beginning to make inroads into the world of applications programming, particularly as an alternative to BASIC in the personal/microcomputer market. Pascal, like BASIC, also suffers from the lack of a strong standard for the language. There are currently several dialects of the language, each with an avid band of users (ISO Pascal, UCSD Pascal, Turbo Pascal, and the IEEE/ANSI Pascal). Most of the differences appear to be in the area of file operations and in extensions to the language defined by its designer, Niklaus Wirth. Thus, with the exception of file processing statements, any Pascal program written according to Wirth's definition is generally portable from dialect to dialect.

FORTRAN, COBOL, BASIC and Pascal have received special attention in this section due to their impact in the marketplace and on education. The other languages listed in Figure 4.1, as well as several that are not listed (for example, APL, SNOBOL, and MODULA-2) are certainly worth study. However, a discussion of many languages is beyond the scope and needs of this book. Additional information on these can be found in volumes dedicated to programming languages, such as those listed in the bibliography.

A FRAMEWORK FOR EVALUATING A LANGUAGE

We now turn to the selection of a framework by which we can evaluate a programming language in some detail to determine if the language is appropriate for a particular application (or set of related applications). This framework can also be used to compare one programming language to another.

PRATT'S MODEL

Terrence W. Pratt proposed such a framework or model in his book *Programming Languages: Design and Implementation* (1975). The Pratt model is based on the concept of an abstract machine (computer) that executes programs written in the given language directly (that is, the machine language of the computer is the programming language). Using this concept of the abstract machine, the Pratt model then separates the attributes of a language into six components for analysis. These components are:

1. Data—the elementary data types and data structures that are defined by the language and can be manipulated directly by basic operations in the language.

2. Primitive operations—the basic operations for the manipulation of data (such as ASSIGN, +, −, READ)

3. Sequence control—mechanisms (such as statements) that control the sequence in which the primitive operations are performed.

4. Data control—mechanisms for controlling the data supplied to each execution of an operation (that is, scope rules, parameter passing, and so on)

5. Storage management—mechanisms for controlling the allocation of storage for programs and data (static or dynamic allocation for variables).

6. Operating environment—mechanisms for communicating with the external environment and data (in a batch processing environment this amounts to file processing).

Other authors of books on programming languages (such as Ledgard and Marcotty (1981) have, in general, examined most of the same aspects of programming languages as are addressed in the Pratt model without the use of an abstract machine concept. Thus, the language aspects are presented in groupings different from the six proposed by Pratt. There is some disadvantage in using a framework that is more or less based on the Von Neumann computer concept in evaluating all languages, as some languages (notably LISP) do not readily conform to this abstraction. However, the majority of the commonly popular applications languages (FORTRAN. COBOL, BASIC, and Pascal) do conform to this concept. Therefore, due to its appropriateness for the most commonly used languages and to its clarity of organization, the framework developed in this chapter is based on the Pratt model with only minor modifications. The six components of the Pratt evaluation model and those additions and/or modifications that will complete our evaluation model are now examined in more detail.

EXPANSION OF EVALUATION MODEL COMPONENTS

Data The data for a language refers to those data types, elementary or structured, that are allowed as operands for basic operations in the language. The types of data that are supported directly by a language can have a major effect on whether the language is appropriate for one class of applications or another. For example, any language that does not support integer and floating point data types for computation is likely to be inappropriate for a large group of scientific applications. Likewise, a language that does not support character strings as a basic data type and records as a structured type is likely to be tedious to use for most commercial applications.

Basic Data Types: A *basic data type* is a data type that cannot be (or, at least, is not meant to be) subdivided into component data types. Examples of basic numeric types are:

- Integer
- Real or Floating point
- Complex
- Packed Decimal
- Display (that is, character decimal)

Other basic data types include:

- Character
- String (sometimes treated as a structured type)
- Boolean
- Pointer

Structured Data Types: A *structured data type* is data type composed of a set of data elements which are valid data types (either basic or structured) that may be treated individually.

Perhaps the most universal structured data types are vectors and arrays. A *vector* is a one-dimensional structure containing a fixed number of contiguous elements, all of the same type. A *one-dimensional array* is a vector. A *two-dimensional array* is a vector of vectors and an *n-dimensional array* is a vector of (n − 1)-dimensional arrays.

If the basic elements of an array are restricted to a single basic data type, then every component within the array will be of this same basic type, and the array is called *homogeneous* (every element in the array must be an integer or every element must be a real; but, a mixture of integers and reals is not allowed). However, if the basic element of the array is allowed to vary in type or if the basic element is a structured data type (such as a record) containing more than one basic data type, then the array is said to be *heterogeneous.*

FORTRAN and BASIC allow only homogeneous arrays (which is awkward for many types of nonnumeric processing), while COBOL and Pascal allow homogeneous or heterogeneous arrays. (See Figure 4.2.)

Records are structured data types whose components can be any combination of valid data types in the language, including records. The record data type is highly desirable for a variety of applications in which there is a need to define and process structured data elements that are not wholly

FIGURE 4.2
HOMOGENEOUS AND HETEROGENEOUS ARRAYS

27	32
45	09
98	18
72	54
16	00

(a)

Two-dimensional homogeneous array of integers

ADAMS, E.	06
CARPENTER, J.	10
ELLZEY, R.	09
MCCOY, W.	12
MEAD, D.	14

(b)

One-dimensional heterogeneous array of records

```
01 EMPLOYEE-RECORD.
   02 EMPLOYEE-NAME    PIC X(20).
   02 EMPLOYEE-SSN     PIC 9(9).
   02 HOURS-WORKED.
      03 REGULAR-HOURS   PIC 999.
      03 OVERTIME-HOURS  PIC 999.
   02 EMPLOYEE-PAY-RATE  PIC 99V99.
```

FIGURE 4.3
COBOL RECORD DATA TYPE

numeric. Commercial applications for records are obvious (see Figure 4.3), but records can also be used to define components in large structures created by the programmer, such as linked lists shown in (Figure 4.4).

Figure 4.4 shows that the Pascal record defines the form of the elements in a linked list. A *list* is a one-dimensional structure containing a variable number of elements all of the same type. Thus, a list is similar to a vector, except that the number of elements is not fixed and they need not be located in contiguous locations. If each element in a list (except the last) contains a pointer to the next element in the list, the list is called a *linked list.* (See Figure 4.5.)

Linked lists are important structures: (1) because they provide a means of establishing logical order among a set of elements without requiring physical order; and (2) because linked lists form the basis for the creation of more complex logical structures, such as trees. Of the languages listed in Figure 4.1, only LISP supports the linked list as a language-defined data type with primitive operations for the creation and manipulation of lists. However, linked lists can be easily created and manipulated by program control in COBOL, PL/1, Pascal, C, and Ada, as well.

Other Language-Defined Data Types: Other language-defined data types such as enumerated data sets (Pascal and Ada) or edited data items (COBOL) are useful for one type of application or another, but these will not be covered individually. A more extensive discussion on language-defined data types can be found in most standard textbooks on programming languages.

```
type
   STUDENT =
      record
         NAME        : NAMETYPE  ;
         ID          : integer   ;
         GRADES      : array[1. .10] of integer;
         AVERAGE     : real;
         NEXTSTUDENT : pointer
      end;
```

FIGURE 4.4
PASCAL RECORD TYPE FOR ELEMENT IN A LINKED LIST

FIGURE 4.5
CONCEPTUAL DIAGRAM OF A THREE ELEMENT LINKED LIST

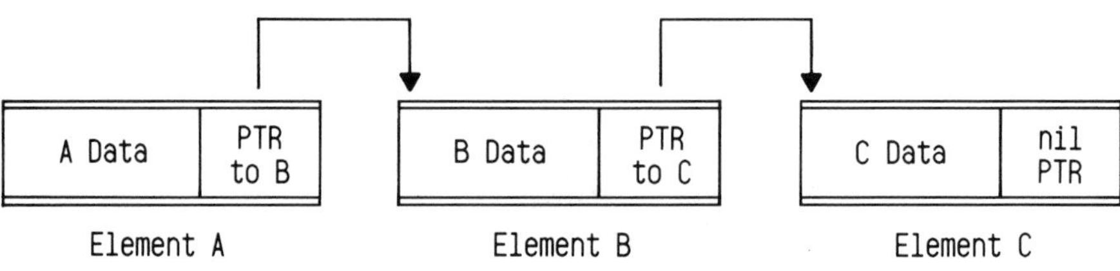

User Defined Data Types: User defined data types are data types that are defined by the programmer but supported in a manner similar to that used for language-defined data types; Pascal and Ada allow user-defined data types. User-defined data types provide programming convenience in that complex data structures can be treated as single data objects. Also, depending on the level of type checking, user-defined data types provide a means of restricting the use of a particular data type, thus reducing the likelihood of programmer errors. For example, in Pascal, a record of type STUDENT could not be assigned to a record of type EMPLOYEE.

Type Checking: Type checking is the process of checking each operation to be executed by a program for the proper number and type of arguments. Type checking done during program compilation is called *static type checking*. FORTRAN, COBOL, and Pascal use only static type checking. Type checking performed during program execution is called *dynamic type checking*.

Even though static type checking can detect a majority of programming type errors, it is of no help for possible data errors that could occur at execution time. Dynamic type checking can detect many run time data errors but the price for dynamic type checking is paid in program overhead. Not only is there considerable execution time overhead in the checking of data types during program execution, but there is also storage overhead for the routines that perform the checking. Both types of overhead also result from associating a type descriptor with each data element instead of maintaining just the value of the data object.

A language in which data types are rigidly enforced is said to be *strong typed*. Very few languages qualify as purely strong typed (only Ada from the list in Figure 4.1), as most languages allow some—if not many—ways to violate type. Therefore, it is perhaps more useful to describe a language in terms of the degree of type checking that is done or whether the language is (in general) "more" strongly typed than another. For example, FORTRAN allows character data to be assigned to integer or real variables by using input statements. COBOL allows any data item to be REDEFINED as a different type (also called *aliasing*) and treats all group items (records) as equivalent types. Pascal is for the most part, strongly typed and does considerably more type checking than FORTRAN or COBOL. However, because of a few minor cases (such as the treatment of variant records), Pascal is not considered strong typed.

Declared versus Undeclared Data Elements: COBOL, Pascal, C, and Ada all require that every variable or named constant be explicitly declared, by name and type, prior to its use in a procedural statement; in each of these four languages there is a declaration section, or sections, that precede and are set apart from the procedures that use them. By contrast, FORTRAN, BASIC, and PL/1 do not, in general, require explicit declarations, and allow a variable to be declared implicitly by its appearance in a procedural statement and, at that time, its type is assigned by default (e.g., FORTRAN) or by its use.

Although having the programmer explicitly declare variables may occasionally cause minor inconvenience, the requirement is generally accepted as a means of reducing program errors, improving program readability, and simplifying program translation. In the case of implicit declarations, a simple case of a misspelled variable name (programmer error) can cause the creation of a new variable causing, possibly, more subtle and time consuming logic errors than the actual coding error that did occur.

Data Conversions: Although type checking is done to prevent inadvertent attempts at performing operations such as assignment with improper operands, there are often times that it is desirable to convert a numeric value from one numeric form to another. FORTRAN, BASIC, and Pascal convert character numeric values (text form) to their declared numeric data types as part of an input operation (the reverse is done for output operations). Yet, none of these languages provides a direct means of converting character data to a numeric form after input, which is a common data processing function in the editing of character data. FORTRAN does allow conversion of integer to real or real to integer through assignment and Pascal will convert integer data to floating point by assignment, but not vice versa.

COBOL, however, does no conversion during input/output operations but allows the conversion of any numeric data type to any other numeric data type through assignment (the MOVE statement) for all numeric types supported by the language: (character numeric (display); fixed point; edited; and, usually, floating point and/or packed decimal).

Conversion of numeric data values is a useful feature in a number of data processing applications, and the programmer needs to be aware of when and how data conversion occurs. However, data conversion should not be confused with a change in the type of a variable or the absence of type checking. It simply means that the assumption has been made that, where allowed, the programmer wishes the language to resolve differences in data types for operations by conversion to a common data type instead of preventing the operation.

Basic Operations *Basic* or *primitive operations* in a language are those operations that are available to operate directly on data elements of the various data types supported by the language. Common examples of basic operations are:

1. Assignment—a value is assigned to a named data element, such as:

```
N  =  1          (FORTRAN, BASIC, C or PL/1)
N :=  1          (Pascal or Ada)
MOVE 1 TO N      (COBOL)
```

2. Arithmetic, such as:

```
+, -, *, /     which are valid for all seven
               languages in the assignment
               example in 1
```

3. Relational, such as:

```
=, <>, <, >, <=, >=
```

Some operations are restricted to a single data type (for example, the DIV operation in Pascal, which is restricted to integer operands). Other operations may be used for a variety of data types (such as, the assignment and relational operations from most languages).

Some languages support primitive operations not commonly found in other languages (for example, the SEARCH and SORT operations in COBOL or the bit-wise shift operations << and >> in C). A language may also provide a common generic operation that is used for a wider or different class of data types than is allowed in another language (such as in FORTRAN, where arithmetic operations are valid for integer, single precision floating point, double precision floating point, or complex numbers, while in Pascal, a "/" operation is only allowed for a real divide).

Closely related to the basic operations of a language are the standard functions defined by the language. While these are not operations per se, they are closely related in that they perform an operation and return a value that can be used as an operand for a basic operation. Standard functions (such as the mathematical functions supplied with FORTRAN or the ORD and CHAR functions in Pascal) can greatly increase the power and convenience of a language for given applications and should not be overlooked.

Because language-supported data types and basic operations are so closely related, much of the pertinent material for basic operations was covered in the previous section on data types and will not be repeated. Indeed, the most valuable part of the support that a language supplies for a particular data type are the operations that can be performed on the data type. Thus, any discussion of one will include aspects of the other.

Sequence Control Sequence control refers to those features of a language that control the sequence in which the basic operations are performed when they are written in a program. Sequence control can be divided into three classes:

1. Sequence control within a program statement (that is, sequence control in evaluating expressions).
2. Sequence control between statements.
3. Sequence control between subroutines.

Evaluation of Expressions: Sequence control for the operations used in the evaluation of expressions is basically similar for every language listed in Figure 4.1 except LISP. For the other nine languages, in each case, an expression is evaluated by performing operations from left to right according to that language's set of precedence rules (see Figure 4.6). The precedence rules may vary slightly from language to language, but in general, the rules for arithmetic operations are the same and in each case, a different or specific precedence can be obtained by grouping an operation together with its operands in a pair of parentheses. In such a case, the parentheses pair carries the highest precedence. In the case of nested pairs of parentheses, the innermost level is performed first.

OPERATOR	PRECEDENCE
NOT	1st
*, /, DIV, MOD, AND	2nd
+, −, OR	3rd
<, <=, >, >=, =, < >, IN	4th

FIGURE 4.6
PRECEDENCE RULES FOR PASCAL

Sequence Control Between Statements: Sequence control between statements refers to the order in which the statements of a program will be performed. How a language provides this control is perhaps the most important factor in the development of the logic for a specific program. For example, if we wish to write structured programs, then a language that includes statements that are equivalent to the three basic Bohm/Jacopini constructs (see Figure 4.7) will be more convenient to use for the expression of structured algorithms than one that does not. More specifically, these three constructs are:

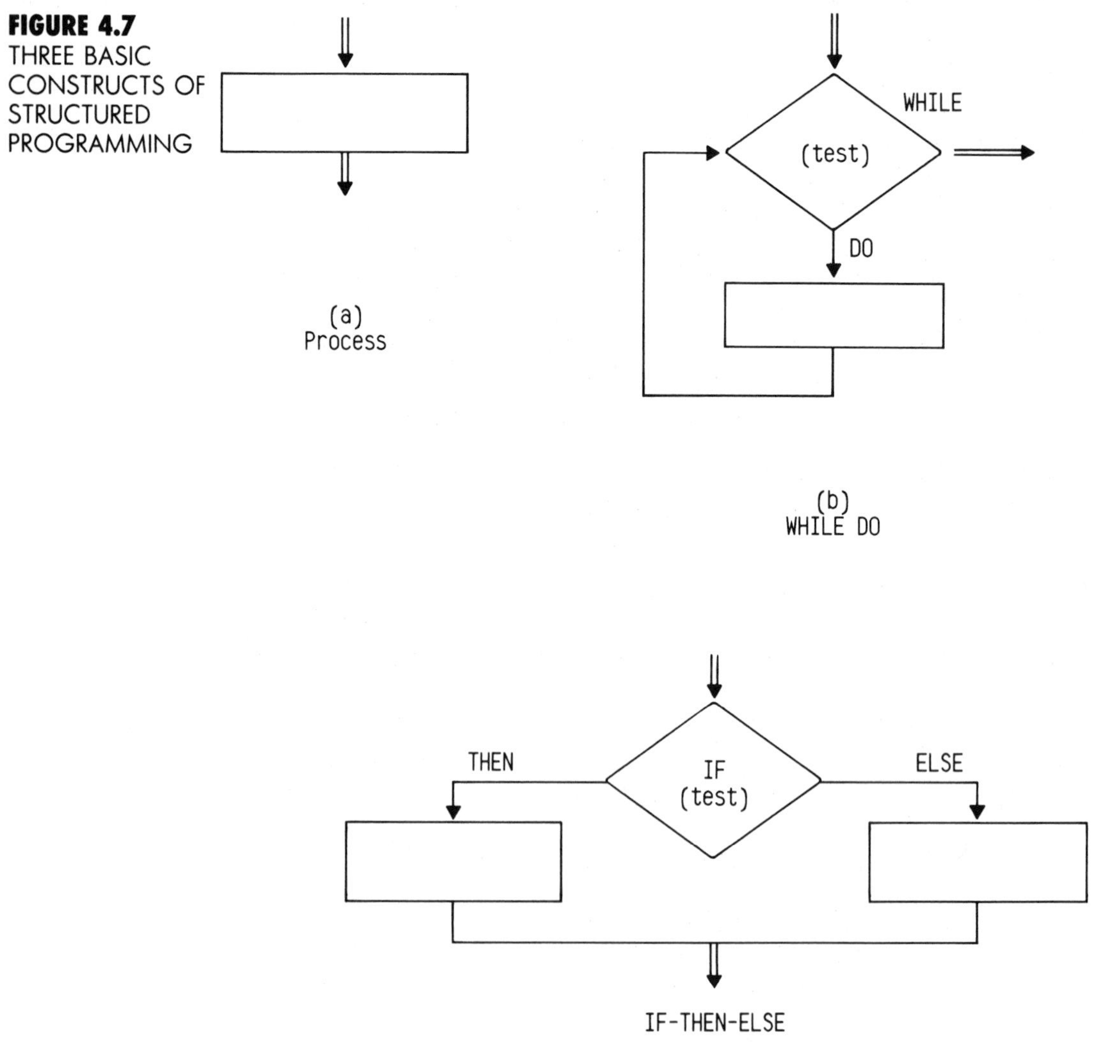

FIGURE 4.7
THREE BASIC CONSTRUCTS OF STRUCTURED PROGRAMMING

1. Single process—after the process is performed, control flows to the next physical statement in the program (for example, assignment, READ, WRITE, subroutine call, and so on).

2. Iteration—a statement or group of statements is executed repeatedly until some specified condition occurs (as with WHILE DO or DO WHILE statements).

3. Binary choice—depending on some specified test, exactly one of two alternative statements is performed (such as an IF-THEN-ELSE statement). Either choice in the statement may be compound or null.

ALGOL, COBOL, PL/1, Pascal, C, and Ada all contain flexible forms of these constructs directly. Although earlier versions of FORTRAN did not contain an IF-THEN-ELSE statement, FORTRAN 77 now includes this statement type. However, the iteration statement (the DO loop) is awkward for loops in which the test is not based on counting. BASIC is restricted to the same type of iteration statement as FORTRAN and, in general, does not include the IF-THEN-ELSE construct.

While some languages such as FORTRAN and BASIC provide only one type of iteration statement, other languages have more. COBOL offers two versions, with alternate forms of the PERFORM (a WHILE DO type and a DO loop type). Pascal has three versions; both types found in COBOL plus a DO WHILE type (the REPEAT-UNTIL), which is similar to the WHILE DO except that the test is performed at the end of the loop (see Figure 4.8).

Another sequence control statement which is available in every procedural language listed in Figure 4.1 is the GO TO statement. Unrestricted use of the GO TO statement has received much criticism by programming

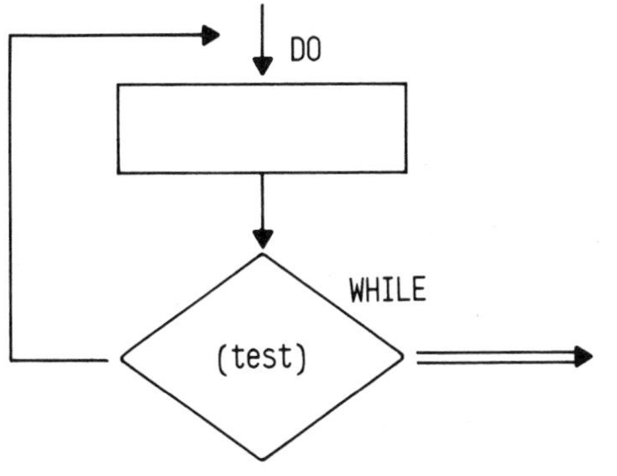

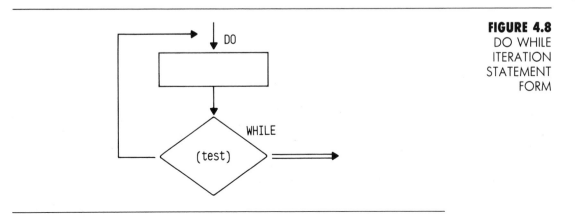

FIGURE 4.8 DO WHILE ITERATION STATEMENT FORM

methodology scholars for a host of reasons; one is an often referred to problem known as "spaghetti logic". In short, the unrestricted GO TO provides no clue as to the future execution sequence of program statements after the GO TO has been executed. This is contrary to the execution of a construct in structured programming, since upon completion of any of these constructs, sequence control will always continue at the next physical textual statement in the program.

FORTRAN and BASIC have relied heavily on the GO TO statement for program control. However, in these languages, the GO TO can be restricted by convention to the creation of structured programming constructs only, thus eliminating (except for mistakes) most of the problems with the statement.

Another statement type which is often useful is the CASE statement (see Figure 4.9). The CASE construct provides a means whereby, depending on a test (usually involving an index), exactly one of several alternative statements or groups of statements is executed, and then, control returns to a common exit point. The CASE statement can provide an alternative to excessive nesting of IF-THEN-ELSE statements. This statement (or some form of it) occurs directly in Pascal, PL/1, C, and Ada, but must be simulated by restricted forms of the GO TO in COBOL, FORTRAN and BASIC.

Sequence Control Involving Subroutines: In this book the function subprogram structure (as is found in FORTRAN and Pascal) is not treated separately. However, most of the discussion of subroutines is generic and would apply to functions as well. Sequence control involving subroutines usually follows the convention that a CALL statement to the subroutine is viewed as a process type statement, and control will return to the next physical textual statement after the CALL statement upon completion of the subroutine. (Coroutines are not considered in this treatment.) Much of the

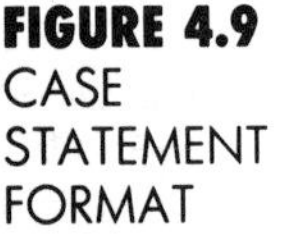

FIGURE 4.9
CASE STATEMENT FORMAT

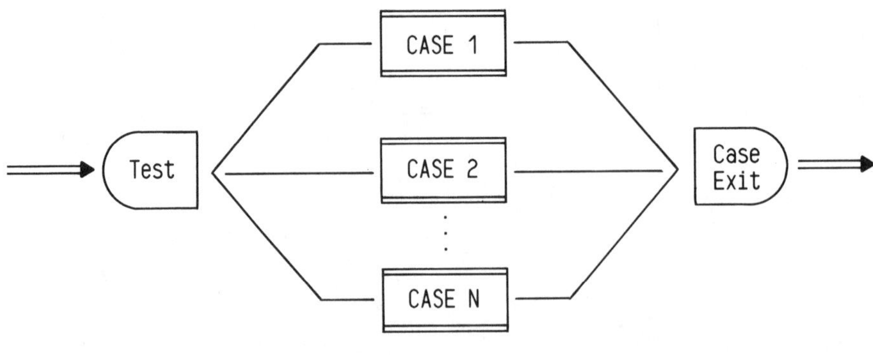

discussion of subroutines in Chapter 2 is appropriate here and will not be repeated.

One additional aspect of subroutines that was not covered in Chapter 2 was whether the subroutines can be recursive. A *recursive routine* is one that can call itself or cause another routine to call it prior to the completion of its execution. In order to support recursive calls to subroutines, a language must provide for a separate referencing environment for each call to a routine that is to be used recursively. Referencing environments will be explained more fully in the next section, but in this case, for each call to a recursive subroutine, a separate set of variable data elements and parameters must be created and preserved until the specific call has been completed. ALGOL, PL/1, Pascal, C, Ada and LISP all support recursion; FORTRAN, COBOL, and BASIC do not. Figure 4.10 shows an example of a recursive subroutine (procedure) written in Pascal, in which given a value for N $\geq$ 0, the routine will compute the sum of the consecutive integers from 0 through N and return the sum at NSUM.

Data Control Data control refers to the manner in which data values are supplied to the operations of a program written in a given language. For example, if we examine:

```
C := A + B                    (Pascal)
C  = A + B                    (FORTRAN)
ADD A, B GIVING C }
or                 }          (COBOL)
COMPUTE C = A + B  }
```

we have seemingly logically equivalent statements in three languages. The meaning in each case is that two data elements identified by A and B are

```
PROCEDURE  SumInt(n : integer; var nsum : integer);
  VAR      temp : integer;

  BEGIN
    IF n < 1 THEN
      nsum := 0
    ELSE
      BEGIN
        temp := n - 1;
        SumInt (temp, nsum);
        nsum := n + nsum
      END
    END
  END;
```

FIGURE 4.10 RECURSIVE ROUTINE WRITTEN IN PASCAL

to be added together, and their sum is to be assigned to a data element identified by C. However, the manner in which the identifiers are associated with their data values could cause entirely different results in each of the three cases, even though at some point A, B, and C refer to equivalent data elements in each of the three programs that contain the statements.

Referencing Environments: This brings us to the concept of a referencing environment. A *referencing environment* is a set of associations between data element identifiers and the data element values. In assembly language, the referencing environment for a program does not change. Symbolic operands (that is identifiers) are simply replaced by addresses from the symbol table, and the address for a particular symbol does not change throughout the program. While programs written in some higher level languages (such as BASIC) also have only a single referencing environment, programs written in other languages (Pascal, for one) may have many.

A *global referencing environment* is a referencing environment that can be used throughout all levels of a program (the main routine and all subroutines). It is created for all data elements declared or used at the program level (highest level) and for most languages, it usually does not change for a given program.

A *local referencing environment* is a referencing environment that is created upon entry to a subroutine for the data elements declared in the subroutine, as well as any parameters or temporary data elements used in the subroutine. Logically, a local referencing environment does not exist prior to entering the subroutine it serves and is discarded upon completion of the subroutine only to be recreated on the next entry.

A *nonlocal referencing environment* is a referencing environment that can exist only in programs written in a language that allows nesting of subroutine definitions (including Pascal, PL/1, and Ada). A nonlocal environment for a given subroutine SUBRTN is the local environment for a higher level subroutine that contains SUBRTN (this will be explained further under block-structured languages).

Many languages (FORTRAN, Pascal, C, PL/1 and Ada for instance) allow the same names to be used for different data elements (such as variables) in different portions of a program. In other words, the same name could be used for a global variable and then used for a local variable in one or more subroutines. Thus, the variable name will appear in more than one referencing environment for a given program, which means that a different association will be in effect for the variable name in different portions of the program. It is, therefore, essential to have rules that determine which referencing environment is to be used for each variable found at each point in a program (see Figure 4.11). These rules are called scope rules.

```
          PROGRAM SCOPEX (input, output);
              .
              .
(1)           VAR  X : integer;
              .
              .
              .
              PROCEDURE SUBRTN (A : real);
                  .
                  .
(2)               VAR X : real ;
                  .
                  .
                  BEGIN
                      .
                      .
(3)                   Z := A * X ; (* local X *)
                      .
                      .
                  END; (* end subrtn *)
                  .
                  .
              BEGIN    (* start program mainline *)
                  .
                  .
(4)               Z := 2 + X ; (* global X *)
                  .
                  .
              END.  (* END SCOPEX *)
```

FIGURE 4.11
SKELETON OUTLINE OF PASCAL PROGRAM WITH GLOBAL AND LOCAL REFERENCING ENVIRONMENTS

Scope of a Variable Declaration: The *scope* of a variable declaration is that portion or region of a program for which the declaration is in effect. The *scope rules* are the rules that determine the scope of a declaration (explicit or implicit).

The scope rules that can be determined from the text of a program are called the *static scope.* Those scope rules which depend on the execution pattern of the program are called the *dynamic scope.* In all of the languages listed in Figure 4.1, except LISP, the scope of a declaration can be determined statically.

An example of static scope rules is shown in Figure 4.11. In this example, a skeleton Pascal program is shown with a global and local referencing environment. The declaration of X at point 1 is part of the global environment and is in effect for the statement at point 4. The declaration at point 2 is part of the local environment of the procedure SUBRTN and is in effect for the statement at point 3 any time that the subroutine (that is procedure) is entered. Thus, because of the scope rules for this language, the X at point 3 refers to a value found in a different location in main memory than the location that contains the value for the X referenced at point 4.

Block-Structured Languages: Pascal, ALGOL, PL/1 and Ada belong to a group known as block-structured languages. A *block-structured language* is a language in which: (1) every program is created as a set of blocks, each with its own local referencing environment; (2) each block begins with a declaration section containing declarations for all local variables, named constants and nested block definitions followed by a statement section, and (3) the blocks can be nested to any level, however, there is one block that contains all other blocks or nests of blocks in the program. The referencing environment of this outer block is the global environment of the program (see Figure 4.12).

Block-structured languages offer a number of advantages for the programmer. For example, they all support recursive subroutines, and they offer a natural means of writing top-down modular programs. Block-structured languages also have the advantage that the referencing environment may be established by static scope rules (see Figure 4.12).

The language C deserves a special mention here. C is very similar to the block-structured languages and actually satisfies conditions 1 and 2 of the previous list of requirements for block-structured languages, but it does not permit the nesting of blocks. All blocks in a C program must be defined at the same level, even though one block must be designated as the *main* block to serve as the logical mainline for the rest of the program.

When referencing environments of a program are established by static scope rules, it does not necessarily mean that the binding of a data element name to a location in memory which contains the value of the data element is also static. As a matter of fact, for block-structured languages, the binding of data element names to memory locations is done dynamically during the program execution for all environments except for the global environment.

Bindings of data element names to memory locations will be discussed more in a later section on storage control.

Parameters: Another aspect of data control is the manner in which parameters are passed between routines and/or subroutines of a program. *Parameters* are data elements whose values are shared between two routines in a program by an explicit listing. We have already seen that programs supporting global or nonlocal referencing environments can share data elements with lower level subroutines directly. However, this technique is unsatisfactory in cases where we want the data element shared with the subroutine to vary (as with recursive calls). Also, reliance on global variables as the

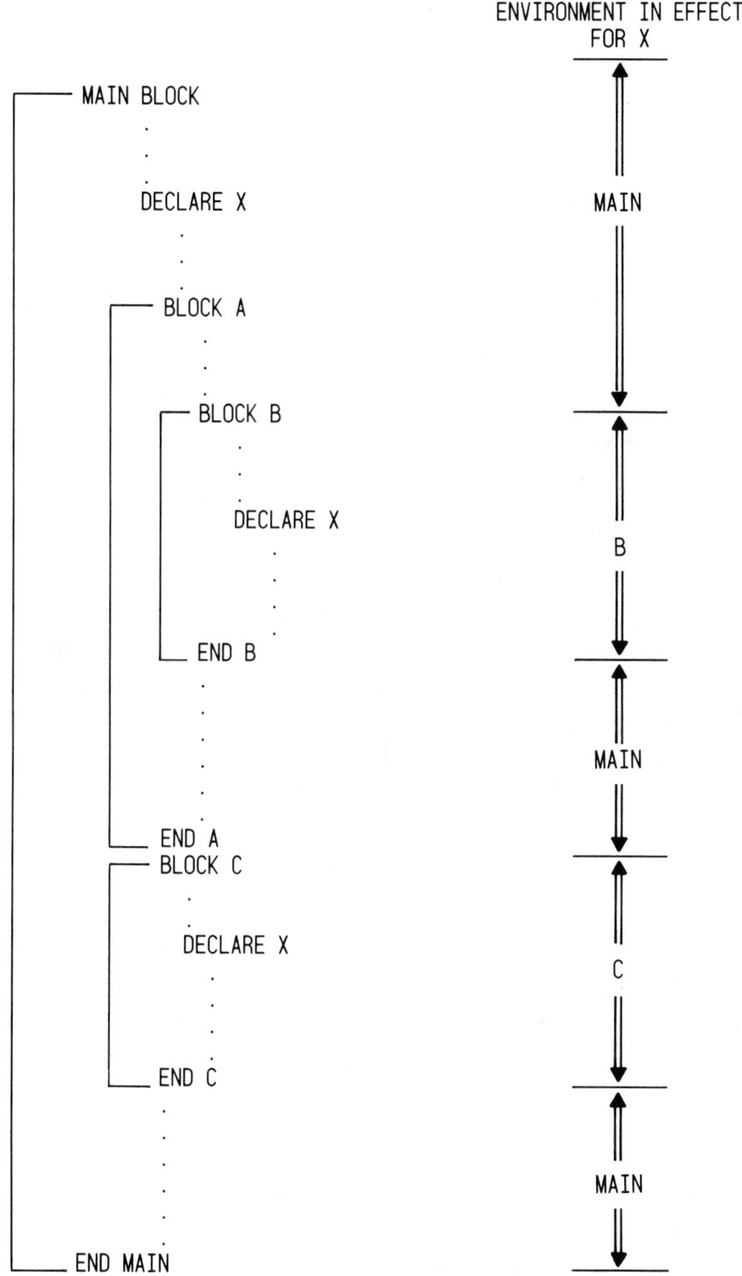

FIGURE 4.12
DIAGRAMS FOR THE REFERENCING ENVIRONMENTS OF A PROGRAM WRITTEN IN A BLOCK-STRUCTURED LANGUAGE

```
Pascal     PAYCOMP (hours, rate, pay)
FORTRAN    CALL PAYCOMP (HOURS, RATE, PAY)
COBOL      CALL PAYCOMP USING HOURS, RATE, PAY
```

FIGURE 4.13
SUBROUTINE CALLS WITH ACTUAL PARAMETERS

principal means of sharing data values between routines can increase the likelihood of program errors. It is, therefore, not considered good programming practice.

The list of parameters to be shared typically appears in the calling statement to the subroutine and in the subroutine definition as well. The parameters in the list in the calling routine are known as the *actual parameters,* as these are data elements that must exist prior to the call to the subroutine. Examples of subroutine calls with actual parameters are shown in Figure 4.13.

In each case, the actual parameters HOURS, RATE, and PAY are to be shared with a subroutine called PAYCOMP.

The parameters in the list which is part of the definition of the subroutine are called the *formal parameters.* These represent data elements that conceptually do not exist until the subroutine is called. The statement section of the subroutine defines how the parameters will be used in the subroutine. However, any binding of a formal parameter name to the location of the data value it represents is incomplete until the subroutine is called. In other words, when the subroutine is translated by a compiler, any address associated with a formal parameter will be generated as an offset to some variable location (such as an offset into an activation record) that will be determined dynamically when the subroutine is called. An example of a Pascal subroutine that corresponds to the call statement in Figure 4.13 is shown in Figure 4.14.

In the example of Figure 4.14, the formal parameters hrs, payrate, and pay correspond to the actual parameters hours, rate, and pay, respectively.

FIGURE 4.14
PASCAL SUBROUTINE WITH FORMAL PARAMETERS

```
PROCEDURE PAYCOMP(hrs, payrate : real; VAR pay : real);
    BEGIN
        IF hrs > 40.0 THEN
            pay := (40.0 + 1.5 * (hrs - 40.0)) * payrate
        ELSE
            pay := 40.0 * payrate
    END;
```

As the formal parameters are part of the local environment of the subroutine, they may or may not have the same names as their corresponding actual parameters according to programmer preference.

There are two common techniques used to pass parameters between two routines at run time. The *passing of parameters* actually refers to the establishing of relationships or bindings between the actual parameters and the corresponding formal parameters.

The first technique is called *passing by reference* (also known as passing by location). In this technique, the addresses of the data values for the actual parameters are passed to the subroutine. The subroutine than equates the addresses for the formal parameters to those of the actual parameters so that the subroutine is performing computations with the exact same memory locations that contain the actual parameter data values. This is the technique that was used in Chapter 2 for parameter passing in assembly language subroutines.

The advantage in passing parameters by reference is efficiency with respect to both execution time and memory requirements. The disadvantage in this technique is in data security. Once the subroutine has the address of the actual parameter, it can then change the value of the actual parameter by intent or by accident. For example, in the subroutine calls in Figure 4.13, we expected and wanted the subroutine to supply a new data value for the actual parameter PAY, but we did not want the subroutine to change the values of HOURS and RATE. Thus, any value passed by reference (location) can be changed, even if it was defined as a constant in the calling routine. FORTRAN and COBOL pass parameters by reference only.

The other common technique for passing parameters is called *passing by value* (with passing by result or value/result as slight modifications to the technique). In this technique, a duplicate data element is established for the corresponding formal parameter in the local environment of the subroutine. The value of the actual parameter is copied into this duplicate element, which is then used by the subroutine for references to the corresponding formal parameter. The advantage of this technique is data security, as the subroutine does not have access to the locations that contain the values for the actual parameters. The disadvantage is in program overhead, first to copy the duplicate element and second in providing storage for the duplicate element, particularly if the parameter involved is a structured element, such as an array.

The C language permits parameter passing by value only. However, C does allow the passing of a pointer variable as a parameter; thus, C programs can simulate passing by reference in this way.

Block-structured languages such as Pascal, PL/1, and Ada allow parameter passing by value or reference as the programmer chooses. In Pascal, those formal parameters designated by "VAR" will be passed by reference; all others will be passed by value (see Figure 4.14).

Storage Management The storage management component of a language refers to those language-dependent features that control the manner in which main memory is allocated to a program for its execution. For this discussion we are concerned only with those storage management features that are functions of one programming language or another. Storage management features of the operating system which may be superimposed over those provided by a particular language will be discussed in Chapter 5.

The applications programmer is not usually concerned with how a particular language implementation provides for storage management. However, the storage management techniques employed in the implementation of a language can have a major effect on capabilities and restrictions of a language that *are* of concern to the applications programmer. For example, a language that does not provide for some form of dynamic storage allocation does not allow recursion. By contrast, writing programs in a language that requires dynamic storage allocation may result in programs that execute more slowly than equivalent programs written in a language that does not require dynamic storage management.

Static Storage Allocation: Storage allocation falls into two basic classes, static and dynamic. *Static storage allocation* is allocation that is performed at translation time and does not change during program execution. For example, when static storage allocation is used for a variable, the relative memory location within the program where the value of the variable is found is fixed at translation time. Therefore, all references to the variable can be resolved at translation time, and no additional storage management is required for the variable at execution time. Going one step further, if a language is designed such that all storage allocation is static, then language processors for the language do not need to provide for any form of storage management at execution time. FORTRAN, COBOL, and compiled BASIC all use static storage allocation exclusively. Interpretive BASIC also uses a form of static storage allocation, because new variables encountered during the interpretive cycle are given fixed allocations for the remaining interpretation of the program.

The main advantage in using static storage allocation is execution efficiency, because the binding of a variable to the storage location that contains the value of the variable is done once, prior to program execution time (for translators). Another possible advantage is that the size of the object program is often less, because routines to perform the run time storage management are not included in the object module. However, this size advantage is not always true. In some cases, dynamic storage allocation can more than make up for the storage overhead needed for the storage management routines. A saving is gained in the reuse of storage areas used for the creation and deletion of local referencing environments.

Dynamic Storage Allocation: Dynamic storage allocation refers to any type of storage allocation that is performed during program execution. Broadly speaking, dynamic storage allocation can be separated into two classes: language-controlled allocation (also called automatic allocation) and programmer-controlled allocation. Both classes of dynamic allocation require the inclusion of storage management routines within the object module of a program to implement the dynamic allocation. However, programmer-controlled allocation routines are invoked only by direct programmer request while language-controlled allocation occurs without direct programmer involvement and is, more or less, transparent to the application programmer.

All block-structured languages (for example Pascal, PL/1, and Ada) as well as C, employ automatic (language controlled) dynamic storage allocation in order to create a local referencing environment upon entry to each program block (or program function, in the case of C). Each of these languages uses a *stack-based* storage management technique to create and maintain all local referencing environments that occur during program execution. The basic properties of stack-based storage management are:

1. An *activation record*, which contains the local referencing environment for a program block or subroutine, is created upon each activation (call) of the subroutine. This activation record (see Figure 4.15) contains, at a minimum:

   a. The return point to which program control will pass after the subroutine has completed its execution. Usually, the return point is the program location immediately after the "CALL" that activated the subroutine.

   b. All local variables (except those that can be declared static, as in PL/1 and C).

   c. All formal parameters.

   d. Any temporary local storage needed for such items as expression evaluation.

Return Point Address	Local Variables	Formal Parameters	Temporaries

FIGURE 4.15 CONCEPTUAL STRUCTURE FOR AN ACTIVATION RECORD

The activation record format is fixed for each subroutine. Thus, all references to the local environment of a subroutine can be resolved at translation time as displacements into the activation record of the subroutine. Then, at execution time, only the location of the activation record is needed to complete the binding of each element in the local environment to its location. When a subroutine completes an execution, the activation record for that execution (or activation) is discarded.

2. All activation records for the entire program are maintained on a common stack structure. Typically, this stack structure is created from a block of storage such that each new activation record is allocated from the next sequential piece of unused storage in the block. This allows the stack to grow from one end of the storage block with all unused (free) storage lying toward the other end. Because the return path from an active set of subroutine calls is a backtracking process, a stack structure offers a simple and natural means of efficient storage allocation. The first subroutine activation to complete its execution must be the last subroutine called; therefore, its activation record is positioned on the top of the stack. Thus, to discard its activation record, the stack is simply "popped," and the discarded storage again becomes part of the free storage block. Meanwhile, the new top element of the stack is the next activation record in the chain of current subroutine activations. If this new top element in the stack is an activation record for a routine called SUBX, it is entirely possible that new activation records will be added to the top of the stack before SUBX completes this execution. However, no routines with activation records, which lie below this activation record in the stack, can complete their executions before this activation of SUBX.
   If a routine is called recursively, there will be an activation record in the stack for each call to the routine (that is for each activation of the routine) not yet resolved. Thus, recursion will result in multiple activation records for the same routine within the stack. However, as each activation of the routine completes, the stack provides the ideal mechanism to backtrack through all previous activations of the routine.

Languages such as Pascal, C, PL/1, Ada, and LISP all allow the programmer to request the allocation and deallocation of storage during program execution. This programmer-controlled storage allocation feature can be useful in the creation and manipulation of structures such as linked lists or trees. The feature can also help reduce program size if several temporary storage structures are used during program execution, provided that too many of these structures are not needed at the same time. It is not convenient or desirable to restrict programmer-controlled allocation of the LIFO (last in first out) regimen of stack-based storage management. Therefore, a more general and flexible technique is needed. A common solution is heap-based storage management.

A *heap* is a block of storage from which pieces may be allocated or deallocated in any order. There are several ways to approach the management of heap storage, however, this discussion is limited to one general approach with two methods of selection: First Fit (in Figure 4.16) and Best Fit.

Let us assume the following properties for the heap:

1. Storage may be allocated from the heap in the form of variable length blocks.

2. Storage must be allocated as one contiguous block.

3. Each block within the heap begins with a fixed-length descriptor that contains two fields:

   a. the length of the block

   b. a pointer field.

   (Initially, the heap appears as one long, free block with a nil value in the pointer field to indicate the end of the list.)

4. All blocks of free storage are linked together on the descriptor pointer field to form a free space list.

5. There is a free space pointer (FREEPTR) which sits apart from the heap and always points to the first block in the list of free storage in the heap.

6. Storage is allocated from the heap using the free space list such that starting from the head of the list, the first free block large enough to satisfy the storage request is used. Any extra storage from the block selected is returned to the space list as a shorter block, provided this short block exceeds the length of a descriptor.

7. Once a block of storage is deallocated, it is added to the free space list as a new free block unless it can be combined with an existing free block (or blocks) to form a longer free block in the free space list.

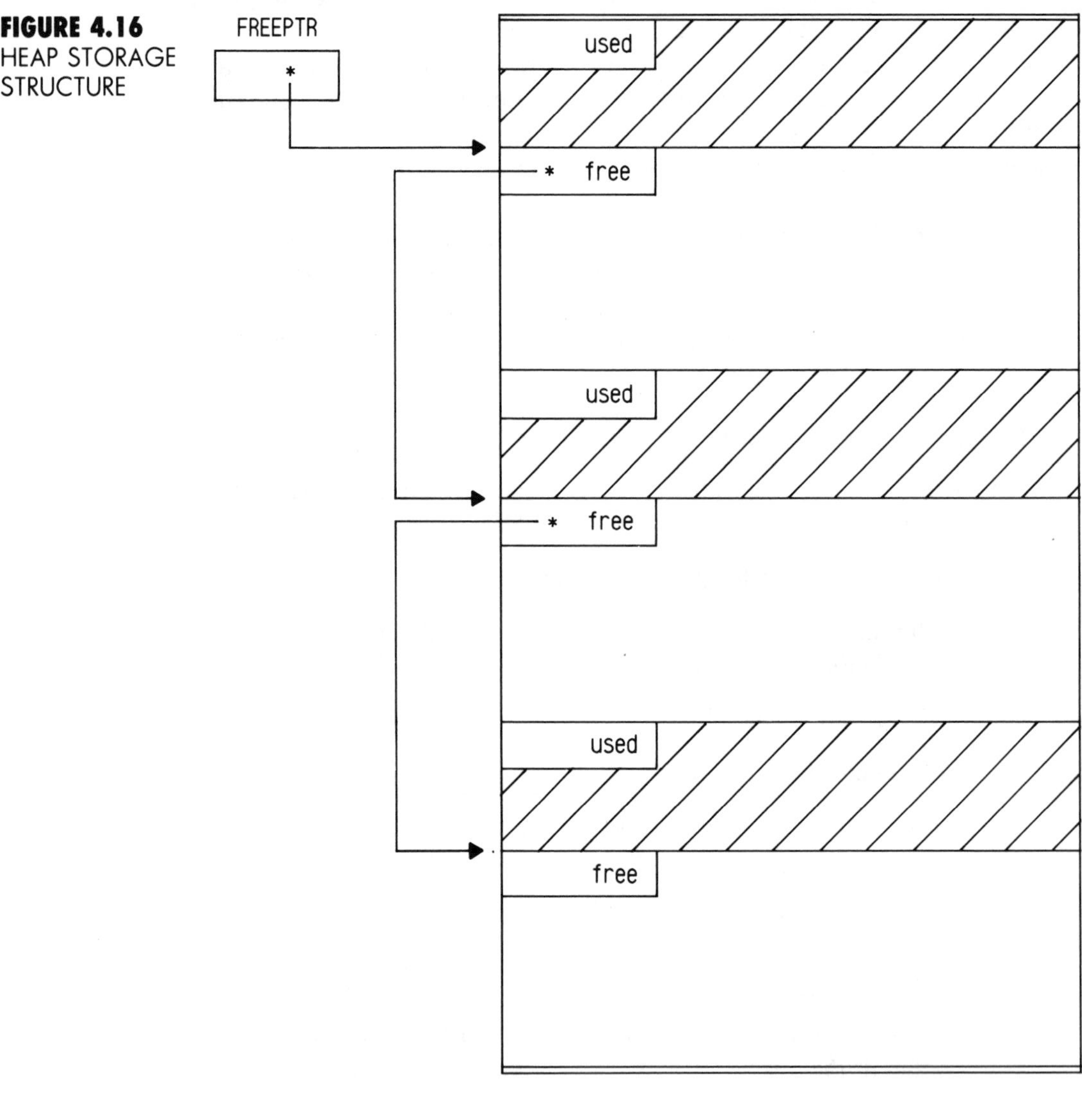

FIGURE 4.16 HEAP STORAGE STRUCTURE

The storage blocks in the free space list are ordered according to the method of selection. In the First Fit method, the free blocks are ordered by location which facilitates the combining of adjacent blocks of free storage in the heap as in Figure 4.16. When the Best Fit selection method is used, the free blocks are logically ordered by size from small to large. This second method will generally provide better utilization of the storage in the heap but will require slightly more effort to combine adjacent free blocks in memory because the list must be scanned for possible combination candidates.

these and other memory management schemes are covered in Chapter 5 under operating system memory management.

To obtain storage from the heap, typically the programmer must supply a description of the format of the storage block (usually done with a record type declaration in Pascal or with a structure declaration in C). Then the programmer must code the request for the storage as part of the program logic. This request is done with a standard procedure (NEW in Pascal), for example. When the request statement or procedure is executed, a pointer to the location of the newly acquired storage block is returned as the value of a pointer variable designated by the programmer.

When the storage block obtained from the heap is no longer needed, it is returned to the heap by a specific request in which a pointer variable that points to the block to be released is supplied (for example the DISPOSED procedure in most versions of Pascal). Usually, the procedure that frees the storage block will destroy the value of the pointer variable that was supplied to it. However, it is the programmer's responsibility to see that all other pointers to the released block of storage are also destroyed, otherwise, dangling references will result. A *dangling reference* occurs when a pointer variable contains a value that points to a block of storage that has been released for reassignment. This can cause serious run-time errors if there are attempts to reuse the storage block under its previous role, as the storage may have been allocated for other purposes.

Another potential problem in programmer-controlled storage allocation is the existence of garbage in the heap. *Garbage* is a block of storage that has been allocated but cannot be referenced. This occurs when all pointers to the block have been destroyed before the block was deallocated. Garbage is not generally as serious a problem as dangling references, but it can cause the termination of a program due to a lack of available dynamic storage.

Figure 4.17 shows a typical run-time storage arrangement for a Pascal program, assuming that the version of the language used supports a programmer-controlled facility similar to that which was previously described. The program shown provides us with an example in which all three types of storage management techniques that were described previously (static, stack-based, and heap-based) are used in combination. The executable code portion of the program is allocated statically. This code portion contains not only the code generated for routines written in the original Pascal program, but also any language-supplied routines needed to manage the stack and the heap. The static portion of the program may also contain the global data elements, but this is not always true. Some machine architectures do not allow the mixing of data elements and machine instructions in a common storage area. The stack which is used for all activation records and the heap which is used for programmer-controlled storage were described previously. However, the stack and heap are designed to "grow" toward each

FIGURE 4.17 STORAGE DIAGRAM FOR A PASCAL PROGRAM AT RUN TIME

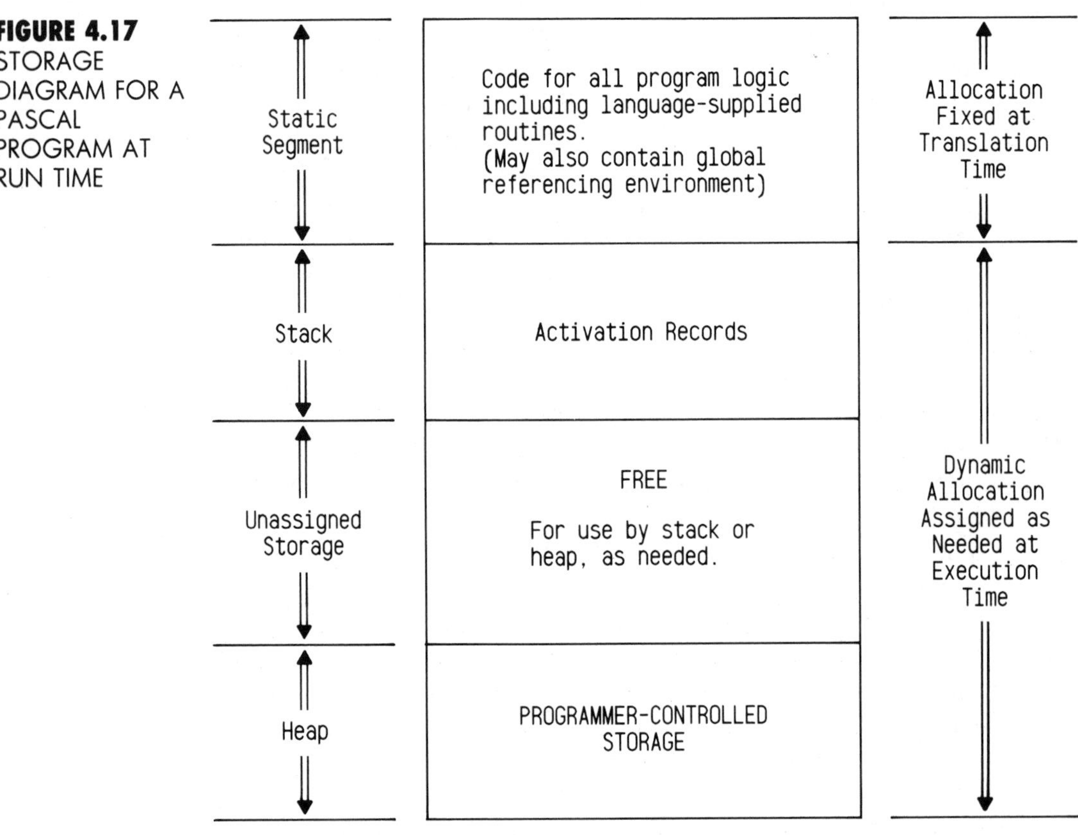

other so that one common dynamic area can be used to accommodate both structures.

I/O and File Processing The features that a language provides for a program to communicate with its external environment form the last of the abstract machine model components for evaluating a programming language. By limiting our discussion of external environment factors to logical I/O and file processing, we have taken a somewhat narrower view of the external operating environment than Pratt (1984). This is not to say that the other factors that could be part of an external operating environment are not important. For example, we do not discuss the factor of embedded system environments, which was a major concern in the design of Ada. But for discussions in this chapter, emphasis is on those factors which have the greatest impact on the largest set of applications—namely, the factors that control the manner in which data is passed between a program and its external environment.

There are two basic ways by which values are transferred between program variables and external media (such as a terminal screen or a disk); list I/O and record I/O. In list I/O, each variable involved in the data transfer must be "listed" explicitly in the I/O statements. Examples of list I/O statements are:

1. Pascal `READLN (A,B,C);`
2. BASIC `READ A, B, C`
3. FORTRAN 77 `READ (5, 100, END=999)A,B,C`
4. COBOL `DISPLAY A, B, C`

In list I/O, data conversion usually occurs automatically as needed. List I/O is convenient when a small number of variables are involved, particularly in an interactive application environment. However, it becomes more and more cumbersome as the number of variables for each I/O operation increases.

Record I/O involves the transfer of a complete logical record for each I/O operation without listing the individual record components. There is no data conversion during record I/O, which has several advantages. First, numeric items routinely needed for computation can be stored in their computational forms (binary or floating point), thus saving conversion time and usually, disk storage as well. Also, there are many programs that perform computation on only a few of the (perhaps) many numeric data items that are contained in a record, even though most, if not all, of the numeric items are listed in reports. In these cases, many unnecessary data conversions are spared for each I/O operation. The last benefit is not readily available in languages which do not support character-to-numeric conversions directly after I/O (such as, Pascal, FORTRAN, and BASIC), but it is appropriate for others such as COBOL, PL/1, or RPG.

Examples of record I/O statements are:

1. COBOL `READ EMPLOYEE-FILE.`
2. Pascal `read (EMPFILE, EMPREC);`

Another I/O feature that is important for interactive applications (programs that communicate with video data terminals during their execution) is whether the language supports terminal interaction directly or not. Most language implementations intended for the mini and microcomputer markets will provide this feature. However, at this time (1985), the most frequently used language implementations for IBM mainframe systems (COBOL, FORTRAN, and PL/1) all require the incorporation of an extensive separate software package (usually CICS) to provide support for routine interactive terminal applications.

We now examine those aspects of a programming language that provide for file processing. For this discussion a *file* is considered to be a data structure that can be defined by the language and that resides on an external storage device (such as a disk).

We are interested in the types of operations that are provided by the language to:

1. create the file
2. delete the file
3. read data from the file
4. change the values in existing data elements in the file
5. insert or delete elements (records) in the file.

Closely related to types of operations that can be performed on the elements of a file are the file organizations defined by the language for which these operations may be applied. A *file organization* is a logical view of the structure of a file based on the logical relationships between the records of the file. In this context, a record is the set of data that forms the basic unit on which all logical file I/O operations are performed. Because a file organization is a logical view of the structure of a file, the physical location of the data (the physical structure of the data) may or may not resemble the logical structure. However, in implementing a file organization, there is normally an attempt to use a physical arrangement of the data which provides the most efficient realization of the logical structure. In addition, the logical view of a file supported by a language may or may not coincide with file organizations already supported by the host operating system. However, it is very advantageous to the implementors of the language of a particular system if the host operating system supports each file organization required by the language. Should an operating system support file organizations that are not part of a language specification, the language implementors have the option of including these organizations as nonstandard extensions to the language, usually with a minor amount of additional work. Conversely, when the language standard requires a file organization (for example, indexed sequential) that is not supported by the host operating system, there may be considerable extra effort involved for the language implementors.

The most common file organizations are:

1. Sequential
2. Relative

3. Direct (also called random)

4. Indexed

Other organizations are more or less extensions and/or combinations of these. A brief description of each of these basic file organizations follows.

A *sequential* file is one that must be processed in the same order each time. For example, after reaching the Nth record in the file, the 99 intervening records must be read in sequence before the N + 100 record can be read. This is the most basic of the file organizations and is supported for practically every language that includes any file processing in the language. For this file type, in most cases, the physical and logical order will be the same in order to provide efficient sequential processing.

A *relative* file is one in which the records may be accessed "directly" by a relative record number. It is not required that the records also be ordered sequentially; but, if they are (as is frequently done in microcomputer systems), records can be located directly by calculating a "record displacement" into the file to access a record which will provide efficient access when random processing of the file is desired. In addition, the sequential order of the records provides for efficient sequential processing when this mode of processing is needed for the same file.

A *direct* file is similar to a relative file, in that individual records can be retrieved in any order. However, a direct file is distinct from a relative one because it is always created by some form of hashing that randomized the locations of the records. Access to any record requires the specification of a record identifier (such as a key), and sequential processing (without specifying the key of each record) is usually not allowed. Access to any single record in a direct file is usually at least as fast as access times experienced with other file organizations. However, processing a direct file by key to achieve sequential processing of the file is usually much slower than processing a similar file with sequential organization, because the random location of the records will usually cause considerable disk head movement (seek time) to process the entire file. It is important to point out that a relative file *may be* a direct file which has been randomized by record number but, in general, direct and relative should not be considered equivalent.

An *indexed* file is a file for which there are one or more indexes which match record keys to corresponding record locations. Typically, each index is ordered by the key to facilitate rapid searching of the index. An *indexed sequential* file is one in which there is one primary index, such that both the index and the corresponding data records are sequentially ordered by the same key. This provides for efficient alternate processing in either a random mode (by key) or a sequential mode in which the index is not used to locate records. Although random retrieval is reasonably efficient for indexed sequential files, it is not usually as fast as for direct files, due to the additional time required to search the index.

The indexed sequential file organization is commonly used for files which are regularly processed in a random fashion (on perhaps a daily basis) but are periodically (perhaps weekly or monthly) processed entirely sequentially. This organization is generally more versatile than the relative/ sequential organization because order can be based on any key field in the record (such as name or social security number) and not just on a record number. Also, indexed sequential files usually allow records to be inserted into the file at any position as long as the logical order is preserved. Relative/ sequential files often allow only additions to the end of the file.

As was stated before, COBOL has the most extensive file handling facilities of any commonly available programming language. It supports three file organizations—sequential, relative, and indexed—and a full set of operations for each organization.

Standard Pascal supports only sequential files that cannot be updated (so that to change records, the file must be recreated). However, Pascal dialects (e.g., UCSD Pascal and Turbo Pascal) support both sequential and relative files, and do allow updating.

Minimal ANS BASIC provides for no data files. However, most extended dialects of BASIC will provide file capabilities to provide for sequential and some form of random processing.

FORTRAN provides for sequential and direct files and some interesting file operations that are carried over from tape-oriented file processing such as BACKSPACE and REWIND.

Some language designers feel that file operations should not be part of the language per se, but should be handled by simply incorporating the file operations supported by the operating system. Such file operations use function or procedure calls to file library routines provided with the operating system. While this approach is workable in languages such as C and MODULA-2 when they are used for the systems programming applications for which they were designed and where file processing normally plays a very minor role, it is less satisfactory for other applications. The main problem is that there is much less standardization between operating systems (particularly in file and I/O operations) than there is between implementations of a specific language.

For example, the COBOL language supports indexed files which is the most appropriate file type in many data processing applications. Therefore, if a programmer designs a COBOL program to use indexed files, there is no need for concern whether this file type is supported directly by the host operating system, nor should there be any serious problems in transporting the program to another operating system which also supports COBOL. There are many operating systems that support indexed files directly; but suppose a programmer wanted to functionally replicate the previous COBOL example program using C in a UNIX operating system environment. Because UNIX does not support indexed files directly, and C depends on the operating system for its file support, the application programmer would be faced with implementing the indexed sequential organization together with simulating any file operations needed to process the file as indexed. Implementing this could easily result in more effort than the rest of the application which uses the indexed files.

Other Considerations In order to complete our evaluation framework, it is helpful to explicitly include several items which were not part of Pratt's abstract machine model but are routinely addressed in treatments of programming languages, including Pratt's.

Design Emphasis: Those aspects of a programming language that are emphasized by design can provide considerable insight as to whether one language or another is more appropriate for a given application. Generally, it is the intended application area(s) that guides the designers of the language to choose which aspects to emphasize. However, there is not always agreement about the needs of a particular applications area. For example, FORTRAN and ALGOL were primarily intended for scientific applications, yet their design emphasis is quite different. Unfortunately, many desirable features for a language oppose one another.

For example:

A language that is very easy to learn (such as BASIC) cannot be comprehensive.

A language that is comprehensive (such as PL/1) must sacrifice some efficiency.

A language that is efficient (such as FORTRAN) must limit the applications for which it is appropriate.

A language that stresses natural language syntax (such as COBOL) cannot be concise.

Thus, the design of every language must involve some compromise. In the case of opposing goals such as speed and flexibility, the emphasis of one will be achieved at the expense of the other.

Syntax: The syntax of a language is often the first distinguishing characteristic of a language that we learn. When faced with a choice of otherwise appropriate languages, this may be the deciding factor. For example, when teaching a beginning programming class, choosing a language with a simple, concise syntax is usually an advantage. In large organizations, where programs are frequently passed on from programmer to programmer for maintenance and/or modification, it is important that the syntax be highly readable in order to minimize the transition time. Likewise, a language that has a syntax that clearly expresses its meaning will be easier to learn and less prone to coding errors.

Miscellaneous: Finally, the miscellaneous category accounts for any other information about the language, for example, whether the language has a widely accepted standard definition or whether the language is generally available for most computing systems used in a particular applications area or class of computers.

Now that the description of our evaluation framework is complete, two examples of a summary analysis performed on COBOL and Pascal are shown using this framework. (See Figures 4.18 and 4.19.)

WASSERMAN'S EVALUATION FACTORS

The evaluation framework developed in the last section focuses primarily on those aspects that describe the components, structure, and implementation of a language. It can be used to evaluate the suitability of a language for a particular application or to simply study languages in general. A brief, more pragmatic scheme to evaluate a language, for a particular application, was described by Anthony Wasserman in his overview to the *Tutorial on Programming Language Design* (1980) in which he proposed six important factors to consider in choosing a language. These factors, which are more closely related to the topics that were covered in the miscellaneous section of the evaluation model, are well worth consideration and are summarized here.

1. Availability
   - (a) Is the language available for the target machine?
   - (b) Is it available for the computers of others who may wish to use it?
2. Uniformity
   - (a) Is the same language likely to be available on any future computers that are acquired by the organization that uses it?
   - (b) Will the language definition remain stable (or at least compatible) with earlier versions?

FIGURE 4.18
SUMMARY ANALYSIS OF COBOL

LANGUAGE PROPERTY	C O B O L
BASIC DATA TYPES	Character (strings) Numbers Display Computational Edited
DATA STRUCTURES	Records Arrays (1 to 3 dimensions) Sequential, relative, & indexed sequential files.
BASIC OPERATIONS	Arithmetic - Add, subtract, multiply, divide including options for assignment, rounding, remainders, etc. Relational - $<$, $>$, $=$, $<=$, $>=$, $\neq$ Boolean - AND, OR, NOT SEARCH - (binary table search) SORT - (sorts external files)
SEQUENCE CONTROL	IF-THEN-ELSE PERFORM, PERFORM-UNTIL, PERFORM-VARYING-UNTIL GO TO, GO TO DEPENDING ON
DATA CONTROL	1. Without subroutines, all variables are global. 2. With subroutines, all variables are local to the module in which they are declared and parameters are passed by reference between modules.
STORAGE MANAGEMENT	Static - all fixed at compile time.
FILE HANDLING	Extensive file handling capabilities for sequential, indexed sequential, and relative files.
MAJOR DESIGN EMPHASIS	1. Hardware independence and transportability. 2. Readability. 3. Execution efficiency. 4. Powerful file handling capabilities.
SYNTAX	1. English-like to the point of being self-documenting. 2. Easy to write but sometimes tedious. 3. Uses reserved words (many) 4. All variables must be declared.
MISCELLANEOUS	Program is separated into four divisions which are: IDENTIFICATION - Program name and commentary information. ENVIRONMENT - machine-dependent information. DATA - declaration of all variables and files. PROCEDURE - specification of algorithms.

FIGURE 4.19 SUMMARY ANALYSIS OF PASCAL

LANGUAGE / PROPERTY	PASCAL
BASIC DATA TYPES	1. integers 2. reals 3. character 4. Boolean 5. enumeration 6. pointer
DATA STRUCTURES	1. arrays 2. records 3. sequential files 4. sets 5. user defined - composite of any other basic type or structures
BASIC OPERATIONS	Assignment, add, subtract, multiply, two divides (integer and real), mod, standard relational and Boolean Operations. Has a good set of predefined functions - 10 for math and 7 others.
SEQUENCE CONTROL	1. All three of the Bohm Jaccopini logical constructs (Process, WHILE-DO, IF-THEN-ELSE) 2. Plus case construct, GOTO, REPEAT-UNTIL (DO-WHILE) FOR-COUNT-DO 3. Allows definitions of function and subroutine (Procedures) subprograms
DATA CONTROL	1. Static scope rules for local and non-local environments 2. Parameters passing by value or by reference 3. Does not allow separately compiled subroutines therefore eliminating those written in other languages.
STORAGE MANAGEMENT	Uses: (1) fixed (static) arrangement for executable code with (2) a stack to manage activation records to control local variables referencing environment and (3) a heap to control programmer dynamic storage requests.
FILE HANDLING	Has very limited file handling capabilities. Limited to sequential files which cannot be updated except through recreation. (UCSD Pascal & Turbo Pascal provide basic file operations for sequential and relative files.)
MAJOR DESIGN EMPHASIS	1. Simple language for teaching programming and for construction of system software 2. Broad range of data types and structures 3. Emphasizes power in expressing algorithms and program clarity over translation and execution efficiency.
SYNTAX	1. block structured. 2. All variables must be declared and are strong typed (for the most part). 3. Uses reserved words. 4. Easy to read and write.
MISCELLANEOUS	Lacks a strong standard followed by most commercially available implementations.

3. Efficiency
   How efficient is this language compared to other languages under consideration?

4. Portability

   (a) What is the availability on other systems?

   (b) Is there an accepted standard language definition?

5. Language Features for the Application

   (a) Does the language include all the necessary features to write the application in a reasonably straightforward manner?

   (b) Does it include additional features that make it especially appropriate for the application?

6. Personal Preference
   Is there a preference for or against the language compared to other possible choices? (This may affect the quality of the programs.)

IMPLEMENTATION OF LANGUAGE PROCESSORS

In the introduction to this chapter the functional characteristics of compilers and interpreters were discussed from an external viewpoint. Now those factors that determine and/or affect the major internal characteristics and structures of these language processors are considered.

In order to process a program or routine written in some particular programming language, both compilers and interpreters must be able to recognize precisely the form (syntax) and meaning (semantics) of the input source language module and identify errors in the expression of the language. Therefore, the definition of the source language must be incorporated within the language processor.

A formal notation for the exact definition of the syntax and semantics of a language would be of great help to the implementor of a language processor. Unfortunately, no such single notation exists, although there are separate formal notations for the definitions of syntax and semantics. Those notations that have been developed for the definition of semantics (such as the Vienna Definition Language, VDL) have not been widely used due to their complexity. Formal notations for the definition of language syntax, however, have been in use since shortly after the development of FORTRAN. It is now common practice to formally specify the syntax of a programming language using a formal notation and to informally specify the semantics of the language, usually by writing them out in English.

GRAMMARS

A formal definition of the syntax of a language is called a *grammar.* If all the structures in the language may be defined without regarding context, the grammar is called *context-free,* otherwise, it is called *context-sensitive.* A context-free grammar, G, consists of four elements such that

```
G = {T, N, R, S}    where:
T = the set of terminal symbols (tokens)
    used to write the language
N = the set of nonterminal symbols which are used
    to describe valid structures in the language.
    For example, in both Pascal and FORTRAN,
    ''expression'' and ''assignment statement'' are
    nonterminal symbols. Nonterminal symbols
    cannot be used in writing strings in the
    language, therefore T and N have no elements
    in common (i.e., T ∩ N = 0).
R = the set of rules for defining the nonterminal
    symbols in the language. Each rule defines
    which symbol or sequence of symbols (either
    terminal or nonterminal or both) can be used
    to replace a particular nonterminal symbol. A
    rule is also called a production because it
    defines the sequence of symbols that may be
    produced by a symbol.
S = a start symbol which is a nonterminal symbol
    that is not used to define any other symbol and
    from which all valid use of the language can
    be derived.
```

It is much easier to state the rules for a context-free grammar formally than it is for a context-sensitive grammar. Fortunately, the syntax for most programming languages is (by design) nearly context-free, therefore, the common practice is to define as much of the syntax as is possible with a formal context-free notation (such as Backus-Naur Form) and then state those few additional context-sensitive aspects informally. For example, a rule that states that a particular identifier cannot be defined (declared) more than once in a procedure is a context-sensitive rule.

The most common notation found in the literature for context-free grammars is the BNF (Backus-Naur Form) notation, which was initially developed by John Backus in 1959 to define the syntax of ALGOL 60. The notation was then improved by Peter Naur shortly thereafter.

The BNF notation is defined as follows:

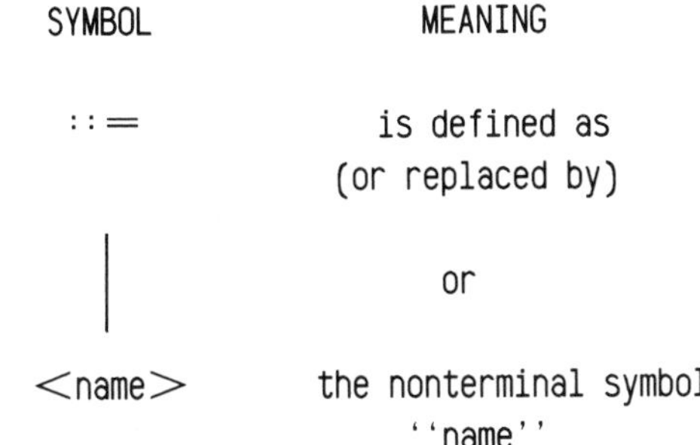

SYMBOL	MEANING
::=	is defined as (or replaced by)
|	or
<name>	the nonterminal symbol ''name''

Example: A BNF definition of a language that consists of unsigned even binary numbers is:

```
<beven>   ::= 0|<bstring> 0

<bstring> ::= <bit>|<bit> <bstring>

<bit>     ::= 0|1
```

In relating this example to the elements of a grammar, S = beven; N = {beven, bstring, bit}; T = {0,1}; and R = the three rules given for the elements of N.

Two other common formal notations for specifying programming language syntax are the COBOL notation (developed for the definition of COBOL) and the Syntax Chart notation (developed by Nicklaus Wirth for the definition of Pascal).

A comparative example of the three formal syntax notations using the Format 1 form of a COBOL MOVE statement is shown in Figure 4.20.

Both the COBOL and Syntax Chart notations offer advantages over the BNF notation in the expression of repetition and in alternative symbol sequences. However, due to the simplicity of the BNF notation and to its prominence in the literature, it is used as the formal syntax notation for the rest of the book.

A grammar can be used to generate "sentences" in a language by starting at the start symbol (S) and through successive applications of the rules (R), arrive at a string of terminal symbols that form a legal sentence in the language. For example, using the earlier definition for a language of unsigned even binary numbers we could generate:

FIGURE 4.20 COMPARISON OF FORMAL SYNTAX NOTATIONS

1. BNF

```
<Move Statement> ::= MOVE <identifier>TO<identifier-list>|
                     MOVE <literal> TO <identifier-list>

<identifier-list> ::= <identifier>|<identifier-
                      list><identifier>
```

2. COBOL Notation

```
MOVE {identifier-1} TO identifier-2 [identifier-3]. . .
     {literal     }
```

3. Syntax Charts

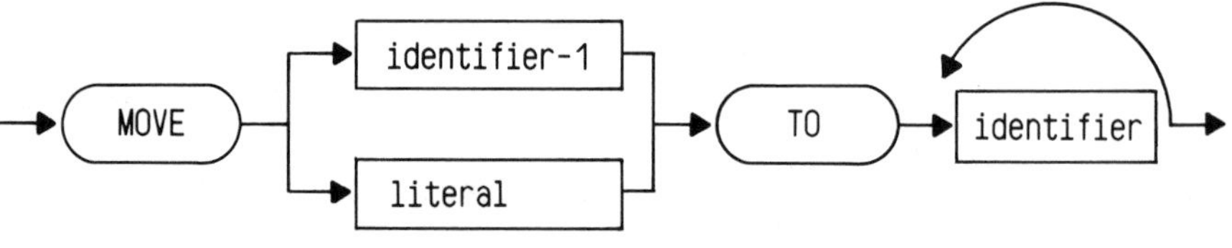


```
<beven>
<bstring> 0
<bit><bstring> 0
<bit><bit><bstring> 0
<bit><bit><bit> 0
  1    0    1   0
```

A derivation tree for this generation is shown in Figure 4.21.

A grammar can also be used to analyze a sequence of symbols to see if they form a valid structure in the language and if valid, to identify what the structure is. The process of recognizing and identifying structures of a language from a given string of symbols is called *parsing.* A derivation tree that represents the parsing of a particular string of symbols is called its *parse tree.* It is only this second use of a grammar (parsing) that is of concern in language processors; therefore, the discussions here accordingly focus on parsing.

The following illustrations are examples of the parsing of "sentences" from two very simple (alright, trivial) languages. A sentence in the first language consists of any nonnegative integer while a sentence in the second language is a single BASIC identifier from minimal ANS BASIC.

Example 1: A BNF definition for a language of all nonnegative integers:

```
<sentence> ::= <integer>
<integer>  ::= <digit> | <integer> <digit>
<digit>    ::= 0 | 1 | 2 | 3 | 4 | 5 | 6 | 7 | 8 | 9
```

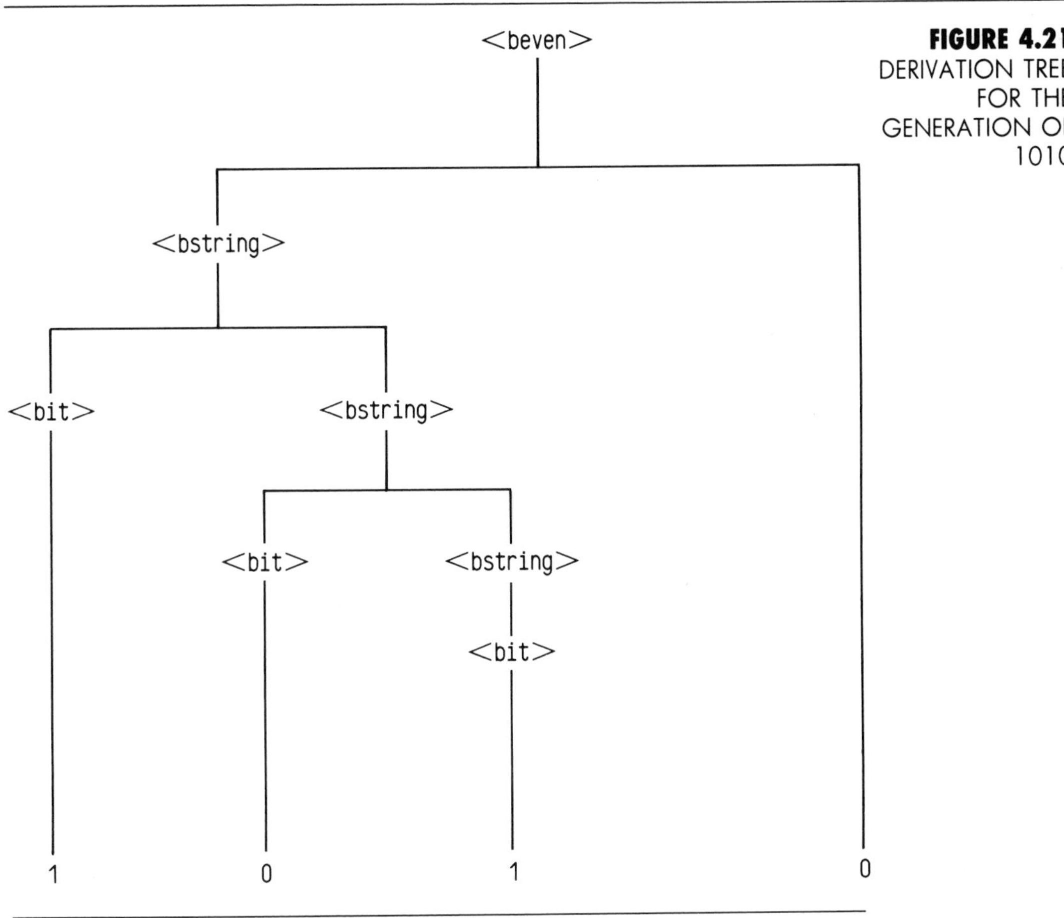

FIGURE 4.21 DERIVATION TREE FOR THE GENERATION OF 1010

Using this definition, the parse tree for the integer 119 is given in Figure 4.22.

Example 2: A BNF definition for a language of BASIC identifiers is:

```
<BASIC identifier> ::= <letter> | <letter><digit> |
                       <letter>$
<letter> ::= A | B | C | D | . . . . | Z
<digit>  ::= 0 | 1 | 2 | 3 | . . . . | 9
```

Using this definition, the parse tree for the identifier C6 is given in Figure 4.23.

COMPILATION

As stated before, a compiler is a language processor that translates a source module written in a programming language into machine language (for ex-

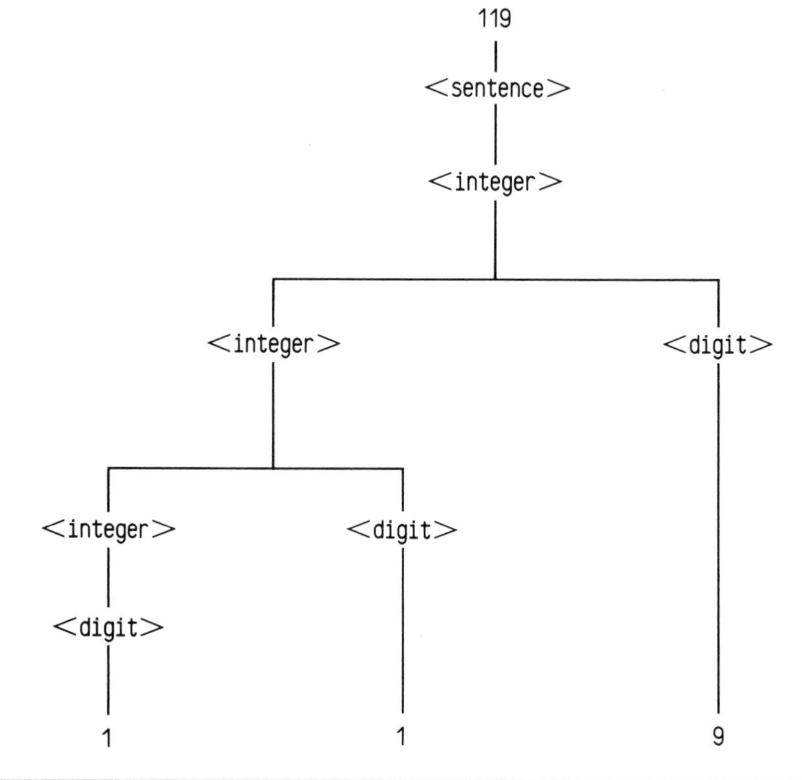

FIGURE 4.22
PARSE TREE FOR THE INTEGER 119

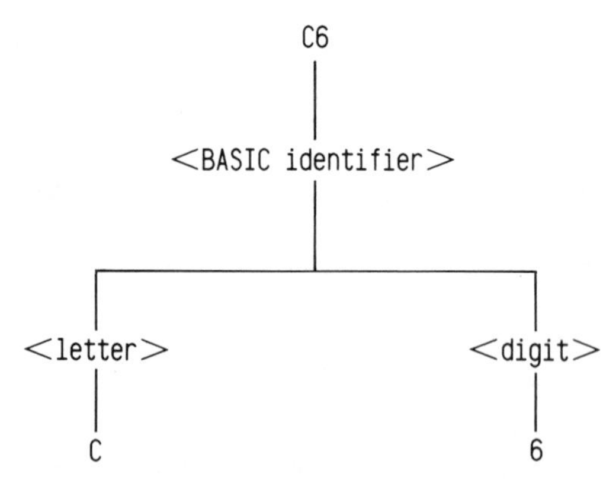

FIGURE 4.23
PARSE TREE FOR THE BASIC IDENTIFIER C6

ample, an object module). Thus, the process of compilation is strictly one of translation from one language into another. It is true that load-and-go compilers initiate the execution of the object program, but this is done in addition to the compilation process, not as part of it.

Compilers and assemblers form a class of language processors known as *translators* because they functionally perform the same role in the life cycle of a program. Therefore, there is considerable similarity in the major tasks performed by compilers and assemblers and in the order that these tasks are performed. This similarity was addressed in Chapter 2 in the discussion of the implementation of assemblers. In turn, this discussion on compilers draws on those concepts developed in describing assemblers.

Both compilers and assemblers perform the same two major tasks: analysis and generation. Even at the next functional level, the subtasks performed under analysis and generation are quite similar for compilers and assemblers (see Figure 4.24) except that assemblers do not employ an optimization subtask. This is because an assembly language program specifies exactly the machine language instructions desired, supposedly. However, when we begin to examine these subtasks comparatively, we find that the implementations are usually considerably more complex for compilers than for assemblers. The reasons for this increased complexity will be explored as the actions and interactions of these major tasks and subtasks for a compiler are traced. Figure 4.25 is a diagram showing the conceptual relationships of the major components of a compiler together with information flow through these components that depicts the translation process. This is not the only possible arrangement for a compiler; for example, the syntactic analyzer could accept the input source and call the lexical analyzer as needed. The model in Figure 4.25 will prove useful, however, for the rest of this discussion on compilers, because it is basically the model followed.

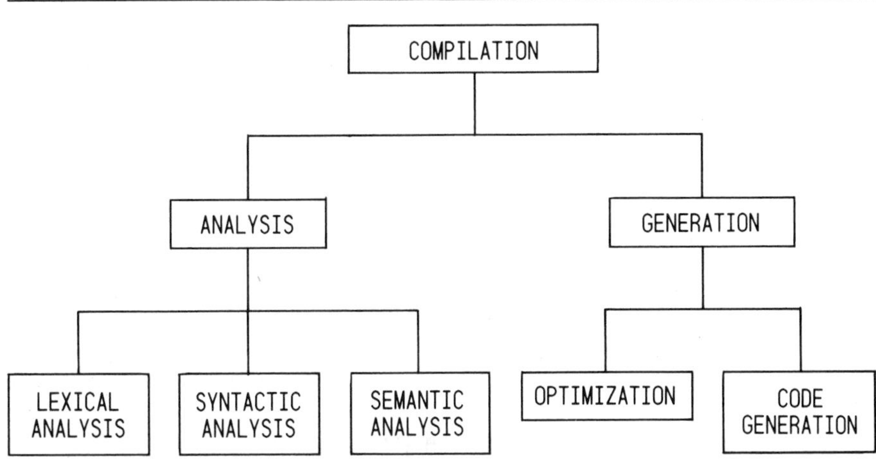

FIGURE 4.24
CONCEPTUAL ORGANIZATION OF THE STRUCTURE OF A COMPILER

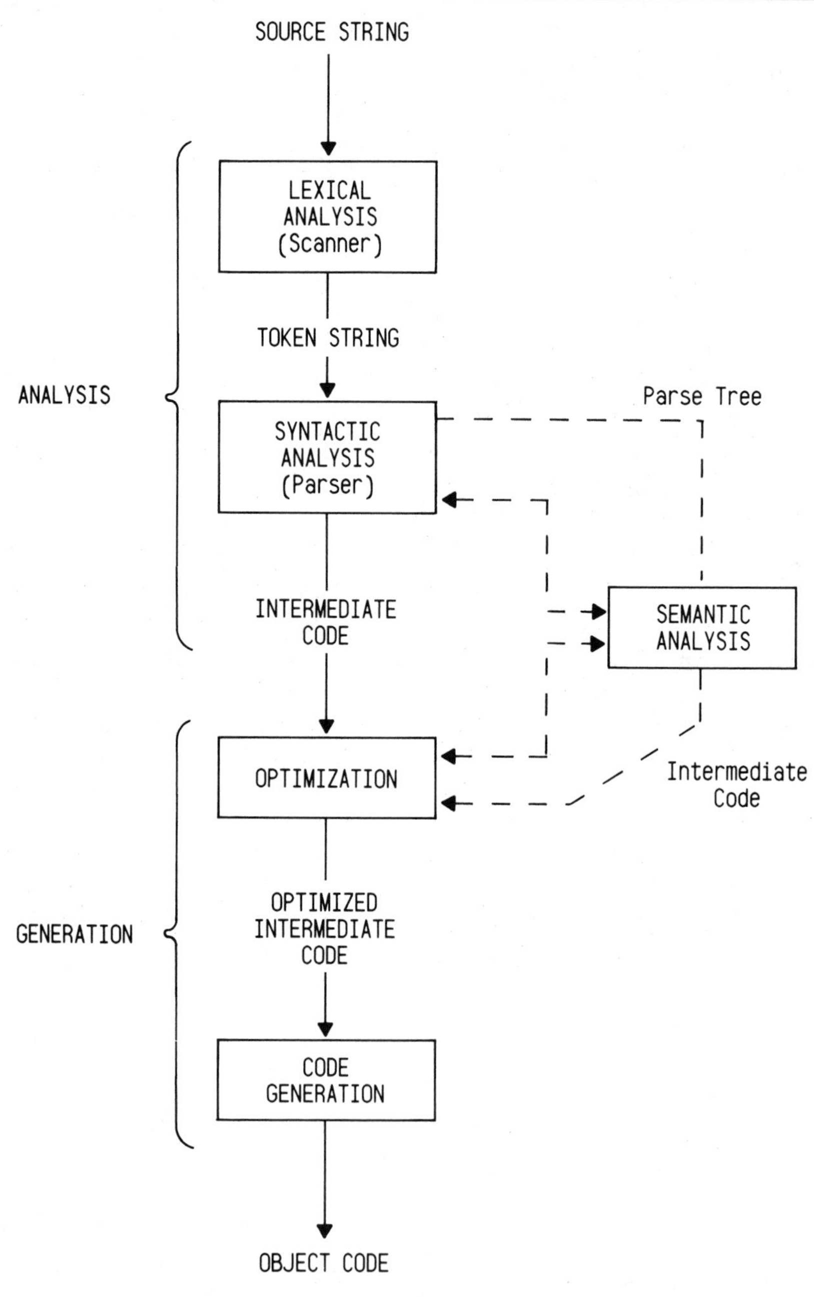

FIGURE 4.25
CONCEPTUAL VIEW OF THE INFORMATION FLOW THROUGH THE MAJOR TASKS OF COMPILATION

For this diagram, semantic analysis is moved from the mainline flow because the placement of this component is probably the most variable aspect of a compiler. In fact, some parts of semantic analysis may occur anywhere from a point in conjunction with syntactical analysis to a point in conjunction with code generation. In general, we can assume:

1. Lexical and syntactical analysis must occur before the generation of the intermediate code.
2. All analysis must be completed before the generation of the object code.

The function of the major components of a compiler are now examined more closely.

Analysis It has been stated several times that the tasks of analysis (i.e., lexical analysis, syntactic analysis, and semantic analysis) are generally much more complex for compilers than for assemblers. There are two principal reasons for this.

First, the statements in an assembly language program can, in general, be analyzed (and generated) on a statement-by-statement basis without regard to other statements, while the statements in a higher level language may often be interrelated. For example, in assembly language, there is no machine instruction for a loop (iteration). There are branching instructions, compare instructions, and so on, but a loop is created by the programmer. Thus the assembler does not need to recognize the instructions that belong to the loop. However, most procedural programming languages have iteration statements; therefore, compilers for these languages must keep track of the statements that form the body of the loop, and other features. This interrelation of statements in programming languages is also true for other statements, such as compound statements, IF-THEN-ELSE statements, and CASE statements.

The second principal reason for the additional complexity is there is usually much more variety in the structure and composition of statements in a higher level language than there is in an assembly language.

For example, a machine instruction in IBM assembly language has a structure which is fixed by the operation. It allows exactly one operation involving a fixed number of operands per instruction, and there is no checking of data types. However, an assignment statement, which is one of the simplest in Pascal or FORTRAN, involves two or more operands involved in one or more operations with data type checking (and possibly conversion). In addition, one or more of the operands may be a subroutine call to a function subroutine.

Other issues affecting analysis of programming languages will be addressed under the discussions of the three phases of analysis.

Lexical Analysis: Lexical analysis is the process of dividing an input source string into a series of tokens where a token is a basic syntactic unit in the language. That is, a token is a terminal symbol in the grammar that defines the syntax of the language. Each token is identified by its type and value. The purpose of the lexical analysis (which is performed by a routine referred to as the *scanner*) is: (1) to identify the tokens as they appear in the input stream, and (2) to arrange these tokens into a convenient form for further processing.

The lexical analysis must be performed using a character-by-character examination of the input stream; however, there are a number of factors which can affect the ease by which the scanner can identify a token. Among these are:

1. Flexibility in the form of statements. In a language where statements have a fixed format for location of token types (such as RPG), a token is identified by checking a fixed field location in the input statement. Other languages are flexible in the location of tokens, but require certain fixed positions in the order for token types in all or most statement types. For example, COBOL requires that the first token in every procedural statement be a reserved word identifying the operation.
   Of course, practically all languages have positional requirements for specific statement types (such as assignment or IF statement). The preceding remarks are directed toward very general rules of structure, because the recognition of specific statement structure is the task of the parser.

2. *Key words and reserved words.* A *key word* is a token type for which a specific value is (except for noise words) a required part of a structure in the language. A *reserved word* is a key word that can only be used as a key word. Some languages, such as FORTRAN and PL/1, allow key words to be used as identifiers, also. This not only complicates token typing, but also structural analysis as well. Other languages, such as COBOL and Pascal, use reserved words instead, which not only simplifies translation but coding and debugging as well.

3. *The use of delimiters to separate tokens.* Languages simplify token recognition through the use of specific delimiters that indicate the end of a token (COBOL, for example uses a space as a delimiter). Other languages require considerable structural analysis before a

token can be isolated and typed. A classic example comes from the analysis of two FORTRAN input strings (remember FORTRAN ignores spaces):

```
(a) DO  50  K = 1,50
```

and

```
(b) DO  50  K = 1.50 (This is, perhaps, the result
                      of a coding error.)
```

String (a) would be analyzed as having the tokens:
DO; 50; K; =; 1; ,; 50
while string (b) would be analyzed as having the tokens:
DO50K; =; 1.50
As a result the parser will determine that (a) is a DO statement while (b) is an assignment statement.

It was mentioned previously that besides identifying tokens, another function of the scanner is to arrange the tokens in a form which is convenient for later processing. Typically, the scanner passes a fixed length token descriptor (see Figure 4.26) instead of the actual token. This token descriptor (or token surrogate) contains two fields. One field contains a code indicating the token type, and the other field contains a pointer into a table of values for tokens of this type or perhaps a table containing the values for two or more related token types.

The token value tables have similarities to those for assemblers (such as a symbol table for identifiers and an operations table for legal operators).

Type Code	Pointer to Token Value

FIGURE 4.26a
DIAGRAM OF TOKEN SURROGATE PRODUCED BY THE SCANNER

01	14

FIGURE 4.26b
TOKEN SURROGATE EXAMPLE

There may also be value tables for key words, constants, and special symbols. Thus, an "IF" token from a Pascal IF-THEN-ELSE statement might be represented in the form shown in Figure 4.26b:
where 01 is the code for token type "keyword" and 14 is the pointer to the 14th entry in the key word value table.

Syntactic Analysis (The Parser): Syntactic analysis is the process that uses the rules of grammar for a language to identify the structures (defined by the nonterminal symbols) represented by the sequential string of tokens produced by the scanner. In addition to the identification of structures, the parser must arrange the tokens in a conceptual representation of the parse tree (for example, the tokens could be arranged in a linear sequence that duplicates a particular traversal order of the parse tree). This representation of the parse tree produced by the parser is used to produce the intermediate code that in turn, is used to generate the object code.

For a more specific example of the basic parsing process used in the identification of structures, consider the rules of grammar in Figure 4.27 which define the syntax for the structures in a "language" of restricted assignment statements from Pascal.

The start symbol for our language of assignment statements is, by definition of a grammar, the nonterminal symbol <assign>. This is the only symbol not found in the right-hand side of a production rule for nonterminals and is a symbol from which all valid "sentences" (that is, assignment statements) in the language can be derived.

The terminal symbols are divided into the five token types shown in Figure 4.28.

Using the grammar defined in Figures 4.27 and 4.28, the derivation (parse tree) for a simple assignment statement is shown in Figure 4.29.

For a more complete example, including the roles of the scanner and the parser, consider the assignment statement:

```
    <assign> ::= <var> := <expression>
<expression> ::= <term> | <term> <OP1> <expression>
      <term> ::= <factor> | <factor> <OP2> <term>
    <factor> ::= <var> | <const> | (<expression>)
       <var> ::= name | name <sub>
       <OP1> ::= + | -
       <OP2> ::= * | / | DIV
       <sub> ::= [<factor>] | [<factor>, <factor>]
     <const> ::= integer | real
```

FIGURE 4.27
RULES OF GRAMMER FOR THE RESTRICTED PASCAL ASSIGNMENT STATEMENTS

Token Type	Type Code	Value
name	1	any valid Pascal name
integer	2	any integer constant
real	3	any real constant
operation	4	:=, +, −, *, /, DIV
punctuation	5	(,), [,], , (A comma is also a valid token.)

FIGURE 4.28 TERMINAL SYMBOLS FOR LANGUAGE OF FIGURE 4.27

```
X := 2 * a + b * (c − d)
```

We will assume that the scanner uses a value table for each token type (see Figure 4.30) and (for simplicity) that this is the first or only statement to be processed.

If we also assume that the scanner processes the entire statement, the following token string will be produced for the parser of which only the (type, value) pairs need be passed.

Token	Type	Value Table Pointer
X	1	1
:=	4	1
2	2	1
*	4	4
a	1	2
+	4	2
b	1	3
*	4	4
(	5	1
c	1	4
-	4	3
d	1	5
)	5	2

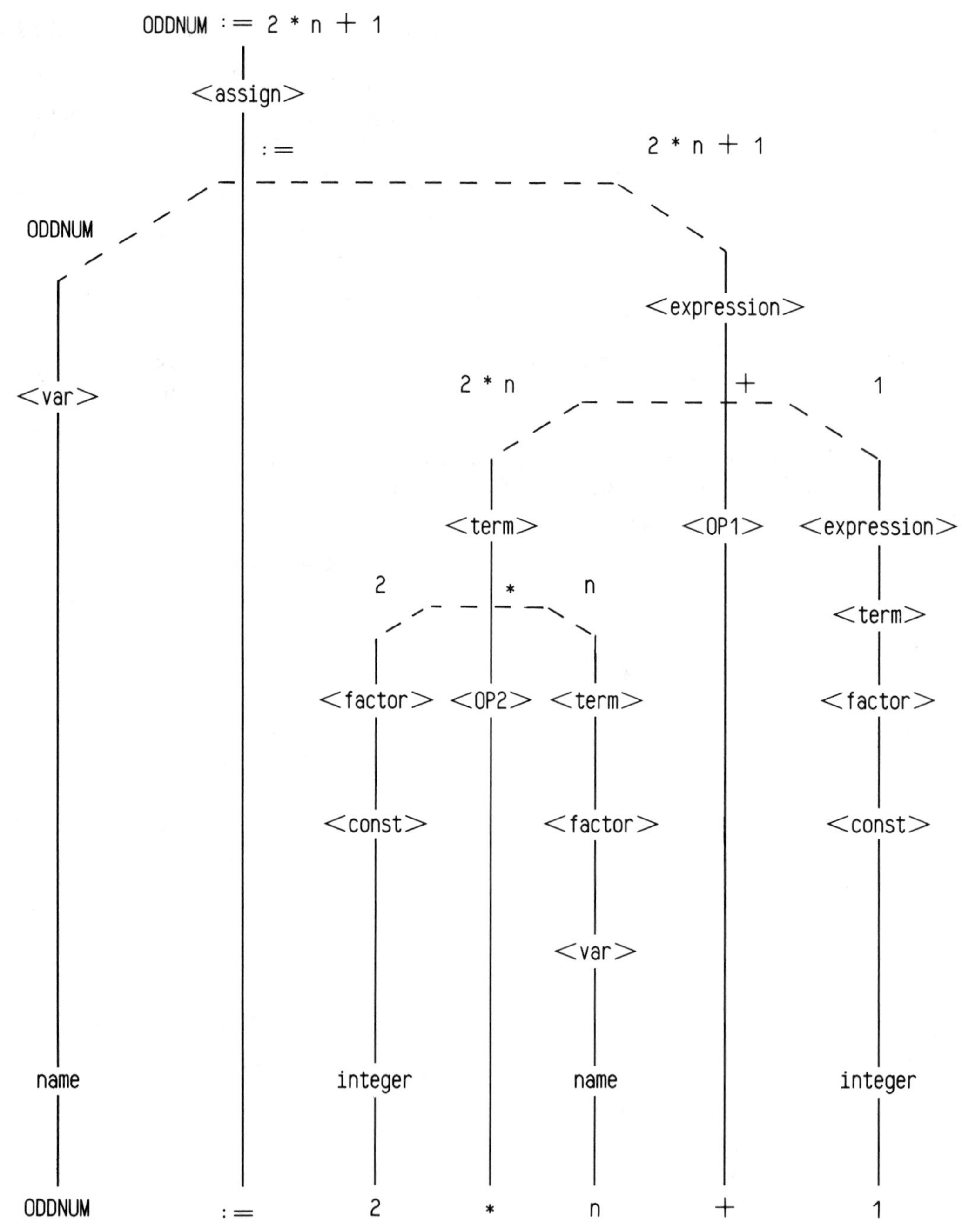

FIGURE 4.29
PARSE TREE FOR ODDNUM := 2 * n + 1

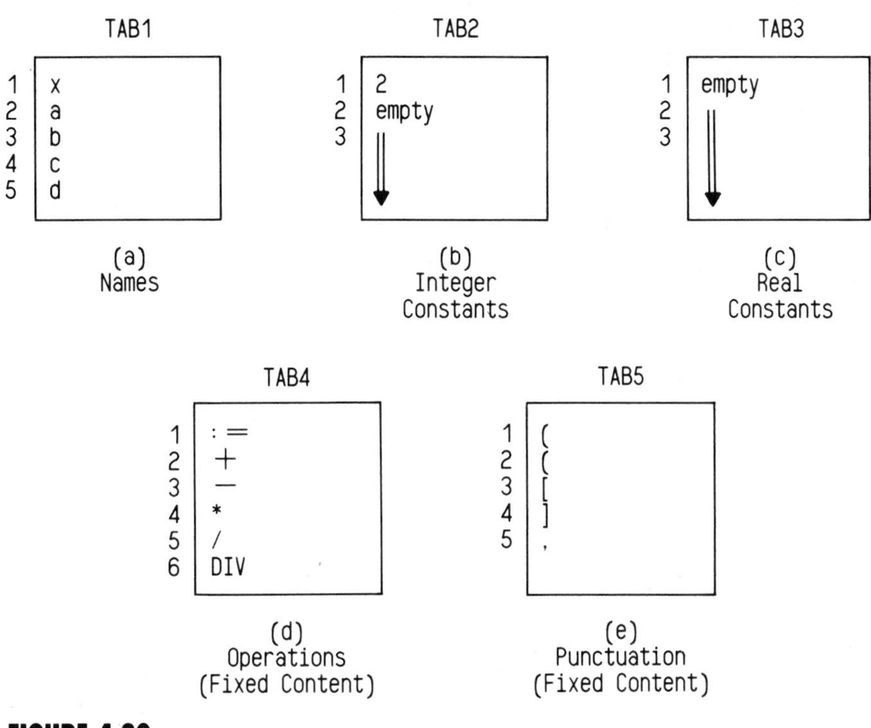

FIGURE 4.30
TOKEN TYPE/VALUE TABLES USED/CREATED BY SCANNER IN ANALYZING X:= 2 * a + b * (c − d)

Using the token string produced by the scanner, the parser must create a representation of the parse tree for the statement shown in Figure 4.31.

There are a number of ways in which the parse tree could be created. Volumes have been written describing various parsing techniques and the development of algorithms to implement these techniques. However, serious treatment of parsing techniques and the accompanying algorithms is beyond the scope and intent of this book. Those who want additional information should consult a more comprehensive reference such as the excellent book by Aho and Ullman, *Principles of Compiler Design* (1979).

In general though, parsing algorithms are classified by two basic approaches to parsing, top-down or bottom-up, but it is not uncommon to find parsers which use combinations of the two.

A *top-down* parser works from the highest goal (that is, a nonterminal symbol) in the structure that it is trying to identify and applies all possible derivations from this goal using the rules of grammar until it identifies the input string (or rejects it due to an error in syntax). For example, in our

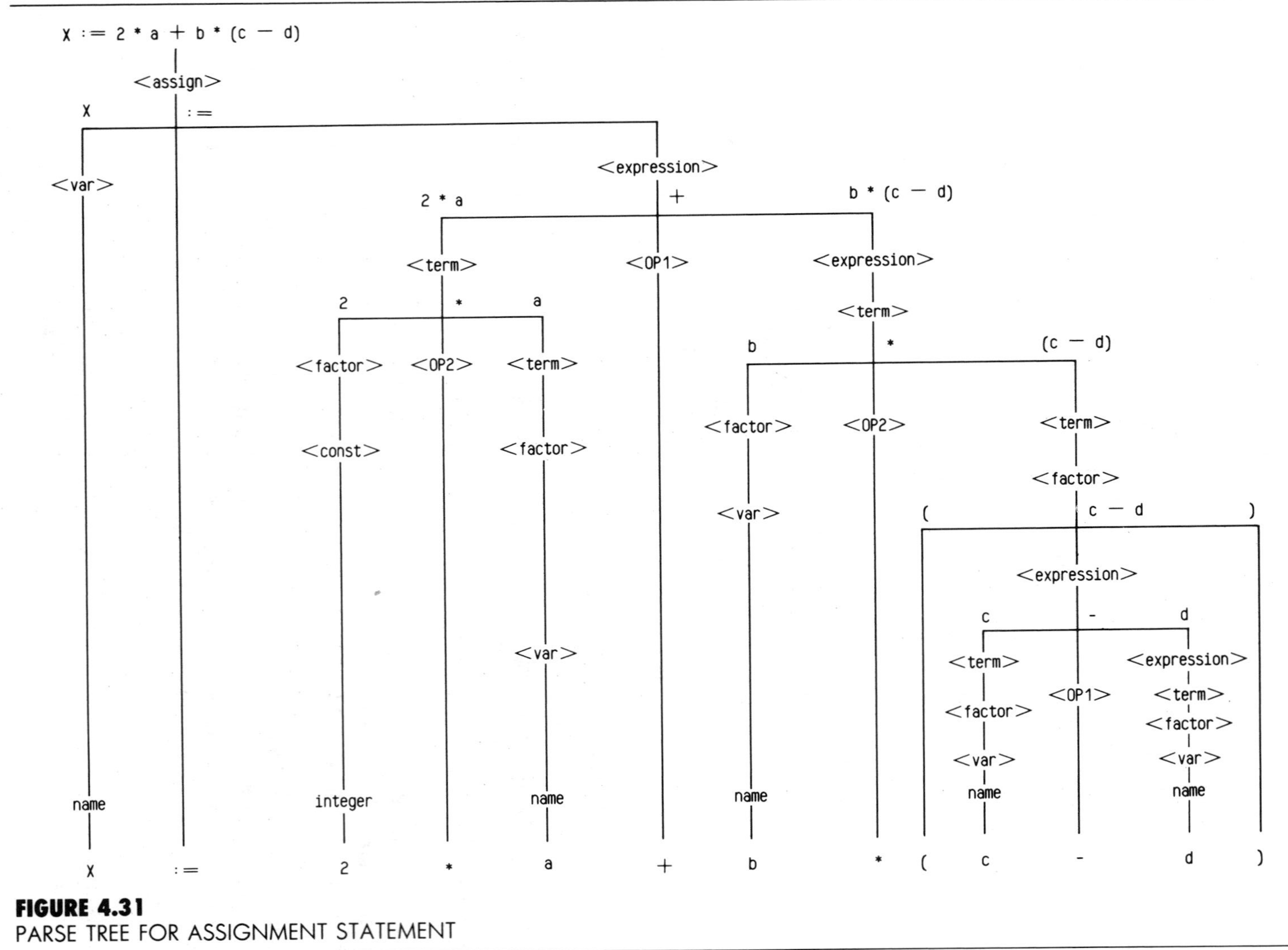

FIGURE 4.31
PARSE TREE FOR ASSIGNMENT STATEMENT

previous example, a top-down parser would assume that an input string was an assignment statement and then once the := token was located, it would attempt to show that the tokens to the left and right of the := form a variable and an expression, respectively.

A *bottom-up* parser works upward from the terminal symbols (that is, the token string) to try and discover larger and larger structures until the "goal" symbol is reached.

Only one very basic algorithm for a parser is shown in this book (see Figure 4.32). This type of parser uses a top-down method known as *recursive-*

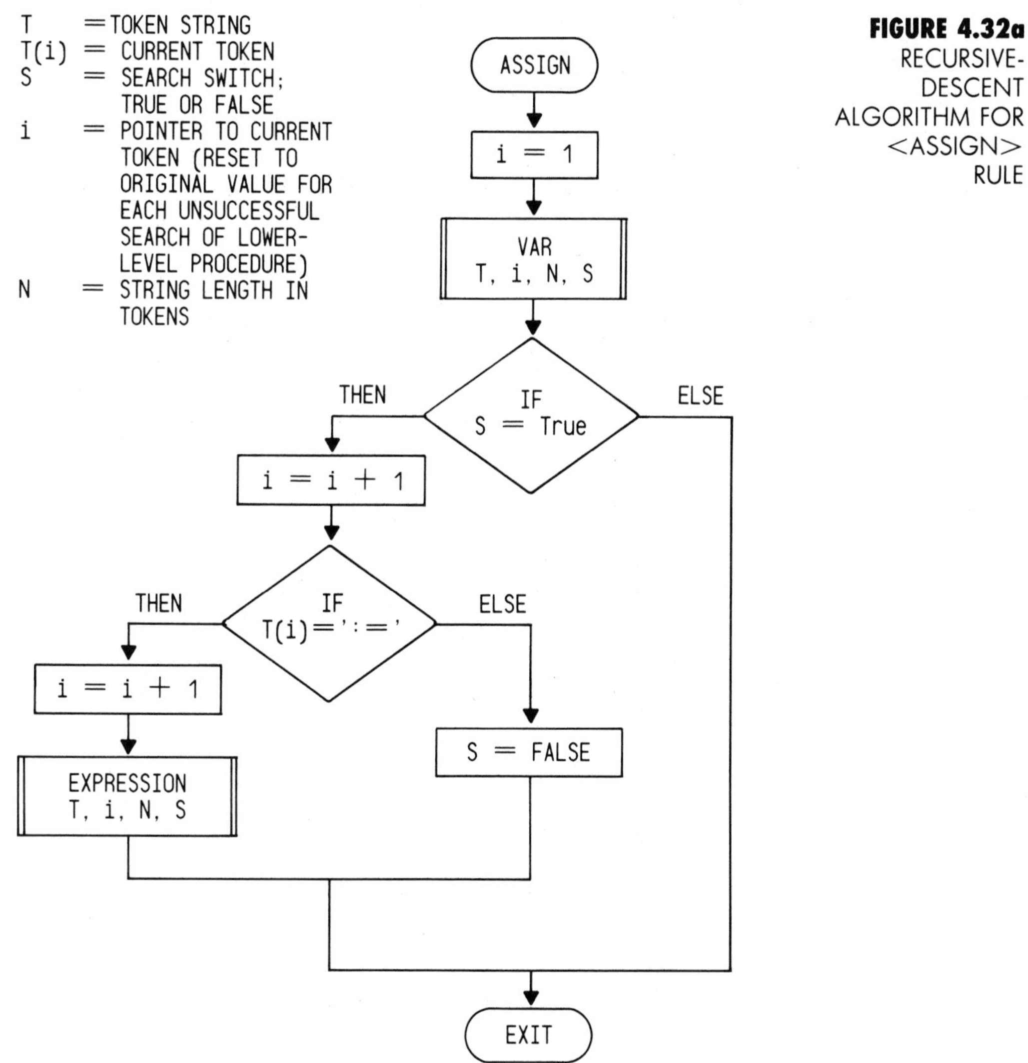

FIGURE 4.32a RECURSIVE-DESCENT ALGORITHM FOR <ASSIGN> RULE

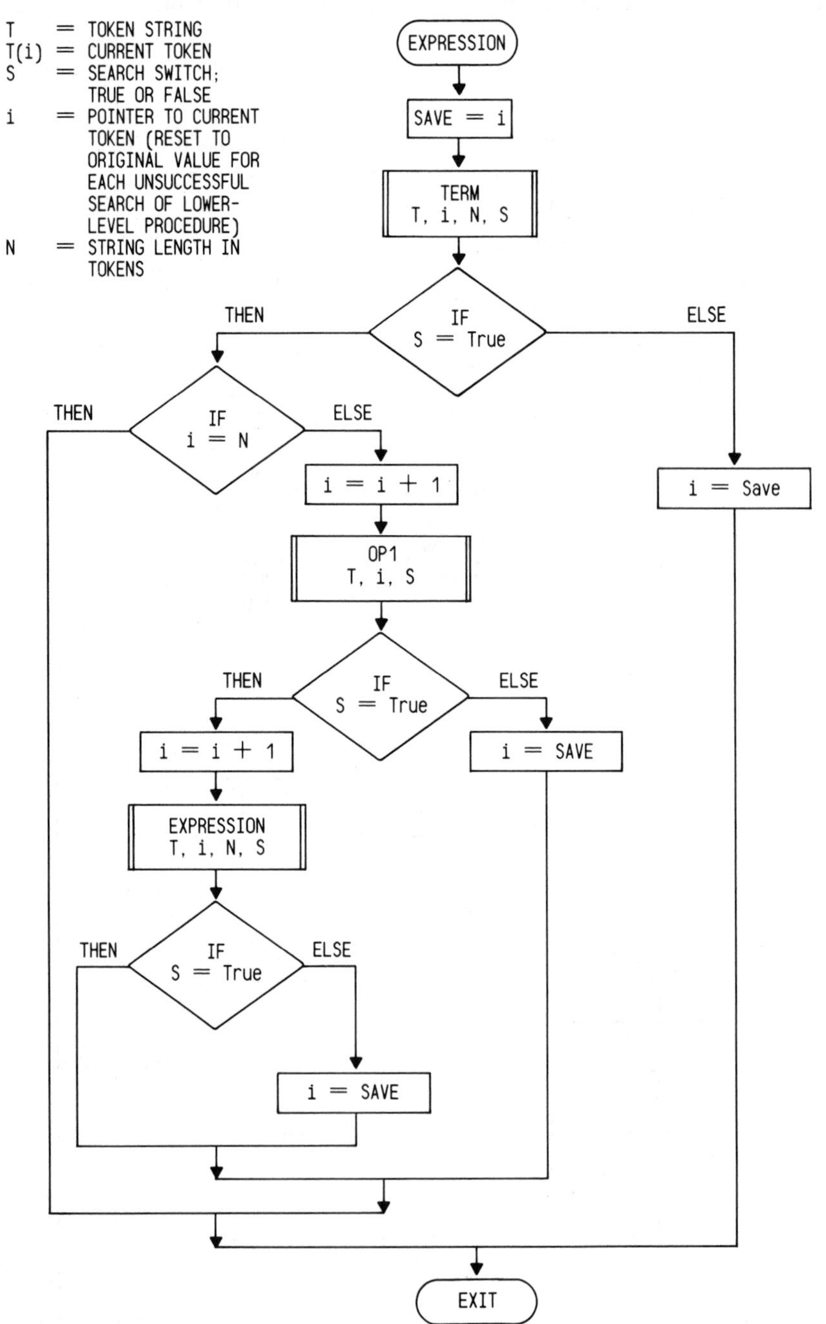

FIGURE 4.32b
RECURSIVE-DESCENT ALGORITHM FOR <EXPRESSION> RULE

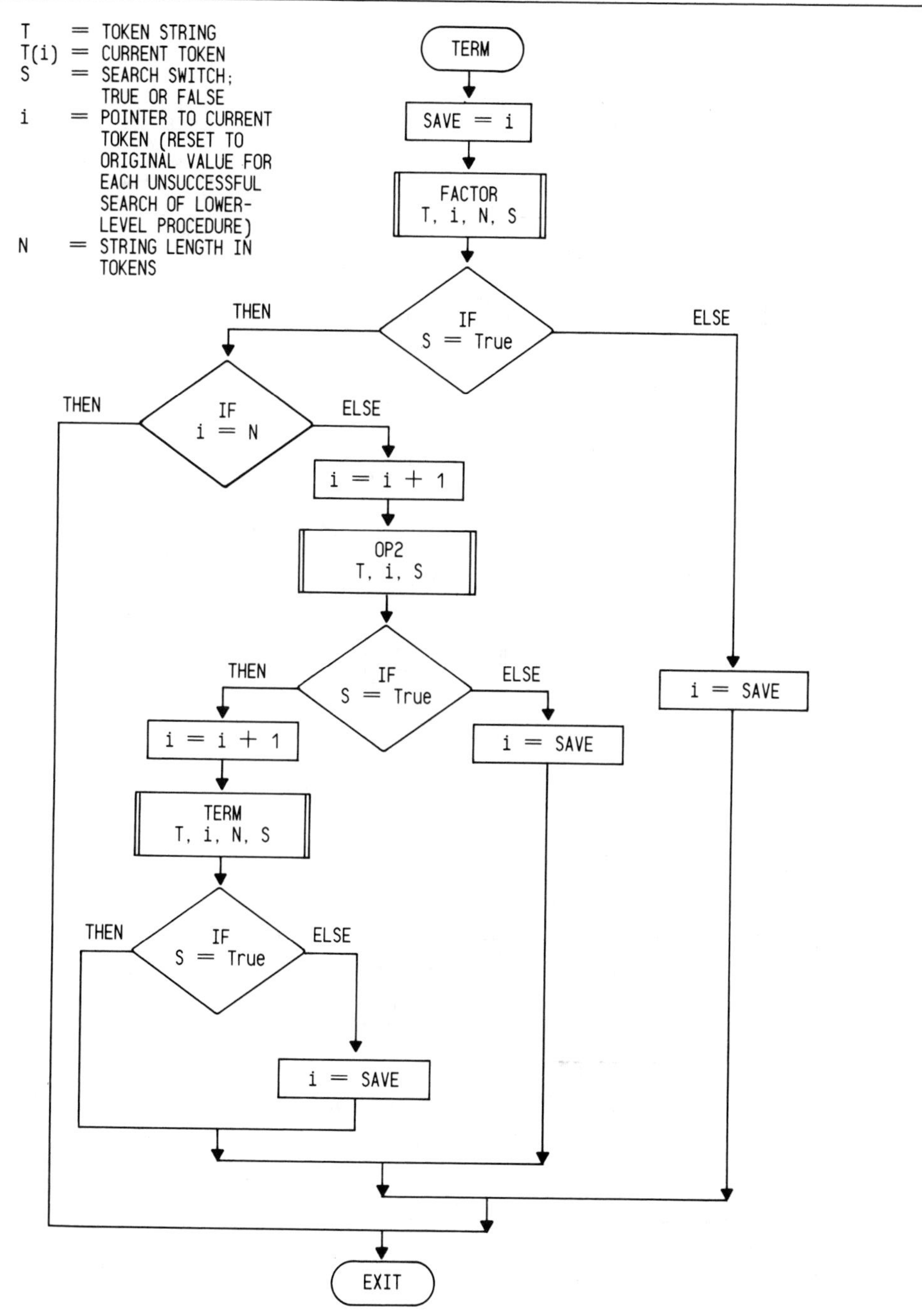

FIGURE 4.32c
RECURSIVE-DESCENT ALGORITHM FOR <TERM> RULE

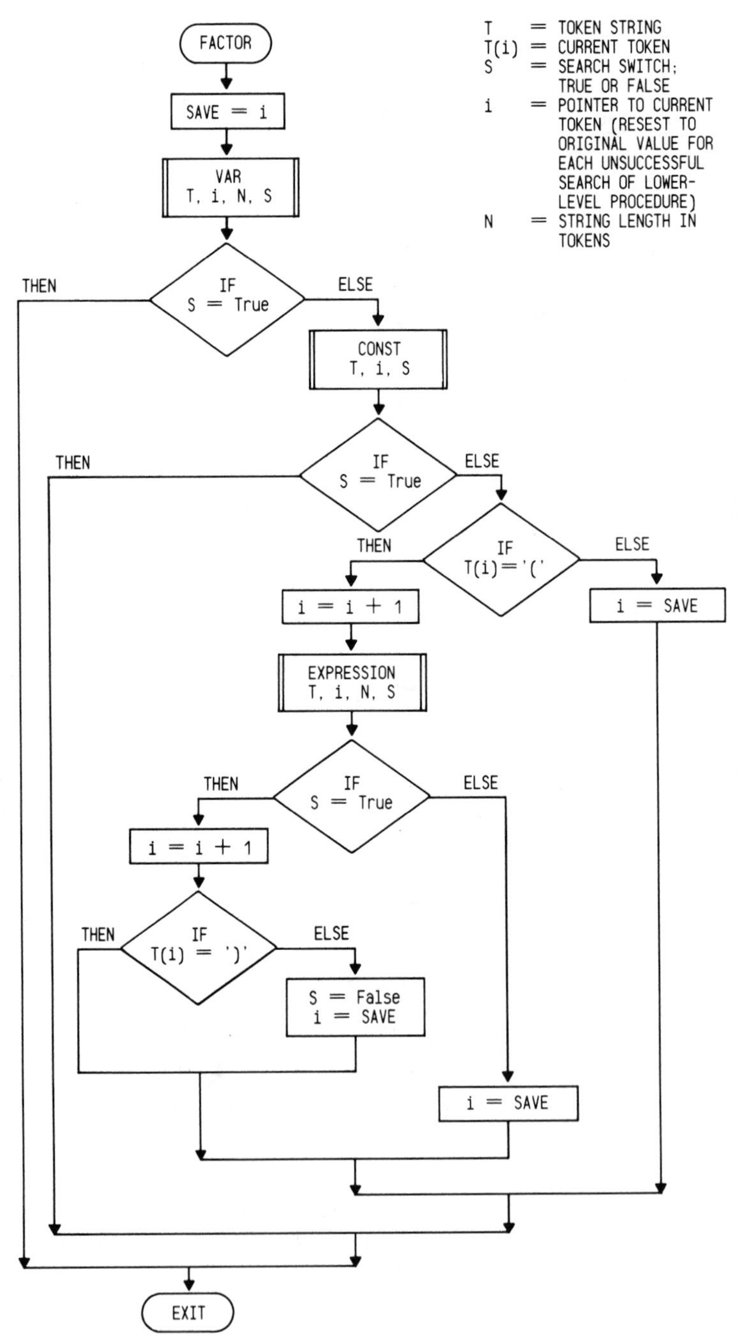

FIGURE 4.32d
RECURSIVE-DESCENT ALGORITHM FOR <FACTOR> RULE

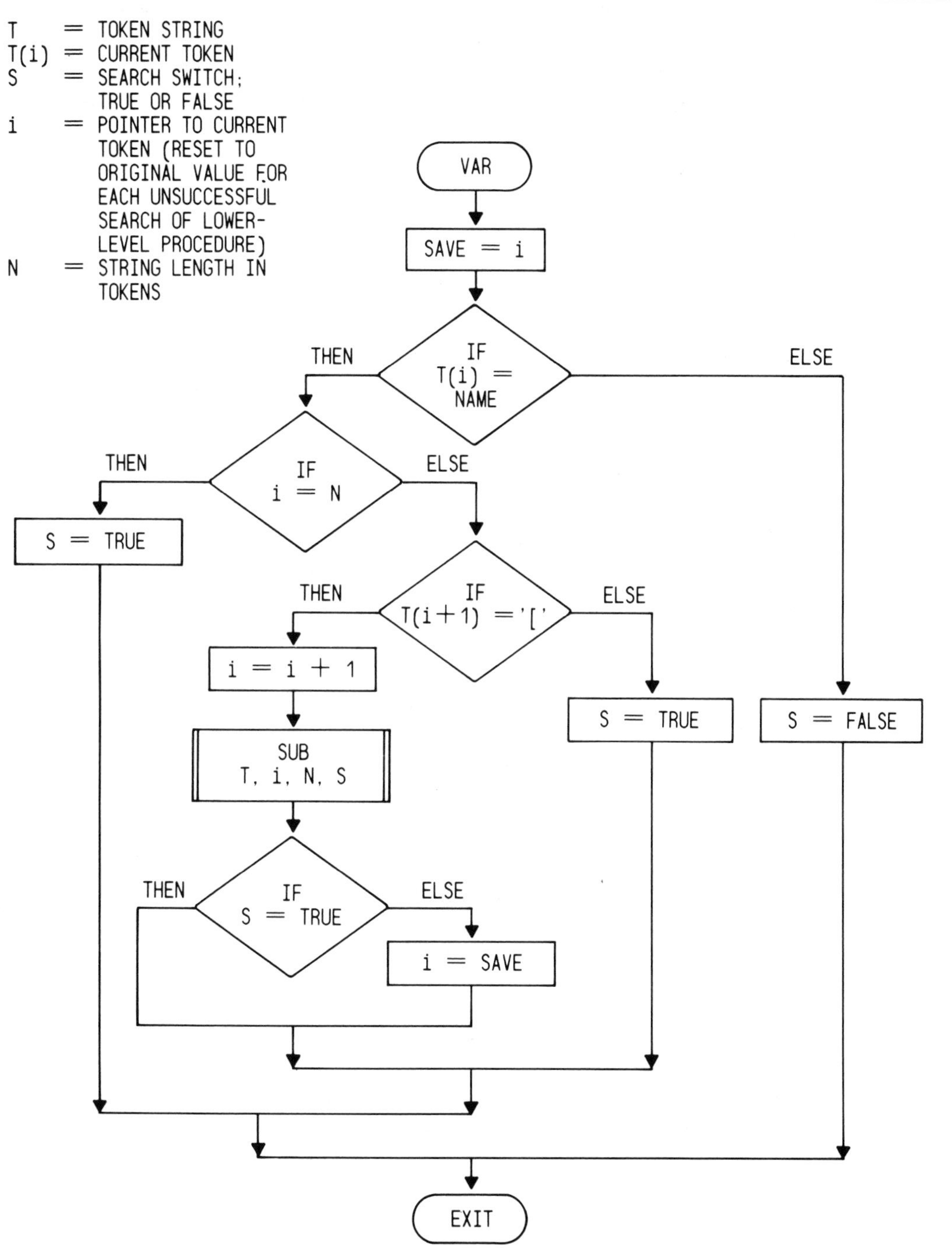

FIGURE 4.32e
RECURSIVE-DESCENT ALGORITHM FOR <VAR> RULE

descent. There is no intent to imply that recursive-descent parsers are superior to others; usually, they are not. While there are generally better parsing techniques than this, an algorithm for this technique is shown because it is relatively more simple than the others and because it is representative of a large general class.

In recursive-descent, there is a routine (or procedure) for each nonterminal symbol in the grammar of the language. The process starts by invoking the procedure for the start symbol which, in turn, calls other lower-level procedures. Any procedure, except the start procedure, may (in general) call itself, hence the name recursive-descent. However, care must be taken in writing the rules of grammar to be used with a recursive-descent parser that *left-recursion* does not occur. A left-recursive rule is one in which a symbol immediately refers to itself as part of its definition, thus resulting in a infinite loop, if called recursively. For example:

```
<term> ::= <term> <OP2> <factor> is left-recursive.
```

While <term> ::= <factor> <OP2> <term> is not left recursive, and allows <term> to be reduced to a simpler form before calling itself.

A recursive-descent parser for the grammar of Figure 4.27 is shown in Figure 4.32. In this algorithm, it is assumed that the parser is working with an entire statement token stream and that the number of tokens in the stream has been counted. As each procedure is called, the token counter i is positioned at the beginning of the sequence of tokens that will be tested to identify a particular structure (such as a term or factor). When a procedure identifies a structure, i is positioned to the last token in the token string that comprises the structure. Otherwise, the procedure will restore i to its original position so that other structures can be tested. Only the five higher level procedures are shown because the four lower level procedures are relatively straightforward after studying those given.

Semantic Analysis: Generally speaking, *semantic analysis* is the process of determining the meaning of the statements written according to the rules of syntax for a language. More specifically, this usually involves using a set of semantic routines (typically, one for each language structure) that are used to convert the parse tree produced by the parser into the intermediate code. The semantic analysis can be performed after the parsing phase or cooperatively during the parsing phase so that the intermediate code is produced as the parser identifies substructures in the input stream. In the latter case, the parse tree is never actually created but is replaced by equivalent intermediate code by the end of the parsing phase.

The form of the intermediate code is usually in some (more or less) machine independent form that is simple enough to be converted into machine code in a single pass, with the exception of any optimization.

For example, consider the assignment statement

```
X := a + b * c
```

and its accompanying parse tree shown in Figure 4.33.

There are several forms commonly used for the intermediate code. Two forms are quadruples and postfix code. In the case of *quadruples*, each quadruple represents an operation, up to two operands, and a destination for the result of the operation. For example, our assignment statement in Figure 4.33 would be represented as:

Operation	Operands	Destination
*	b c	T1
+	a T1	T2
:=	T2	X

Quadruples are not only appropriate to represent binary operations (such as +, *) and unary operations (such as :=), but they can be used to represent simple branching or conditional branching operations from which higher level control structures are built. In the case of branches, the target of the branch is the quadruple indicated by its sequential number. Conditional branches test the result of the most recently processed quadruple. For example, consider the IF-THEN-ELSE statement:

```
IF N < 100 THEN
   C := N * R1
ELSE
   C := N * R2
```

This could be represented as shown in Figure 4.34:

In the case of postfix code, the code represents the result of a post order traversal (for example RLN) of a tree in which the leaves (terminals) represent operands and the higher level nodes represent operations. For example, the parse tree in Figure 4.33 (without bringing down the operations to leaf level) in postfix code from right to left would be:

```
c b * a + x :=
```

Branching in postfix code is handled as it was with quadruples, in that each element in the postfix code is associated with a number (address) that can be the object of a branching operation. There are many other aspects

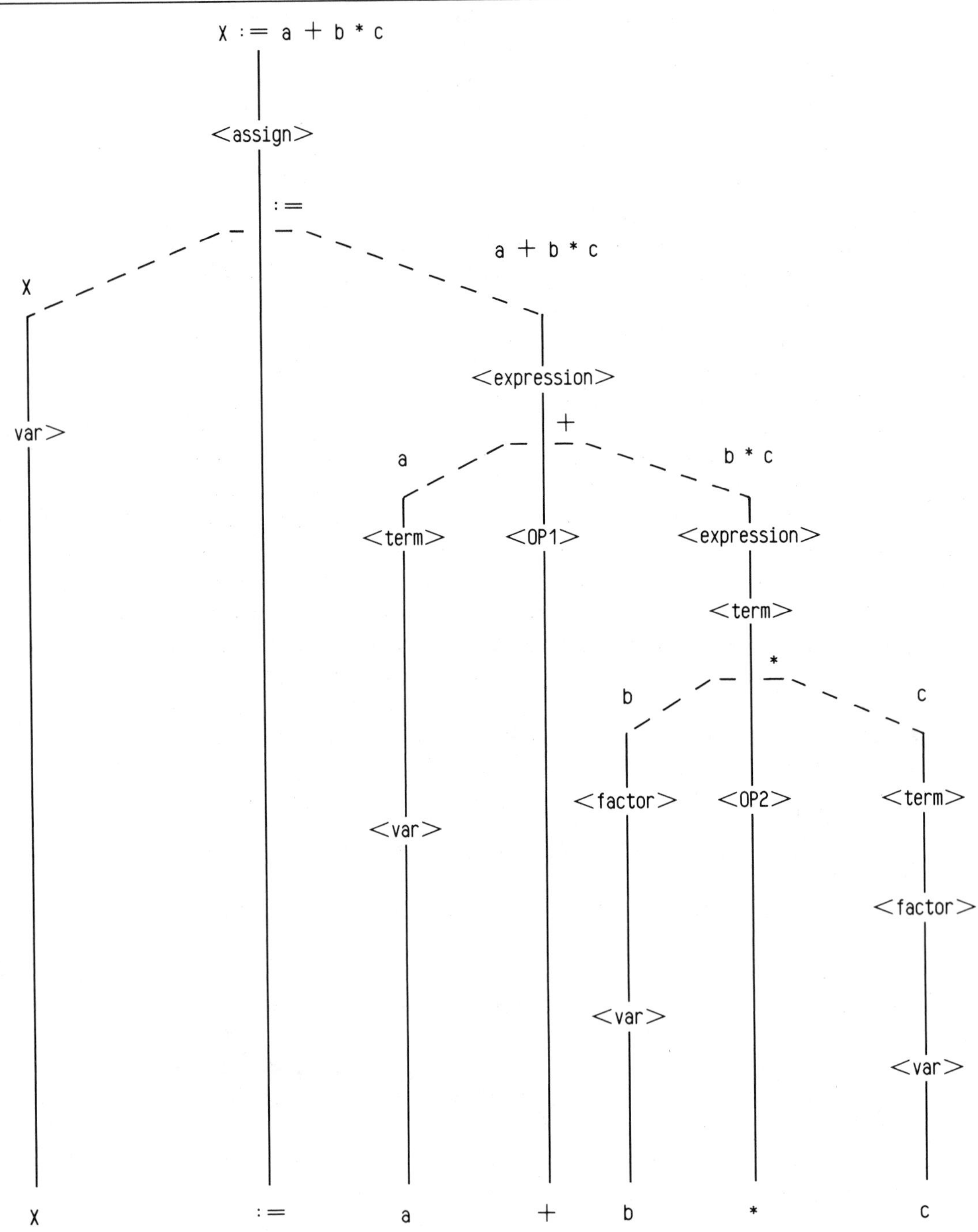

FIGURE 4.33
PARSE TREE FOR X := a + b * c

Number	Operation	Operands		Destination
1	-	100	N	T1
2	BNP	T1		#6
3	*	N	R1	T2
4	:	T2		C
5	B			#8
6	*	N	R2	T3
7	:=	T3		C
8	- - -	- - -	- - -	- - -

FIGURE 4.34 INTERMEDIATE CODE FOR IF-THEN-ELSE STATEMENT

to the semantics of a programming language. For example, a legal operation between two numeric data objects may also imply a data conversion if the data objects are of different numeric types. This is clearly a semantic issue, but the point during the compilation process at which the data conversion issue is handled is quite flexible. In fact, it is this highly flexible manner in the way that semantic analysis as a whole is treated in compiler implementations, together with the lack of a concise notation for describing semantics (such as BNF for syntax), that make discussions of this phase of analysis difficult.

It is not the intent here to present all the information needed to write a compiler, but to offer an appreciation for the basic processes involved in compilation and to provide a basis for comparing the general complexity of compilation as compared to the assembly process described in Chapter 2. Therefore, a complete discussion of semantic issues will not be attempted.

Generation After the analysis phase has been completed, the next major phase of compilation is the generation of the object code. Generation can be broken into three subtasks:

1. Storage allocation for data objects.
2. Optimization
3. Production of object code

Storage Allocation: In order to generate object code from the intermediate code, we must be able to replace references to symbolic operands with the locations of the operands. Once the location of a data object (e.g., a variable) has been assigned, this location can be placed in the appropriate symbol table, and references to the data object can be resolved by accessing the symbol table in a similar manner previously described in Chapter 2 for symbolic assemblers. In fact, as long as the data objects are allocated statically (as is done with FORTRAN, COBOL, and BASIC), the process is practically the same as previously described in allocating storage for literals in the assembly process.

When allocating storage for dynamic data objects, additional actions are required. For example, if the data object is part of an activation record, then its location can be treated as a displacement into the activation record, which will be created dynamically during execution time. It should also be noted that the use of activation records will require the insertion of "calls" at the proper points in the object code to invoke the routines that create and maintain activation records.

Optimization: Optimization is not required in the compilation process, but some attempt at optimization is usually desirable. There are basically two kinds of optimization: machine-independent and machine-dependent.

Machine-independent optimization is performed on the intermediate code and produces an optimized intermediate code. This involves such tasks as the reduction and/or elimination of redundant or unnecessary computations. It may also involve replacing a section of intermediate code, with functionally equivalent code that is more efficient. An example of reducing redundant computation is to move a computation that yields a constant value outside of a loop.

Machine-dependent optimization involves such tasks as assuring the efficient use of registers to eliminate unnecessary storing and immediate reloading of the same operand.

Production of Object Code: Object code production is the final state of compilation, in which the machine code (or other target code) is produced. For an example of the production of object code from intermediate code consider the intermediate code from Figure 4.34 and the resulting code, shown in Figure 4.35. We will assume that the data objects are allocated statically and that each is in fullword binary form. (Operands are represented symbolically, however these would be resolved at this point.)

INTERPRETATION

The alternative to compilation is interpretation. The treatment here of interpretation is rather brief, for two reasons. First, the advantages and disadvantages of interpretation were covered in the comparative discussion of compilers and interpreters earlier in the chapter. Second, a substantial part of the interpretive process is a duplication of activities discussed in the compilation process.

More specifically, an interpreter (like a compiler) can be described in terms of two major activities; namely, analysis and synthesis. The analysis

FIGURE 4.35 PRODUCTION OF OBJECT CODE

Quadruples				Object Code		
-	100	N	T1	L	5,N	
				S	5,=F'100'	
				ST	5,T1	
BNP	T1		#6	BNP	*+28	(skip next 6 instructions)
*	N	R1	T2	L	5,N	
				M	4,R1	
				ST	5,T2	} ST 5,C (optimization)
:=	T2		C	L	5,T2	
				ST	5,C	
B			#8	B	*+24	(skip next 5 instructions)
*	N	R2	T3	L	5,N	
				M	4,R2	
				ST	5,T3	} ST 5,C (optimization)
:=	T3		C	L	5,T3	
				ST	5,C	
				-		

phase is essentially the same process that was described for compilers, from lexical analysis through the production of an intermediate code form for each statement in the program. The major difference is that interpreters perform the analysis-synthesis cycle on a statement-by-statement basis, while compilers tend to delay synthesis until the whole program (or at least much larger segments of it) has been analyzed.

The synthesis portion of interpretation is the immediate execution of each statement in the source program as soon as it has been analyzed. Typically, there is an interpretive routine for each statement type in the language (such as assignment) that simulates the execution of the statement from the intermediate form of the statement produced by the analysis phase. In a purely interpretive scheme there can be no optimization, because interpretation is performed on a statement-by-statement basis and no object code is generated or saved. However, because data objects cannot be handled on a statement-by-statement basis, symbol tables are maintained and storage is allocated on a program or routine level, depending upon the requirements of the language used. In BASIC, for example, data objects are allocated statically on a program basis while in Pascal, there is static and dynamic allocation of storage.

In practice, many commercial "interpreters" combine interpretation with compilation so an intermediate form of the whole source program (or large pieces of it) are produced and saved. This larger, intermediate form provides a reduction in the interpretation cycle overhead and also allows for some optimization, if desired.

FIGURE 4.36
BASIC ALGORITHM FOR AN INTERPRETER

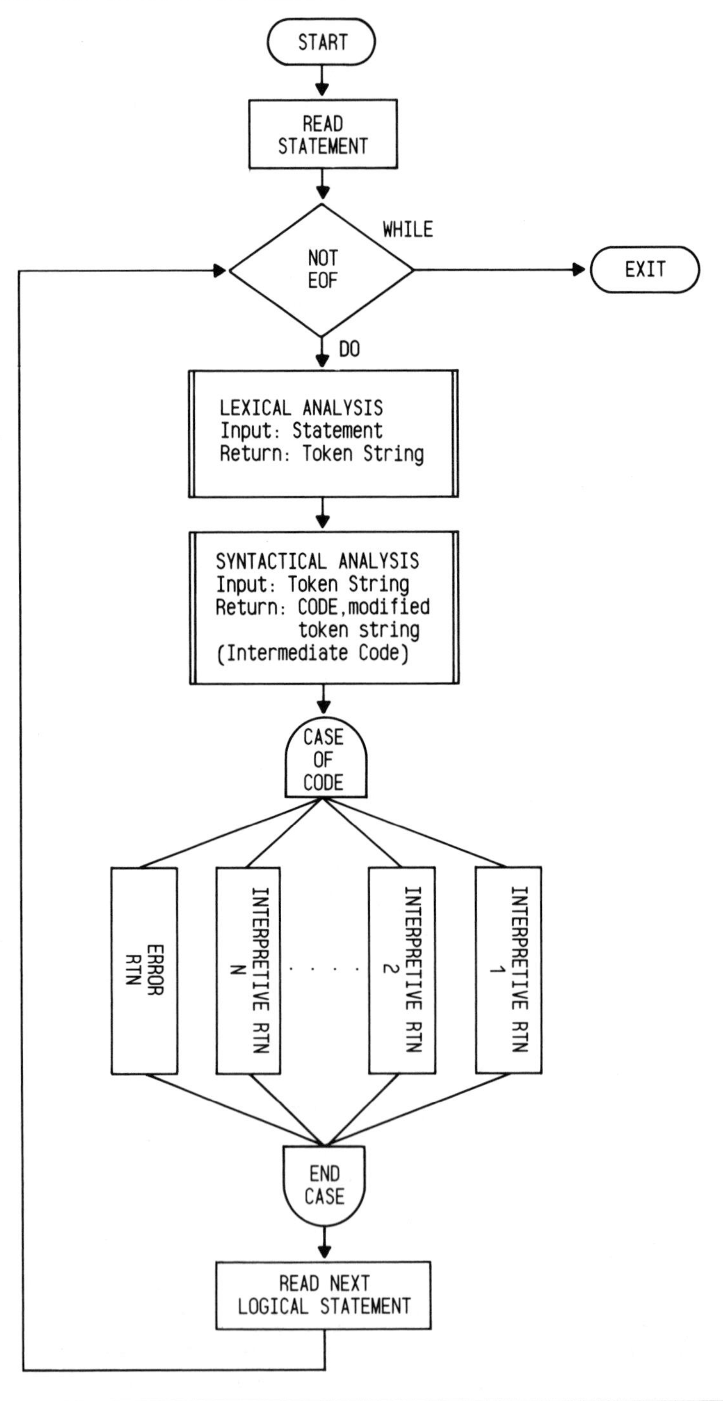

Interpretation can be summarized as an iterative process involving three repetitive steps:

1. Read a statement
2. Analyze the statement
3. Execute the statement

These steps are the basis for the high-level algorithm for an interpreter shown in Figure 4.36.

Review Questions and Exercises

1. Define or explain briefly.
   a. Procedural language
   b. nonprocedural language
   c. Compiler
   d. Interpreter
   e. Homogeneous array
   f. Strong typing
   g. Referencing environment
   h. Local referencing environment
   i. Static scope
   j. Block-structured language
   k. Actual and formal parameters
   l. Activation record
   m. Garbage
   n. Grammar
   o. Parsing
2. Compare and contrast the following pairs of terms.
   a. Passing parameters by reference and by value
   b. Static and dynamic storage allocation
   c. Compilation and interpretation
3. Explain the storage management needed to support recursive subroutine calls in a programming language.
4. Describe under what conditions garbage or dangling references can occur in programs written in a language that supports programmer-controlled, dynamic storage allocation.
5. The following grammar defines a language of even, nonnegative integers.

```
<even-int>     ::= <even-digit> | <integer> <even-
  digit>
<interger>     ::= <digit> | <digit> <interger>
<digit>        ::= <even-digit> | <odd-digit>
<even-digit>   ::= 0 | 2 | 4 | 6 | 8
<odd-digit>    ::= 1 | 3 | 5 | 7 | 9
```

a. Show the derivation (parse tree) for 96.
b. Show the parse tree for 2034.

6. Define a grammar using BNF notation for a language of floating-point numbers written in scientific form

   sd.ddddEs*d*

   where s is a sign ±; d is a digit that can be repeated if underlined.
7. Show the parse tree for the assignment statement

   ```
   X := (a + b) * (c − d)
   ```

   using the grammar given in Figure 4.27.
8. Show a representation of intermediate code in quadruple form that would be generated from the parse tree in problem 7.
9. Show the object code that would be produced from the intermediate code in problem number eight. Assume no optimization is performed and represent the object code in symbolic assembly language format with symbolic main storage operands.
10. Use the modified Pratt evaluation scheme to analyze a programming language other than one of those analyzed in this book.

OPERATING SYSTEMS

In Chapter 1 the history of the development of operating systems was briefly traced, and it may be of interest to review that material at this point before continuing. A key point in that earlier discussion was that operating system development has historically been in response to developments in hardware. For example, the invention of the interrupt and the development of I/O processors were central to the development of effective multiuser operating systems.

In this chapter, attempts are made to point out other parallels in hardware/operating system development where they seem appropriate and pertinent to the discussions of operating systems. For the most part, however, discussions will concentrate on what relatively modern operating systems are, rather on what they have been.

BASIC FUNCTIONS AND CONCEPTS

As we approach the study of operating systems, it s natural to ask the questions: What is an operating system? What does it do? How do you get it to do what it does? How does it do what it does?

DEFINITION OF AN OPERATING SYSTEM

The first step toward defining an operating system is to describe it as a set of programs whose purpose is to improve the useability and efficiency of a computer.

Useability refers to useable for humans, because without an operating system, we humans would be forced to communicate with a computer at machine language level. Were this the case, progress in computing applications would be only a tiny fraction of what it is today, because even what we recognize as a simple report program would represent a tedious, if not formidable task.

In its broadest sense, an operating system includes any programs and/or routines that aid in the development of other programs and that contribute to the orderly and efficient execution of programs once they have been developed. This would include language processors, utilities, and what is sometimes called the "control program"; however, the more prevalent view of an operating system is to equate an operating system to the *control program.* Thus, in this view, the operating system is the set of routines that provides service and control for programs (primarily application programs) during their execution. Therefore, to the operating system, the language processors and utilities are just special-purpose application programs.

This latter and more restrictive view of an operating system is the one chosen for this book. The larger view is what we call system software and is the reason that the title of this book refers to system software, instead of just operating systems.

Efficiency may seem a rather incompatible goal for an operating system since, with the exception of initiating or performing I/O functions, an operating system is pure overhead with respect to computer applications and does not directly produce any useable work for the user of a computer. On the other hand, even though it produces little or no useable work, what it does is extremely useful, for without the operating system, we humans would have to manually perform many functions that are done by the operating system. This manual operation is incredibly slow compared to computing speeds and would create a situation in which the computer is idle whenever the human must perform a task. As the number of tasks for the human to manage increases, the greater is the loss of *potential* use of the computer, and the greater the likelihood of errors. Since computers can perform well-defined tasks quickly and accurately, the solution to improved efficiency is to allow the computer to manage its own activity with a minimum of human intervention. Thus an operating system is actually a manager of system resources.

In Chapter 1, an *operating system* was defined as an integrated set of routines that function together to manage the resources of a computing system during its operation. These routines are usually implemented as software, and this discussion treats them totally as software; however, advances in microprogramming technology have allowed some operating system functions to migrate to firmware. The primary resources managed by the operating system are:

1. The CPU(s)
2. Main memory
3. I/O devices (including the I/O processors to which they may be attached)
4. Files

In each case, the operating system must control who gets to use the resource, how much of the resource they get, and how long they can use it. In other words, in order to manage a resource, the operating system must control the allocation of the resource. This is particularly important in a system that allows concurrent execution of more than one program or task, because the operating system must control the allocation of a resource in order to resolve the problem of two programs in execution contending for the same resource.

THE PURPOSE OF AN OPERATING SYSTEM

Management and control of resources are means to an end and are not the actual purpose of an operating system. As described earlier, the purpose of an operating system is to make a computer system more convenient to use and to improve the efficiency of the system.

Convenience. In using a computer system, convenience is achieved by deferring to the operating system many functions which are not dependent on the application program that requests the function and are above the level of a single machine language instruction. Examples of these functions are:

1. I/O operations—the reading of a record from a particular I/O device does not depend on the nature of the program requesting the READ. By allowing the operating system to perform the READ procedure, the application programmer is spared a tedious task that would be duplicated in every program requiring the same type of READ.

2. Error handling—detection and processing of error conditions are not required of the application programs. In the case of a fatal program error, the operating system can terminate the errant program without interfering or halting the execution of other programs.

3. File handling—allocation of external storage, cataloging of files, and label checking to provide file security are all functions that are performed by the operating system.

4. Automatic transition within and between jobs—without this function, a great deal of manual intervention would be required to initiate the execution of each program.

Efficiency. Improvement in the efficient use of a computer system is accomplished largely through the operating system's management of tasks which can be performed concurrently. Obviously, when the operating system is in control of the CPU, other programs cannot execute; thus, as was stated before, from the viewpoint of useful work (applications), the operating system is mostly overhead. However, due to the fact that I/O operations are much slower than CPU speeds, many programs spend most of their job time waiting for I/O instead of using the CPU (assuming that the computer has the capability to perform I/O independently of the CPU, which is the case in all but the simplest microcomputer systems). By monitoring the periods when a program is waiting for an I/O operation, the operating system can allow other programs to use the CPU. Thus, the execution of several programs can progress concurrently; this is called *multiprogramming* (see Multiprogramming versus multiprocessing in this chapter). Therefore, the real time for the execution of the set of programs is often much less than the time that would be required to execute each of them to completion one at a time.

To illustrate the concept of the concurrent execution of programs, consider the two programs shown in Figures 5.1a and 5.1b that are executed on a single CPU system with an I/O processor or DMA. For simplicity, this

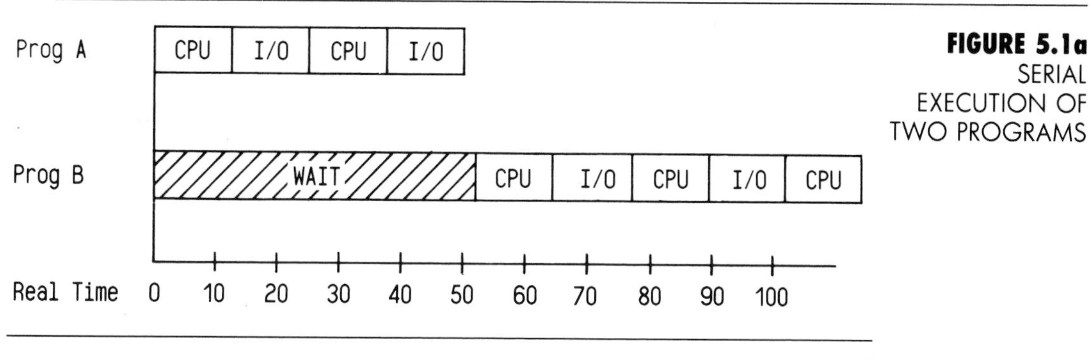

FIGURE 5.1a SERIAL EXECUTION OF TWO PROGRAMS

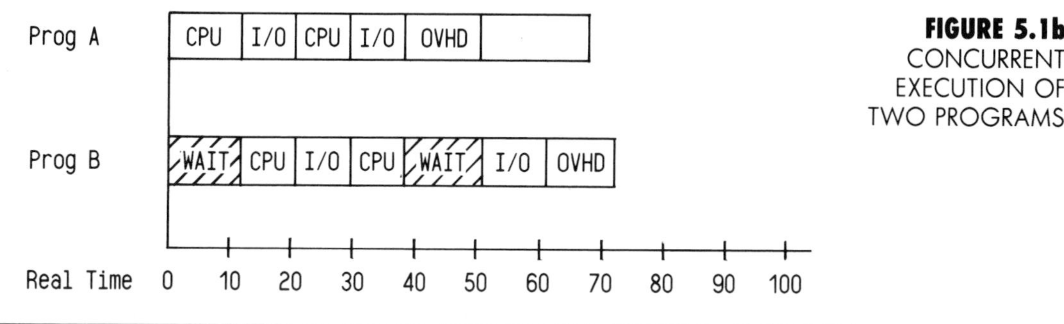

FIGURE 5.1b CONCURRENT EXECUTION OF TWO PROGRAMS

figure combines the periods of CPU activity and I/O activity into large blocks which are representative of the percentage of time spent in the two activities respectively. Actually, there would be many very short intervals of activity alternating between CPU usage and I/O, but this would be difficult to illustrate and tedious to read. Figure 5.1a shows the serial execution of the two programs (which would be required without an operating system). Figure 5.1b shows the concurrent execution of the same two programs. Notice that the total CPU time and I/O time is the same in both cases, but there is a significant savings in real time or elapsed time (actually, there will be a slight increase in CPU time due to the execution of the necessary operating system routines, but in most cases this will amount to an increase of no more than a few percent). Figure 5.1b shows the operating system overhead added to both programs, but only program B has a block of WAIT time. In this example, it is assumed that program A has priority over program B. Since it is highly unlikely that we could get a perfect match in the alternating activities of both programs, when both programs need the CPU at the same time, program B will wait.

As stated already, using the operating system to provide automatic job transition adds to the convenience of using a computer system. In addition, it will also improve the efficiency in the use of the computer system, since any form of human intervention is orders of magnitude slower than even the slowest computer implementation of the same function.

The operating system can also improve the efficiency of the use of a computing system by a single program by performing multiple buffering on I/O requests for sequential files. This is a technique where more than one I/O buffer is used in a program for a particular file. The operating system can then initiate the filling or emptying of one or more alternate buffers by an I/O processor in anticipation of future processing needs while the application program is using the CPU to process the contents of the current primary buffer. When the application program finishes its processing of a particular buffer, that buffer now becomes an alternate, and the buffer containing the next sequential record or block becomes the current primary buffer (see Figure 5.2).

The use of multiple buffering is of greater value in systems in which there are relatively few users running programs concurrently, because the concept is based on the assumption that without this technique, the CPU and I/O processor(s) spend a significant percentage of available time waiting for each other. However, as the number of concurrent users increases, there is a greater probability that some programs will be waiting to use a resource (the CPU or I/O processor) as soon as it is released by the current user. Thus, the benefits due to multiple buffering begin to disappear as the number of active programs increases and may serve only to needlessly enlarge the size of the programs involved.

FIGURE 5.2a
PROGRAM WITH SINGLE BUFFER

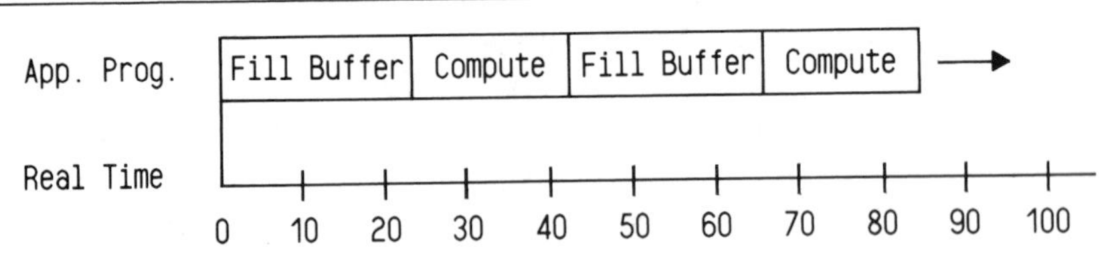

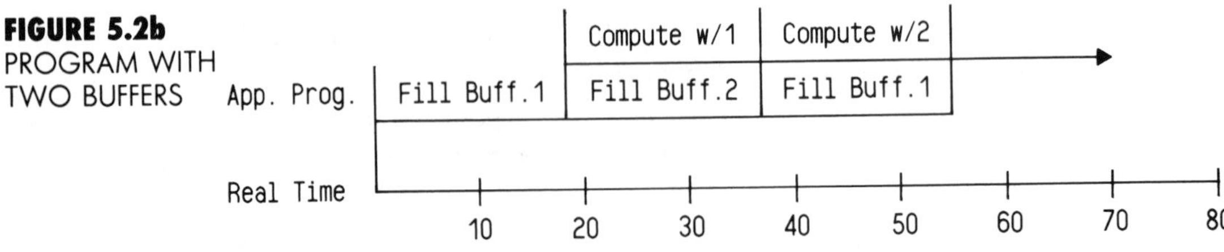

FIGURE 5.2b
PROGRAM WITH TWO BUFFERS

CONCEPTUAL VIEW OF AN OPERATING SYSTEM

In studying the types of functions that an operating system performs in order to improve convenience and efficiency, we may conclude that the operating system provides a means of extending the basic capabilities provided by the instruction set of a computer. In fact, when it comes to views of a computer as a machine, only the operating system "sees" the physical, unenhanced machine. The application program "sees" an enhanced machine that is the logical combination of the physical machine and the operating system. A user of a computer sees the enhanced machine through the further enhancement of the application program (that is, a user in a business office may view the computer as a payroll machine for that application). Figure 5.3 illustrates these views.

Now that the concept of what an operating system is has been discussed in general terms, we need to address the question of where it resides. In order to perform some of the functions that were described earlier (and others that will be described later) at least part of the operating system must be present in main memory at all times that the computer is in operation. In systems where only a portion of the operating system is memory resident, the memory resident portion is called the *nucleus* or *kernel* of the operating system. Other less critical routines, as well as those that are not in frequent use, can be brought into a common or transient area on a demand basis, much as application programs are brought into the user area of memory as

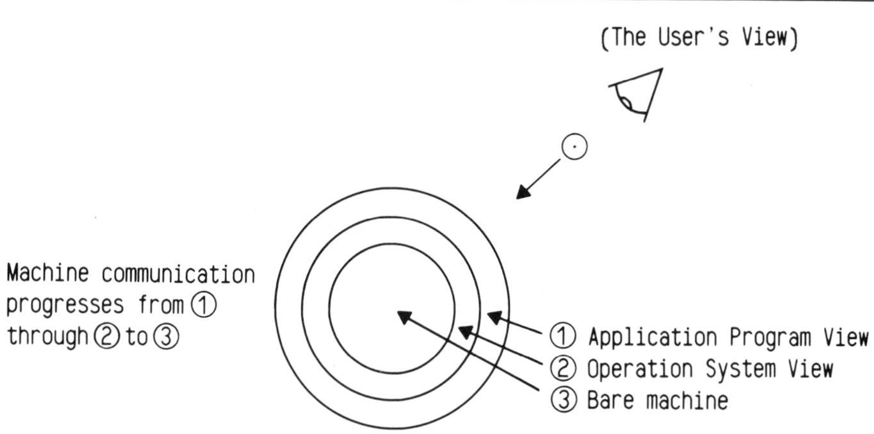

FIGURE 5.3
CONCEPTUAL VIEWS OF A COMPUTER THROUGH LEVELS OF SOFTWARE

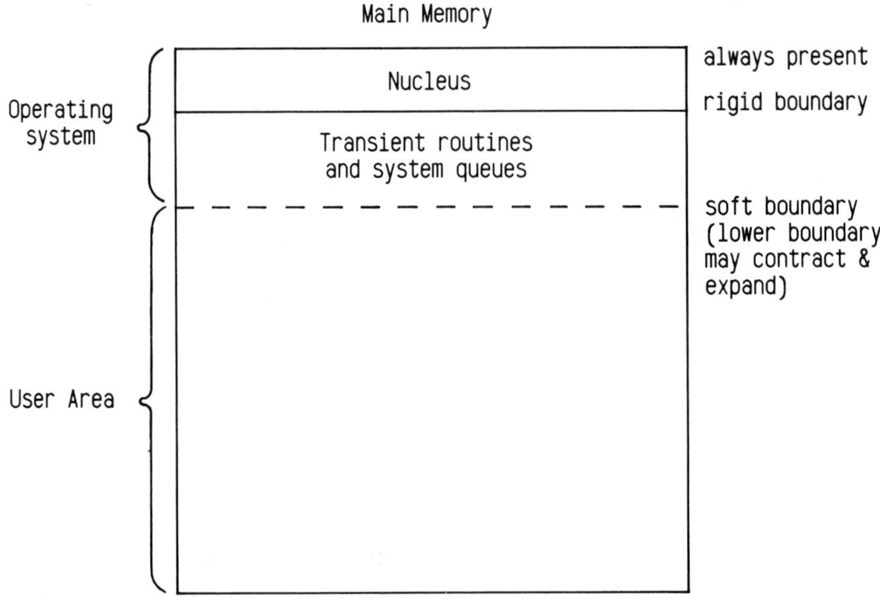

FIGURE 5.4
BASIC ARRANGEMENT OF MAIN MEMORY IN A COMPUTER WITH AN OPERATING SYSTEM

needed (see Figure 5.4). In some cases, it is possible for the entire operating system to reside in main memory, but this would typically place unnecessary restrictions on the amount of memory available for application programs and is not likely to be the design approach used in any but the most primitive single user system.

But how does the operating system, or more specifically its nucleus, get into main memory in the first place? All but the most primitive computers have a short-load procedure built into the CPU hardware or resident in its microcode. Immediately after turning on the computer the operator presses a "load button" on the computer console that activates and causes a single record from a predetermined device to be read into fixed locations in main memory. (In most personal computers, this process occurs automatically when the computer is turned on). This single record is itself a simple absolute loader (commonly called the *bootstrap loader*), which in turn loads the rest of the nucleus into fixed locations in main memory. This initial loading of the operating system nucleus is called the Initial Program Load (IPL) and upon its completion, the operating system is ready to process requests from the operator and application programs.

COMMUNICATION WITH THE OPERATING SYSTEM

Now that we have addressed the questions of what an operating system is and, in very general terms, what it does, we now turn to the question of how we get it to do the things it does. In other words, how do we communicate our needs to the operating system? Basically, there are two means of communication; through the command language of the operating system and through interrupts.

THE COMMAND LANGUAGE

Every operating system which is designed to provide humans with interprogram communication with the operating system has some form of command language. The command language may be simple and "friendly," as is the case in most popular personal computer systems, or it may be complex and not so friendly, as is the case in IBM's OS-type operating systems. Command language statements request specific services from the operating system such as: EXEC (execute) a certain program or LIST the contents of a particular directory. The operating system interprets each command language statement as it is received and immediately schedules the request for service. Because of the immediate interpretation of the command language, it is highly desirable for the main logic of the command language interpreter to be a memory resident, therefore, it is usually part of the nucleus. (UNIX, with its command interpreter "shell," deviates from this somewhat).

Command language statements can be broken into two groups: operator commands and job commands. *Operator commands* are those that request actions affecting the overall operating environment or the status of the environment; for example, a status request for the amount of free storage available in the system or a request for a list of active jobs in the system. *Job commands* provide interprogram requests for services for a particular user, such as a request to execute a program or a request to allocate space for a file. In a single-user operating system, the user is usually also the operator, so all of the operator and user commands are available to the user. However, in a mainframe environment, the operator commands are available only to the console operator terminal(s), and other users are restricted to the portion of the command language that deals with job control (for example, IBM's JCL).

INTERRUPTS

Most modern operating systems are interrupt driven, whether they are large or small, multiuser or single-user systems. *Interrupt driven* means that all communication with the operating system (except for portions of file management) is initiated through an interrupt. Even processing of operator command language statements must begin with an interrupt from the operator console or terminal, at which time the operating system will accept command language statements. Since the role of the operating system is one of service, the philosophy behind an interrupt driven system is that the operating system will remain dormant until some user or condition needs service. The interrupt is a means of automatically notifying the operating system that service is needed and of passing control to the operating system.

Returning to the discussion of how a user communicates with the operating system, communication from an executing program (intraprogram communication) occurs by executing a machine language instruction that requests service from the operating system by causing an interrupt. The specification of the service needed was placed in a register or control block or both before the instruction was executed, thus the operating system can analyze the request and then provide the service. For IBM mainframe computers, this instruction is a SVC (SuperVisor Call), which is also the name of one of the primary interrupt classes.

SVC interrupts provide a program with the capability of requesting an I/O function, a program dump, or several other services that could be performed by the operating system in direct support of an executing program.

SUBROUTINE CALLS TO SHARED ROUTINES

Reentrant (also reenterable) routines are routines that do not modify themselves in any way during execution. Thus, multiple programs can use the same copy of the routine concurrently without interfering with each other. Subroutine calls to shared reentrant routines—such as access method routines—are special cases in this view of operating system communication. For this discussion these routines are not considered as part of the operating system proper, since they run as subroutines under the control of the application program that uses them. However, they are often provided with the operating system and, in the case of access methods, figure heavily in the file management functions of the operating system. But, since these routines are: (1) part of a subroutine library which is common to all users, (2) problem state routines (cannot execute privileged instructions) and are (3) indistinguishable to the control program from the application programs that use them, we will view these routines as a means of providing standard interfaces between the application programs and the operating system and as a means of making requests for basic services more convenient.

CLASSIFICATIONS AND MEASURES OF OPERATING SYSTEMS

Before continuing the discussion of operating systems, definitions are needed for the various classifications by which operating systems are designed, and by which their performance is judged.

OPERATING SYSTEM PERFORMANCE

The three common measures of operating system performance are: throughput, response time, and availability. *Throughput* is the amount of work (in application program terms, such as the number of a certain type of records read or records written) in a given time period (real or elapsed time). Obviously, for an accurate comparison of throughput for two systems, the systems should be tested on an equivalent set of the same application programs (a benchmark test).

Response time is the time interval from the instant a request is sent to the system until the first character of the reply appears to the user making the request.

Availability refers to the probability of the system being available when a user from the target population requests access. Low availability for a system due to system failure would be highly undesirable for any system. However, a system that allows a single user to capture control of the CPU for long uninterrupted periods of time would not rate well with respect to availability for a target population requiring service to many users concurrently.

Other means of measuring performance are:

• *turnaround time*—the total time required from job submission until job completion (*job* is a set of one or more programs which are executed sequentially in order to achieve some goal, for example a compile, link and execution).

• *security*—the security of one user's files and programs from unauthorized access by another user

• *demand on resources*—the physical resources such as main memory and disk storage that are required to effectively use the system.

BATCH VERSUS INTERACTIVE SYSTEMS

A *batch* operating system is one in which the user has no means of communication with the operating system to affect the execution of the job while the job is being processed. Job commands, programs, and data are "batched" together and run as a single unit of work without intervention by the user. These features are typical of older systems in which the user was expected to enter a job by means of punched cards that defined a complete job stream and not by "interacting" with the system. Batch systems tend to stress throughput over other measures of performance.

An *interactive system* is one in which the user can submit command statements to the operating system during a job, as each job function or program is completed on a dynamic basis as needed. These systems are typical of modern systems in which users work from terminals and have the opportunity and desire to interact with the operating system so that a job can be redirected because of intermediate results instead of having to abort or rerun it in its entirety.

Interactive systems need to stress good response time even at the expense of throughput; otherwise, terminal users will become inpatient (if not irate).

SINGLE-USER VERSUS MULTIUSER SYSTEM

A *single-user* system is one in which the operating system recognizes only one active "user" or application at one time. It is possible for a single application program to interact with several terminals. But the operating system interprets this as a single user, since the multiple-user interaction is the function of the application program and not the operating system (all users are sharing the same single application). This concept does not differ greatly from a program using multiple disk drives. Single-user operating systems are typically used in personal computer systems; popular examples are CP/M and MS-DOS.

A *multiuser* system is one that allows more than one application program to be active during a time period. The operating system recognizes these programs as distinct tasks which can compete for the computing system's resources and allows their execution to proceed concurrently. Nearly all mainframe operating systems are multiuser systems.

MULTIPROGRAMMING VERSUS MULTIPROCESSING

Multiprogramming refers to the concurrent execution of two or more programs. Concurrent does not imply simultaneous execution of machine instructions by more than one program since in any single-CPU computing system, only one program can be in control of the CPU at any given instant.

Multiprocessing refers to computing with more than one CPU. In this case, two or more programs can be executing machine instructions simultaneously. Multiprocessing usually implies multiprogramming but not vice versa.

TIMESHARING

Timesharing is a computing environment in which the users of the computing system are all forced to take turns in sharing the system resources on a regular basis, so that no user can control the CPU for more than a fixed, brief time limit on any turn. The time limit is set by a timeslice mechanism which is enforced by the hardware and governed by the operating system. A *timeslice* is a short amount of time (usually measured in milliseconds) during which a program can control the CPU; if the program does not release the CPU (for example, by requesting an I/O operation) before the timeslice has expired, the system will be interrupted at the end of the timeslice and control will pass to the operating system in order to allow the next user to run. Timesharing is intended for an interactive multiprogramming environment in which typically many users need modest computing service. Although the very nature of any multiprogramming implies a sharing of system resources, it is, in general, the absence of the short, enforced execution turns that differentiates simple multiprogramming from timesharing. Timesharing was developed in response to a terminal-based computing population as opposed to the machine room or batch processing population that had prompted the development of the earlier multiprogramming systems.

In a batch processing environment, there is little concern that a program may monopolize system resources (particularly the CPU) for a longer period of time, as long as resources are generally used efficiently while the system is in operation. Conversely, in an interactive environment, if one program monopolizes the CPU, the majority of the users are left staring at unresponsive terminals. Thus, timesharing provides a means whereby there is a much more equitable sharing of resources during any time interval. Therefore, a major goal in the design of a timesharing system is to provide an environment in which each user has the feeling of a dedicated system; thus, from a performance standpoint, response time is usually stressed over throughput.

REAL-TIME

Real-time refers to a computing environment in which processing must be performed according to strict time constraints. This type of system is used for applications in which timely feedback from a program in execution will affect its continued execution. This is typical of process control applications. Operating systems that are intended to support an environment in which real time applications can be effectively implemented are referred to as real-time operating systems. Instead of stressing throughput or response time over one another, the real-time operating system must be able to distinguish a real-time task from other tasks (that is, it must have a priority system) and once a real-time task is initiated, the task must be allowed to run to completion with a minimum of interruption.

GENERALIZED FUNCTIONAL MODEL OF AN OPERATING SYSTEM

We now turn to the question of how, in general, an operating system does what it does. Obviously the specifics will vary from system to system, but when we view an operating system as a manager of the major resources consisting of the CPU, main memory, I/O devices and files, we have a functional model by which we can study and compare how most operating systems perform their tasks.

CPU MANAGEMENT

Surely no resource is more important for the operating system to manage than the CPU, since no program can execute without it. For this discussion, it is assumed that we have a single-CPU computer. Since the CPU is a resource that must be assigned in its entirety, the management of the CPU is basically concerned with two functions: deciding which program gets to use the CPU and then actually assigning the CPU to the selected program. Of the two functions, assigning the CPU is usually much simpler. In order to accomplish this the operating system simply updates status information in one or more well-defined control blocks, reloads program registers (if the program was running previously), and then loads the program counter with the address of the next instruction to be executed in the program. Once the program counter has been loaded, the CPU assignment is complete, and execution will proceed in the selected program.

In order to decide which program will get to use the CPU, one or more assignment strategies are involved. In a single-user system this strategy can amount to little more than assigning the CPU to the operating system when it is needed (this is largely done automatically through interrupts). Otherwise, the CPU is assigned to the user program. If the operating system in a single-user system contains routines (programs) that can compete for the

CPU among themselves, then strategies similar to those for the multiprogramming system, described next, must be used.

CPU ASSIGNMENT STRATEGIES IN A MULTIPROGRAMMING ENVIRONMENT

We now examine briefly, several of the more common CPU assignment strategies. In practice, an operating system may use one or more of these (or close variations or extensions thereof) in making a selection for CPU assignment.

FIFO In the first in, first out (or first come, first served FCFS) strategy, an entry for each of the active programs is placed in a queue, and CPU assignment is performed according to normal queue processing (that is, assignment is made from one end and additions are added to the other). The queue can be arranged with entries for only those programs that are ready to use the CPU based on the order in which they became ready, or it can be arranged as the list of all programs that have entered the multiprogramming session but have not completed their execution. In the latter arrangement, the programs are ordered as they became active, and each entry in the queue must carry an indicator of whether the program is ready to use the CPU or not (for example, a program may be waiting for an I/O operation to complete, thus it is not ready to use the CPU again). The queue can be serviced so that the top program is always checked for assignment first (thus we have the same assignment order each time) or by making this queue circular, programs can be checked on a round-robin basis.

Priority Queue This strategy is similar to the FIFO strategy, in that assignment is made from a queue. However, instead of placing new requests for assignment at the end of the queue, new requests are placed in the queue according to some priority scheme. In other words, programs ready for assignment are placed in a list ordered by priority, and the list is processed as a queue for assignment. Priorities can be assigned in a number of ways such as: (1) by program identification, (2) by the operator at load time, (3) by the class of program such as real time, interactive or batch, or (4) by demand on resources.

Demand on Resources Demand on resources is usually centered around the demand on the CPU, since this is the resource to be assigned. Demand is based on how much time the CPU is needed. One strategy is to give the program needing more CPU time a higher priority than one requiring less time. This is referred to as longest job first (LJF). However, this technique is not generally satisfactory, since short jobs spend a great percentage of their active lives waiting, and also because this scheme can allow a compute bound program to severely limit the benefits of multiprogramming. The opposite scheme, shortest job first (SJF) is generally better. It provides for better program participation in the multiprogramming, less average wait time, and better throughput, although it does slow down the turnaround time of the programs with longer CPU requirements.

Both SJF and LJF strategies suffer from the problem of finding a reliable method of distinguishing the actual CPU needs. Users can be asked to estimate the time needed, but this is difficult at best and may be intentionally underestimated once the users realize that the low estimate will affect their turnaround time (unless there is a penalty system for poor estimates, but this further complicates the scheme). SJF and LJF schemes can be based on past demands of their respective programs under the assumption that new demands will be similar to past demands. This assumption can have many exceptions and must be implemented carefully if it is to be effective.

Multilevel Queues The concept of selecting programs from a single queue of programs that are ready to use the CPU can be extended to a selection scheme utilizing multiple queues. *A multilevel queue* scheme is one in which programs that are ready to use the CPU are assigned to one of several selection queues based on the highest level of distinction or classification for programs in the system. Selection is then made according to a priority scheme among the queues which governs the order in which the queues are serviced. Possibly, a weighted amount of service is provided to each queue. For example, a program in a higher queue might be allowed twice as much CPU time as a program in a lower queue or, in a weighted round-robin scheme, a higher level queue might be checked for service twice as often as a lower level queue. Of course, the simplest scheme involving multilevel queues is to always start selection with the highest level queue and proceed downward to a lower level queue only when all higher level queues are empty.

There are several ways by which programs are placed in a particular queue. In systems that do not use feedback from the execution cycles of the programs in the system, queue assignment is made when a program enters the system, and this assignment does not change. Two methods of making this type of assignment are: (1) *user designation*, in which the user (programmer) or console operator (in a mainframe environment) designates the classification by which the program will be assigned to a queue; (2) *program type*, in which a program is assigned to a queue according to its type—real-time, interactive, or batch.

Finally, there are feedback, multilevel queue systems in which assignment of a program to a particular queue will vary during its execution cycle according to the execution behavior of the program. In these systems a program moves upward or downward in the queue hierarchy according to an execution code of behavior monitored by the operating system. For instance, in a timesharing system attempting to service many users concurrently, a compute-bound program is not as desirable as an I/O-bound program, which rarely uses up its timeslice before giving up control of the CPU. Therefore, the compute bound program is moved to a lower level queue, which is checked less frequently than the others. If, after a period of banishment to the lower queue, the initially compute-bound program begins to exhibit behavior that is more acceptable, it will be elevated to a higher level queue. Banishment of a program to a lower level queue can result in another problem, called *starvation.* This is a situation in which there is so much activity from the higher level queues that a program is blocked from completing execution because of a lack of attention (that is, service). A possible solution to starvation is to routinely elevate a task to a higher queue after a period of banishment. Thus, any program can eventually run to completion even if there are repeated instances of banishment.

Processes Much of the study of CPU management has been formalized by examining processes and their interaction. A *process* is defined as a program in execution. In this view, two executions of the same program that are active concurrently are two separate processes. A process is further defined to exist in one of three states: running, ready, or waiting (see Figure 5.5). In the *running state,* a process is executing machine instructions, therefore, it is in control of the CPU.

In the *ready state,* a process is ready to use the CPU and is awaiting assignment. In other words, it is ready to run but has not yet been given control of the CPU.

In the *wait state,* a process is waiting for some event (such as an I/O operation) to complete before it can be ready to use the CPU. While a process is in the wait state, it is blocked from using the CPU. In fact, sometimes the term *blocked* is used instead of wait.

By analyzing how processes move from state to state and how they must interact with each other, allocation of the CPU and any other resource can be studied at a higher level of logic before reducing the logical steps to machine level.

Figure 5.5 shows the basic transitions between states for a process. The transition from state to state is not generally symmetrical, and any sequence of states for a particular process must follow three basic rules.

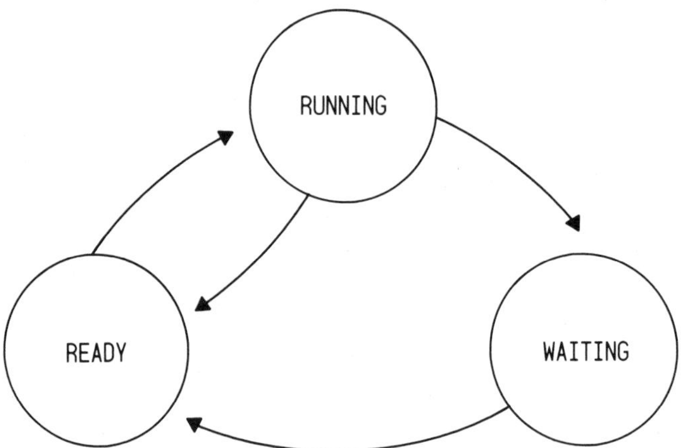

FIGURE 5.5
CONCEPTUAL DIAGRAM OF THE TRANSITION OF STATES FOR A PROCESS

1. A process in the running state can move to either the ready or waiting state. (An example of a change from running to ready state occurs when the operating system gains control of the CPU in order to service an interrupt that is not associated with the process that was running. An example of a change from the running state to the wait state occurs when a process initiates a request for service, such as an I/O request.)

2. A process in the wait state can only move to the ready state. An example of this occurs when the I/O for which a process was waiting has been completed.

3. A process in the ready state can change only to the running state. (This occurs any time the operating system selects a process for assignment of the CPU.)

A major concern in the study of processes is the avoidance of deadlocks. A *deadlock* is a condition in which a process is waiting for an event that cannot occur. The classic example of deadlock is called the "*deadly embrace*". In this situation, two processes (which are cleverly referred to as PROC1 and PROC2) each requires two resources (RES1 and RES2) to complete their execution, however, the two processes request the resources in the opposite order. Through a normal progression of states between PROC1 and PROC2, the situation occurs in which PROC1 has acquired RES1 and is waiting for RES2 to reach completion, while PROC2 has acquired RES2 and is waiting for RES1 to reach completion; thus, the deadly embrace. The operating system must have a policy for resolving deadlocks when they occur. Otherwise, the deadlocked processes are blocked indefinitely. It follows that any other process which is waiting for a resource that is held by a deadlocked process is also deadlocked.

There are several general policies used to avoid deadlocks. One policy is to prevent any process from starting until it can acquire all of the resources it will need to run to completion. Another policy is to simply break deadlocks when they occur by cancelling one process (to be rerun later) so that the other process can continue. There are other possible approaches to the problem of deadlocks, but every useable operating system involving concurrent processes must have a workable solution.

The operating system manages processes by associating a process control block (PCB) with each process. The PCB contains status information about the process (such as its execution state) and usually all information needed to re-enter the running state at the point at which its execution was last suspended (for example, CPU register contents). The PCBs form the elements of the queues from which processes (executing programs) are dispatched, and the PCBs are also the primary physical units used by the operating system to control processes instead of the actual programs that parented the processes. In the larger, more complex operating systems, the PCB and its functions may be split into several control blocks, but the basic concept is the same.

MEMORY MANAGEMENT

Just as no program can execute its instructions without control of the CPU, the CPU cannot fetch instructions for execution unless they reside in main memory; therefore, the management of main memory is a primary concern of an operating system. However, there is a major difference in the way that main memory and the CPU are allocated. The CPU, as described before, is a resource that must be allocated in total to a single program or process. By contrast, main memory is a resource that can be divided and allocated to several programs which are executing concurrently (that is, existing in one of the three process states).

The basic goals of memory management are to:

1. Allocate enough memory to a set of programs so that they can be executed. (In a single-user system this set amounts to one program.)

2. Allow members of the executing program set to be replaced by new programs. In other words, once a program completes its ex-

ecution, reallocate its memory to a new program on a continuing basis.

3. Accomplish goals 1 and 2 with a minimum waste of available main memory.
4. Accomplish the first three goals while providing an efficient use of the computing system resources. We must avoid the situation in which an operating system spends so much CPU time achieving the first three goals that only a small amount of time is left for the application programs.

Single-User Systems In a single-user system, main memory management is relatively simple. It basically amounts to allocating to the operating system the portion of memory that it needs and then allocating the rest to the currently active program. With respect to the allocation of memory to the operating system, a fundamental design choice must be made. Either place the entire operating system in memory such that the portion of memory allocated to the operating system remains constant, or allocate memory in terms of a fixed portion called the nucleus (or kernel) and a variable part. The variable part can then change with respect to content and size during program execution (see Figure 5.6).

The choice of placing the entire operating system in main memory is often referred to as the *resident monitor* approach. The advantages of this approach are that it is simple for the designers to implement, and it performs services efficiently. The efficiency comes from the fact that since all operating system routines are memory resident, any request of the operating system can be processed immediately without possibly having to fetch the necessary routine(s) from secondary storage. The disadvantages come in the areas of flexibility and in the scope of service that can be expected of a resident monitor. Because additional services require additional routines—and thus additional memory requirements—services must be kept to a minimum. Otherwise, the operating system would require so much main memory that very little (if any) would be left for the user. For this reason, resident monitors are usually found only on basic single-user systems such as may be found in some personal computers (CP/M is nearly an example of this design, but even in this case there is some overlaying of routines). It is very unlikely that a memory resident operating system design would be considered for more than a single user, because the overhead associated with multiple users could easily exhaust far too much of available main memory. However, even a moderately sophisticated single-user system will usually employ the design choice that follows.

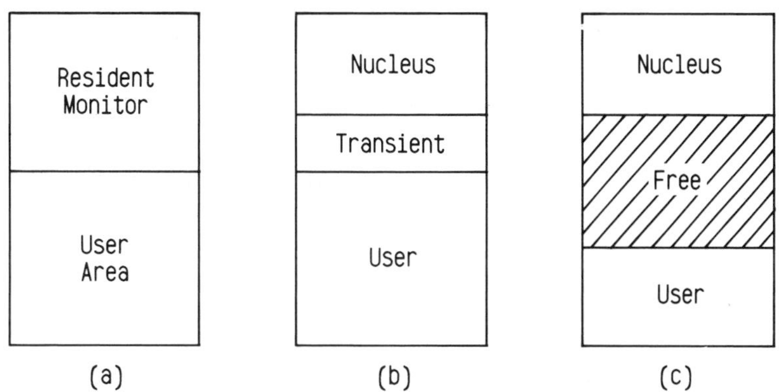

FIGURE 5.6
THREE DESIGNS FOR MEMORY ORGANIZATION IN A SINGLE-USER OPERATING SYSTEM

The second choice is to divide the operating system allocation into a memory resident nucleus and a transient area. The nucleus contains all routines that must be memory resident, such as the first-level interrupt processing routines and other routines which are commonly used by most programs. Other routines are read into the transient area from secondary storage as needed. This approach allows operating system services to be greatly expanded with only a slight decrease in the speed of processing most functions, if the operating system structure is designed properly. Figures 5.6b and 5.6c show two variations of this concept. In Figure 5.6b, the operating system allocation is fixed in size (at least during program execution), but there is a portion of this area in which the contents will vary as needed. In Figure 5.6c, the nucleus is in low memory, and the user program is loaded from the other end of memory downward. The operating system or user program may expand into the free area as needed.

Multiuser Systems Practically all multiuser systems use some variation of the memory resident nucleus with supporting transient routines as their approach to that part of memory management which concerns the operating system itself. This concept has been discussed at two other points in this chapter and will not be pursued further, except to mention that some operating system routines can run in the user area. In this case, the routines are treated in the same manner as application programs (with possibly a higher priority) and are subject to the same rules that govern memory management for user programs.

We now approach the problem of memory management in the user area with multiple users (programs). Perhaps the simplest scheme is to divide the user area into several areas of fixed size (IBM calls these *partitions*) and allocate memory to a program by one of the partitions. In this way the partition is treated as a unit resource, and allocation is done on a "all-or-none" basis. The operating system keeps track of whether a partition is free or not and when available, allocates the entire partition to a program waiting for execution. Partition size is usually determined at system generation or at IPL time and cannot usually be changed during normal operation of the system (IBM's DOS and its derivatives are examples of this type of system). The main disadvantages of this approach are the potential memory waste due to the fixed size allocation and the restriction of larger programs to certain larger partitions. For example, if a 2K program is loaded into a 60K partition, 58K of memory is wasted until the 2K program completes its execution and the partition can be reassigned. To make matters worse, while the 2K program is executing, let us suppose that we want to execute a 50K program, but the largest available partition is 40K. We now find ourselves in the situation of having 108K of unused memory between the two partitions discussed (and probably more among the other partitions), while being unable to load our 50K program for execution (see Figure 5.7).

The advantage in the fixed partition approach is in the reduction of operating system overhead, but the burden of using main memory effectively is placed largely on the user instead of the operating system. In other words, the user must schedule the order in which programs arrive for execution in order to make reasonably efficient use of main memory.

The next approach is to allocate memory in variable amounts according to program size. In this case, the operating system must still keep account of the location and size of each free area of contiguous main memory, just as with fixed partitions. However, with variable allocation of memory, both the location and size of the free blocks vary dynamically. This adds overhead to the operating system, but usually provides for a better utilization of main memory and a gain in performance as the number of users increases. When a request is made to the operating system to load a new program for execution, the operating system must search its list of free memory areas and find a free block that will accommodate the new program. Since the choice of the free memory area that will be used for the loading of a new program will rarely result in an exact fit, a strategy for selecting a free area of memory must be chosen which will minimize memory fragmentation.

Fragmentation: is the condition in which a number of free areas exist in memory that are collectively large enough to accommodate one or more programs waiting to run, yet none of the areas is individually large enough to accommodate another program. Fragmentation is more or less built into a memory management scheme using fixed partitions. By the very nature of such a design, there is little that the operating system can do (other than

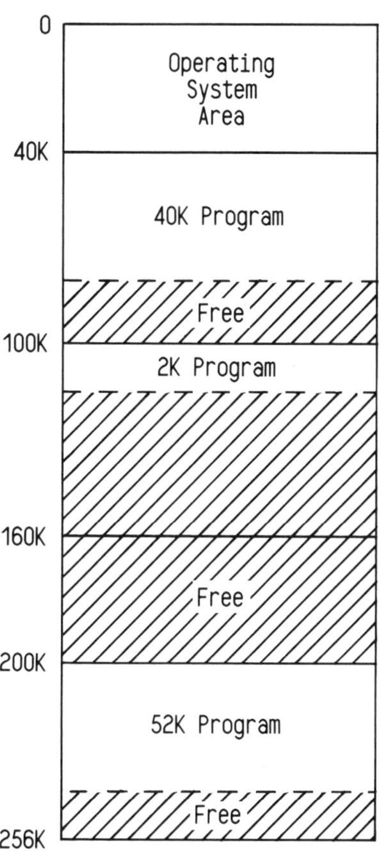

FIGURE 5.7 MULTIUSER SYSTEM WITH A FIXED PARTITION ALLOCATION

use the best fit strategy described later) and the burden of improving the situation is left to the user.

In a system in which memory allocation is based on the size of the program to be loaded, there need be no fragmentation at all when a set of programs are loaded together. The fragmentation problem occurs later as programs complete their executions in a more or less random order (or at least different from the order in which they were loaded). Areas of free memory now exist between active programs that are highly variable in size; but the areas usually will be reassigned, in part, to other programs, and the cycle continues. This can lead to fragmentation (see Figure 5.8). Figure 5.8 depicts a memory assignment sequence that shows how fragmentation occurs. By the time the condition in Figure 5.8c is reached, a 30K program cannot be loaded.

Assignment Strategies: The choice of a strategy for selecting a particular block of free memory to use for loading a new program can have some

FIGURE 5.8
PROCESS BY WHICH FRAGMENTATION OCCURS

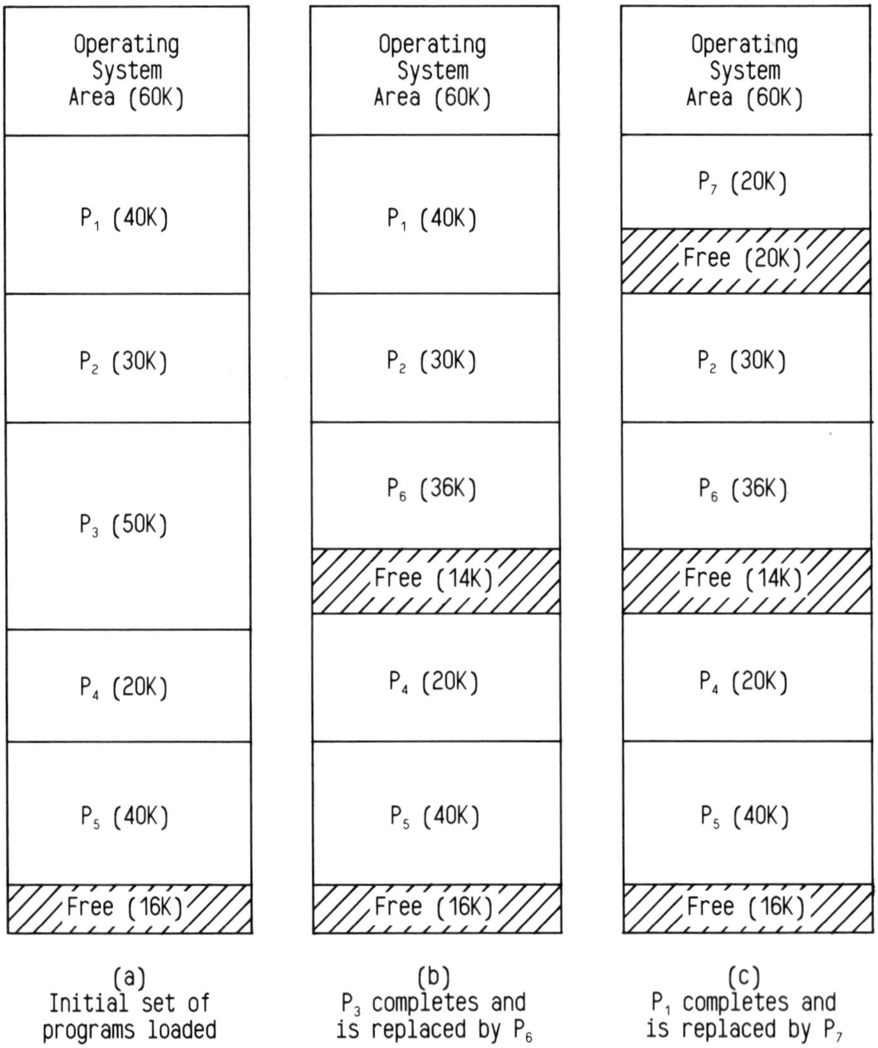

(a) Initial set of programs loaded	(b) P_3 completes and is replaced by P_6	(c) P_1 completes and is replaced by P_7
Operating System Area (60K)	Operating System Area (60K)	Operating System Area (60K)
P_1 (40K)	P_1 (40K)	P_7 (20K)
		Free (20K)
P_2 (30K)	P_2 (30K)	P_2 (30K)
P_3 (50K)	P_6 (36K)	P_6 (36K)
	Free (14K)	Free (14K)
P_4 (20K)	P_4 (20K)	P_4 (20K)
P_5 (40K)	P_5 (40K)	P_5 (40K)
Free (16K)	Free (16K)	Free (16K)

effect on how quickly fragmentation will occur. Three common program placement strategies are now examined.

The simplest strategy is called *first fit*. In this strategy, the operating system scans the list of free memory areas and chooses the first one large enough to hold the new program. As with any of the strategies in a variable allocation system, any unused part of the free area is returned to the free memory list as a smaller block for possible reassignment.

The next placement strategy is called *best fit*. In this strategy the entire list of free memory areas is searched and the block leaving the smallest amount of unused memory is selected. This approach has the advantage of leaving larger blocks of memory for assignment to larger programs, but the amount of unused memory that is returned to the free space list is likely to be too small to be used for another program.

The third strategy is called *worst fit*. This strategy uses the opposite approach of the best fit method, in that the free block providing the greatest amount of unused memory is selected. The philosophy here is that the larger the block of unused memory that is returned to the free memory list, the more likely it will be large enough to accommodate another program.

No matter which strategy is used, if the list of free memory areas is ordered by location, whenever free blocks of adjacent areas of memory occur, they are combined into a single contiguous block, which helps alleviate the problem of fragmentation.

The problem of fragmentation can be eliminated (at least periodically) if the memory management system employs the technique of program *compaction*. In this scheme, whole programs are (periodically) shifted next to each other so that the available free memory exists as one contiguous pool. While largely solving the fragmentation problem, the operating system overhead incurred can be quite costly in terms of CPU time, since it involves not only the physical movement of programs but the relocation of all load-dependent addresses. As long as the programs involved are each physically contiguous, the relocation problem can be solved by the use of a program origin register (POR), which always carries the beginning address of the program that is currently running. In this case, all loaded machine language programs carry zero relative addresses in place of absolute addresses. Therefore, the CPU can create the necessary absolute address by simply adding the zero relative address to the contents of the POR during execution. The POR is transparent to the application programmer and is accessible only in the privileged mode; its contents are updated by the operating system as each program is allowed to run. This scheme was used on the CDC 6600 system, and variations have been implemented on other machines, but a more general form of address mapping known as virtual memory (discussed later) is currently more popular.

Another means of dealing with fragmentation is to provide for some form of scatter loading of a program into several free blocks which are not contiguous to each other. This scheme raises havoc with most real memory addressing modes, so that even relative addresses would have to be changed. The scheme is not generally practical unless some form of address translation is available at execution time. Since address translation is covered in detail under virtual memory, this approach is not discussed further here.

Segmentation and Overlays In previous discussions of memory management, it was assumed that a program is loaded into memory as a single unit into a contiguous area of main memory. This is the case in most real memory systems, but there is a technique that involves both the programmer and the operating system that allows a program to execute from an area of memory that is smaller than the complete program.

The programmer must design the program as a set of segments arranged logically in a tree structure, where each segment is a node in the tree. The topmost node in the tree is called the *root segment* and must be memory resident throughout execution of the program. Any other segment need not be memory resident except for its own execution, at which time the segment plus all other segments along the branch from the executing segment to the root segment must be resident. Segments are designed to overlay sibling segments at each level of the tree below the root (see Figure 5.9), so that the minimum size of memory needed to execute a segmented program is equal to the maximum of the sum of the root and the maximum segment from each level of the tree. If the load points for the nonroot segments can vary, the memory size needed can equal the maximum sum of the segments in any branch of the tree. In either case, a nonroot segment is loaded into memory dynamically by the operating system as it is called by the program.

Figure 5.9 depicts a 38K program consisting of eight segments arranged into a tree of three levels. At any given time, only one segment from each of the levels can be memory resident. If memory allocation is based on segment size, then the program can run in as little as 16K of memory. If segment allocation is done according to fixed size overlay areas, then 18K will be needed.

Virtual Memory All of the memory management techniques that have been discussed so far are intended to provide better utilization of the main memory of a computer. Under a particular set of conditions, each is preferable to the others, but under general conditions, none is totally satisfactory. Two of the basic problems that we face when we approach the choice of any memory management strategy still remain: (1) provide enough memory to allow for optimum use of the other components in our computing system (particularly the CPU) and (2) choose a strategy that minimizes the waste of the memory provided (this will in turn help solve the first problem).

The first problem deals with a condition in which the computer is said to be *memory bound.* This situation arises in a multiprogramming environment in which we have the following three factors: (1) all available memory of useable size has been allocated to active application programs, (2) there are other application programs which are prevented from running because of the lack of memory and (3) the CPU is operating well below full capacity.

The second problem (the waste of memory) has been discussed before, but it usually arises because of fragmentation of available memory or be-

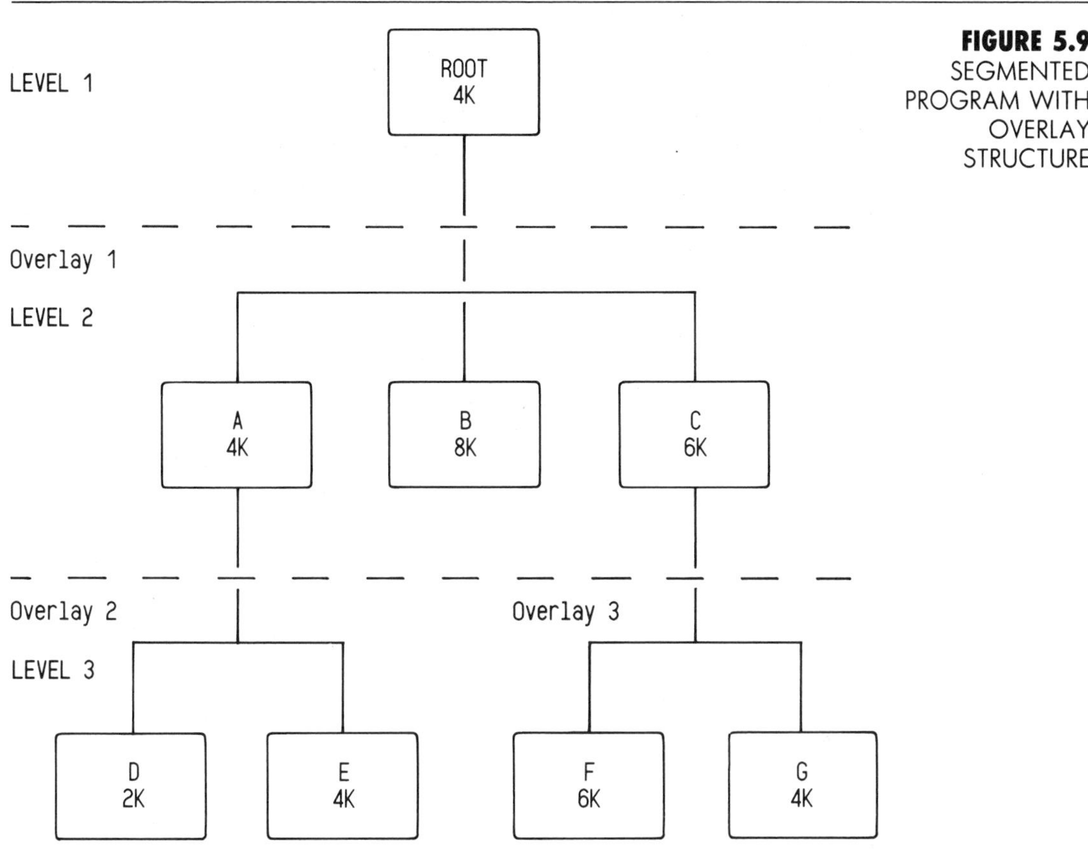

FIGURE 5.9 SEGMENTED PROGRAM WITH OVERLAY STRUCTURE

cause memory has been allocated according to rigid, preset "partitions."

A memory management strategy known as virtual memory offers a solution to both of these problems (although sometimes not very efficiently). *Virtual memory* is a strategy by which the programmer is provided with a logical view of main memory that is called a "virtual memory"; this virtual memory is mapped onto real memory at or during execution. When using a virtual memory system, all activities associated with main memory which support the execution of programs appear to take place in the virtual memory. These activities include: program loading, address modification, subroutine linkage, and the maintaining of the current image of a program during its execution. Since a virtual memory is only a logical view of main memory, it is possible to provide multiple virtual memories within a given system, each of which is mapped onto the same real memory. However, in order to support a multiple virtual memory scheme, more operating system overhead is required. Therefore, for some operating systems such as IBM's DOS/VSE, all users are restricted to a single virtual memory.

Virtual memory (as the name implies) is not real memory; it is a logical concept of a real memory. On the other hand, a program cannot execute nor access data until both are resident in real memory. So it is reasonable to ask just where this virtual memory is. After all, programs and data are represented by a series of bits which must be stored somewhere, even if we are using a logical view of memory. Theoretically, the logical view could reside totally in real memory, and while it would help solve part of problem two (fragmentation), it would not help solve problem one (lack of sufficient memory). Also, the added operating system overhead would probably offset any possible benefits. In practice, the virtual memory initially resides at least partially, if not totally, on an external random access storage device such as disk or drum storage; this external storage is commonly referred to as *backing storage* or *auxiliary storage.* The common practice is to maintain a complete copy of the virtual memory on the auxiliary storage and map from the auxiliary storage to real memory on a demand basis as needed as programs progress through their executions.

The mapping from virtual to real memory could be performed totally by software, but this would lead to such a degradation in execution time that most virtual systems use a combination of hardware and software techniques to perform the mappings. As stated before, in order to initiate the execution of an application program, the program is first loaded into a continuous portion of virtual memory allocated for the program. For this reason, all absolute addresses within the executable code of a program are stored as virtual addresses. The virtual to real mapping is then usually accomplished by loading the object program with its virtual addresses in real memory. Then the virtual addresses are translated dynamically on an instruction-by-instruction basis as the program executes. This address translation is performed largely if not totally by hardware, and designers of the virtual memory operating system make every attempt to minimize any software involvement in the translation process.

One of the great benefits in using a virtual memory scheme is that programs can be divided into "pieces" that can be mapped individually into similar sized blocks of real memory as needed. Furthermore, even though these program "pieces" form a single block of contiguous locations in the virtual memory, they need not be mapped into sections of real memory that form one contiguous block; thus, fragmentation is "virtually" eliminated. Schemes for dividing and mapping virtual memory are described as follows:

Paging: A *page* is a fixed size block of memory. In this scheme, virtual memory is divided into pages, and real memory is divided into *page frames* of page size to hold the pages as they are "paged" in. Pages are contiguous in virtual memory but the corresponding page frames in real memory to which they are assigned are not necessarily contiguous (see Figure 5.10).

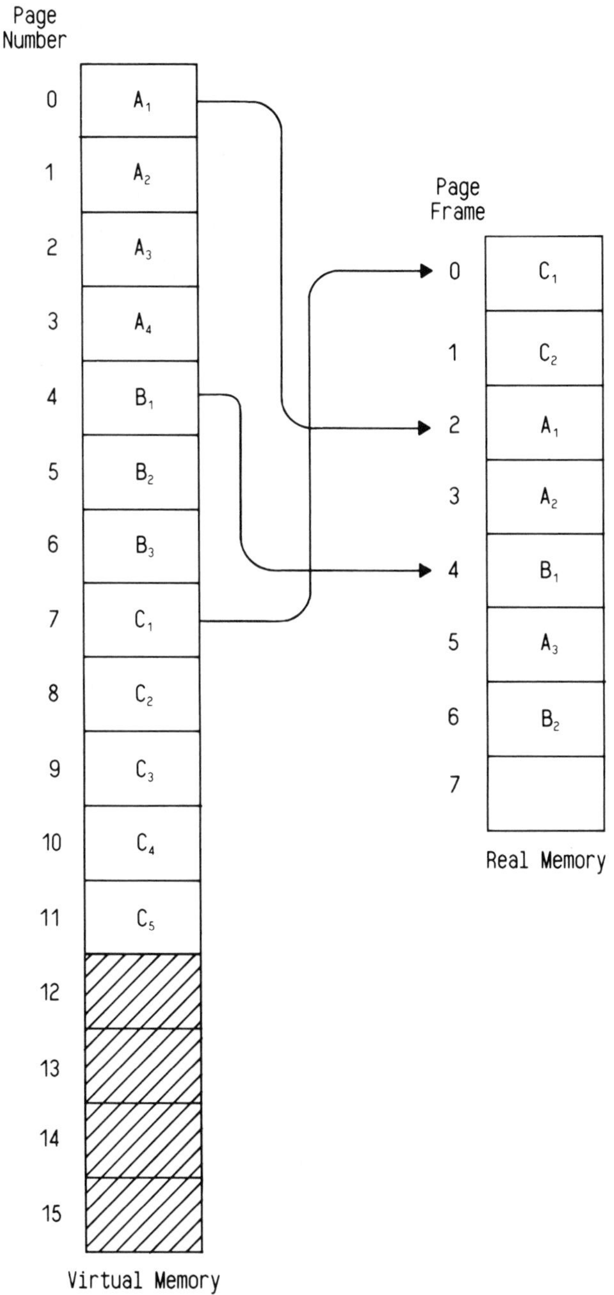

FIGURE 5.10
DIAGRAM OF THREE PROGRAMS (A, B, AND C) WHICH ARE LOADED IN CONTIGUOUS PAGES OF VIRTUAL MEMORY AND MAPPED INTO NON-CONTIGUOUS PAGE FRAMES IN REAL MEMORY

IBM uses page sizes of 2K or 4K bytes, which are not radically different from page sizes used by other vendors (for example, DEC uses 512-byte pages for the VAX-11 machines). In general, a larger page size can result in less paging activity because, with fewer pages needed to contain a program, there will normally be fewer instances of crossing page boundaries during program execution. Thus, the likelihood of needing a nonmemory resident page is reduced during program execution (although much of this effect can be achieved by clustering pages of smaller size). Conversely, a smaller page size generally reduces the waste of real memory, because the virtual memory allocation for a program must be made in whole pages. Therefore, the last page of the set allocated to a program will be, on the average, only half used. When this last page is loaded into a page frame, there is a "mini" form of fragmentation. Thus, the smaller page size reduces this type of fragmentation. In practice, system designers must choose a page size that achieves an acceptable balance of benefits from the two extremes. Regardless of the page size, there is a general scheme for the selection of which page frames will be used for paging virtual memory pages in and out of real memory. The most active pages in the immediate past tend to be used again, and thus an attempt is made to allow these pages to remain in real memory. However, before any page is paged out and its page frame reassigned, the page must be checked to see if it was changed during its current stay in real memory (indicated by status bits). If the page was not changed while in real memory, its page frame can be reused with no further action. Otherwise, the page must be copied out to its virtual memory image on the backing store before it can be overlaid. It is obviously more efficient with respect to execution time to be able to reuse page frames without having to first copy out a changed page. Therefore, page frame selection also involves an attempt to minimize paging out activity.

The process by which a virtual address is translated into a real address under a virtual memory scheme using paging is described in the following paragraphs.

In this scheme, each virtual address is divided into two parts—a page address and a displacement within the page (see Figure 5.11). By using a page size which is equal to some power of two such that page size = 2^n, the low order n bits of the virtual address always specify the displacement within the desired page. The remaining high-order bits of the address specify the number of the page in the virtual memory. This page number corresponds to the view that the virtual memory is organized as a sequential string of numerically consecutive pages just as real memory is viewed as a sequential string of numerically consecutive words.

Translation of the virtual address to its run time real address is therefore accomplished by simply replacing the page number portion of the address

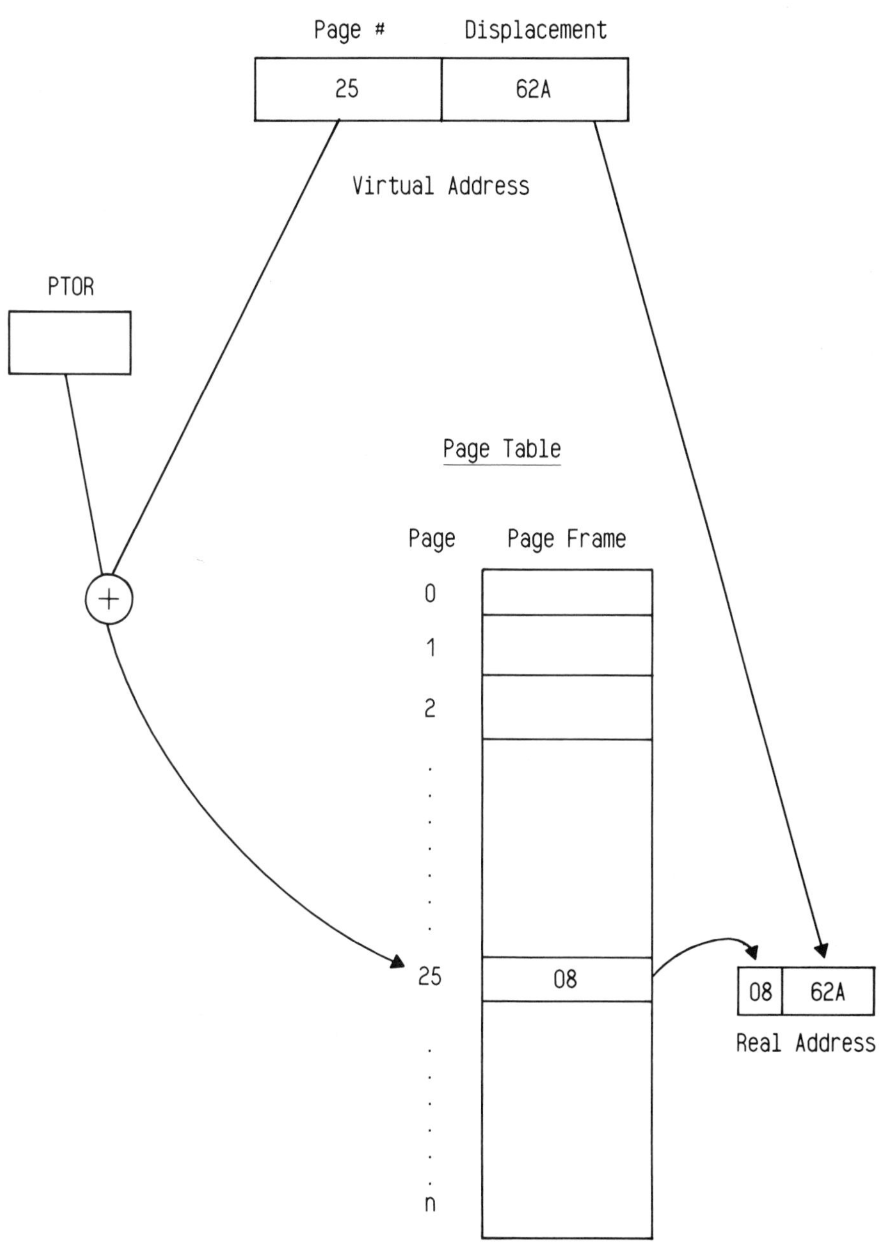

FIGURE 5.11
DIAGRAM OF CONVERSION OF VIRTUAL ADDRESS 2562A TO REAL ADDRESS 0862A USING A VIRTUAL MEMORY SCHEME WITH PAGING.

by the corresponding number of the real memory page frame that holds the page.

The basic procedure for accomplishing this is to maintain a page table in real memory ordered on page numbers in which there is an entry for each page in the virtual memory. Each page table entry contains the number of the page frame that holds the page (if the page is in main memory) and a valid/invalid status bit that specifies whether the desired page is currently in real memory or not. The CPU contains a register that points to the beginning of the page table (the Page Table Origin Register). The PTOR allows address translation to be performed automatically by the hardware (assuming the page is currently loaded into real memory). The CPU can simply use the page number as a displacement which can be added to the contents of the PTOR and thus fetch the desired page frame number from the page table.

Depending on the addressing scheme of the computer involved (that is, byte addressable or word addressable) the page number can be multiplied by bit shifting in order to derive the proper page table displacement. Thus, for pages currently residing in main memory, a virtual address is translated with a single additional main memory fetch, some very minor machine operations, and no software involvement. The operating system does not become involved in the translation process unless the page is not in main memory.

If an address translation is attempted for a page which is not in main memory, a *page fault* interrupt occurs, and control passes to the operating system so that it can bring the desired page into memory from the backing store before continuing with the execution of the program that caused the page fault. Page faults are detected by the CPU when it fetches a page table entry that has the valid/invalid bit set to "invalid." When a virtual system reaches a condition of excessive paging, it is said to be *thrashing*. Thrashing is a major concern in the design and implementation of virtual systems. When this condition occurs, the operating system spends so much of the available system time in control of the CPU to perform the paging that very little useable work is accomplished.

Segmentation: In this scheme, a program in the virtual memory is organized into logical segments which are variable in length. The mapping from virtual to real memory is performed on whole segments instead of fixed size pages. In concept, this process is similar to the segmentation scheme used for overlays in a pure real memory environment, except that the roll-in/roll-out sequence is performed totally by the operating system and is transparent to the user. Also, in this segmentation scheme, the segments can all be totally disjoint in real memory and no memory resident root segment is required in order to execute other segments. Although segmentation provides a means of extending memory, it is less satisfactory in solving the problems of fragmentation. Fragmentation is still a problem, because real memory must be allocated in variable size blocks of contiguous memory that can vary greatly in size. Therefore, memory must be assigned using a strategy such as best fit, worst fit, or first fit, just as was done in a pure real memory system. On the other hand, combining segmentation with paging is highly satisfactory.

Paged Segmentation: This third scheme for implementing virtual memory, achieves most of the advantages of both the segmentation and paging schemes described previously. Programs in the virtual memory are organized in segments containing an integral number of pages. Usually the number of pages in a segment is variable (and should be for true segmentation), but some vendors have used fixed size segments in addition to fixed size pages (an example was the RCA Spectra 70/46 System). Mapping from virtual memory to real is done on a segment-by-segment basis. However, the pages within a segment need not be loaded into contiguous page frames in real memory. This greatly improves the fragmentation problem in real memory, since only the last page in a segment is subject to less than full utilization. Normally, the operating system will try to load complete program segments, which gives the programmer some control over the likelihood of the occurrence of page faults, but this is not a necessary condition for a program to execute. Even if a complete segment is initially loaded, page replacement strategies may cause the reallocation of page frames to other segments prior to the completion of the original segment's execution.

Since each segment consists of logically contiguous locations, each segment must be accompanied by its own page table. Therefore, each time a segment is loaded into real memory, its page table must also be loaded and made current. This scheme requires a two-level translation process. Thus, every virtual address is composed of three parts; a segment number, a page number, and a displacement.

Address translation is achieved by using a Segment Table Origin Resister (STOR), which points to the beginning of a table containing an entry for each segment in the virtual memory. Each segment table entry contains the beginning address of the page table for the corresponding segment, together with a valid/invalid bit indicating if the segment (or at least part of it) is currently memory resident. In a process similar to that described for paging, the CPU adds the segment number from the virtual address to the STOR to gain the displacement into the segment table. Then the CPU adds the page number from the virtual address to the page table address found in the segment table to obtain the desired page frame number from the corresponding page table entry (see Figure 5.12). This process requires three memory fetches to obtain a main memory operand instead of the one fetch required for a real memory system. Therefore, the main disadvantage in

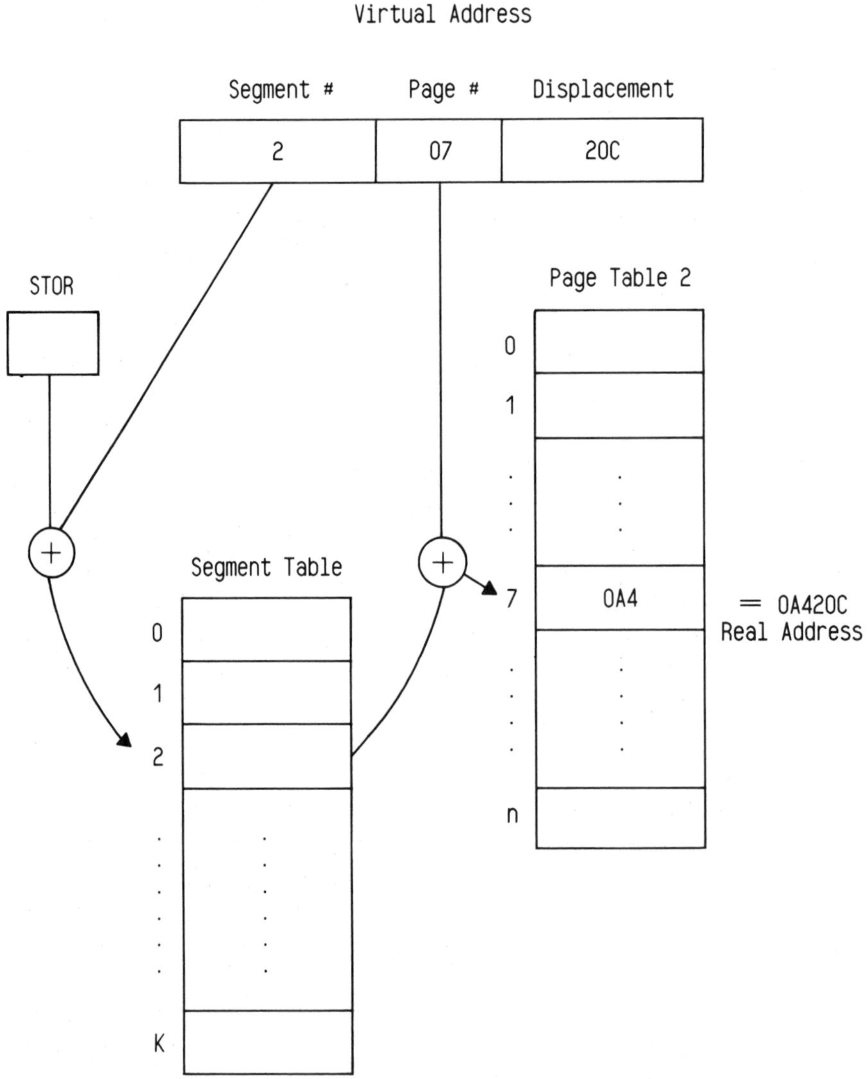

FIGURE 5.12
TRANSLATION OF VIRTUAL ADDRESS 20720C TO REAL ADDRESS 0A420C IN A PAGED SEGMENTATION SCHEME OF VIRTUAL MEMORY

this scheme is in system performance (namely, slower execution speed). Fortunately, this situation can be greatly improved by the use of associative array registers or some sort of cache memory.

Once again, the translation process is accomplished by a hardware (or a combination of hardware and firmware) procedure and the operating system does not become involved unless there is a segment fault or a page fault within a partially resident segment. When this occurs. the operating system must execute the necessary procedures to bring the missing segment or page into memory from the backing store.

As mentioned before, in using only the basic translation technique, a virtual memory system that employs just paging or just segmentation requires an extra memory fetch for every virtual address that must be translated. Likewise, a virtual system using the paged segmentation combination needs two extra memory fetches per translation. Compared to an equivalent real memory system in which most main memory operands themselves are obtained with a single fetch, the overhead can cause the number of fetches in retrieving a simple operand to double or triple due to translation. Thus, the speed of the host computer is significantly degraded. One technique that greatly improves this situation is the use of *associative array registers* (AARs).

AARs comprise a high speed associative memory within the CPU (that is, all registers can be accessed simultaneously by the CPU). These registers contain the page frame locations of the most recently referenced pages currently residing in main memory (or some other active subset of the resident pages). Translation for an address within one of the pages referenced by the AARs can be completed (approximately) an order of magnitude faster than using the page and segment tables. Unfortunately, it is currently not usually considered cost effective to provide enough AARs to cover every possible page of real memory. Therefore, a compromise scheme is normally used. (Actually, RCA used a design on the Spectra 70 virtual machines that did cover every page in memory with a register for immediate translation, but the design for these machines involved another compromise that required a fixed-size real memory on which fixed-size virtual memories were mapped.) Studies have shown that by providing a relatively modest ratio of AARs to real memory page frames, a considerable improvement in address translation time is usually accomplished. Because the CPU can perform a search of the AARs in parallel with initialization of the search through the segment and/or page tables, and the table search can be aborted if translation is successful in the AARs. Otherwise, the slower process is continued to completion. The improved address translation time comes from the sequential nature of programs which results in a high probability that the next address to be translated will lie within a page from a small set of the most recently used pages. In the System/370 computers, IBM used 16 to 128 AARs, depending on the product model.

A final comment on virtual memory is needed before we move to the discussion of the management of the next major resource. There has been an effort to show how virtual memory can greatly reduce, if not solve, the problems of memory fragmentation and lack of main memory (a memory-bound system). These problems needed solutions in order to improve the degree of multiprogramming that could be achieved with a given system. However, the implication that the more programs we have multiprogramming the better, is not necessarily true. In fact, anytime the CPU is near full utilization (saturation), the addition of more programs to the multiprogramming activity will simply increase the operating system overhead and, therefore, degrade system performance instead of improving it. Thus, as it turns out, multiprogramming is just one more activity that is best practiced in moderation; otherwise, the results can be most disappointing.

DEVICE MANAGEMENT

In Chapter 1 a general description was given of how data is passed between main memory and its external environment (through I/O processors, DMA controllers, or CPU-directed I/O). However, the emphasis in that discussion was on the functions of the primary subsystems, not the I/O devices that form the external environment. This approach was appropriate then, because if we ignore the individual characteristics of specific I/O devices, we can treat I/O operations generically and concentrate on basic concepts first. In reality, there is great variation in the physical characteristics of specific types of I/O devices, and these characteristics directly affect the manner in which we can access the devices and the manner in which data is transferred to and from them.

For example, consider some of the differences between a line printer and a disk drive. The printer is a relatively slow-speed device that can only be used for physically sequential output of fixed length records and should not be shared by concurrent processes. Conversely, a disk drive is a relatively high-speed device that can be accessed randomly (at least at the track level) for input or output involving fixed or variable length records and can be shared by concurrent processes. Both the line printer and disk drive require control information, but the control information that directs printer spacing is normally carried as part of the output record (for example, the first byte of the print record), whereas a disk drive requires separate control commands (for such tasks as positioning the access arm) before any I/O occurs.

Any routine that controls the I/O operations for a particular device must be designed to accommodate the kinds of differences that were just described. In addition, more primitive functions involving the synchronization of I/O operations must also be performed. For example, many I/O devices or their controllers contain storage buffers that can hold a physical record. The purpose of these buffers is to allow the I/O processor (channel), DMA controller, or even the CPU to send (or receive) a complete physical record (data block) to the buffer at a relatively high speed and then allow the device to work with the data in its buffer at its own speed. Thus, the faster component is freed for other tasks. In order for this buffered I/O process to function properly, the device must be checked to see if the buffer is free to receive data or ready to send data, as the case may be. Otherwise, a channel could overlay print records in the buffer faster than they could be printed, resulting in an abbreviated, chaotic, and highly unpredictable form of the intended output (in other words, a grand mess)!

By now, it should be evident that routines which directly control I/O operations are not trivial and are highly device-dependent. Fortunately, I/O control routines (sometimes called *I/O drivers* or *device drivers*) are not dependent on the applications that use them (that is, any process that needs to write a line of output to the same printer can use the same driver). Therefore, by including in the operating system an I/O driver for each device type attached to a computing system, the operating system can perform all low-level and device-dependent functions. Thus the applications programmer can be spared much of this tedium that was partially described and can write programs that function at a higher logical level, while the lowest level functions are left to the device drivers. Actually, there are typically one or more logical levels between the device drivers and the application programs, but these relate to file management, which is covered in the next section.

Physical Device Tables In order to provide the necessary I/O services and also to control the allocation and use of I/O devices, the operating system must have a complete description of all the I/O devices attached to the computing system it serves and controls. There are several variations on how this information can be provided to the operating system, but one basic technique is to provide the operating system with a global physical device table (PDT) that contains an entry for each device attached to the computing system, and a separate device descriptor table (DDT) for each type of device used (see Figure 5.13). Each entry in the PDT will contain basic information

Device	Physical Address*	On Line Flag	Pointer to Request Queue	Pointer to DDT
CDRDR	004	Y	FREE	A(DDT1)
PRNTR1	006	Y	A(PRTQ)	A(DDT2)
PRNTR2	007	N	NULL	A(DDT2)
DISK1	141	Y	A(DK1Q)	A(DDT3)
DISK2	142	Y	FREE	A(DDT3)
.	.	.	.	.
.	.	.	.	.
.	.	.	.	.

*In this scheme, the first, second, and third characters represent the I/O channel, the device controller (if any), and the I/O port (or slot) respectively.

FIGURE 5.13
PHYSICAL DEVICE TABLE

concerning the physical location of the device (such as the channel and/or port to which it is attached), the availability of the device, and the location of the DDT that supplies the information concerning the individual characteristics of the device. Normally, a queue of requests pending for the use of each device is maintained by the operating system so that a request for a device which is currently busy can be scheduled for service when the device becomes available. If a device (such as a disk drive) can be used by more than one process concurrently, this information is carried in the DDT for the device, and its use is scheduled accordingly.

When an I/O request is made for a particular device, the operating system can first check to see if the device is on line. Then, if the device is free, the request can be processed immediately. Otherwise, the request will be placed on the request queue for that device for service later.

Logical and Virtual Devices Allowing the operating system to handle requests for the use of I/O devices certainly improves the useability of a computing system. However, the process that was described in the previous section requires that the operating system be informed of the specific physical device that is needed (such as which printer or which disk drive). This may be simple enough on a personal computer system, but on a large mainframe system it is often inconvenient, if not undesirable, for the applications programmer to specify this information. After all, the applications programmer does not usually care which physical device is assigned to provide a particular service, as long as the service is provided correctly. In addition, if a particular process requests a certain physical device, the process will have to wait until the exact device that was requested is available for use, even though there may be other devices of the same type which are free for use. Clearly, this would greatly affect system performance and efficiency.

This problem is greatly reduced, and programming convenience is improved by the use of logical devices. A *logical device* is a device that is defined by the programmer and whose characteristics form a subset of at least one of the physical devices attached to the computing system. In this way, the operating system can assign the logical device to an appropriate physical device at run time. Often logical devices are required to have special names, such as: SYSIN, SYSOUT, SYSLST, or SYS005. In any case, the operating system will maintain a scheme whereby logical device names are recorded with their current physical device assignments.

Virtual devices carry the concept of logical devices one step further. A *virtual device* is a logical device whose mapping to a physical device does not necessarily preserve the individual characteristics of the logical device. A common use of virtual devices is SPOOLing (where SPOOL is an acronym for Simultaneous Peripheral Operation OnLine). In a multiuser system with one printer, if requests for printed output were assigned directly to the printer on a process-by-process basis, it is possible that frequently, several active processes would be prevented from concurrent execution due to the necessity of the dedicated assignment of the printer. On the other hand, if each process could be allowed to send its printer output to a temporary storage area on a disk drive that is used to simulate a printer for each process, then the processes could execute concurrently to completion (that is, multiprogram) and at a higher speed (disks are faster than printers). Later, the simulated printer output for each process can be directed to the real printer by the operating system at maximum printer speed, since the computation required to produce the output has already been performed, and an improved utilization of system resources is gained.

Device Independence The real goal of the use of logical devices is to provide the programmer with device independence. Device independence means that the programmer is freed from any involvement with the assignment of physical devices. At the very least, this implies independence from selecting a particular device from a set of the same type. On a more general level, it can mean that device assignments will be made at run time by the operating system to any device that satisfies the minimum logical requirements specified by the programmer. In other words, an output file could not be directed to a card reader, but it could be directed to any one of several different, appropriate output device types. Device assignment may be, and often is, redirected by the terminal or system operator at run time. However, this does not affect the device independence afforded the programmer.

Some operating systems such as UNIX, with its stream-directed I/O, provide a very high degree of device independence. IBM's OS-derived systems basically limit device independence to a device class, and their DOS/VSE offers little more than moving devise assignment to the job command language (JCL).

FILE MANAGEMENT

The last section explained how device management by the operating system can improve the convenience and useability of the computer. But, if the operating system limited its service to just device management in obtaining data from external devices for executing programs, the applications programmer's job would be far from convenient. For example, the creation and/or completion of I/O processor routines (such as the channel programs described in Chapter 1) is not a function of device management, since these routines are, in general, application-dependent. Device management handles the allocation of I/O devices and those low-level functions for communicating with the devices that are not application-dependent. By contrast, many I/O functions such as the completion of channel programs that we as applications programmers have grown accustomed to, are indeed application-dependent. These application-dependent functions, as well as any others that allow us to impose or conform to logical organizational structures for external sets of data (files), form the basis of the file management portion of the operating system.

In this functional model of an operating system, file management has one distinct difference from the other three resource managers. CPU management, memory management, and device management are primarily concerned with the management of the physical resources of a computing system (namely, the CPU, main memory, and the I/O devices), while file management is primarily concerned with the management of a set of logical resources known as files.

A *file* is an organized collection of information (usually directed toward some purpose) that is defined by the programmer and recognized by the operating system. The basic organizational unit of a file is a *logical record* (record for short), which represents the set of data transferred to or from a file for logical level file operations (such as READ, and WRITE). A *physical record* is the block of data actually transferred to or from an I/O device. On unit record devices such as card readers and line printers, the logical and physical records are usually the same, but on mass storage units such as disks and tapes there is often a considerable difference. For example: mass storage units require that each physical record be separated from its neighbors by gaps in order to allow proper location and transfer of the block. When logical records are relatively short (such as card images), it is common practice to combine several logical records into one physical record. This process is called *blocking* (see Figure 5.14a). Blocking can improve the utilization of available space on the device and can reduce the number of physical I/Os required to process a file (the value of this is explained later).

Another example of the difference between logical and physical records occurs when disk tracks are divided into sectors. In this case, every physical

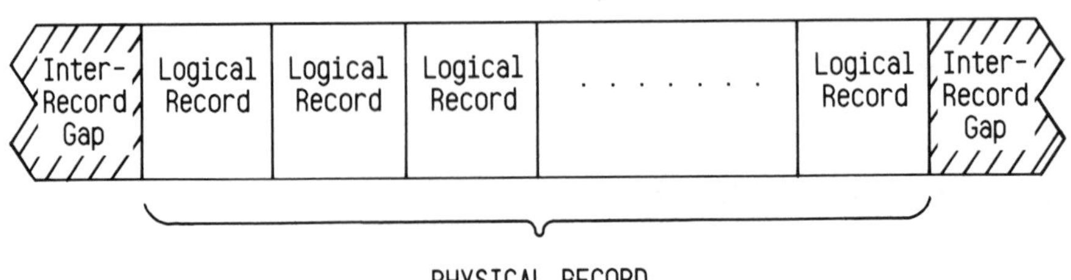

FIGURE 5.14a
BLOCKING OF LOGICAL RECORDS INTO ONE PHYSICAL RECORD

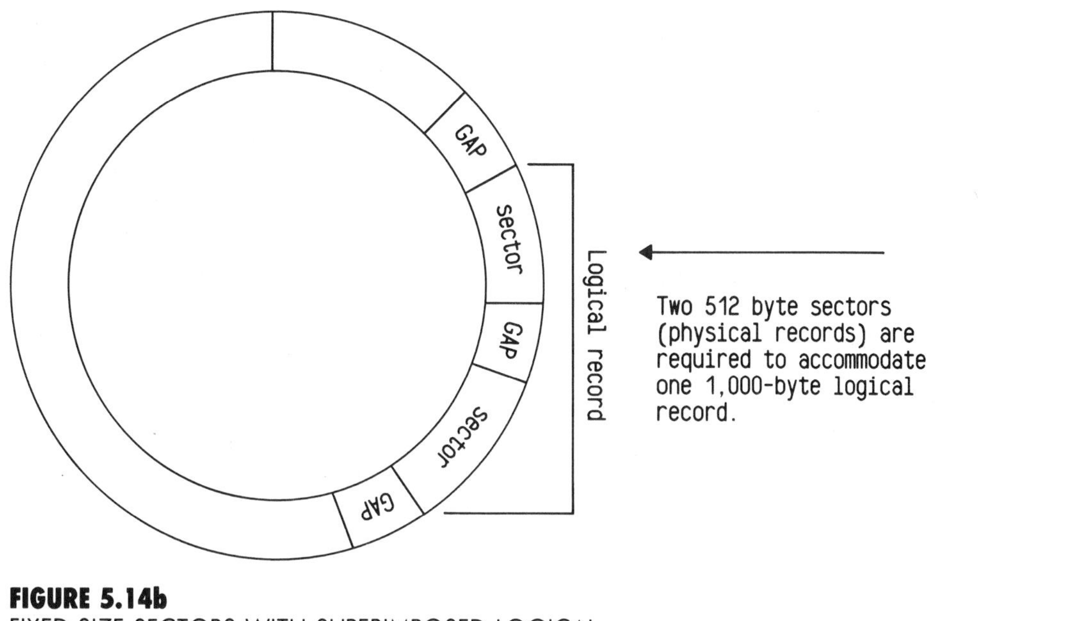
GAP
Sector
GAP
Sector
GAP
Logical record
Two 512 byte sectors (physical records) are required to accommodate one 1,000-byte logical record.

FIGURE 5.14b
FIXED-SIZE SECTORS WITH SUPERIMPOSED LOGICAL RECORD OF LONGER LENGTH

record on the disk drive is exactly the size of the sector size (for example, 512 bytes). Logical records are then superimposed within or across sectors, as the case may be (see Figure 5.14b).

Just as each of the major resource managers of the operating system controls the allocation and use of the resources they manage, file management must control the allocation and use of files. But in order to provide this service, the file management software must create and maintain a logical view of the physical data that can be used by the applications programmer. Therefore, file management should be considered functionally as a layer of software between device management and the application program that maps the programmer's file-oriented view of the data onto the physical representation of the data.

The concept of multiple layers of software within the operating system can be carried much further. Indeed, Madnick and Alsop (1969) defined a modular file system (typical of mainframe operating systems) that contained six distinct sublayers. These functional refinements, which reveal the many sublayers within an operating system, must be considered in the design of an operating system. This chapter does not go into this much detail, however, it will occasionally be useful to view file management in terms of two sublayers. For the most part, this discussion will treat file management as a single (although possibly thick) layer of software through which an application program communicates with the basic operating system layer containing the other resource managers in order to obtain file-level operations.

The position that file management occupies compared to the other components of an operating system becomes more evident when we consider that for most operating systems, it is possible for the applications programmer to bypass file management functions altogether and request services directly from the I/O device manager. However, this would require the programmer to create his or her own file system (if a logical system were desired) or to operate purely at the physical I/O level.

For example, using the IBM mainframe model developed in Chapter 1, at a minimum, the programmer would have to write the necessary channel programs required for each I/O operation and then issue a SVC instruction requesting I/O service when needed. However, this would provide only physical level I/O. Any services involving a logical structure for the external data would require substantial, additional programming. Clearly, for most applications it is more convenient and faster (not to mention safer) to leave file management to the operating system.

From the user's perspective, the principal functions of file management are:

1. Creation and maintenance of file directories
2. File creation and deletion
3. Support for file processing
4. Allocation and protection of files

Creation and Maintenance of File Directories Each of the principal functions listed previously, as well as other internal functions of file management that are not immediately obvious to the user, involve the use of directories. A minimal *directory* is a data structure that is used to link symbols (or indentifiers) to their respective locations. Thus, file directories must link file names (or identifiers) to their respective locations, and in addition to the locations, they usually include descriptive information about each file as well.

Directories provide the principal means by which an operating system can locate and/or identify a particular file. Therefore, any file processing activity requires, at least initially, the use of a directory to locate and gain access to the file. This brings up another point. Typically, information concerning who may access a file and in what mode (READ, WRITE, or UPDATE) is carried in the directory. The operating system uses this information to allow or deny access to the file by a given user.

Directories are also involved in both the creation and deletion of files. Because directories are the primary means by which a file is located or identified, the creation of a file requires the addition of an entry to the proper directory(ies), while the deletion of a file requires the removal of its directory entries.

There are a number of variations as to the organization, location, and content of file directories, but the basic concepts involved are derived from two general types of file directories: the device directory and the master file directory.

A *device directory* is a file directory of all the files located on a particular device (or volume for that device, such as the current floppy disk mounted in a disk drive). IBM has traditionally referred to a device directory as a Volume Table Of Contents (VTOC). Practically all operating systems use device directories, since the more common mass storage devices allow interchangeable volumes to be mounted on the device (such as a disk drive or tape drive). In a small computing system such as a personal computer, device directories may be the only directories used by the operating system. This is because there is likely to be only a small number of relatively low-capacity storage devices attached to the system and typically the system will only serve one user at a time. Generally, the device directory will be constructed as a one-dimensional table (a list), as in Figure 5.15.

If a multiuser system with larger and more numerous mass storage devices relied solely on device directories, the time to locate a particular file would be substantially increased. Therefore, the usual solution to this problem is to use a Master File Directory (MFD), which is based on a logical organization of all files, in conjunction with the device directories.

Volume ID		
File 1 ID	Location	Description
File 2 ID	Location	Description
File n ID	Location	Description

FIGURE 5.15
DEVICE DIRECTORY

The MFD will then contain the logical information about the file such as its name, the owner, the type of file, and protection information about access to the file. As to the location of the file, the MFD will simply carry the identification of the volume on which the file resides and possibly a pointer to the appropriate entry in the device directory for the volume. The device directory contents generally relate to the physical properties of the file, such as its physical location and how it was allocated (contiguous, linked blocks, or whatever). In addition the device directory may possibly duplicate some of the protection information.

A typical organization of the MFD is based on file ownership, so that each user has a subdirectory (or directories) based on the files that he or she has created (see Figure 5.16). In order to provide uniqueness in file identification, usually the name of each file created by a particular user is formed by prefixing the user name or ID to the file name selected by the user (for example, user SMITH's TAXFILE has the name SMITH.TAXFILE). Figure 5.16 can be generalized into a tree structure of several levels, each denoting classification refinement.

File Creation and Deletion In order to create a file, file management must perform three basic tasks:

1. Allocate space for the file.

FIGURE 5.16 TWO-LEVEL MASTER FILE DIRECTORY

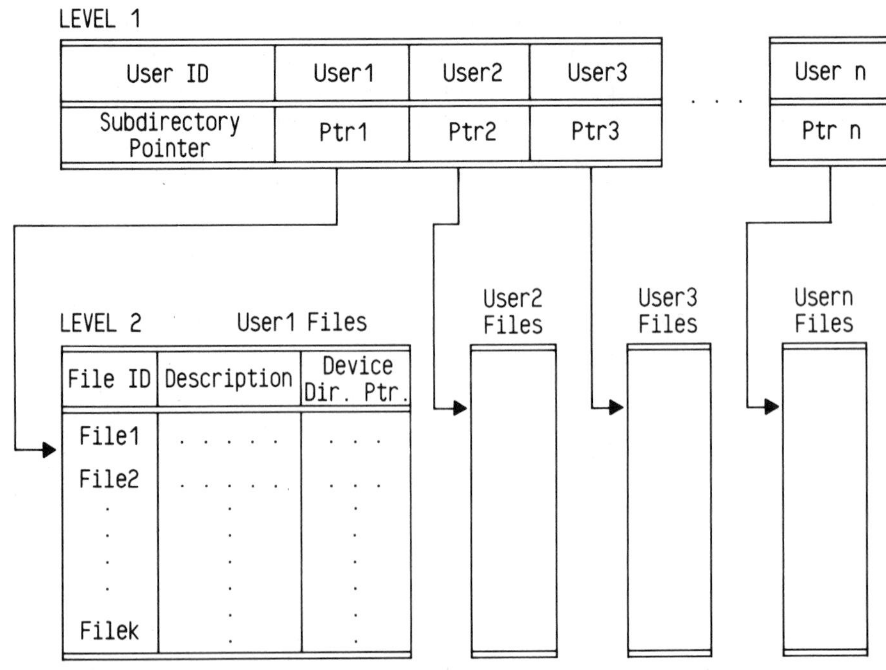

2. Build the appropriate directory entries for the file (described in the previous section).
3. Load the initial set of records into the file for processing (this may be viewed as part of file processing activity, but it will be introduced here).

In order to allocate storage for the file, file management must maintain a list (or other structure) of the free space available for allocation. If the required storage is available (or if a predetermined minimum amount of storage is available to start file creation) the process continues.

External storage allocation may be limited to physically contiguous allocation (as is required for any tape volume) but some systems (particularly larger mainframe systems) allow linked and/or indexed allocation of external storage.

Contiguous allocation is the simplest for the operating system to support, but it presents the same disadvantage that we encountered with main memory allocation, namely fragmentation. Fragmentation can be reduced and momentarily eliminated through periodic compaction of all valid files into one contiguous area of the device. For mass storage devices, this is usually achieved by copying the files from a volume on one device to a similar volume on another device of the same type. However, this procedure can be very time consuming (and thus inefficient) in a multiuser system where many files are created and destroyed on a continuing basis. In addition, contiguous allocation poses a problem for file growth, so that the file owner is basically given two choices. Either the file must be recreated in order to expand it, or the initial allocation during file creation must provide for extra storage for possible file growth. The first choice leads to wasted system time, while the second choice can result in a poor utilization of available space on a given device.

The problem of fragmentation is greatly reduced if linked allocation is used. In this case, storage is allocated to a file in terms of relatively smaller, fixed-size pieces or blocks (such as a single disk track or track segment). Each block carries a pointer to its successor, so that the file blocks form a linked list. The device directory carries pointers to the first and last blocks of each file so that the file can be located or extended with minimum effort. There is a small amount of storage overhead required for the pointer in each block. However, the major disadvantage of linked allocation is, that unless the system also provides for indexing, the only type of file processing that is efficient is sequential processing; and, random processing is essentially impractical. By contrast, contiguous file allocation accommodates random file processing fairly easily.

The third type of allocation is indexed allocation. In this scheme, for every file that is created as an indexed file, file management will create an index (or directory) that matches each record ID with its physical location. The index is designed for rapid searching (for example, it has a structure like an ordered table or tree), so that when random processing of a file is desired a record is obtained by locating its entry in the index and then retrieving the record (or the block that contains it) with one access to the random access device. Of course, the index itself may reside on the storage device and in this case, one or even a few additional READ operations from the device may be required to locate the record entry in the index. This is generally acceptable with respect to efficiency and is a vast improvement over the alternative of locating each random record by sequential searching. There is the disadvantage of the storage overhead required to store the indexes and system time required to create and maintain them.

Operating systems designed to support large files will generally support indexing, while operating systems designed for personal computers and non-commerical, minicomputer systems generally do not. For example, all of the IBM mainframe operating systems support indexing, while MS-DOS and UNIX do not.

The initial load of a new set of records into a file can be treated as the file processing activity of writing new records to a previously empty file. However, an initial load phase of file creation can often be much more efficient than simply inserting records into a file that was initially created as empty, particularly if the file is to be ordered and/or indexed. Since the index itself is usually ordered, it is usually much more efficient to allow the operating system to create the major portion of an index or ordered file as a single comprehensive activity. In this way, the physical location of records and index entries can be chosen to provide the most efficient processing of the required logical order. For example, if a logically sequential file is created such that logically adjacent records are normally located in corresponding adjacent physical locations, any sequential processing of the file will be much more efficient than if the logical and physical order of the records have little correlation.

The deletion of a file is relatively straightforward and is achieved by simply returning the space allocated to the file to the free space list and removing the entries for the file from the directory system.

File Processing Operations The typical logical level operations that support file processing include:

1. OPEN and CLOSE files for processing.
2. READ a logical record from the file.

3. WRITE a logical record to the file (either to replace an existing record or to add a new record to the file).

Implied functions that must be performed in order to support the logical operations include:

1. I/O buffer control.
2. Blocking and deblocking of logical records.
3. Logical level error handling (for example, supplying an invalid record ID to a READ operation).
4. Building or completing I/O programs (such as channel programs) to implement a logical-level operation.

Of the implied functions, only I/O buffer control and blocking need further explanation here. Earlier in this chapter it was explained how multiple buffering can reduce the real time that a program takes to complete its execution. I/O buffers for each file are created in the main memory space allocated to a program for its execution, and the locations of these buffers are maintained in a file control block (FCB) also located within the program area. (In some cases, buffers are assigned to a file from a pool of buffers on a dynamic basis, but when this approach is used, the buffer location in the FCB is updated as needed). Each I/O buffer is the size of a physical record for the file or the most convenient size not less than the size of a physical record (in some cases the buffer may be used for more than one size of physical record). File management keeps track of the location and size of buffers currently assigned to a particular file and uses this information to complete I/O programs as needed (for example, place the buffer locations in the appropriate CCWs, as explained earlier). File management also controls the cycle of choosing the current buffer when a multiple-buffering scheme is used.

File management must also perform the mapping of physical to logical records and vice versa. For example: suppose that a file is composed of physical records containing ten logical records per block. After the appropriate I/O program has been executed to read a physical record into an I/O buffer, file management maintains a logical record pointer that always points to the next available logical record in the buffer. A logical READ in the application program either moves this next logical record into a work area for processing or makes the portion of the I/O buffer that contains the next logical record visible to the requesting program. (A COBOL program provides examples of both of these techniques. When a record is READ into an area of WORKING-STORAGE, the first option is in effect. When the record is accessed using the record description in the FILE SECTION, the access is to the I/O buffer.)

A great benefit of blocking logical records into one physical record is that in the case just cited, in which there were 10 logical records per block, only one I/O program was executed for every 10 logical records read. Intermediate logical READ operations from the requesting program resulted in the execution of a relatively simple routine, which made the next logical record available to the program without going to the inner layers of the operating system. This avoided the cycle involving system interrupts, reassigning the CPU, and so on, that is set in motion for each physical I/O.

A similar example could be developed for logical WRITE operations. When blocking is used, a physical WRITE occurs only when the block (the I/O buffer) is full or when the file is closed. Of course, both of these examples are only valid for files processed sequentially.

Since all transfers to and from an I/O device are performed in terms of physical records, any change to a logical record (such as posting one or more fields in a record) must result in the replacement (REWRITE) of the complete physical record that contained the altered record. For a disk drive, the original record is changed by first reading the required block, making the desired changes, and then writing the block back to its original track address to overlay its old image. However, on a tape drive that allows updating in place, this requires a backspace and then a physical write to replace a record. Most of this activity is made transparent by file management routines.

The manner in which new records are added to a file depends largely on the file type. For a sequential file, records are simply added to the end. For random or indexed files, the physical position for a new record is derived from the record key or ID (for example, the relative record number), and then the record is inserted accordingly. To achieve this, the requesting program usually needs to specify only the record ID and the operation needed (that is, WRITE), and file management handles the rest.

A brief comment is needed for the OPEN and CLOSE procedures. When a file is opened either explicitly (as in COBOL programs) or implicitly (as in Pascal programs), file management usually performs several actions, such as checking to see if the file is available and if the user is allowed access to it. It is also a common practice to maintain a working directory for all currently opened files in order to reduce the time required for directory searches for currently active files. When the file is closed, any pending physical writes are completed (an output buffer may be only partially filled and a short logical block must be written). Any required status information is posted in the appropriate directories, and the file entry is removed from the directory of active files.

Protection and Allocation of Files Access to a particular file is controlled by file management routines. When a user tries to OPEN or initially access a file, the directory entry for the file that denotes ownership and access restrictions is checked, since this information will determine which users can access a given file (this may be unrestricted) and in what mode (READ, WRITE, or both). If these conditions are satisfied, additional checking may be required to see if the file is currently in use (opened) and if multiple user access is allowed (for example, it is usually undesirable to allow two users to update a file concurrently).

It is possible on some devices, such as floppy disk drives, to prevent all WRITE operations to a particular volume by hardware convention. This can only control writing and also prevents every user, including the owner, from updating the file. In general, however, file allocation and protection are controlled by software.

EXAMPLES OF PROGRAM/OPERATING SYSTEM INTERACTION

The primary goal of the last section in presenting the functional model of an operating system was to describe the various functions that an operating system typically performs in managing the resources of a computing system. A secondary goal was to impart an appreciation for the amount of activity (the number of functions that must be performed) that is required to provide routine services to the user of a computing system, so that the conveniences that have come to be expected are available.

By now it should be clear that even a routine request for service of the operating system (such as a request to read a record from a disk drive) is not accomplished by the execution of one or two basic routines. Indeed, most requests require the execution of several to many routines before control is returned to the program that initiated the request. The exact number of routines required varies from operating system to operating system, but in general, the number of routines needed tends to increase with the size of the operating system.

Two specific examples borrowed from typical IBM mainframe operating systems are given at the end of this section to illustrate the scope of activity that is typical of operating systems. In these examples only the major conceptual steps are given, but in reality, there are a number of substeps (functions) used in the process. The first example examines the major points of interface with the operating system by an executable program called DEMO during its execution life cycle—from its entrance into the computing system to its normal termination.

The second example focuses on the steps performed by the major routines of an operating system required in responding to a single request for service by a program. Specifically, this example traces the major routines and events required to READ a single record for a program named DEMO (see Figure 5.18).

In order to understand these two specific examples involving an IBM mainframe operating system environment, it may be helpful to briefly describe a few of the characteristics of the operating system(s) that are relevant to the examples. The main memory organization of the IBM operating system shown in Figure 5.17 is basically the organization used for OS/MVT;

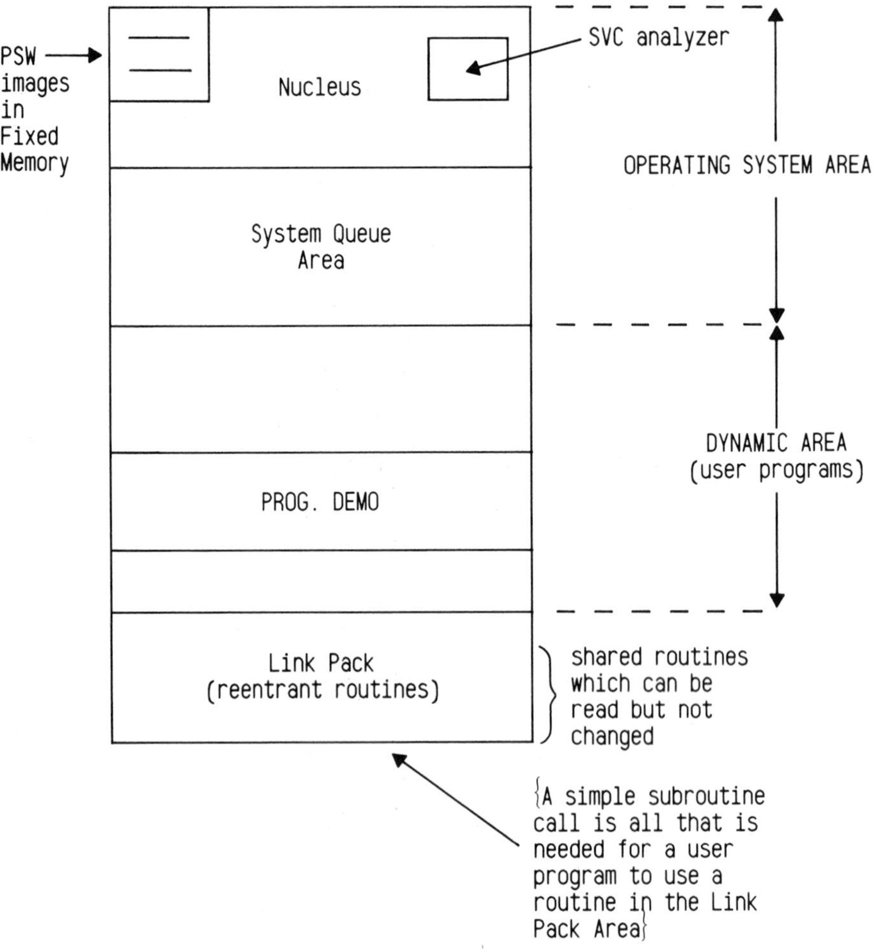

FIGURE 5.17
CONCEPTUAL MAIN MEMORY DIAGRAM FOR A TYPICAL IBM OS-TYPE MAIN FRAME OPERATING SYSTEM

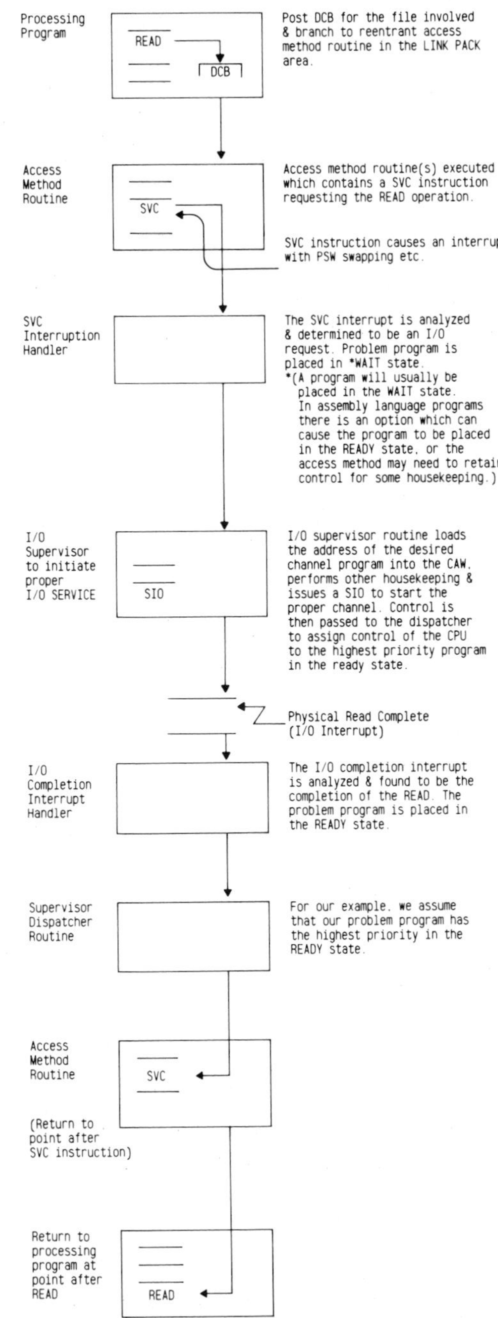

FIGURE 5.18
SEQUENCE OF MAJOR ROUTINES REQUIRED TO SERVICE AN INTERRUPT GENERATED BY A REQUEST TO READ A RECORD

however, it is conceptually similar to any of the OS-type operating systems—OS/MFT, OS/VS1, OS/VS2–1—and is also generally similar in function to a single virtual memory view in MVS (OS/VS2–2). For the level of these examples, specific differences between systems is not a significant factor.

All OS-type systems use three basic control statements to provide interprogram communication with the operating system during a job. These are:

JOB, which identifies the job to the system.

DD, which defines any file needed by a program.

EXEC, which causes the loading and execution of a named program or cataloged set of control statements.

EXAMPLE 1. Chronological Account of Program Execution (IBM Mainframe Environment)

1. The operating system (OS) reads a EXEC job control statement directing it to execute a program named DEMO.
2. The OS loads and relocates program DEMO in the designated region of memory.
3. The OS then creates a control block called the Task Control Block (TCB), which is the principal source of status and other pertinent information used by the OS to supervise the execution of the program. The TCB is attached to the queue of active tasks and is marked as ready for execution.
4. The OS now allows the highest priority program in the active queue in the ready state to start execution (this amounts to posting the new status in the program's TCB and then dispatching control of the CPU to it). If DEMO was not the highest priority ready program, it would eventually get its turn, so we can proceed to its execution.
5. As long as there are no conditions which cause interrupts (errors, I/O completions, and so on), DEMO will remain in control of the CPU and execute machine instructions.
6. Suppose an interrupt occurs from a source external to DEMO? PSW swapping occurs and control passes automatically to the OS interrupt analyzer routine for the particular type of interrupt. This routine immediately stores in the TCB of DEMO all information

needed to restart it at the point of the interrupt, and changes its execution status to ready.

7. When the OS later determines that DEMO should continue to run, it reloads the general-purpose registers and the PSW contents from the save areas in the TCB for DEMO. Thus, DEMO is running once again, starting at the point at which it was last interrupted. (Floating-point registers (FPRs) have not been considered in the abbreviated mainframe model, but, in general, these must be saved and reloaded as needed also).

8. Later, during its execution, DEMO needs to READ a record. The machine language READ routine in DEMO is simply a call to an access method routine in the pool of reentrant routines found in the LINK PACK area of memory. The access method routine is a generalized routine that can be shared by all programs. Since it is reentrant, all variable information must be external to it. The variable information, in this case, refers to the actual I/O areas (buffers), the I/O channel program to perform the I/O (written in the machine language of the channel), and a block of descriptive information about the file involved, all three of which are located within the program area of DEMO. The address needed to locate the descriptive block is passed to the access method routine in a register. The access method routine then completes the I/O channel program (which is located in DEMO) required to perform the READ and issues an SVC (SuperVisor Call) instruction to request the OS to initiate a READ.

9. The SVC causes an interrupt, which is initially processed as in Step 6, except that DEMO is placed in the WAIT state. Control is then passed to the OS routine that supervises I/O (appropriately called the I/O supervisor).

10. The I/O supervisor loads the Channel Address Word (CAW) in fixed memory with the address of DEMO's I/O channel program to perform the READ (a series of CCWs), and then issues a SIO (start I/O) instruction to the proper channel. While the channel is executing the I/O program for DEMO, DEMO remains in the WAIT state, and control of the CPU is passed to the highest priority program in the READY state.

11. The channel executes the channel program in DEMO, which reads the desired record into the I/O area (buffer), also located in DEMO. Upon completion of its channel program, the channel then causes an I/O completion interrupt.

12. The OS analyzes the interrupt, determines that the I/O service for which DEMO was waiting has been completed, and changes DEMO's execution status to READY.

13. When control is returned to DEMO, execution resumes immediately after the SVC instruction in the access method subroutine that requested the READ, whereupon the subroutine returns control to DEMO via a normal subroutine return. All is as before, with the record now in place.

14. Eventually, normal termination of DEMO's execution is accomplished by a call (or return) to a subroutine in the reentrant routine pool (LINK PACK), which in turn issues a SVC instruction requesting the operating system to terminate DEMO by removing its TCB from the list of active tasks (programs).

REVIEW QUESTIONS AND EXERCISES

1. Define or explain briefly:
   a. multiprogramming
   b. multiprocessing
   c. multiple buffering
   d. operating system nucleus
   e. interrupt driven
   f. re-entrant routine
   g. response time
   h. throughput
   i. availability
   j. batch system
   k. interactive system
   l. time sharing system
   m. process
   n. deadly embrace
   o. fragmentation
   p. memory bound
   q. page fault
   r. thrashing
   s. physical record
   t. logical record

2. Indicate which of the following sequences of states for a process are valid.
   a. ready, waiting, running
   b. ready, running, waiting
   c. running, ready, waiting
   d. running, waiting, running
   e. running, waiting, ready
   f. waiting, running, ready
   g. waiting, ready, waiting
3. Suppose we want to run two programs (A and B) concurrently. Program A is the more important of the two and is basically compute bound in that it requires two hours of CPU time and five minutes of I/O time, mostly at the end of the run. Program B has just the opposite characteristics, in that it requires five minutes of CPU time spread evenly throughout two hours of I/O time.
   a. If we want to run both programs together in the shortest clock time, which program should be given priority?
   b. Which program should be given priority if program A must complete its execution in less than three hours?
   c. Draw diagrams showing the approximate clock times if program A has priority over program B and then showing the time if program B has priority over program A.
4. Compare the three basic memory management strategies used in a real memory operating system.
5. Given that a virtual memory system uses 4K pages and no segmentation, what would the resulting real address for a virtual address of 00602C be using the accompanying page table?

PAGE TABLE

000	000
001	000
002	000
003	002
004	004
005	005
006	003
007	000
008	006
009	001
00A	000

6. Explain how AARs (associative array registers) are used to improve address translation time.
7. Explain the effect that CPU saturation has on multiprogramming.
8. Explain how an operating system provides for file protection.
9. What are the benefits provided by a file directory system maintained by the operating system?
10. Explain how blocking of logical records can save program execution time.

PROGRAMMING EXERCISE

The following exercise is intended to illustrate the effects of blocking and multiple buffering on CPU time and turnaround time for a particular application. It assumes that the operating system used supplies CPU and/or job times for programs run on the computing system.

The program requirements are easily satisfied using COBOL or PL/1 in most any operating system environment. The requirements are also straightforward, using assembly language in an IBM mainframe environment (although a knowledge beyond that presented in this book is required).

STEP 1. Create a sequential disk file containing 1000 unblocked records (use relatively short records; 20–80 bytes). Write a program that simply copies the file to another identically formatted disk file using single buffering for the two files. Record the time required to run the program.

STEP 2. Recreate the disk file from Step 1 using a blocking factor of 10 or greater. Modify the program to copy the file again to a similarly blocked image file. In addition, use multiple buffering for this second execution. Record the execution time and compare the results. (You may want to compare blocking and multiple buffering separately.)

NOTE: In COBOL, the USE INTEGER AREAS clause in the SELECT statement is used to obtain a specific number of I/O buffers for a file. In PL/1 or IBM mainframe assembly language, the number of buffers is part of the file description.

APPENDIX A
MACHINE LANGUAGE INSTRUCTIONS FOR IBM 4300 PROCESSOR FAMILY

Instruction Name	Mnemonic	Instruction Type	Sets Condition Code	Op Code
*ADD	AR	RR	X	1A
*ADD	A	RX	X	5A
ADD DECIMAL	AP	SS	X	FA
ADD HALFWORD	AH	RX	X	4A
ADD LOGICAL	ALR	RR	X	1E
ADD LOGICAL	AL	RX	X	5E
ADD NORMALIZED (extended)	AXR	RR	X	36
ADD NORMALIZED (long)	ADR	RR	X	2A
ADD NORMALIZED	AD	RX	X	6A
ADD NORMALIZED (short)	AER	RR	X	3A
ADD NORMALIZED (short)	AE	RX	X	7A
ADD UNNORMALIZED (long)	AWR	RR	X	2E
ADD UNNORMALIZED (long)	AW	RX	X	6E
ADD UNNORMALIZED (short)	AUR	RR	X	3E
ADD UNNORMALIZED (short)	AU	RX	X	7E
*AND	NR	RR	X	14
*AND	N	RX	X	54
AND (character)	NC	SS	X	D4
AND (immediate)	NI	SI	X	94
*BRANCH AND LINK	BALR	RR		05
*BRANCH AND LINK	BAL	RX		45
*BRANCH ON CONDITION	BCR	RR		07
*BRANCH ON CONDITION	BC	RX		47
*BRANCH ON COUNT	BCTR	RR		06
*BRANCH ON COUNT	BCT	RX		46
BRANCH ON INDEX HIGH	BXH	RS		86
BRANCH ON INDEX LOW OR EQUAL	BXLE	RS		87

Instruction Name	Mnemonic	Instruction Type	Sets Condition Code	Op Code
CLEAR I/O	CLRIO	S	X	9D01
CLEAR PAGE	CLRP	S		B215
*COMPARE	CR	RR	X	19
*COMPARE	C	RX	X	59
COMPARE (long)	CDR	RR	X	29
COMPARE (long)	CD	RX	X	69
COMPARE (short)	CER	RR	X	39
COMPARE (short)	CE	RX	X	79
COMPARE AND SWAP	CS	RS	X	BA
COMPARE DECIMAL	CP	SS	X	F9
COMPARE DOUBLE AND SWAP	CDS	RS	X	BB
COMPARE HALFWORD	CH	RX	X	49
COMPARE LOGICAL	CLR	RR	X	15
*COMPARE LOGICAL	CL	RX	X	55
*COMPARE LOGICAL (character)	CLC	SS	X	D5
*COMPARE LOGICAL (immediate)	CLI	SI	X	95
COMPARE LOGICAL CHARACTERS UNDER MASK	CLM	RS	X	BD
COMPARE LOGICAL LONG	CLCL	RR	X	0F
CONNECT PAGE	CTP	RS	X	B0
*CONVERT TO BINARY	CVB	RX		4F
*CONVERT TO DECIMAL	CVD	RX		4E
DECONFIGURE PAGE	DEP	S		B21B
DIAGNOSE				83
DISCONNECTPAGE	DCTP	S	X	B21C
*DIVIDE	DR	RR		1D
*DIVIDE	D	RX		5D
DIVIDE (long)	DDR	RR		2D
DIVIDE (long)	DD	RX		6D
DIVIDE (short)	DER	RR		3D
DIVIDE (short)	DE	RX		7D
DIVIDE DECIMAL	DP	SS		FD

Instruction Name	Mnemonic	Instruction Type	Sets Condition Code	Op Code
EDIT	ED	SS	X	DE
EDIT AND MARK	EDMK	SS	X	DF
*EXCLUSIVE OR	XR	RR	X	17
*EXCLUSIVE OR	X	RX	X	57
EXCLUSIVE OR (character)	XC	SS	X	D7
EXCLUSIVE OR (immediate)	XI	SI	X	97
EXECUTE	EX	RX		44
HALT DEVICE	HDV	S	X	9E01
HALT I/O	HIO	S	X	9E00
HALVE (long)	HDR	RR		24
HALVE (short)	HER	RR		34
*INSERT CHARACTER	IC	RX		43
INSERT CHARACTERS UNDER MASK	ICM	RS	X	BF
INSERT PAGE BITS	IPB	RS		B4
INSERT PSW KEY	IPK	S		B20B
INSERT STORAGE KEY	ISK	RR		09
*LOAD	LR	RR		18
*LOAD	L	RX		58
LOAD (long)	LDR	RR		28
LOAD (long)	LD	RX		68
LOAD (short)	LER	RR		38
LOAD (short)	LE	RX		78
*LOAD ADDRESS	LA	RX		41
*LOAD AND TEST	LTR	RR	X	12
LOAD AND TEST (long)	LTDR	RR	X	22
LOAD AND TEST (short)	LTER	RR	X	32
LOAD COMPLEMENT	LCR	RR	X	13
LOAD COMPLEMENT (long)	LCDR	RR	X	23
LOAD COMPLEMENT (short)	LCER	RR	X	33
LOAD CONTROL	LCTL	RS		B7
LOAD FRAME INDEX	LFI	RS	X	B8

Instruction Name	Mnemonic	Instruction Type	Sets Condition Code	Op Code
LOAD HALFWORD	LH	RX		48
*LOAD MULTIPLE	LM	RS		98
LOAD NEGATIVE	LNR	RR	X	11
LOAD NEGATIVE (long)	LNDR	RR	X	21
LOAD NEGATIVE (short)	LNER	RR	X	31
LOAD POSITIVE	LPR	RR	X	10
LOAD POSITIVE (long)	LPDR	RR	X	20
LOAD POSITIVE (short)	LPER	RR	X	30
LOAD PSW	LPSW	S	X	82
LOAD ROUNDED (extended to long)	LRDR	RR		25
LOAD ROUNDED (long to short)	LRER	RR		35
MAKE ADDRESSABLE	MAD	S	X	B21D
MAKE UNADDRESSABLE	MUN	S	X	B21E
MONITOR CALL	MC	SI		AF
*MOVE (character)	MVC	SS		D2
*MOVE (immediate)	MVI	SI		92
MOVE INVERSE	MVCIN	SS		E8
MOVE LONG	MVCL	RR	X	0E
MOVE NUMERICS	MVN	SS		D1
MOVE WITH OFFSET	MVO	SS		F1
MOVE ZONES	MVZ	SS		D3
*MULTIPLY	MR	RR		1C
*MULTIPLY	M	RX		5C
MULTIPLY (extended)	MXR	RR		26
MULTIPLY (long)	MDR	RR		2C
MULTIPLY (long)	MD	RX		6C
MULTIPLY (long to extended)	MXDR	RR		27
MULTIPLY (long to extended)	MXD	RX		67
MULTIPLY (short to long)	MER	RR		3C
MULTIPLY (short to long)	ME	RX		7C
MULTIPLY DECIMAL	MP	SS		FC

Instruction Name	Mnemonic	Instruction Type	Sets Condition Code	Op Code
MULTIPLY HALFWORD	MH	RX		4C
*OR	OR	RR	X	16
*OR	O	RX	X	56
OR (character)	OC	SS	X	D6
*OR (immediate)	OI	SI	X	96
*PACK	PACK	SS		F2
RESET REFERENCE BIT	RRB	S	X	B213
RETRIEVE STATUS AND PAGE	RSP	SS	X	D8
SET CLOCK	SCK	S	X	B204
SET CLOCK COMPARATOR	SCKC	S		B206
SET CPU TIMER	SPT	S		B208
SET PAGE BITS	SPB	RS	X	B5
SET PROGRAM MASK	SPM	RR	X	04
SET PSW KEY FROM ADDRESS	SPKA	S		B20A
SET STORAGE KEY	SSK	RR		08
SET SYSTEM MASK	SSM	S		80
SHIFT AND ROUND DECIMAL	SRP	SS	X	F0
SHIFT LEFT DOUBLE	SLDA	RS	X	8F
*SHIFT LEFT DOUBLE LOGICAL	SLDL	RS		8D
SHIFT LEFT SINGLE	SLA	RS	X	8B
*SHIFT LEFT SINGLE LOGICAL	SLL	RS		89
SHIFT RIGHT DOUBLE	SRDA	RS	X	8E
*SHIFT RIGHT DOUBLE LOGICAL	SRDL	RS		8C
SHIFT RIGHT SINGLE	SRA	RS	X	8A
*SHIFT RIGHT SINGLE LOGICAL	SRL	RS		88
*START I/O	SIO	S	X	9C00
START I/O FAST RELEASE	SIOF	S	X	9C01
*STORE	ST	RX		50
STORE (long)	STD	RX		60
STORE (short)	STE	RX		70
STORE CAPACITY COUNTS	STCAP	S		B21F
STORE CHANNEL ID	STIDC	S	X	B203
*STORE CHARACTER	STC	RX		42

Instruction Name	Mnemonic	Instruction Type	Sets Condition Code	Op Code
STORE CHARACTERS UNDER MASK	STCM	RS		BE
STORE CLOCK	STCK	S	X	B205
STORE CLOCK COMPARATOR	STCKC	S		B207
STORE CONTROL	STCTL	RS		B6
STORE CPU ID	STIDP	S		B202
STORE CPU TIMER	STPT	S		B209
STORE HALFWORD	STH	RX		40
*STORE MULTIPLE	STM	RS		90
STORE THEN AND SYSTEM MASK	STNSM	SI		AC
STORE THEN OR SYSTEM MASK	STOSM	SI		AD
*SUBTRACT	SR	RR	X	1B
*SUBTRACT	S	RX	X	5B
SUBTRACT DECIMAL	SP	SS	X	FB
SUBTRACT HALFWORD	SH	RX	X	4B
SUBTRACT LOGICAL	SLR	RR	X	1F
SUBTRACT LOGICAL	SL	RX	X	5F
SUBTRACT NORMALIZED (extended)	SXR	RR	X	37
SUBTRACT NORMALIZED (long)	SDR	RR	X	2B
SUBTRACT NORMALIZED (long)	SD	RX	X	6B
SUBTRACT NORMALIZED (short)	SER	RR	X	3B
SUBTRACT NORMALIZED (short)	SE	RX	X	7B
SUBTRACT UNNORMALIZED (long)	SWR	RR	X	2F
SUBTRACT UNNORMALIZED (long)	SW	RX	X	6F
SUBTRACT UNNORMALIZED (short)	SUR	RR	X	3F
SUBTRACT UNNORMALIZED (short)	SU	RX	X	7F
*SUPERVISOR CALL	SVC	RR	X	0A
TEST AND SET	TS	S	X	93
TEST CHANNEL	TCH	S	X	9F00
TEST I/O	TIO	S	X	9D00

Instruction Name	Mnemonic	Instruction Type	Sets Condition Code	Op Code
TEST UNDER MASK	TM	SI	X	91
TRANSLATE	TR	SS		DC
TRANSLATE AND TEST	TRT	SS	X	DD
*UNPACK	UNPK	SS		F3
ZERO AND ADD	ZAP	SS	X	F8

(* Indicates included in the 47 instruction subset used for this book.)

APPENDIX B
FULL TABLE OF EBCDIC CHARACTER CODES

CHARACTER	EBCDIC CODE Binary	Hex
space	0100 0000	40
¢	0100 1010	4A
.	0100 1011	4B
<	0100 1100	4C
(	0100 1101	4D
+	0100 1110	4E
¦	0100 1111	4F
&	0101 0000	50
!	0101 1010	5A
$	0101 1011	5B
*	0101 1100	5C
)	0101 1101	5D
;	0101 1110	5E
	0101 1111	5F
-	0110 0000	60
/	0110 0001	61
,	0110 1011	6B
%	0110 1100	6C
_	0110 1101	6D
>	0110 1110	6E
?	0110 1111	6F
:	0111 1010	7A
#	0111 1011	7B
@	0111 1100	7C
'	0111 1101	7D
=	0111 1110	7E
"	0111 1111	7F
a	1000 0001	81
b	1000 0010	82
c	1000 0011	83
d	1000 0100	84
e	1000 0101	85
f	1000 0110	86
g	1000 0111	87
h	1000 1000	88

CHARACTER	EBCDIC CODE Binary	Hex
i	1000 1001	89
j	1001 0001	91
k	1001 0010	92
l	1001 0011	93
m	1001 0100	94
n	1001 0101	95
o	1001 0110	96
p	1001 0111	97
q	1001 1000	98
r	1001 1001	99
~	1010 0001	A1
s	1010 0010	A2
t	1010 0011	A3
u	1010 0100	A4
v	1010 0101	A5
w	1010 0110	A6
x	1010 0111	A7
y	1010 1000	A8
z	1010 1001	A9
{	1100 0000	C0
A	1100 0001	C1
B	1100 0010	C2
C	1100 0011	C3
D	1100 0100	C4
E	1100 0101	C5
F	1100 0110	C6
G	1100 0111	C7
H	1100 1000	C8
I	1100 1001	C9
}	1101 0000	D0
J	1101 0001	D1
K	1101 0010	D2
L	1101 0011	D3
M	1101 0100	D4
N	1101 0101	D5
O	1101 0110	D6
P	1101 0111	D7
Q	1101 1000	D8
R	1101 1001	D9

CHARACTER	EBCDIC CODE	
	Binary	Hex
\	1110 0000	E0
S	1110 0010	E2
T	1110 0011	E3
U	1110 0100	E4
V	1110 0101	E5
W	1110 0110	E6
X	1110 0111	E7
Y	1110 1000	E8
Z	1110 1001	E9
0	1111 0000	F0
1	1111 0001	F1
2	1111 0010	F2
3	1111 0011	F3
4	1111 0100	F4
5	1111 0101	F5
6	1111 0110	F6
7	1111 0111	F7
8	1111 1000	F8
9	1111 1001	F9

BIBLIOGRAPHY

Aho, Alfred V., and Ullman, Jeffrey D. *Principles of Compiler Design.* Reading, Mass.: Addison-Wesley Publishing Company, 1977.

Barron, D. W. *Assemblers and Loaders.* 2d ed. London: Macdonald & Co. (Publishers) Ltd., 1972.

Barron, David. *Computer Operating Systems for Micros, Minis and Mainframes.* 2d ed. London: Chapman and Hall, 1971.

Beck, Leland L. *System Software An Introduction to Systems Programming.* Reading, Mass.: Addison-Wesley Publishing Company, 1985.

Bell Telephone Laboratories, Inc. *UNIX Programmer's Manual Volume 1.* Rev. ed. New York: Holt, Rinehart and Winston, 1983.

Borland International. *Turbo Pascal 2.0 Reference Manual.* 3d ed. 1984.

Bowles, Kenneth L. *Beginner's Guide for the UCSD Pascal System.* Peterborough, NH: Byte Books, 1980.

Brown, Douglas L. *From Pascal to C: An Introduction to the C Programming Language.* Belmont, Calif.: Wadsworth, Inc., 1985.

Calingaert, Peter. *Assembler, Compilers and Program Translation.* Potomac, Md.: Computer Science Press, 1979.

Calingaert, Peter. *Operating System Elements.* Englewood Cliffs, N.J.: Prentice-Hall, 1982.

Coffman, Edward G. Jr., Denning, Peter J. *Operating Systems Theory.* Englewood Cliffs, N.J.: Prentice-Hall, 1973.

Davis, William S. *Operating Systems.* 2d ed. Reading Mass.: Addison-Wesley Publishing Company, 1983.

Deitel, Harvey M. *An Introduction to Operating Systems.* Rev. ed. Reading, Mass.: Addison-Wesley Publishing Company, 1984.

Digital Equipment Corp. *VAX Architecture Handbook.* 1981.

Donovan, John J. *Systems Programming.* New York: McGraw-Hill, 1972.

Ellzey, Roy S. *Data Structures for Computer Information Systems.* Chicago: Science Research Associates, 1982.

Feurer, Alan R., and Gehani, Narain H. "A Comparison of the Programming Languages C and PASCAL." *ACM Computing Surveys* 14, no. 1 (March 1982).

Flores, Ivan. *Assemblers and BAL.* Englewood Cliffs, N.J.: Prentice-Hall, 1971.

Fraser, Christopher W., and Hanson, David R. "A Machine-Independent Linker." Software-Practice and Experience 12 (September 1981), pp. 351–66.

Freeman, Peter. *Software Systems Principles.* Chicago: Science Research Associates, 1975.

Gear, William C. *Computer Organization and Programming.* 3d ed. New York: McGraw-Hill, 1980.

Ghezzi, Carlo, and Jazayeri, Mehidi. *Programming Language Concepts.* New York: John Wiley & Sons, Inc., 1982.

Graham, Robert M. *Principles of Systems Programming* New York: John Wiley & Sons, Inc., 1975.

Gries, David. *Compiler Construction for Digital Computers.* New York: John Wiley & Sons, Inc., 1971.

Hansen, Per Brinch. *Operating System Principles.* Englewood Cliffs, N.J.: Prentice-Hall, 1973.

Hamacher, Carl V.; Vranesic, Zvonko G.; and Zaky, Safwat G. *Computer Organization.* 2d ed. New York: McGraw-Hill, 1984.

Holt, R.C. Graham, G.S., Lazowska, E.D., and Scott, M.A. *Structured Concurrent Programming with Operating Systems.* Reading, Mass.: Addision-Wesley Publishing Company, 1978.

Hsiao, David K. *Systems Programming Concepts of Operating and Data Base Systems.* Reading, Mass.: Addison-Wesley Publishing Company, 1975.

IBM. *IBM 4300 Processors Principles of Operation for ECPS:VSE Mode.* GA22–7070–0.

IBM *DOS Full American National Standard COBOL.* GC28-6394.

IBM. *DOS/VSE Assembler Logic.* SY33-8567.

IBM. *OS/VS—VM/370 Assembler Programmer's Guide.* GC33-4021.

IBM. Personal Computer Computer Language Series, *UCSD Pascal Reference for the UCSD P-System Version IV.0,* Jan. 1982.

IBM. *IBM System/370 Principles of Operation.* GA22–7000–6.

IBM. *OS/VS—DOS/VSE—VM/370 Assembler Language.* GC33–4010–5.

IBM. *IBM System/370 Reference Summary.* GX20–1850–2.

Jensen, Kathleen, and Wirth, Niklaus. *Pascal, User Manual and Report.* 3d ed. Revised by Andrew B. Mickel and James F. Miner. New York: Springer-Verlag, 1985.

Jones, Douglas W. "Assembly Language as Object Code." *Software-Practice and Experience,* 13 (June 1981), pp. 715–25.

Kaisler, Stephen H. *The Design of Operating Systems for Small Computer Systems.* New York: John Wiley and Sons, 1983.

Katzan, Harry, Jr. *Computer Systems Organization and Programming.* Chicago: Science Research Associates, 1976.

Katzan, Harry, Jr. *Operating Systems.* New York: Van Nostrand Reinhold, 1973.

Knuth, Donald E. *The Art of Computer Programming,* vol. 1 Reading, Mass.: Addison-Wesley Publishing Company, 1969.

Koffman, Elliot B. *Problem Solving and Structured Programming in Pascal.* 2d ed. Reading, Mass.: Addison-Wesley Publishing Company, 1985.

Kudlick, Michael D. *Assembly Language Programming.* 2d ed. Dubuque, Ia.: Wm. C. Brown Co., 1983.

Ledgard, Henry, and Marcotty, Michael. *The Programming Language Landscape.* Chicago: Science Research Associates, 1981.

Leestma, Sanford and Nyhoff, Larry. *Pascal Programming and Problem Solving.* New York: MacMillan Publishing Co., 1984.

Levy, Henry M., and Eckhouse, Richard H. R. *Computer Programming and Architecture: The VAX-11.* Digital Press, 1980.

Lister, N. M. *Fundamentals of Operating Systems.* 2d ed. New York: Springer-Verlag, 1979.

MacEwen, Glenn H. *Introduction to Computer Systems Using the PDP-11 and Pascal.* New York: McGraw-Hill, 1980.

MacLennan, Bruce J. *Principles of Programming Languages: Design, Evaluation, and Implementation.* New York: Holt, Rinehart and Winston, 1983.

Madnick, Stuart E., and Donovan, John J. *Operating Systems.* New York: McGraw-Hill, 1974.

Madnick, S. E., and Alsop, J. W. "A Modular Approach to File System Design." Proc. AFIPS 1969 SJCC 34: 1–12.

Peterson, James L. and Silberschatz, Abraham. *Operating System Concepts.* 2d ed. Reading, Mass.: Addison-Wesley Publishing Company, 1985.

Pratt, Terrence W. *Programming Languages Design and Implementation. 2d ed. Englewood Cliffs, N.J.: Prentice-Hall, 1984.*

Presser, Leon, and White, John R. "Linkers and Loaders." ACM Computing Surveys 4, no.3 (September 1972).

Pyramid. *PYRAMID 90x: The Supermini Designed for UNIX.* 4010-0015B. Printed USA #584.

Ralston, Anthony, and Reilly, Edwin D., Jr. *Encyclopedia of Computer Science and Engineering.* 2d ed. New York: Van Nostrand Reinhold, 1983.

RCA. *Time Sharing Operating System (TSOS) Data Management System Reference Manual.* DJ-001-2-00.

RCA. Spectra 70. *70/46 Processor Reference Manual* Cherry Hill, N.J.: Marketing Publications, 1970. BE-002-2-00.

Scanlon, Leo J. *6502 Software Design.* Indianapolis, In: Howard W. Sams & Co., 1980.

Shaw, Alan C. *The Logical Design of Operating Systems.* Englewood Cliffs, N.J.: Prentice-Hall, 1974.

Siewiorek, Daniel P.; Bell, Gordon C., and Newell, Allen. *Computer Structures: Principles and Examples.* New York: McGraw-Hill, 1982.

Stone, Harold S., (ed.), Chen, Tien Chi, et.al. *Introduction to Computer Architecture.* 2d ed. Chicago: Science Research Associates, 1980.

Struble, George W. *Assembler Language Programming.* 3d ed. Reading, Mass.: Addison-Wesley, 1984.

Wasserman, Anthony I. *Programming Language Design (Tutorial)* New York: IEEE Computer Society Press, 1980.

Wexelblat, Richard L. (ed.) *History of Programming Languages.* New York: Academic Press, 1981.

Yates, Jean L., and Emerson, Sandra L. *The Business Guide to the UNIX System.* Reading, Mass.: Addison-Wesley Publishing Company, 1984.

Yourdon, Edward. *Techniques of Program Structure and Design.* Englewood Cliffs, N.J.: Prentice-Hall, 1975.

INDEX